Dear Reader,

Probating an estate is a common legal task that every family must face one day. If you are asked to probate the estate of a beloved spouse, sibling, parent or friend, will you be ready?

You could turn the job over to a lawyer—as many choose to do—but that can be unreasonably expensive. Handling probate is a gold mine for the legal industry. In 1999, for example, *The Washington Post* estimated that the transfer of wealth from the World War II generation to its heirs will be the most ever, exceeding $10 trillion. Lawyers stand to claim millions of those dollars often for performing routine tasks that almost anyone can do.

As *The Executor's Guide* explains, settling the estate of a loved one does not have to be a complex, intimidating process. While it is time-consuming and sometimes cumbersome, in most cases probate does not require legal research, writing or adversary proceedings. If the value of the estate is less than the federal estate tax limit ($1.5 million in 2004-05), and the estate plan is straightforward and not being questioned by possible heirs, then almost anyone with basic arithmetic skills and the ability to follow instructions can handle probate.

The Executor's Guide shows you how. It provides the roadmap of what steps you need to take first and what can wait until later; what to do if there's no will; how to determine if the estate qualifies for a simplified "nonprobate" procedure; and how to pay taxes, handle trusts and work with family members.

Providing the best resources to help you navigate the legal system is just one part of HALT's mission. We also advocate reforms to make the legal system more consumer-friendly. In probate, we work to simplify procedures, and urge courts to provide consumer-friendly assistance to help people avoid unnecessary legal costs. Finally, the dollar limits on small estate administration are far too low in most states. HALT advocates a limit of $225,000, which would ensure most easily probated estates could use this less costly and more efficient procedure.

Settling an estate doesn't have to turn into an overwhelming second job. Armed with the legal fundamentals detailed in this book, consumers can assure their loved one's wishes are honored as they would have wanted—an invaluable service and a final gift to a loved one.

Sincerely,

James C. Turner
Executive Director
HALT, Inc.
September 2004, Washington, DC

Read This First

The information in this book is as up to date and accurate as we can make it. But it's important to realize that the law changes frequently, as do fees, forms, and procedures. If you handle your own legal matters, it's up to you to be sure that all information you use—including the information in this book—is accurate. Here are some suggestions to help you:

First, make sure you've got the most recent edition of this book. To learn whether a later edition is available, check the edition number on the book's spine and then go to Nolo's online Law Store at www.nolo.com or call Nolo's Customer Service Department at 800-728-3555.

Next, even if you have a current edition, you need to be sure it's fully up to date. The law can change overnight. At www.nolo.com, we post notices of major legal and practical changes that affect the latest edition of a book. To check for updates, find your book in the Law Store on Nolo's website (you can use the "A to Z Product List" and click the book's title). If you see an "Updates" link on the left side of the page, click it. If you don't see a link, that means we haven't posted any updates. (But check back regularly.)

Finally, we believe accurate and current legal information should help you solve many of your own legal problems on a cost-efficient basis. But this text is not a substitute for personalized advice from a knowledgeable lawyer. If you want the help of a trained professional, consult an attorney licensed to practice in your state.

1st edition

The
Executor's
Guide

Settling a Loved One's Estate or Trust

by Mary Randolph

First Edition	MAY 2004
Illustrations	MARI STEIN
Cover Design	TONI IHARA
Book Design	SUSAN PUTNEY
Production	MARGARET LIVINGSTON
Proofreading	ROBERT WELLS
Index	THÉRÈSE SHERE
Printing	DELTA PRINTING SOLUTIONS, INC.

Acknowledgments

I would like to give my heartfelt thanks to:

My friends Shae Irving and Jake Warner, who edited many drafts of this book. Each one added so much style and substance that I can't imagine the book without them. What a gift to have not one but two editors who are knowledgeable, thoughtful, hard-working, and funny.

Julia Nissley, author of *How to Probate an Estate in California*. I've had the pleasure of working with Julia since I came to Nolo many years ago, and her wonderful book was an invaluable help.

Twila Slesnick, coauthor of another excellent Nolo book, *IRAs, 401(k)s and Other Retirement Plans: Taking Your Money Out*, who patiently read (and corrected) what I wrote about retirement plans.

Liza Weiman Hanks, an estate planning attorney of FamilyWorks law practice in San Jose, California. Her energy, knowledge, and encouragement helped me run this marathon.

Virginia Palmer, an estate planning attorney with Fitzgerald, Abbott & Beardsley in Oakland, California, who generously gave me the benefit of her extensive experience with trusts.

Ella Hirst, Nolo's indefatigable researcher and keeper of information, who was always willing to keep digging.

Lulu Cornell, who read more drafts of this book than she probably cares to remember as she entered corrections and comments and added some of her own.

Stan Jacobsen, who provided a steady stream of helpful articles that I never would have found without him.

My husband, for his support through the long process of writing this book.

Susan Putney and Margaret Livingston, who designed and laid out the book, and Toni Ihara, who designed the cover.

And finally, my girls, for their encouragement, patience, and love, and for making me laugh every single day.

Table of Contents

1. Overview

2. If You're Asked to Be an Executor or Trustee

3. The First Week

4. The First Month

5. Claiming Life Insurance, Social Security, and Other Benefits

6. Making Sense of the Will

7. If There's No Will

8. Taking Inventory

9. Managing Assets and Paying Bills

10. Caring for Children and Their Property

11. Taxes

12. Property That Doesn't Go Through Probate

13. Transferring Joint Tenancy and Other Survivorship Property

14. Transferring Community Property

15. Claiming Money in Retirement Plans

16. Claiming Payable-on-Death Assets

17. Special Procedures for Small Estates

18. The Regular Probate Process

19. Wrapping Up a Simple Living Trust

20. Managing a Child's Trust

21. Handling a Bypass (AB) Trust

22. Researching the Law Yourself

23. Lawyers and Other Experts

Appendix: State Information

Glossary

Index

PART

Getting Ready

CHAPTER 1

Overview

Most people, at one time or another, must wind up the affairs of a spouse, close relative, or friend who has died. They become responsible for collecting and distributing the deceased person's worldly goods, following the instructions in the will and state law.

If you find yourself in this position, your new legal obligations may seem overwhelming. You may be thrust into the unfamiliar world of probate courts and lawyers, asked to read complicated documents that make your eyes glaze, and made responsible for supervising the transfer of valuable property.

All of this happens at a very difficult time, of course. You've lost someone important to you—perhaps the most important person in your life or the person you always turned to for support and advice. If the circumstances of the death were especially painful, as when a young person dies, just getting through daily life may feel daunting—never mind taking on extra legal and practical tasks. You may feel that you simply do not possess the energy necessary to sort through records, make phone calls, and make decisions.

It may, in fact, take some time before you can attend to all these matters. And it will also take time, diligence, and patience. But you can do it, with information (from this book and other sources) and help from family, friends, and professionals.

You may be surprised to find that working your way through the elements of your job as executor, steadily tying up loose ends, is in some ways satisfying. It is a way both of

honoring the wishes of the person who has died and of performing an unquestionably useful service to those still living. It is a way of saying good-bye and moving on.

YOU'RE NOT ALONE

In the next 20 years, executors and trustees will manage the transfer of more than $4.8 trillion in wealth from one generation to the next. (Douglas Wilson, "Providing Guidance to Executors and Trustees," *Journal of Accountancy*, Oct. 1997.)

A. What Executors Do

In a nutshell, if you're named as executor you must:

Gather the deceased person's assets. This part shouldn't be hard, especially if the person's assets were of the ordinary kind: perhaps a house, a car, and some bank accounts and investments. If, before the person died, you got a handle on what he or she owned, it will be even easier.

Take care of them. You must safeguard the deceased person's property (both real estate and personal property) until you hand it over to beneficiaries. This may involve making investment decisions or even managing business property.

Pay debts and taxes. You aren't personally liable for the deceased person's debts (unless you were married, in which case you may be); you'll pay them from the deceased person's assets. You will have to file income tax returns on behalf of the deceased person and possibly (if the amount of property left is large) on behalf of the estate.

Distribute what's left. You'll transfer assets to the people who inherit them under the will, under state law, or by contract. This may involve going to probate court, but many assets can be transferred without probate. In recent years, many states have simplified probate significantly, so even if probate is required, it won't drag on like a court case in a 19th-century novel.

The whole process of winding up an estate will probably take from six to 18 months, depending on the circumstances and the law in your state. (Chapter 2 explains all these elements in more detail.) Here's how it usually goes:

- **First week:** Immediate practical decisions

- **Next few months:** Financial and legal matters

- **One (occasionally two) years:** Taxes.

Unless the estate includes exceptionally complicated property or there are serious family conflicts, none of an executor's tasks requires out-of-the-ordinary financial or legal skill. You just need to be honest, careful, and willing to put the interests of the estate above your own. When you need advice from an expert—for example, a lawyer, investment advisor, or tax preparer—you can get it and pay for it with estate assets.

There's one skill you do need, and that's communicating with people. Unless you inherit everything, you'll have to deal with beneficiaries who may run the gamut from selfless to greedy. Family relationships may be strained. And you'll probably have to work with businesses, institutions, courts, and government agencies during the process. Doing this successfully takes patience, common sense, and persistence.

B. What Trustees Do

More and more people are using living trusts as substitutes for wills. Trusts let people leave their property but avoid probate; certain kinds of trusts also reduce or avoid estate taxes. And some trusts are created in wills, as a way to manage property if the deceased person didn't want the people who inherited it (children or other beneficiaries) to have complete control over the property.

Trustees have the same general duties that executors do: gathering trust property and seeing that it gets to the beneficiaries who inherit it. They also have the same legal responsibility to be honest and prudent when handling the deceased person's property.

Whether or not a trustee has an easier job than an executor depends on what kind of trust you're dealing with. Trusts are discussed in detail later in the book, but here are the three kinds you're most likely to run into:

Simple living trust. A simple living trust is one that has only one purpose: to avoid probate. If you're wrapping up this kind of trust, you can probably carry out your duties in a few weeks or months. All you do is transfer trust property to the people named in the trust document. The probate court won't be involved.

Bypass (AB) living trust. This kind of trust, made by affluent couples who want to avoid estate tax, can last for years after the first spouse dies and involves complex tax planning. You'll need expert help.

Child's trust. These trusts are set up so that an adult can manage property left to a child (often a grandchild). If you're the trustee, you'll have to invest and spend trust property until the children are grown. Especially if the trust is for more than one child, you'll have a lot of decisions to make.

C. How Hard Will It Be?

Increasingly, people are naming family members—not lawyers, banks, or trust companies—as executors, even for relatively large estates. As you might expect, people who have served as executors have different but strong opinions about whether or not this trend is a good thing.

More than anything else, the difficulty or ease of an executor's job depends on how much preparation is done before the death. After the death, there's not much you can do. If the deceased person was organized, if you're familiar with his or her finances and property, and if family members are reasonably cooperative, your job will still take effort, but it shouldn't involve any big headaches.

But if you inherit a mess—poor records (or none at all), unclear instructions, and squabbling family members—then obviously you have a harder row to hoe. You'll be able to do it, but it will take a good deal longer.

Again, keep in mind that you can hire (with estate assets) experts to advise and help you. Most executors and trustees do need professional help from time to time.

If you're worried about botching the job and ending up personally liable for your mistakes, you can relax. You are very unlikely to create personal legal problems if you act in good faith and follow a few basic rules. The law requires that you always be scrupulously honest, never take advantage of your position for personal benefit, and treat all beneficiaries and creditors fairly and impartially. It's not an impossible standard to meet. (More on this in Chapter 2.)

PAYMENT FOR SERVING AS AN EXECUTOR OR TRUSTEE

You are probably entitled (under the will, trust, or state law) to reasonable compensation for your work as an executor or trustee. Many family members, however, feel uncomfortable accepting money and don't take a fee. There's also a practical reason to decline a fee: it's taxable income. If you're inheriting everything anyway, you're better off waiving the fee and instead inheriting the money, which won't be subject to income tax.

D. Emotional Concerns

Unless you're a professional, handling an estate or trust is much more than just a legal and financial job. When you're acting on behalf of a family member or close friend, you must deal with powerful and sometimes complicated feelings about the loss. Your grief may debilitate you, at least for a while.

These emotional and spiritual issues are, of course, profoundly important and long-lasting. This book focuses on the legal and practical aspects of the executor's situation, but there are many sources of emotional sustenance—books, websites, organizations, counselors—in addition to your own network of family and friends. Every resource has its own tone, philosophy, and advice; you'll have to find what speaks to you.

As executor or trustee, you will probably also have to work with the emotions of others. The demands of other beneficiaries and family members may weigh more heavily on you than probate court paperwork and investment decisions do. On the other hand, you may garner much-needed support from the network of family and friends.

Beneficiaries will be understandably concerned about what's happening, which means you may have to field a lot of anxious questions. Why is it taking so long to distribute the assets? Shouldn't you sell the deceased person's stock (or car or house) before its value drops? Why can't I take the rocking chair Mother always told me she wanted me to have? What are you going to do about Susan, who's taken things from the house?

You'll have to develop your own strategies for dealing with difficult family members. (One good use of a lawyer can be as a buffer between you and them.) A few simple actions, however, are always helpful:

- Keep beneficiaries informed about what's happening (or not happening) with regular letters or email.

- Make sure you have legal authority for everything you do.

- Keep careful records of all actions you take.

Probably the best way to head off spats, and even lawsuits, is regular communication. You may think you don't have anything to report—but that may be the time beneficiaries most want to hear from you. They will appreciate knowing, for example, that you must wait another month for a court-imposed deadline before you can distribute property to them. Even brief email messages, sent regularly, can calm people's anxieties.

Some executors find it helpful to hold family meetings to discuss ongoing issues. Others avoid such gatherings like the plague, because they know they will only ignite smoldering problems. Some families enlist the aid of a family counselor or therapist who can help people talk—and listen—to each other and work through problems. You'll have to discover, through trial and error, what works for you and your family.

E. How This Book Can Help

This book provides a roadmap that will help you navigate an unfamiliar land of legal procedures and confusing terminology. It will help you know what to expect, what decisions you'll need to make, when to get help, and what questions to ask.

But it is not a complete how-to book. It's impossible for one book to explain, for example, every state's procedure for transferring joint tenancy property to the surviving owner or how to conduct a probate court proceeding in every state. So although there are instructions to help you find out the details you need, and an appendix outlining some key part of the probate laws of every state, you'll almost certainly need assistance and information beyond what you find here.

As you use this book, you'll notice that although the executor's job may seem daunting as a whole, you can take your duties one step at a time. Yes, the law imposes deadlines here and there, but for the most part you are free to take things at a pace that is manageable for you. You can and should honor your own feelings and needs at the same time you honor the wishes of the person who trusted you with this responsibility.

Icons Used in This Book

 Warning: A potential problem you should consider carefully.

 Tip: A bit of practical advice.

 Expert: Time to consult a lawyer or other expert.

 Fast Track: A chance to skip some material that doesn't apply to your situation.

 Personal Story: A real-life anecdote that illustrates a point.

 Cross-Reference: Related information in another part of this book.

 Resource: Sources of more information about the topic discussed in the text. ■

CHAPTER 2

If You're Asked to Be
an Executor or Trustee

After a relative or friend has died, you may be surprised to learn that you were chosen to be the executor of the deceased person's estate or the successor trustee of a living trust. You may feel pleased to have a chance to do a final and important favor for someone you loved. On the other hand, you may accept this responsibility because you conclude you have little choice.

In fact, you do have a choice. Even if you feel an obligation to the deceased person—who has both honored and burdened you by choosing you for the role of executor or trustee—you may decline the job and let it pass to someone else. And although chances are that you have a good reason—poor health or other consuming commitments, for example—the law does not require you to explain it to anyone.

If you're lucky enough to know in advance that you have been chosen, you'll have some valuable time to think about your options. If you decline, the person will have the chance to choose someone else. And if you accept, there are many things the person who has appointed you can do, while he or she is still alive, that will make things much easier when your services are needed. After all, your job will be to carry out that person's wishes. It makes sense to take the opportunity to work together now, to clarify what is intended and how best to accomplish the task.

This chapter discusses how to decide whether or not to accept the job of executor or successor trustee—and how to make it easier if you do.

A. Executor or Trustee?

You may be asked to be the executor of a will, the successor trustee of a trust, or both. Many of your responsibilities will be the same no matter which position you occupy. The key difference is that if you are an executor, you may need to conduct a probate court proceeding to transfer the deceased person's property.

This chapter explains each job in much more detail, but here is a quick look at each one:

Executor. The executor is named in the will or, if there's no will, appointed by a judge. The executor gathers the deceased person's property, pays debts and taxes, and distributes what's left to the beneficiaries. The executor may or may not need to conduct probate court proceedings—it depends on what kind of property the deceased person owned, how much it's worth, and how much planning was done ahead of time.

Successor trustee. The successor trustee is named in the document (commonly called a trust declaration or trust instrument) that creates a living trust. Officially, the successor trustee's job is just to collect property that was held in the living trust and distribute it to the beneficiaries named in the trust document. Probate court proceedings are not necessary. However, if the deceased person did not name an executor, it usually falls to the successor trustee to do all the other jobs that traditionally belong to an executor: pay debts, file tax returns, and transfer property that wasn't held in trust. Being a trustee is usually easier than being an executor, but there is still work to be done.

Many people pick the same person to fill both roles. It makes sense—that way, one person is in charge of all the deceased person's property, whether or not it was held in trust.

B. The Executor's Role: An Overview

As an executor, you will be in charge of property that belongs to other people (beneficiaries and creditors), and you will be following instructions left in the will by someone who has died. Because such a situation leaves a lot of room for mischief by a dishonest person, the law requires executors to act with the highest ethical standards and to follow a set of well-established rules and procedures. For your efforts, you are entitled to reasonable financial compensation. But your true reward must be the satisfaction of performing an important task well.

1. Winding Up an Estate

Simply put, the executor's job is to gather and take care of the deceased person's assets, pay valid debts, and distribute what's left to the people who inherit it. Sounds pretty straightforward, and in many instances it is. But all these parts of the job can come with their own complications.

Some good news is that you may be able to transfer all the deceased person's property without probate court proceedings. Many estates pass without probate because property was held in joint tenancy, payable-on-death accounts, or other ways that let you pass it directly to the surviving co-owner or named beneficiary. And all states now offer simplified probate for "small estates." What qualifies as a small estate may surprise you: In some states, estates worth hundreds of thousands of dollars can slip under the wire, depending on how the assets were owned and how much estate planning was done before death.

Gathering assets. This part shouldn't be hard if, before the person dies, you become familiar with the deceased person's financial affairs. But if you're unprepared, and the deceased person leaves behind murky finances and jumbled records, you may have a tough time knowing what property you're supposed to be taking charge of. (Chapter 4 offers help for finding and making sense of financial and other records—but the best strategy is to get things straightened out before the death. See Section E, below.)

Taking care of assets. You must safeguard the deceased person's property until you hand it over to beneficiaries. For example, if a house or condo is empty, and a car is parked at the curb, you'll need to make sure both are secure. You may also have to decide whether or not to sell certain assets, either to raise cash or to avoid losing significant value. When it comes to managing investments, your main duty is not to turn a big profit, but to avoid losing money. You should invest estate assets in only the safest places. (Chapter 9 discusses this further.)

SUMMARY OF AN EXECUTOR'S DUTIES

- Find the will, if any.
- Notify the post office, utility companies, credit card companies, banks, and other businesses of the death.
- Notify the Social Security Administration and any agencies from which the deceased person was receiving benefits.
- Inventory all assets and, if necessary, have valuable ones appraised.
- Determine whether or not probate is necessary; if it is, conduct the probate court proceeding or hire a lawyer to do it (or help you).
- If there's a living trust, work with the successor trustee to coordinate bill-paying, property management, and other tasks.
- Notify beneficiaries named in the will, or people entitled to inherit under state law.
- Take good care of estate assets until you turn them over to the beneficiaries.
- Solicit beneficiaries' input on and consent to important decisions such as selling assets or changing investments.
- Collect money owed to the estate—for example, final wages or insurance benefits.
- Pay bills owed by the estate.
- File final income tax returns for the deceased person.
- If the estate was large, file estate tax returns.
- Distribute the assets.

Paying debts and taxes. Most people don't leave behind outsized debts or tax bills, so this isn't normally a problem. But if the estate doesn't contain enough money to go around, it can be a headache. You won't, however, be personally liable for debts the deceased person owed alone. (Executors can, however, be personally liable for losses they cause to the estate through mismanagement or dishonesty.) You will have to file income tax returns on behalf of the deceased person and, if the estate goes through probate and receives income, on behalf of the estate. Very few estates require federal or state estate tax returns.

Distributing what's left. As you might guess, this can be the trickiest part, especially if there are lots of beneficiaries—commonly, though, just a few people inherit. Whether or not the probate court is involved depends on what property the deceased person left and how much estate planning he or she did before death. These days, many kinds of assets can be transferred without going through probate court. For example, individual retirement accounts, payable-on-death bank or brokerage accounts, and life insurance policies usually go directly to beneficiaries the deceased person named in a document other than a will. For other property, if there's a will, you must make sense of its terms. If there's no will, you must make sense of state law that gives property to close relatives.

Working with others along the way. Unless you inherit everything, you'll have to deal with relatives, who may be cooperative and patient—or grasping and unhelpful. Lots of families stick together and accept the deceased person's wishes, but in others, family relationships are tested.

You'll also have to work with businesses, institutions, courts, and government agencies. Doing this successfully requires a large measure of patience.

Finally, you may find yourself helping beneficiaries with matters that aren't, strictly speaking, within your authority as executor. For example, life insurance proceeds aren't part of the estate, but a beneficiary might want you to help claim policy proceeds.

2. The Executor's Duty of Trust

An executor acts in place of the deceased person and owes the estate a duty to be absolutely trustworthy. This is called a "fiduciary duty." It means that you must always act in the best interest of the estate—not your own interests. For example, if you and the deceased person owned a business together, and you want to buy the deceased's half-interest, you would have to follow a scrupulously fair, open, and competitive process to offer the business interest for sale. The process would have to be run solely for the estate's benefit, not yours.

Here are a few examples of acts that violate an executor's fiduciary duty and could get you into trouble:

- wasting or stealing estate money

- benefiting personally at the expense of the estate—for example, selling yourself estate property

- selling an asset during probate if you don't have authority

- investing estate assets recklessly—for example, in a volatile stock or start-up company, or

- arranging things so that one beneficiary ends up with an unfairly larger share than another.

3. Compensation

You are entitled to compensation for your work as executor.

Just how much you're entitled to depends on the terms of the will and your state's law. Most wills don't set out a specific fee or hourly rate, but under state law in most places, you can claim a "reasonable" fee. It's up to you to decide what's reasonable. If beneficiaries or creditors object, they can complain to the probate court, which will review the fee. Some states, however, let executors claim a percentage of the value of the estate. Still a few others give executors a percentage of the money that flows in and out of the estate, to try to reflect the amount of work the executor must do managing assets.

Most executors don't accept payment unless their responsibilities are onerous or long-lasting, because they are close family members who inherit under the will anyway. There are also tax considerations. If you accept an executor's fee, the money is taxable income for you. If you're going to inherit the money anyway, it's usually better to take it as an inheritance, which isn't taxed. (The exception to this rule comes if estate tax will be due, and your personal rate is lower than the estate's; in this situation, it may be wise to take the payment as compensation. If the estate is large enough to owe estate tax, you should be consulting a tax expert anyway, so ask about the executor's fee.)

If you're not a close relative or friend, you may feel perfectly comfortable accepting a fee for your work. You may have been chosen because of your special skills—perhaps you can manage the deceased person's business until it can be sold, or you have the enviable ability to calm rancor among family members—and it's only fair that you be compensated.

C. The Successor Trustee's Role: An Overview

If you're in charge of wrapping up a simple living trust, your job is in many ways similar to that of an executor. (See Section B, above.) Your primary task is to distribute property held in the trust to the beneficiaries. And you have the same duty to be scrupulously honest in all your dealings, and to always put the beneficiaries' interests first. You may also have to expend time and energy dealing with beneficiaries who are anxious, uninformed, or downright annoying. Whether or not you are entitled to compensation depends on what the trust document says.

Again, if you're the only person acting on behalf of the deceased person—that is, no one else has been named as executor—you must also fulfill the broader duties of an executor.

But generally, serving as a successor trustee is easier than serving as an executor. If your only responsibility is a simple living trust, you can probably finish your duties as successor trustee in a few weeks or months. That's because you don't have to go through probate court, with all its requirements about notifying creditors and heirs that the estate is being settled.

Your duties may, however, last quite a long time if the trust is more than a simple living trust. For example, if you are trustee of a children's trust, your responsibility may last until the beneficiaries are young adults. (For more on the special concerns that apply to taking on a job as a long-term trustee, see Chapters 20 and 21.)

SUMMARY OF A SUCCESSOR TRUSTEE'S DUTIES

- Prepare some simple paperwork to document that fact that you're taking over as trustee, in case people or institutions you deal with want a record of your authority.

- Determine what property is held in trust.

- Notify beneficiaries that you're now in charge of the trust.

- Get valuable property appraised, if necessary.

- Pay debts and expenses related to the trust, if any.

- Transfer trust property (or in some cases, the proceeds of its sale) to beneficiaries named in the trust document.

D. Should You Accept the Job?

If you're asked to be an executor, a successor trustee, or both, or if you learn through the family grapevine that you've been named to the post, you don't have to accept or decline now. You can decide later, when it's actually time to serve. But if you already know—or are pretty sure—that you can't or don't want to take the job, it's most helpful to announce your decision right away, so that the person who sought your help can choose someone else.

You may feel that you don't really have a choice about whether or not to serve. If your spouse or parent asks you to step in, you probably feel duty-bound to take on the role, even if you'd love to say no. But it can be a wrenching decision, especially in families with a history of turmoil and disagreement. Even if the family situation is relatively calm, the job may be just too large a burden. If you're not willing and able to handle it, and someone else is, you're not doing anyone a favor by accepting.

This section discusses some legal and personal aspects of the job to take into account as you make your decision. It also discusses the option of suggesting, if you conclude the job is too much for you, that you be appointed as coexecutor with another person or an institutional executor.

1. Legal Restrictions on Executors

Every state has laws about who may serve as an executor of an estate that's probated in the state's courts. So even if you're willing to take on the job, it's possible—though not likely—that you won't qualify under state law. These rules do *not* apply to the successor trustee of a living trust, who is not usually involved in any court proceedings.

Generally, any adult who hasn't been convicted of a felony can serve as an executor. But a fair number of states impose special requirements on out-of-state executors. For example, even if the will says it's not required, you may have to post a bond—a kind of insurance policy to protect beneficiaries—in case you mishandle estate assets. Some insist that you appoint someone to be your in-state "agent" as well, so there is always someone around who is subject to the jurisdiction of the local court and can receive legal papers on your behalf.

To find out whether your state puts any special burdens on out-of-state executors, check your state's information page in the appendix. If something looks problematic, the person who wants you to serve may need to name an in-state coexecutor or take other measures to make things work smoothly.

2. Skills an Executor or Trustee Needs

The best executors and trustees are people who are careful, patient, unquestionably honest, well-organized, and committed to doing a good job. They must get along with people—especially the other beneficiaries. And they need a good bit of spare time, too. You can expect to spend many, many hours, probably for six months to a year, to do the job.

You don't, however, need to be a financial wizard or legal expert. You can always get professional or personal help with your tasks. For example, perhaps a sibling, even one who isn't serving as your official coexecutor or cotrustee, could help you with the time-consuming jobs of sorting through papers or making phone calls. (This can work especially well if the helpers are recruited in advance by the person who is naming you as executor or trustee.) And you have legal authority to hire accountants, tax preparers, lawyers, real estate brokers, and others whose professional expertise you need. Their fees will be paid from estate funds, not your own pocket. For example, some executors happily turn over the whole probate process to a lawyer; others do much of the routine work themselves and consult experts from time to time, to get over rough spots.

3. Your Situation

Every estate and every family situation is unique. The difficulty of serving as executor or trustee depends on many factors: the size of the estate, your state's laws, and the complexity of the deceased person's financial affairs, to name a few. Two personal factors also loom large: how smoothly family members get along and how well-organized the deceased person was.

a. Complexity of the Job

The size and complexity of the estate count for a lot. If the person will probably leave property of modest value, with a few major assets and no estate tax issues, accepting the executor's or trustee's job may not be such a big deal.

If you've already been helping manage someone's finances, handling things after death may be a natural extension of your duties. But if you're unfamiliar with the person's affairs, you may face as many practical problems as legal ones: finding the will, untangling investments, digging up insurance policies, and the like.

If you're being asked to be an executor, the complexity of your state's probate system also matters. The trend is to make the process simpler, but unfortunately not every state has jumped on this bandwagon. (Chapter 18 discusses state differences in probate procedures.)

b. Personal Factors

If you'll inherit most or all of the property, you have a strong incentive to serve as executor or trustee. You'll be in charge of what will shortly be your own property, and you won't have other beneficiaries to worry about.

If you're one of several beneficiaries, however—for example, one of three children who will share everything—it may be helpful to ask yourself some questions about the reality you will face.

- If you live far away, will it be too difficult or expensive for you to handle the estate? If there is a responsible and appropriate person living close by, that person may be a better choice.

- How likely are family members to let you do your job without second-guessing every decision? It's one thing to agree to wind up an estate, quite another to try to mediate the miseries of a dysfunctional family.

- How likely are other inheritors to bicker among themselves and with you? Would conflict be reduced or intensified if someone served as coexecutor or cotrustee with you? Sometimes it prevents hurt feelings and future conflict to name two siblings, for example, as cotrustees, even if only one of them is suited to the part—and will likely end up doing the lion's share of the work.

- If you're worried about taking time away from work to perform your executor's duties, what payment will you be legally entitled to collect for your services? Especially if you stand to inherit only a small portion of the estate, you'll want to charge a reasonable fee that reflects the responsibility you've taken on.

- Is there anyone else willing and able to do a conscientious job or at least share the work as a coexecutor or cotrustee?

Even if the answers to some of these questions are discouraging, it doesn't mean you should turn down the job. After all, there are ways to constructively deal with many potential problems. But thinking about them now will help you prepare mentally for the challenges ahead, and maybe prompt you to figure out creative ways to avoid problems.

Finally, you may find that the process of winding up a loved one's affairs is unexpectedly therapeutic. There is satisfaction in knowing that you're doing what the deceased person wanted. And whether or not it's true, many of us feel that we didn't do quite enough for a person who has died, and that now it's too late. Maybe not.

A COMPROMISE FOR LARGE ESTATES

For large estates—worth more than about $1 million—that face state or federal estate tax issues, an executor's job may be truly burdensome. One choice is to accept the executor's post only if a professional trust company is named as coexecutor. That way you will be set up in advance to pay pros to handle most of the paperwork and other details while you keep an eye on the big picture.

c. If You Don't Serve, Who Will?

If you decline the job after the person who names you has died, or resign after serving for a while, someone else must take over. How that person is chosen depends on whether you're serving as an executor or as a successor trustee.

If you're a trustee of a living trust, the trust document probably names another person to take your place as successor trustee if you resign. If not, it will be up to the beneficiaries to choose someone.

If you're an executor and you haven't yet begun probate, you should simply notify the alternate executor named in the will. If there isn't anyone, someone must either take over informally or begin probate proceedings and ask the court to be appointed an executor.

If you resign as executor after having started probate court proceedings, you can submit your resignation to the probate court. You must give the court a written record of what, if anything, you have done—property you have distributed, bills you have paid, and so on.

The court will then appoint someone to take your place. If the will names an alternate executor, that person will get the nod. If it doesn't, the court will appoint someone. In some states, if you are the surviving spouse or child, you can choose the person who will be appointed.

EXAMPLE: *Eleanor's will appoints her son Harry as her executor, but Harry is unable to serve. The will does not name an alternate executor. Under state law, Eleanor's daughters Victoria and Vanessa are next in line to be executors. Victoria declines to serve and instead nominates a close friend of her mother's. If Vanessa wants to serve, the court will appoint her. If she doesn't, the friend nominated by Victoria would get the job, even if more distant relatives wanted it.*

If the choice is up to the court, many states' laws direct judges to appoint people in roughly this order:

- surviving spouse (or, in California, Hawaii, or Vermont, an unmarried partner, if the couple registered with the state)

- children

- grandchildren

- parents

- siblings

- another beneficiary of the will

- a creditor (one who hopes to get paid from the estate may request the position).

If there are absolutely no interested parties, the court hires someone, commonly called the "public administrator," to take over.

E. Making the Job Manageable

A key to how easy or difficult it will be to serve as executor or trustee is the amount of preparation done beforehand. If you have the chance, getting the will-maker to do some planning can smooth out what would otherwise be a bumpy ride. Three areas deserve particular attention:

- **Organization.** Getting organized will make it easier for everybody, now and later. But if you take over a welter of papers, you may spend more time than you ever thought possible sorting them out.

- **Probate avoidance.** It's not hard to own most property in a way that does away with the need for probate—making it possible for you to eventually transfer it to inheritors with a minimum of fuss. (If you're asked to be a successor trustee, then obviously probate avoidance is already being addressed.)

- **Family relationships.** Tending a simmering stew of family disagreements will exhaust and probably exasperate you. But if people understand and accept the person's wishes before the death, you are much less likely to face arguments later.

If someone does you the honor of asking you to be an executor or trustee, promptly arrange to have a talk about these crucial matters. You can't take these steps; it's up to the person who has asked you to serve. If he or she isn't willing to do some work now to save you a lot of hassle later (and ensure that his or her wishes will actually be carried out), you may have a sound reason to respectfully decline.

HAVING THE CONVERSATION

Many people, understandably enough, prefer to steer clear of the subject of death—especially their own. So it's common for someone to ask you to serve as executor, but then put off your questions with vague assurances that whatever you do will be fine. Don't settle for that. Persist, politely, until all your questions are answered. Stress that to do what he or she wants and avoid family dissension, you must have clear directions to follow.

It's best to get information in writing, as discussed below. Otherwise you won't remember everything, and if anyone challenges you, you won't be able to back up your opinions. Keep the documents with the will or other important papers, in a place where you can get at them immediately after the death.

10 WAYS THE WILL- OR TRUST-MAKER CAN MAKE THE EXECUTOR'S JOB EASIER

To make your job easier, ask the person who has named you as executor or trustee to take these steps:

1. Make a list of significant assets, and keep it current.

2. Write a simple, clear will (and perhaps a simple living trust).

3. Hold as much property as possible in ways that will avoid probate.

4. Set out, in writing, the final arrangements he or she wishes.

5. Make sure documents such as the will, tax returns, deeds, insurance policies, and so on are accessible to the executor.

6. If he or she owns (or might, after the death of a spouse) assets worth more than $1.5 million, investigate ways to avoid federal estate tax.

7. Settle any lawsuits or major disputes.

8. If the estate will contain hard-to-sell assets such as complicated investments or a family business, make a clear plan for the executor to follow.

9. Get a handle on debts.

10. Head off disputes by explaining the estate plan to family members and asking them to respect it.

Getting organized. *Nolo's Personal RecordKeeper* provides an easy, systematic way to list all assets that are significant for financial or sentimental reasons, their locations and values, as well as much miscellaneous information that will help survivors sort things out. Because the information is on a computer, it can be easily updated and shared. (For more information, visit www.nolo.com.)

1. Get a List of Assets

It can be a great help to have the person whose estate you will handle draw up a list of assets; it may help you avoid overlooking something valuable later.

First, the person should list each piece of property that is significant for either financial or personal reasons. Then answer these key questions:

- **Where is it?** If that's not obvious (for instance, jewelry that's been tucked away in an odd spot for safekeeping), you will need guidance.

- **How much is it worth?** Again, if it's not obvious—for example, in the case of art or collections—find out what it cost and where you could get it appraised or sold.

- **Where are important documents?** Track down, for example, title slips to cars or boats, other ownership documents, maintenance records, and receipts for valuable items of personal property.

The "Information for My Executor" form, below, provides a way to list assets and some other helpful information. You may want to give this information to the person who has named you as executor. For much more thorough prompting, and space to include almost unlimited information, check out the Nolo software designed for this purpose, *Personal RecordKeeper.*

A list of assets is not in any way a substitute for a will or trust. It is for the convenience of the executor and does not legally control who will inherit property.

COMMON KINDS OF VALUABLE PROPERTY

Animals

Antiques

Art

Books/CDs/Videos

Business interests

    - Sole proprietorship

    - Corporation

    - Limited liability company

    - Partnership

Business property (if a sole proprietorship)

Cameras

Cash accounts

    - Certificates of deposit

    - Checking

    - Money market funds

    - Savings

China, crystal, silver

Coins, stamps

Collectibles

Computers

Copyrights, patents, trademarks

Electronic equipment

Furniture

Jewelry

Life insurance and annuity policies

Limited partnership

Precious metals

Real estate (house, farmland, time-share, dock space, mobile home, vacation home)

Retirement accounts

    - 401(k) or 403(b) plans

    - IRAs, Roth IRAs

    - Keogh plans

Royalties

Securities

    - Bonds

    - Mutual funds

    - Stocks

Tools

U.S. bills, notes, bonds

Vehicles

INFORMATION FOR MY EXECUTOR

To help my executor, here is information about my significant assets, including those that may hold sentimental value to my family members and friends, and other information that my executor may need.

Valuable Property

Real estate _____

_____

Vehicles _____

Retirement accounts (account numbers and name and address of administrator)

_____

_____

Cash accounts (account numbers and name and address of bank)

_____

_____

Investments _____

Life insurance and annuity policies (policy numbers and name of company)

_____

Other _____

Where to Look for Documents and Other Items

Will, trust _____

Checkbook _____

Deeds _____

Financial records _____

Property tax returns and records _____

_____

Marriage certificate _____

Divorce decree _____

Car keys _____

House keys (garage, storage space, etc.) _____

Valuable jewelry _____

INFORMATION FOR MY EXECUTOR, *continued*

Credit cards _____

Insurance policies (vehicle, homeowners') _____

_____

Birth certificate _____

Military service records _____

Social Security records _____

Address book _____

Money market account information _____

Bank statements _____

Income tax returns and records _____

Other Information My Executor May Find Helpful

Social Security number _____

Lawyer _____

Tax preparer _____

Investment advisor _____

Real estate agent _____

Stockbroker _____

Accountant _____

Appraiser for my collection of _____

Passwords for online accounts _____

Password for email access _____

Safe Deposit Box

Location of safe deposit box _____

Location of key _____

Contents _____

You may also want to ask the person for information you or other close family members might need in an emergency, or a situation in which the person couldn't easily communicate with you. Strictly speaking, this information isn't for the executor, but many executors also find themselves with many practical decisions to make in an emergency.

INFORMATION FOR EMERGENCIES

Health Care Providers: Contact Information

Physicians _____

Dentist _____

Insurance _____

Location of medical records _____

Pharmacies _____

Legal documents _____

Financial power of attorney (name of agent or attorney-in-fact, location of document)

_____

Health care power of attorney (name of agent or attorney-in-fact, location of document)

_____

Advance medical directive (living will) _____

_____

Emergency Care of Children, Pets, and Houses

Children (names, birthdates, emergency caregivers' name and address, care information)

_____

_____

Pets (names, emergency caregivers' name and address, medical information)

_____

House _____

POWERS OF ATTORNEY AND MEDICAL DIRECTIVES

If you have time to help the person who plans to name you as executor do some more estate planning, by all means have the person look into documents called "powers of attorney." They give some-one—probably you—authority to make health care and financial decisions on the person's behalf if they become incapacitated before they die. A will can't do that. Here are the documents everyone should have:

- **Durable power of attorney for finances,** to give you (or someone else) authority to manage the person's assets and finances if someday he or she can't. (If, however, the person has a living trust, the successor trustee probably has authority over trust assets if the person becomes incapacitated.) Having this document at the ready can be a great help if the person who signed it becomes seriously ill and unable to take care of day-to-day financial affairs. It can also make the executor's job easier, because you have a chance to become familiar with managing the assets you will need to marshal and distribute after the person dies. If you have questions, you can ask them now, while it's still possible to get an answer.

- **Advance medical directive** (living will), which lets people instruct physicians about their wishes for end-of-life health care.

- **Durable power of attorney for health care,** to give you (or someone else) authority to make medical decisions for the person if someday he or she can't.

Making durable powers of attorney and health care directives. *Quicken WillMaker Plus* (software developed and published by Nolo), lets you make financial and health care powers of attorney and medical directives, as well as other estate planning documents.

Medical Directives & Powers of Attorney for California, by Shae Irving (Nolo), contains everything California residents need to make these vital documents.

2. Make Sure There's an Up-to-Date Will or Trust

If there isn't a will, or if it's not up to date, ask the person to make a new one. A lawyer can do it, or it can be done with a good self-help resource, a few of which are listed below.

Just having a will, however, isn't enough—having one that covers all important issues and is easy to understand is the important part. Because so many wills fail this test, you may want to look at it, to see whether or not there are any wonky bits. Check for:

- The executor clause. Start with the basics: Are you sure you've been appointed executor?

- Potentially ambiguous provisions, such as gifts to "my children." If you find such language, encourage the person to make a new, clear will listing the children's names. It could avoid expensive and bitter arguments later. (For an explanation of the potential problems this kind of language can cause, see Chapter 6.)

- If the person has young children, a provision naming someone to raise them if neither parent could.

- Provisions almost sure to lead to controversy. For example, if the will tries to disinherit the spouse or a child or makes seemingly bizarre gifts (for example, a very large sum for the care of a pet or a huge gift to a caregiver at the expense of close blood relatives), you should discuss it. There may be good reasons for these provisions, but they may spawn unpleasantness—or even lawsuits—after the death.

Making a will. *Quicken WillMaker Plus* (software developed and published by Nolo), provides a reliable and inexpensive way to make a valid will, trust, power of attorney, medical directive, final arrangements document, and other legal documents.

Nolo's Simple Will Book, by Denis Clifford, lets you choose a will form or assemble a customized will from a selection of clauses. All the forms are included as tear-outs and on a CD.

3. Encourage Steps to Avoid Probate

For most people, it's also extremely worthwhile to do some estate planning that goes beyond (or around) making a will. At bottom this is because most wills must go through probate unless the estate is small enough to qualify for your state's simplified probate process. (More about that, of course, in Chapter 17.)

What's wrong with probate? Volumes have been written on that subject—but the short answer is that it's a slow, clunky, and expensive way to transfer property to the people who inherit it. From an executor's point of view, it's simple: Probate will weigh you down for anywhere from six months to a year and a half. By contrast, if probate is avoided, you can probably wind things up in a month unless the estate is so large that you must file estate tax returns.

Fortunately, there are many simple ways to avoid the probate of common kinds of assets such as bank accounts and securities accounts. For example, if a bank account owner designates (on a form provided by the bank) a payable-on-death (POD) beneficiary, the account funds won't need to go through probate. Neither does joint tenancy property, when the first co-owner dies. And simple living trusts can avoid probate for any kind of property.

Make out-of-state real estate a priority. One probate is bad enough—no executor should have to handle two of them. But that's what could happen if the estate contains real estate in two states; real estate is always subject to the laws of the state it's located in. So advocate for at least avoiding probate of the out-of-state property, by using joint ownership, a living trust, or a transfer-on-death deed (valid in only a few states, listed in Chapter 12). It will save you a lot of headaches.

More on planning ahead to avoid probate. Here are some books and software that can help with planning to avoid probate.

8 Ways to Avoid Probate, by Mary Randolph (Nolo), explains simple ways to avoid probate, to simplify and speed the process of getting property to the people who inherit it.

Quicken WillMaker Plus (software developed and published by Nolo), lets you make a valid living trust to avoid probate, as well as many other estate planning documents.

Plan Your Estate, by Denis Clifford and Cora Jordan (Nolo), covers estate planning in depth, from probate avoidance to dealing with children to sophisticated trusts aimed at avoiding federal estate tax.

Make Your Own Living Trust, by Denis Clifford (Nolo), explains how to make a simple revocable living trust to avoid probate, and a more complicated "AB" trust for couples concerned about estate tax.

4. Get Wishes for Final Arrangements in Writing

Surviving family members must often make decisions about issues such as organ donation, burial instructions, funerals, and many other matters immediately after a death—sometimes within hours. So it's especially useful to have advance information about what the person wanted.

A will, which is usually not read for days after a death, is not the best place for instructions on these matters. So try to get directions—in as much or as little detail as is comfortable—in a separate, easily accessible document. For information on options involving organ or body donation, cremation or burial, and a host of related issues, see Chapter 3.

Making final arrangements. *Quicken WillMaker Plus* (software developed and published by Nolo) includes a "final arrangements" section that prompts users to set out their wishes regarding burial or cremation and memorial services.

5. Make Sure You'll Have Access to Documents

The best-organized records in the world won't do you any good if you don't know where they are or can't get to them. Insist on knowing where important documents are and having access to them. A will, for example, shouldn't be kept in a safe deposit box unless you are a co-owner with access to it. A fireproof box or metal file cabinet works just fine for paper documents such as a will. If records are on a computer, get either a copy or directions on how to find what you need on the original computer. If other people have already been given some estate planning documents (copies of a will, for example), get a list of who has what.

6. Encourage Efforts to Avoid Estate Tax, If Necessary

Only a tiny percentage of estates actually owe federal estate tax. But the estate of someone who isn't married and leaves a large amount of property—worth more than $1.5 million—may have to pay. (All property left to a surviving spouse who is a U.S. citizen passes tax-free; however, if the second spouse later dies owning a large estate, tax may be due.)

Because of changing tax laws, estates that aren't large enough to owe federal estate tax may still owe state estate tax. Check out your own state's rules by talking to a knowledgeable tax lawyer or preparer. You may also find some useful information online, on your state's official website. (State website addresses are listed in the appendix.)

If estate tax is a possibility, it's worth investigating tax-avoidance strategies. If you, as executor, have to file an estate tax return, it will both delay settlement of the estate and increase its cost, because you'll have to hire an expert to prepare the complicated tax return.

More information on estate tax. *Plan Your Estate*, by Denis Clifford and Cora Jordan (Nolo), discusses various strategies to reduce or avoid federal and state estate tax.

7. Urge Settlement of Lawsuits

Most people, thankfully, aren't ever involved in a lawsuit. But if it looks like the person whose estate you will handle will be embroiled in a court case at his or her death, encourage every effort to settle it out of court. (More than 90% of lawsuits are settled, eventually—so why not sooner than later?) If that doesn't seem possible, and you are an inheritor and stand to benefit or lose based on the outcome, meet with the lawyer handling the case and educate yourself about it.

8. Get a Plan for Hard-to-Sell Assets

If the person owns an active business, has unconventional investments, or owns an unusual and valuable collection, it's a good idea to do some thinking about what should happen to them.

Probably no one is going to be better at selling these assets than their original owner. If he or she is ill or elderly and no one in the family will take over, it may be better to sell now. But if you will be burdened with the task, you'll need good information. For example, if you'll need to sell a collection of first-edition 18th-century English novels, a list of appraisers and other collectors would help.

9. Get a Handle on Debts

Debts aren't a big problem for most estates. Most people leave only routine personal debts such as utility bills and credit card balances. A mortgage is transferred along with the real estate and doesn't have to be paid off at death.

Again, being executor or trustee does not make you personally responsible for the deceased person's debts. (If you and the deceased person incurred the debts together, however, you are liable for them.) You pay them from the estate property. If, however, you expect to be dealing with large debts, it may be wise to investigate how those debts will be paid after the death. For example, how a couple holds title to their property (joint tenancy, tenancy by the entirety, community property, and so on) can determine whether or not the surviving spouse must pay a debt that the deceased spouse incurred alone. Large debts can also disrupt a carefully constructed estate plan.

EXAMPLE: *Marvin's will leaves certain property to his children and everything else (the "residue," in legal lingo) to his wife. His will (as many do) also instructs that debts be paid from the residue of the estate—that is, what his wife inherits. This works fine as long as there are no large debts—but if there are, they could eat up his wife's inheritance, frustrating Marvin's plan.*

10. Try to Head Off Family Fights

This may be the most important step of all. Deaths, unfortunately, do not always bring out the best in families. Long-dormant tensions may burst out, triggered by tussles over seemingly trivial items of property or by major issues such as whether to sell or keep the family home. Problems can be exacerbated if siblings think one child has been favored unreasonably (especially if the others believe the deceased person was manipulated). You definitely do not want to be in the middle, trying to mediate among relatives who have

their hearts set on Mom's relish plate—or on control of the family business.

Here are a few ideas for preventing family strife while the estate planner is still alive. One or more of them may work in your situation.

a. Talk

A frank conversation (or two) with all interested persons together in one room can go a long way to clear up questions and encourage cooperation and communication between you (the future executor) and other family members. But one word of caution is in order: Even well-meaning and scrupulously honest people often recall conversations differently. It's possible that varying memories of what Mom said could create problems where you had hoped to avert them. Talk is great—but the person who has chosen you as executor or trustee should back it up with clear, legally binding written instructions in a will or living trust.

b. Decide Who Gets Items of Sentimental Value

One important part of creating a successful estate plan is recognizing that it's not all about money at all—often, people's feelings are more important. So be sure that it's clear who is to receive family memorabilia, jewelry, photo albums, antiques, and other items people may squabble over. And think ahead—how are family members likely to accept these decisions?

These items can be disposed of in a will or living trust, or even given away while the owner is alive. Different strategies work for different families.

Some families go ahead and get the possibly troubling divisions out of the way now, while parents are still there to mediate sibling squabbles. One way to do this is to make up a long list of assets and circulate it among the kids, or gather everyone in the house and have them put post-it notes on precious objects.

One big advantage of this method (in addition to the parents' presence, which can act as a damper on pettiness) is that it may reveal surprises. Who knew that one sister coveted the old china (and thought it had been promised to her), while the other preferred inexpensive trinkets from a long-ago family vacation?

c.   Write Instructions

A will, trust, and other legal documents will give you legal guidance on how to distribute major assets when it's time to do your job as executor or trustee. But they usually don't—and shouldn't—try to cover everything, down to who gets every teacup or what to do if an argument erupts over family photos or Sparky's "heirloom" dog dish. Especially when a surviving parent dies, the will may simply leave everything to be shared equally among the children.

You can forestall countless hassles if you can persuade the person making the will to take two steps:

1. Use the will (or living trust) to name specific beneficiaries for all items that have particular value, either monetary or emotional, to survivors. (In many states, the will-maker can make a separate list of items and their disposition, and refer to it in the will; see Chapter 6.)

2. Write nonbinding instructions that explain (in as much detail as seems wise) how and why these things have been left and that provide a framework for solving any disputes that erupt. Unlike the terms of a will, these instructions are not legally binding—and again, it's important that they not contradict the will or trust. But they have a moral force that can sway even stubborn offspring.

The person who's doing all this planning should also be encouraged to write an explanation of any will provisions that may surprise or disappoint certain family members. For example, if one child will inherit more than another, the parent may want to explain that

Family surprises. After our mother died, my brother and I divided up the items left in her house. As we sorted through things, it came out that he wanted a certain oil painting, and I had my heart set on the stone deer in the back yard. There were no arguments over these items—but neither of us would have ever guessed what the other wanted.

this is because the other child has already been given property. Or the parent may explain although she loves each equally, she is leaving one a larger share because of health or other problems.

The letter of explanation should include a little guidance about divvying things up. The instructions will depend, of course, on what the person wants. Here are a few examples, based on the common scenario of two or more children and a will that leaves them everything in equal shares but doesn't specify who gets what.

Personal Belongings and Keepsakes

Here, give a little guidance about divvying things up. The instructions will depend, of course, on what you want. Here are a few examples, based on the common scenario of two or more children and a will that leaves them everything in equal shares but doesn't specify who gets what.

EXAMPLE 1: *When my worldly possessions are shared among my children as my will provides, I intend for each child to end up with assets of roughly equivalent value. I have left valuable property through my will, but my offspring must divide the rest of my personal belongings them-selves. I trust them to do this amicably and fairly. If they encounter problems along the way, I instruct that they take turns choosing items, from a list of all my assets left to them, until each has*

selected items with a value equal to that person's share of the total value.

EXAMPLE 2: *I trust my children to divide my personal belongings and family heirlooms among themselves fairly and with a minimum of fuss. If they encounter problems, I instruct my executor to decide who gets what.*

EXAMPLE 3: *If my children cannot agree on who should take a particular object, I instruct that they bid on it in a private auction conducted by the executor or a disinterested third person. The final price shall be paid to the estate and be divided as my will instructs.*

The person may also want to include a few words about his or her decisions.

EXAMPLE: *I love all my children deeply, but I have not left my property to them equally for several reasons, which I hope they understand. First, I have already given Robert substantial amounts of money, which he needed to get his business off the ground. I was very happy to do this, but feel it is fair that my other children should receive a larger share of the property I leave at my death. Second, I am leaving Melissa a slightly larger share to acknowledge her efforts to help me with many day-to-day matters over the last few years, including shopping, doctor visits, and much more. Sacrificing her own time when I needed help, despite her own demanding schedule, she made things much easier and more pleasant for me.* ∎

First Steps

CHAPTER 3

The First Week

When someone very close to you dies, leaving you in charge, you probably won't have a quiet interval in which to plan, consult experts, and generally ponder the best course. You must act. Certain things simply must be taken care of immediately. Arrangements must be made for burial or cremation, relatives and friends must be notified, and often a funeral planned, to mention just some of what must be done.

All this can easily seem overwhelming at a time of grief, and the fatiguing and stressful days just after a loved one dies often pass in a blur. Don't add to your burdens by trying to make any important legal or financial decisions. Leave them for later. For now, do only what's absolutely necessary to cope with immediate concerns and marshal your energy for taking care of yourself and those close to you.

This chapter outlines how to take some first practical steps. Obviously, how you and family members handle this transition period will depend on your own religious, cultural, and family traditions.

The decisions that must be made immediately after a death are traditionally (and legally) the responsibility of the closest surviving family members. If the will names you as executor, but you are not a member of the immediate family, you won't have an official role in these matters. If you are a relative or very close friend, though, the fact that the deceased person chose you as executor signals that he or she looked to you to be a leader. Any help you can give the immediate family may make a difficult time at least a little easier for them.

A. Organ, Tissue, and Body Donation

The first question that arises after a death is likely to involve anatomical gifts, especially if the person who died was relatively young and healthy.

1. Kinds of Donations

Anatomical gifts can be made for two purposes: transplant or research. Healthy people killed by accidents or brief illnesses are the main source of organs for transplant. Tissues useful for research, however, can be taken from many donors.

It is also possible to donate an entire body to a medical school for research or teaching purposes. (Bodies from which organs have been removed cannot be donated for these uses.) Usually, someone who wants to donate his or her body makes arrangements with a particular institution in advance, but you may be able to arrange something after the death. If you are interested in pursuing this alternative, you'll need to contact a nearby medical school or the National Anatomical Service at 800-727-0700.

More information about organ donation. See the Health and Human Services Department's website at www.organdonor.gov or call 800-55-DONOR (800-553-6667).

2. Presumed Consent for Organ Donation

Generally, doctors must have permission, in the form of a donation card signed by the deceased person or consent from the family, before removing organs or tissues. In many states, however, coroners may remove some organs or tissues without explicit authorization under certain circumstances. In practice, these laws come into play only if the death is sudden—for example, in a car accident—and medical personnel cannot reach any family members.

The laws that allow this fall into two general categories:

- laws that presume consent for the removal of tissues—generally corneas and the pituitary gland—if there is no known objection to organ donation, and

- laws that require the coroner to make reasonable efforts to get permission from the next of kin or confirm that the deceased person signed an organ donation form before removing certain organs. These "reasonable efforts" laws usually allow removal of any body part.

Under either kind of law, these rules apply:

- There must be a request for the organ by a qualified recipient.

- The removal must not interfere with any pending investigation or autopsy.

- The removal must not alter the deceased person's facial appearance.

In states that have no presumed consent laws, organs may not be removed for donation without explicit consent. Each state's law is summarized in the appendix.

3. Giving Consent

To be useful for transplant, organs must be taken quickly after death. So shortly after the death occurs (or before, if it appears imminent), an attending physician or someone else from the hospital will probably ask the family whether or not they wish to authorize donation of organs or tissue from the body. If no one contacts you, and you believe the deceased person would have wished to donate organs or tissue, mention it to the doctor who oversaw the patient's care.

Even if the person signed a donor card or left other clear instructions allowing donations, most hospitals won't go ahead without written permission from the surviving spouse or closest relative. This is a family decision; it doesn't come under the executor's authority.

If you know that the deceased person ever indicated a clear preference for or against donation, you must honor that wish. (A law called the Uniform Anatomical Gift Act, adopted by every state, requires it.) But if you aren't sure what the person thought about organ donation, you'll need to try to figure it out. Unfortunately, you'll probably have only a few hours in which to arrive at a decision. Here are some ways to go about it:

- Look for a donor card. In many states, these accompany a driver's license.

- If the deceased person left a health care directive (living will) or power of attorney for health care, read over these documents to see whether or not organ donation is mentioned.

- If your state keeps a computerized donor registry (many do), the hospital should be able to check to see whether the deceased person registered. If the person recently moved, it might pay to check the former state.

- Check the person's will, if you have it. Although it's not recommended, because wills aren't usually read immediately after a death, it might contain instructions about donation.

- Talk to others who were close to the person, to see whether or not they ever discussed the matter.

STATE DONOR REGISTRIES

Many states have donor registries, where residents can sign up to donate any usable organs or tissues at their deaths. These registries, which are run by the state or by a nonprofit organization, provide computerized, confidential lists to authorized medical personnel 24 hours a day. They provide clear evidence of a person's wish to donate organs; however, hospitals may still discuss the donation with surviving family members.

If you are the closest relative, you may find yourself making a decision without any clues as to what the person thought about donation. It is, of course, a very personal matter. The

need, however, is great. More than 80,000 people are waiting for organs in this country. Each day about 60 of them receive a transplant, but another 16 people on the waiting list die because not enough organs are available, according to the U.S. Department of Health and Human Services.

It does not cost the family anything to donate an organ. The recipient pays the expenses, usually through insurance, Medicare, or Medicaid. Donation does not disfigure the body and does not interfere with having a funeral, even an open casket service.

MINORITIES AND ORGAN DONATION

Because patients' bodies are less likely to reject transplanted tissue or organs donated by someone who is genetically similar, there is a need for organs from people of all kinds of ethnic backgrounds.

But there is a special need for donations from people who are members of racial and ethnic minorities in the United States, because certain diseases of the kidney, heart, lung, pancreas, and liver occur more frequently in these minority populations than in the general population. For example, African-Americans, Asian and Pacific Islanders, and Hispanics are three times more likely to suffer from end-stage kidney disease than whites. Native Americans are four times more likely than whites to suffer from diabetes. Sometimes, organ transplant is the best—or the only—way to treat these diseases.

B. Physician's Certification and Death Certificate

Within a day or two after someone dies (the deadline depends on state law) a doctor must sign a certification of death. That's no problem in a hospital, but if the death occurs at home you'll need to call the person's personal physician or, if that's not possible, the county medical examiner or coroner.

Within the next few days, someone at the funeral home or cremation organization will prepare the death certificate. This document contains information about the deceased person. The specifics vary from state to state, but these elements are commonly required:

- address

- birth date

- birthplace

- father's name and birthplace

- mother's name and birthplace

- Social Security number

- veteran's discharge or claim number

- education

- marital status and name of surviving spouse, if any

- date, place, and time of death.

When the certificate is entirely filled in, it must be signed by the physician and filed with the county before the body can be buried or cremated. Usually the mortuary, or whoever else is in charge of the person's remains, files the certificate. (Later, you'll need certified copies of the death certificate. Chapter 4 explains how to get them.)

C. Autopsy

Autopsies—a doctor's examination of a body to determine what caused death—used to be routine. Today, they are seldom conducted unless doctors are puzzled by the cause of death or an autopsy is mandated by law. State law generally requires an autopsy if the death appears to have been the result of an accident or of violence, or if the person had not seen a doctor in some time (from a few days to about a month, depending on state law).

The thought of an autopsy can be disturbing to survivors. But autopsies often reveal surprising facts about the cause of death. What the doctor learns from this investigation may help others at risk of death from similar causes—perhaps even family members, if they share a medical condition with the deceased person.

An autopsy that's required by law will probably be performed by the county medical examiner in the first few days following a death, after which the body is released for cremation or burial. (The autopsy report may not be available until weeks later, however, if tissue is sent to a lab for testing.) The procedure does not preclude an open-casket funeral; a funeral home can disguise signs of the autopsy if necessary.

D. Burial, Cremation, Funerals, and Memorial Services

After a death, surviving family members must contact a mortuary (funeral home) for help with disposing of the body. Which one should you call? It depends on how much (if any) planning has already been done, and on what you want—a traditional funeral and burial, cremation and a memorial service, or some different combination.

Unfortunately, survivors must sometimes make this difficult decision quickly, under pressure from a hospital or nursing home. Try not to let the pressure influence you. An institution cannot, legally, dispose of the body without the consent of the next of kin. You may cause it some inconvenience if you can't provide instant instructions—but that's better than making a poor decision.

In many families, survivors know what to do, either because there is a family tradition or because the deceased person discussed it with them. If you're not sure, see whether or not the deceased person left you some guidance. Look through his or her papers to find evidence of:

- a prepaid burial plan
- membership in a memorial society
- written instructions regarding funeral arrangements
- ownership of a burial plot.

Instructions about burial, cremation, and ceremonies are usually left in a separate document, sometimes called "final arrangements." But if there's a will, and you know where it is, check it—although it's not common, a will may contain instructions for body disposition or memorial services. The deceased person's durable power of attorney for health care may also contain instructions.

If the deceased person made some plans in advance, you'll need only to call the mortuary or memorial society to set events in motion. But more likely, you'll need to choose the mortuary and decide what happens next.

Take what planning you can get. My dad doesn't want to talk about planning his funeral—he just waves me off when I mention it. But he did let me know that he has a paid-for spot in a church graveyard in his home town. I'll need to arrange the details of getting his body there, but even though we've never really discussed it, we have most of a plan.

HANDLING THINGS WITHOUT A PROFESSIONAL

You can take charge of disposing of a loved one's body without a mortuary, if you follow state and local laws. (For example, there are likely to be strict health laws that govern where and how a body can be buried.) For guidance, check out *Caring for the Dead: Your Final Act of Love*, by Lisa Carlson (Upper Access Press). It will help you figure out what laws apply, and what permits you need and how to get them. The Funeral Consumers Alliance can also provide help. You can get information on its website, www.funerals.org or contact the FCA at 33 Patchen Road, South Burlington, VT 05403, 802-482-3437.

1. Your Options

There are two aspects to the first decisions you'll need to make after a death: what to do with the body (burial or cremation) and how to honor the memory of the deceased person with an appropriate service. More and more, these are separate decisions—for example, just because you want the body cremated doesn't mean you can't have a traditional funeral in a church, funeral home, or other location. However, when they're planning, people usually think about body disposition and funeral or memorial service together.

There are two common choices. The first is to have a traditional funeral within a few days after the death, followed immediately by burial in a cemetery. The second is to have the body cremated soon after death, and then to hold a memorial service some weeks (or longer) later. There's no reason, however, that you couldn't have a conventional funeral followed by cremation, or cemetery burial and a later memorial service.

Both of these options, and a few others, are discussed next.

A FEW TERMS YOU MAY RUN INTO

Funeral: A ceremony honoring the deceased person, traditionally held within a few days after the death at a church or funeral home, usually with the body present.

Memorial service: A gathering of friends and relatives to honor the deceased person, usually some time after the body has been buried or cremated.

Shiva: In the Jewish tradition, a seven-day period of mourning observed after a close relative's funeral.

Visitation: A time set aside, days or hours before a funeral, during which friends come to a funeral home to be with surviving family members and, commonly, to view the body. Sometimes called a viewing.

Wake: Similar to a visitation, but more festive—a party in honor of the deceased person. It may be of more emotional significance than the funeral itself.

a. Traditional Funeral and Burial

If you decide on a traditional funeral and burial, a mortuary will help you through the process. It will collect the body, prepare it for burial, and store it until a funeral service is conducted. Usually, the body is available for viewing a day or two before the service. After the service, the mortuary will transport the body to the cemetery for burial. It also commonly makes arrangements with the cemetery the family chooses.

The mortuary also usually obtains copies of the death certificate for the family. It may help with other tasks as well, such as notifying the local newspaper and the Social Security Administration of the death.

Most funerals are brief ceremonies, held at a mortuary chapel or a church. The body is usually present, but the casket may be open or closed. Sometimes it is open before the service so people who attend can view the body. The choice is entirely up to the family.

Burial entails several costs that aren't necessary with cremation, including:

- storing the body before burial

- a grave liner or burial vault (not re-quired by law, but by most cemeteries), and

- opening and closing of the grave.

You may notice that this list does not include embalming. If the body needs to be temporarily protected from decay—say for a few days until a funeral—refrigeration usually accomplishes the goal effectively. Embalming (replacing body fluids with a chemical preservative) is another method, but is rarely necessary or required by law. (Embalming gained popularity during the Civil War, when soldiers' bodies were shipped over long distances. It was later promoted by the funeral industry.)

Embalming, which generally costs about $300 to $700, may be required by law in very limited circumstances:

- when a body will be transported by plane or train from one country or state to another

- when it will be a relatively long time—usually a week or more—until burial or cremation, and

- in rare cases, when the death was caused by a communicable disease.

The casket is probably the biggest expense you'll face; prices range from a few hundred to many thousands of dollars. (The mark-up is commonly from 200% to as much as 2,000%.) Making the choice at such a tough time is not easy. The people who sell caskets (they dislike the older, earthier term "coffin") are well aware of the complicated emotions at play, and many do their best to push people toward expensive, high-profit options and make them feel bad for preferring something simple. Of course, you want to honor the person you loved. But is the price tag on a coffin the best evidence of your feelings? Perhaps the deceased person would have preferred a modest coffin, with the money saved going to a favorite charity.

Don't go it alone. It's a good idea to take someone with you when you shop for a casket and other funeral services. If possible, go with someone who knew the deceased person and his or her wishes, so you'll have a second opinion about the long list of decisions you'll have to make.

Because of these pervasive pressures, most states now require that caskets on sale in a funeral home showroom (or a catalogue) be labeled with the price, a description of the composition, and an identifying model number.

Also keep in mind that you don't have to buy the casket from the mortuary. If you find a model you like, shop around a little. Many independent casket makers and sellers offer their goods online, making comparison shopping and buying easy. (Next-day delivery is standard.)

Some states don't let you shop around. Unfortunately, some states' anticompetitive laws prohibit anyone but a funeral director from selling caskets or similar goods. For example, in Georgia, only a "funeral director" working in a "funeral establishment" can sell "funeral merchandise." (Ga. Code Ann. § 43-18-1.) Some of these laws are being challenged in the courts.

If you do buy a casket from someone other than the mortuary, be aware that it is illegal for a mortuary to charge any kind of "handling fee" for bringing in a casket from outside.

Finally, remember that the function of a casket is to transport the body to a grave. Even the most expensive casket in the world won't preserve a body very long—and there is really no reason to try.

b.   Cremation and Memorial Service

Cremation is an increasingly popular alternative to burial. In 1963, cremation was used in just 4% of U.S. deaths; by 2000 that figure had increased to an estimated 26%.

If you choose simple cremation, the mortuary or crematory will call for the remains, place the body in a modest container, and see that it is cremated according to legal requirements. The cost of cremation varies widely from place to place, but generally runs from $100 to $500. You'll probably have to pay separate fees for:

- transporting the body

- a simple casket or container for moving the body (if the body is to be on display before cremation, you may be able to rent a casket, which you can use with a cloth-covered cardboard liner that you buy; after the viewing, the body is moved to an inexpensive pressed cardboard container)

- a certificate from the medical examiner releasing the body for cremation (in some places)

- removing a pacemaker, if any, from the body before cremation (it can explode and damage the facility), and

- handling charges (paid to the crematory).

During cremation, a body is heated at a very high temperature until it is reduced to a few pounds of ash and bone fragments. The crematory will either dispose of the ashes or return them to survivors in a small inexpensive container, according to your preference. (If you plan to keep the ashes, you'll want to buy a permanent receptacle.) The mortuary may provide a few copies of the death certificate as well.

WITNESSING THE CREMATION

Especially in the wake of recent scandals involving remains of different bodies being mixed, or bodies not being properly cremated, a family member may want to witness the cremation. Many crematories allow it, and it lets survivors be confident that the body has in fact been cremated and that the ashes they receive are those of the deceased family member.

It will be up to family members to plan a memorial service they think is appropriate. (See Section F, below.) Some crematories are located next to cemeteries and have chapels available for memorial services.

Many people choose cremation, in part, to escape pressure and hype from funeral homes, with their pricey caskets and hard-sell tactics. But unfortunately, mortuaries that handle cremations may also try to sell you expensive caskets or urns you don't need. Be prepared.

Many people who decide they want their remains cremated also express a wish about

where they'd like their ashes scattered or buried. There are plenty of laws and regulations about where ashes can legally be scattered, but few families pay much attention to them. Ashes are commonly scattered in favorite woods, lakes, or state parks, or buried at a favorite spot that may serve as an unmarked but well-known place for surviving family members to pay their respects.

c. Direct Burial

Some mortuaries offer a "direct burial" option that skips some of the more expensive aspects of the traditional process such as embalming and fancy caskets. The funeral director calls for the remains and places the body in a simple wooden container. The survivors arrange any memorial service they want, and deal with a cemetery regarding the burial.

If you want the burial to be somewhere other than a cemetery—on private land, for example—it may be possible. Check with local health or zoning authorities to find out whether state and local regulations allow it.

2. Choosing Between Burial and Cremation

If you're left to decide on final arrangements without instructions from the deceased person, you'll have to weigh both emotional and financial elements. If the deceased person ever expressed an opinion—even if it wasn't in the form of explicit instructions—you should of course do your best to respect it.

In this country, most bodies are still buried. But cremation is widely accepted as a less expensive alternative, and one that allows survivors greater freedom in creating an appropriate way to honor the memory of a loved one.

The decision will involve your attitudes toward the body, desire for ritual, and spiritual beliefs. Just about everybody has a strong opinion about how human remains should be handled—and these opinions vary widely depending on cultural and religious traditions. It's best, of course, when survivors agree about how to dispose of the body and hold an appropriate memorial service.

If survivors cannot agree about whether a person's remains should be buried or cremated, however, state law gives the surviving spouse the right to make the decision. (In California, a surviving registered domestic partner has the same right a surviving spouse would have; the same is true in Hawaii for reciprocal beneficiaries and in Vermont for partners in a civil union.) Next in priority come children, then parents, and then next of kin. If you absolutely can't work things out and want to see what your state law says, you can look it up online. Start at the Legal Research Center on www.nolo.com.

3. Choosing a Mortuary

You probably won't have much time to shop around for a mortuary, but it's a good idea to make at least a few phone calls—or have a close friend do it for you—before you make a commitment. You want to find people you feel comfortable with, who don't pressure you to buy more than you need or want, and who offer the kinds of services you're looking for.

Funerals can be very expensive, and grief (not to mention pressure from funeral home staff) often prompts people to spend more than they really want to. Don't be afraid to ask what kind of money you're talking about before you get into the details. You may find substantial price differences—hundreds or thousands of dollars—for similar services. Mortuaries are required by federal law (the Federal Trade Commission's "Funeral Rule") to provide itemized prices for their services, and they must furnish them over the phone if you request it. But you are free to negotiate for the services you need; you do not have to buy a package that includes things you don't want.

One very good place to go for help is the local nonprofit memorial society, if there's one in your area. (They're also called funeral consumers organizations in some areas.) These nonprofit, nonsectarian organizations, usually run by volunteers, help their members get dignified, affordable memorial services. They often negotiate with mortuaries for deep discounts for their members. Members pay a very modest one-time or yearly fee.

Although the idea is to join a memorial society while you're alive (typically, new members get information about powers of attorney, organ donation, a wallet-sized membership card, and information about local funeral costs), at least some societies allow you to join on behalf of a family member after a death. You'll still get the discounted fees that participating mortuaries offer to members. Just as important, you'll gain an ally—an organization that knows which funeral homes are generally helpful and which ones aren't. And if you encounter problems with the funeral home, the memorial society can help. For example, what if the funeral director tells you that the body must be embalmed as a public health measure? The memorial society has successfully refuted this false claim before and can help you do it, too.

Another recent development is that companies that sell caskets online may refer you to local mortuaries that have agreed to discounted prices. You may want to shop around to find a mortuary that's affordable and where you feel comfortable.

Finding a memorial society. The nonprofit Funeral Consumers Alliance maintains a national list of nonprofit funeral societies. Its website, www.funerals.org, contains a wealth of information for anyone who must deal with a mortuary. You can also contact the FCA at 33 Patchen Road, South Burlington, VT 05403, 802-482-3437.

4. Who Pays the Mortuary or Crematory

Commonly, the surviving spouse or whoever will inherit much or most of the estate pays the costs associated with burial or cremation. In fact, these expenses are often paid out of a joint account with the deceased person's name on it.

If that's not workable in your situation, it's normal for a surviving relative to make financial arrangements with the funeral home. Typically, one of three things happens:

- The relative pays out of pocket, and is later reimbursed from the deceased person's property.

- The funeral home agrees to wait for payment from estate funds after probate begins.

- The funeral home agrees to wait for payment, but insists that the relative agree to be legally responsible for the bill if the estate can't pay.

Unless the estate is very small (or the deceased person was in debt), the estate will probably be able to pay the bill. When debts are paid during the probate process, funeral expenses are given a very high priority, right up there with taxes and probate court fees.

Courts do sometimes allow executors to refuse to pay some of the bill if the court finds it outrageous or concludes that the mortuary exerted unethical pressure on the person who agreed to it.

Whatever is bought, and however it is paid for, you have one important job as executor: keep meticulous records. Get copies of all contracts, bills, and receipts. You'll need them later when you're sorting out the estate's finances.

You may be able to get help with funeral costs. Unions, some fraternal groups, and maybe even the Department of Veterans Affairs may pay some funeral benefits. (See Chapter 5.)

5. Veterans

Veterans of the armed services are eligible for several benefits associated with burial.

PRESIDENTIAL MEMORIAL CERTIFICATES

Presidential Memorial Certificates are engraved paper certificates, signed by the current president, in honor of and gratitude for the service of honorably discharged deceased veterans.

The deceased veteran's family and other loved ones may request certificates; the Department of Veterans Affairs (VA) will issue more than one. You can apply in person at any VA regional office, or fax or mail (email requests are not accepted) a request to the VA in Washington, DC.

There is no form to fill in; just write a letter asking for a certificate and saying that you are a loved one of the deceased veteran. Include a copy (not the original) of the veteran's discharge and of the death certificate.

Mailing address:
Presidential Memorial Certificates (402E12)
Department of Veterans Affairs
810 Vermont Avenue, NW
Washington, DC 20420-0001
Fax number: 202-565-8054

a. Burial Flags

The U.S. Department of Veterans Affairs (VA) provides a United States flag, at no cost, to drape the casket or accompany the urn of a veteran who served honorably in the U.S. Armed Forces.

The next-of-kin (or a friend, if there is no family) can apply for a flag by completing VA Form 21-2008, *Application for United States Flag for Burial Purposes*. You'll need to know the dates of the veteran's service, and his or her military serial number. You can get the form, and a flag, at any VA regional office or U.S. Post Office. (The form is also available online, at www.cem.va.gov/bflags.htm.) Generally, funeral directors help with getting it. The application form explains how to display and fold the flag.

b. Burial for Veterans and Their Families

Veterans (unless they were discharged dishonorably) and their spouses and minor children are entitled to burial in one of the country's 114 national cemeteries, free of charge. Some of these cemeteries have no more room for casket burials, but still accept cremated remains. The government does not arrange funerals, but veterans' groups may help families. The cemeteries do provide headstones and markers.

For more information, contact a local office of the federal Department of Veterans Affairs (listed in the phone book) or check out its website at www.va.gov/cemetery/index.htm.

c. Grave Markers

The family of a deceased veteran can request a free headstone from the VA. The markers are provided by the government for the grave of any deceased eligible veteran in any cemetery around the world.

Any veteran who died while on active service or was discharged under conditions other than dishonorable is eligible for a marker. (There are a few exceptions to the rule; for example, veterans convicted of a capital crime or of "subversive activities" are not eligible.) If the death occurred before September 11, 2001 a headstone or marker is available only if the grave is not marked with a private headstone. (38 U.S.C. § 2306(d).)

For information, call the VA Memorial Programs Service at 800-697-6947. You can get an application online at www.cem.va.gov.

E. Other Tasks During the First Few Days

In addition to planning for a final resting place, a bewildering number of decisions and questions will likely be thrown your way during the first few days after a loved one's death. You'll be unusual if you don't feel overwhelmed—dealing with all these details at the same time you're coping with a personal loss is extremely difficult for anyone. Making use of the list below may help you keep track of things.

You may also want to use this list to help you delegate tasks. Don't try to do everything yourself. Those close to you will want to help in some concrete way but probably won't know what to do without guidance from you. They will be happy to pitch in if you can tell them what you need.

- **Call (or fax or email) close friends and relatives to tell them about the death.** Start with the people you know, and then get help from the deceased person's address book. It's often helpful to delegate this difficult task, at least in part, to a close friend. Otherwise, dealing with the grieved reactions of a long list of friends and relatives can be too much to handle.

- **Start making a list of others you'll notify later.** There may be lots of people—former coworkers or neighbors, for example—who you'll want to notify eventually. For now, don't worry about it. There will be plenty of time later to send letters, emails, or printed announcements.

- **Contact clergy, if you wish.** You may want just to talk, or to ask someone to preside over a funeral or memorial service.

- **Arrange for child care, if necessary.** Unless the death was totally unexpected, arrangements have probably already been made for children, but it's important that they not be overlooked when the grownups are busy with practical concerns.

- **Choose an organization to receive gifts.** People may ask you where they can donate money in honor of the deceased person; if you wish, you can name, for example, a hospice, library, church, nonprofit organization, or school.

- **Establish a fund for young children.** If the person left young children, consider establishing a fund for their benefit. Friends and acquaintances will be happy to give what they can. Especially if there is no insurance or other source of money, the funds raised will be a great help.

- **Collect information for a death notice and obituary.** For a small fee, you can insert a short death notice in the local paper, announcing the death and where and when the memorial service will be held. An obituary is a news article about someone's life; the newspaper decides whether or not to write one. In small towns, almost everyone gets an obituary; in Los Angeles or New York City, a tiny percentage does. The smaller the town, the more likely you may be asked by the local paper to help compose the obituary. If so, you'll need to know basic facts about the deceased person's life, such as place of birth, cause of death, occupation, high school and college attended, organization memberships, military service, outstanding work, marriage, children, and grandchildren. The funeral home or newspaper may have a form that will help you organize this information. You can also look at examples in the paper to get an idea of how it's done.

- **Choose people to answer the door and phone.** Again, spare the surviving spouse these draining tasks. Ask the people who take calls and visitors to write down the names of people who check in.

- **Ask someone to arrange to supply food for a few days.** Family members won't have time or energy to cook, and you'll need to feed visitors, probably before and after the funeral.

- **Ask someone to arrange accommodations for out-of-town guests.** People coming in will need a place to stay and will appreciate some help.

- **Keep a list of people who help out or send cards or flowers.** Later, you can send them thank-you notes.

- **Safeguard portable valuables.** Lots of people will probably be coming and going, and things can disappear. So if the deceased person's home contains cash, valuable jewelry, art, collections, or other similar items, make sure they are locked away. (You may need to reassure some people that you have secured them, not grabbed them for yourself.)

- **Ask someone to collect the mail.** Either have the deceased person's mail forwarded (see Chapter 4), or get a box and toss all the mail that comes for the deceased person into it. You can sort through it later.

- **Stop newspaper subscriptions.** If the deceased person's house is now unoccupied, you don't want newspapers to pile up outside.

- **Arrange for pet care.** If the deceased person didn't make arrangements in advance, you'll need someone to take pets until you can make long-term arrangements. Don't drop pets at a shelter trusting that they will find homes—overcrowded shelters commonly euthanize many adoptable pets. Instead, contact a rescue group, which will keep animals until it finds them a permanent home—surely what the animals' owner would have wanted. No matter where you live, there is probably one close by. Look online or call a local humane society for information.

- **Arrange for yard care.** You may need to get someone—perhaps a neighbor's teenager—to mow the lawn or shovel snow.

- **Decide what to do with flowers after the funeral.** Even if you ask for charitable donations in lieu of flowers, you'll probably get lots anyway. You might donate them to a church, hospital, or nursing home, for example.

- **Ask a friend to stay at the house during the funeral.** This will guard against break-ins while the family is away. Sad to say, some burglars scan newspaper death notices and target houses they expect will be empty because of a funeral.

- **Find the will or living trust and put it in a safe place.** Any important papers you come across should be locked away. (More on this in Chapter 4.)

During the period immediately after the death, your main job is to preserve things as they were at the time of death. Don't give away any items of property, pay bills (especially if there may not be enough money to pay all of them), or empty a safe deposit box.

Unfortunately, it is not uncommon for relatives or friends to pressure you (or other family members) to let them take a "keepsake," or something they say was promised to them.

Worse, they may even help themselves. If you encounter this behavior, explain that it's your legal responsibility not to let even the smallest item out of the house. Tell them that you're not giving anything to anyone else, either, until the proper procedures are followed. And then stick to your guns.

F. Arranging a Memorial Service

A memorial service, unlike a traditional funeral, usually takes place some weeks or months after the death. Obviously, that gives you more time to plan it, but you may want to start thinking about it soon after the death.

It's rare that someone leaves instructions for a memorial service—so if there is to be one, it will fall to you and others closest to the deceased person to organize it. Increasingly, memorial services are occasions for people to share their memories of the person they loved—a story that evokes something special about the deceased person, or a song or poem that had special meaning for the person who has died.

Your goal should be to come up with a ceremony that suits the deceased person—not necessarily one that suits you. Although it's true that commemorative services are for the survivors, what is likely to help the survivors most is something that feels in character with the person they are mourning and celebrating. You may want to contact fraternal or religious organizations that conduct or participate in memorial services.

In her own words. My grandma was a war bride who came to this country from England after World War II. A few years before she died, she wrote down the story of meeting my grandpa during wartime and leaving her big family to start a brand new life. At her memorial service, each of her children and grandchildren stood up and read from her story. Many people told us it was one of the most moving ceremonies they'd ever been to, and that they had felt as if my grandma was right there with us.

PLANNING A MEMORIAL SERVICE: THINGS YOU MAY WANT TO ARRANGE

- Time
- Place
- Leader
- Speakers
- Readings
- Printed program
- Flowers
- Photographs
- Food
- Guest book
- Music
- Someone to videotape the ceremony

Planning help from nonprofit memorial societies. Funeral and memorial societies often have helpful advice about creating meaningful memorial services. For some ideas, contact a local group or look online. For example, the website of the People's Memorial Association (www.peoplesmemorial.org/memorial.html) has many ideas. ∎

CHAPTER 4

The First Month

After the first shock has worn off and you've taken care of immediate concerns, you may feel ready to wade into the piles of papers and belongings that must be dealt with, somehow. Then again, you may not feel ready. The period after immediate matters are handled, when relatives go home and friends start to drift back to their everyday responsibilities, can be a difficult time. The grief and plain loneliness you may feel after losing your spouse, parent, or other loved one can surface with surprising and disconcerting strength.

But to their surprise, many people find that dealing with some tangible items and handling some financial matters actually makes them feel better. The hardest part is getting started.

This chapter assumes you're entitled to act on behalf of the deceased person's estate, either because:

- the will named you as executor

- a living trust named you as successor trustee (in which case you have authority over trust assets, but nothing else)

- there is no will and under state law, you (as surviving spouse, only child, or closest relative) are first in line to serve, or

- no probate is necessary (because there is so little property or because everything was owned in a way that avoids probate) and everyone concerned agrees that you are the right person to take charge.

Even if you haven't yet received the probate court's blessing to proceed (and may never receive it, if probate isn't necessary), you can go ahead with some important tasks.

You probably won't have to do everything discussed in this chapter. Still the thought of tackling so many tasks may feel daunting. It sounds trite, but the best advice is to try to take things one day at a time. You don't have to do everything at once, and although you may want to start many of these processes in the first month after the death, it's okay to wait longer, too. Do what you need to do to look after yourself and your family. Most legal matters really can wait.

Tackling financial matters. Especially for surviving spouses, getting access to money for immediate living expenses can be a worry. Chapter 5 discusses how you may be able to get cash from life insurance policies, Social Security, and other sources.

A. Set Up a Filing System

To succeed as an executor, it's crucial to begin your duties by setting up a system to keep track of all the paperwork that will shortly come your way. A good filing system will keep you from wasting hours later, searching for things you need, and it will also make it much easier to answer the inevitable questions from beneficiaries, banks, insurance companies, accountants, and others. You get the idea.

A computer is not essential, but it can be a great help on the organizing front. It's a perfect place to keep lists, copies of letters, and so on. But because you'll be shuffling so many documents, you also need a paper-filing system.

A simple way to get started is to buy a package of file folders and a container (file box or drawer) in which to keep them. Hanging files are the easiest to use. Look at the list below and label the folders you think you'll need before you need them. You can add others later.

Computerizing your records. If you want to keep key information about the estate in a simple database on your personal computer, you may want to use Nolo's *Personal RecordKeeper* software. It lets you keep track of bank account numbers, real estate information, and much more—even family history. You can share the information with other family members if you wish. Learn more about *Personal RecordKeeper* at www.nolo.com.

What should go in all these files? Obviously, you want to keep anything and everything that could later be important to you in your capacity as executor. For example, if you find in a desk drawer a 20-year-old insurance policy that seems to have lapsed, you'll still want to save it, so later—maybe even months later—you can call the company to check on whether or not any insurance is still in force.

It's just as important to keep a copy of everything that goes out—every letter you send and form you file. (If you file a form online, remember to print out a copy and keep it, too.) Why? To be sure you have been thorough, to

FILES YOU MAY NEED

- Appraisals
- Bank Account–Estate
- Bank Accounts–Personal
- Bills–Unpaid
- Bills–Paid
- Correspondence With Beneficiaries
- Death Certificates
- Employment
- Family Facts, Photos, and Historical Documents
- Funeral and Cremation or Burial
- Life Insurance
- Living Trust

- Medical Expenses
- Military Service/Veterans Benefits
- Pensions/Survivors Benefits
- Probate Court
- Property Inventory
- Real Estate
- Retirement Accounts (IRA, 401(k), 403(b), Keogh)
- Social Security
- Stocks and Bonds
- Tax Returns–Estate
- Tax Returns–Personal
- Will

RECORDS TO LOOK FOR

- Annuity policies
- Bank statements
- Birth certificates (of the deceased person and of any minor children)
- Brokerage account statements
- Business co-ownership agreements
- Checkbooks
- Child support documents
- Credit card statements (these days, when people have many bills on autopay and use credit cards at the dentist's office, the grocery store, and nearly everywhere else, a credit card statement can be a hugely important source of information)
- Disability-related documents
- Divorce papers (including property settlement agreements)
- Health insurance policies
- Immigration and citizenship documents
- Investment records
- Life insurance policies and premium payment records
- Marriage license (if you don't have a copy, order one from the county where the wedding took place)
- Military service records (branch, dates of service, discharge or "separation" papers)
- Pension records
- Prenuptial agreement
- Real estate deeds and tax records
- Registration papers for vehicles or boats
- Retirement account statements
- Social Security records
- Tax returns
- W-2 form (showing wages for the most recent year)
- Workers' compensation paperwork

show others that you have been, and because if you have future dealings with the recipient, you'll want a record of what's been said.

You never know which documents you'll need later, but surely there will be some. If you're having trouble getting something done, having documentation may help you press your point.

B. Order Copies of the Death Certificate

As you wind up the deceased person's affairs, you'll need a number of certified copies of the death certificate, which will serve as official evidence of the death. For example, you'll need one whenever you claim benefits or property that you or someone else becomes entitled to because of the death, such as union, veterans, or other funeral and burial benefits, life insurance proceeds, payable-on-death bank accounts, or Social Security benefits.

Typically, the mortuary arranges for you to receive some certified death certificates. It's a good idea to ask for at least ten, more if the deceased person owned many types of property.

1. Where to Order

If you need to order death certificates yourself, you can contact either the state or county vital records office. The county office is probably your best bet, because it receives the documents sooner. Typically, there is a lag time of several months before certificates are available from a central state office.

The county vital records office is called by a variety of names. In Texas, for example, it's the "local registrar," but in Michigan you go to the county clerk.

Each county sets the cost of certificates, so prices vary widely. Expect to pay from $10 to $15 for the first certified copy; if you order multiple copies at one time, the rest are likely to be cheaper. If you don't pick them up in person, you may also be charged a mailing fee. You can pay for them yourself, and later get reimbursement from the estate.

Ordering from the state. If you want to order death certificates from your state's agency, you can learn where to order and how much copies cost at the website of the National Center for Health Statistics: www.cdc.gov/nchswww/howto/w2w/w2welcom.htm.

2. Who May Order

In an increasing number of states, not just anyone can get a certified copy of a death certificate. (These restrictions are aimed at preventing identity theft; thieves use birth and death records to get and misuse personal information.) But as the executor or a member of the immediate family, these rules should pose no problem for you. For example, in Illinois, death records are restricted to relatives or people who have a financial interest in the deceased person's estate. And in California, you must submit a sworn statement with your request, saying that you are the executor or a close family member.

3. Ordering in Person

You can always go in person to the county records office to get certified copies. Just call ahead to find out how much they cost.

4. Ordering by Mail or Fax

If you order death certificates by mail, fax, or online, you'll probably receive them in the mail in a few weeks. If you want to order by mail or fax, call the local office first to find out the total price for the copies and the mailing fee. Then send a check and a simple cover letter like the one below.

Before you write your cover letter, however, you may want to check the county website (see Section 5, below); it may include a form that you can fill in, print out, and mail or fax. If you use the office's own form, you'll know you're providing all the information necessary.

SAMPLE LETTER REQUESTING DEATH CERTIFICATE

June 10, 20xx
Lane County Recorder
P.O. Box 350
Montgomery, OR 97553
Re: Kathleen Laura Smith, Deceased

Date of death: June 2, 20xx
City of death: Montgomery
Age at death: 84
Last address: 392 Washington Court, Montgomery, OR 97547

Please send me ten certified copies of the death certificate of my mother, Kathleen Laura Smith. I have enclosed a check for $125.00 to cover the cost of the certificates and regular postage.

Thank you.

Sincerely,

Jeremy M. Smith
465 Laurel Street
Martinez, CA 94552
(510) 555-1234

---

5. Ordering Online

More and more counties allow people to order death certificates online: instead of printing out a request form, you can submit it electronically and pay by credit card. To find out whether or not online ordering is available in the county where the death occurred, go to the county's official website. You can usually find it by

using this formula, replacing "XX" with the state abbreviation:

www.co.COUNTY_NAME.XX.us.

EXAMPLE: *You can find the website for King County, Washington, at www.co.king.wa.us.*

C. Find the Will

You need to find the will, if there is one. The will is the basis of your job as executor, because it both says who should inherit what and puts you in charge of making it happen. (Remember, though, that some—perhaps most—of the deceased person's property may pass outside of the will. Section D, below, tells you what other important documents, such as living trust documents, you need to look for.)

Lots of Americans never write a will. If your search doesn't uncover one, it's not a problem. Other documents—for example, living trusts, beneficiary designations, or joint ownership deeds—will give you at least some of the instructions you need, and state law will step in to supply the rest. (Chapter 7 discusses the rules.)

1. Where to Look

If you don't know where the will and other key documents are, start your search in the obvious places such as file cabinets, desk drawers, and closets. Check at home and, if the deceased person had an office, look there too.

If that turns up nothing, here are some other avenues to try:

Check safe deposit boxes. If you're a co-owner of the box, you'll have no problem opening it. If you're not a joint owner, but you are an immediate family member, the bank will probably give you access to the box, in the presence of a bank official, to look for a will. (Some states require banks to give the spouse or next of kin access to the safe deposit box for this purpose; in others, it's up to the bank.) You won't be allowed to take anything else out, however, until you have authority from the probate court. If the bank won't cooperate, you can ask the probate court for an order allowing you access to the box only for the purpose of finding the will.

Call around to find the boxes. If you don't know whether or not the deceased person rented a box, call the banks where the deceased person had accounts. Not all bank branches have safe deposit boxes, so you may need to explore a little.

Call the deceased person's lawyer. If a lawyer drafted the will, call to see whether the lawyer has the original or a copy. If you don't know the lawyer's name, go through checkbooks for the last few years and look for payments to an individual lawyer or firm. If you know the lawyer's name but don't have an address or phone number, the state bar association may be able to help—call the headquarters or check its website. In most states, the law requires anyone who has possession of a will to promptly turn it over to the executor named in the will or to the local probate court. (The lawyer is *not* automatically entitled to handle the probate work, even if that's what the deceased client intended; whether or not to hire the lawyer is up to you, the executor.)

Ask the local probate court. It's not common, but some people deposit their wills with the probate court while they're still alive.

Ask the legal community. Place a notice in a local legal newspaper or county bar association publication, asking any lawyer who has the will to quickly turn it over to you. A sample notice is shown below.

SAMPLE NOTICE SEEKING WILL

Survivors of Henry Louis Whitman, who died at age 88 on March 3, 20xx, are seeking his will. His last address was 9982 Ardmore Street, Apt. 35, Indianapolis, IN 52134. If you have the original or a copy of the will, please promptly contact William G. Whitman, 52 Evelyn Drive, Indianapolis, IN 52133, 405-555-1234.

Help for Idaho residents: Check the state will registry. Your state has a will registry, where people can pay $10 to record the whereabouts of their will with the Idaho Secretary of State. (Idaho Stat. § 15-2-1001.) After the death, family members and other interested parties can search the registry. You won't get the will itself, but should get information that will help you find the will.

2. What You're Looking For

You'll probably recognize the will when you find it: a plain-looking document, typed or printed from a computer, labeled "Last Will and Testament" or just "Will of _____ ." It may be stapled to a stiff piece of colored paper, or in an envelope labeled "Will."

Sometimes, however, wills don't look like wills. Handwritten wills may look more like letters or lists. But about half the states allow handwritten, unwitnessed wills, which are called "holographic" wills. (Chapter 6 explains which documents qualify as wills.)

If you plan to take the will through regular probate, you need the *actual* document the person signed. (Whether or not you'll need to go through a formal probate proceeding is discussed in Chapter 12.) Courts generally do not accept photocopies. If all you can find is a copy, you may eventually get the document accepted by the court, but doing so will likely be a large-scale hassle. There will be a court hearing, with witnesses who testify about the circumstances under which the will was made and signed, and that it was never revoked. You're right if you suspect that such a process involves paying lawyers to help sort out the confusion.

Here are some other will-related documents to look for:

Lists of property items. In about half the states, a will can refer to an outside document to dispose of items of tangible personal property—that is, anything tangible except real estate. So if you find *any* document that lists items and who should inherit them, hang on to it. (Chapter 6 discusses what to do with all the papers you find.)

Codicils. Also keep your eye out for any document labeled "Codicil." A codicil is document that revises or adds to an earlier will. It must be signed in front of witnesses, just like an original will. These days, codicils are rare. Most wills are created on computers, so people who want to change something commonly make a whole new will, which specifically revokes all earlier ones.

UNOFFICIAL CODICILS

Although formal, witnessed codicils are no longer common, you may find a handwritten note attached to a will, with some instructions for you. Perhaps the person intended to make one more gift but never got around to revising the will—or simply thought that a note was as legally binding as the will. It's not. Any document that tries to leave property as a will does must satisfy the legal requirements, under state law, for a will.

Still, if you and any other beneficiaries all conclude that the note truly conveys what the deceased person intended, you may want to honor it. You can't change the will itself, but there is nothing to stop you and other beneficiaries from making gifts out of your own inheritance to fulfill the deceased person's wishes.

3. You Know It Exists But Can't Find It

Sometimes, everyone knows a will was drawn up and signed, but it simply can't be found. You may be left with no will at all, or with an old one that you believe the lost one revoked.

You may be able to prove the existence of a lost will—and perhaps even its terms—to the satisfaction of a probate court. Many states have specific procedures—for example, you may need to produce all the witnesses who signed the will and come up with convincing evidence of what the will said.

It's not easy, and you'll almost certainly need a lawyer's help, but in some circumstances it can be done. In one Texas case, for example, a man claimed that his mother had written a will that revoked her earlier will, which had left everything to his sister. He produced a witness who had heard the terms of the will, but he couldn't produce the will. After hearing all the evidence, the court found that the later will did in fact exist, was valid, and left the mother's property as the son claimed. The court also concluded that the daughter had taken the later will, making it impossible for the son to produce it. So the court admitted the later will to probate. The daughter appealed, but lost. (*Cason v. Taylor*, 51 S.W.3d 397 (Tex. App. 2001).)

Similarly, a Georgia probate court accepted a copy of a missing will, based on testimony of the lawyer who had prepared it and the notary who had certified ("acknowledged") the affidavit signed by the witnesses. (*Westmoreland v. Tallent*, 549 S.E.2d 113 (Ga. 2001).)

Getting someone to come up with the will. If you have good reason to think that someone has the deceased person's will but does not intend to present it to the court as required by law, you can start a lawsuit to force the person to file the will. A lawyer should be able to help you assess the likelihood of success in the particular circumstances. Obviously, someone up to no good might promptly "lose" the will if pressured.

4. After You Find It

It probably goes without saying that once you get your hands on the original, signed will, you should keep a very close eye on it. Immediately make some photocopies and then put the original in a safe place, such as a locked file drawer.

Your next step is to file the original will with the probate court. Depositing the will with the court does not mean you are beginning probate proceedings. You may, in fact, decide later that regular probate is unnecessary. But most states' laws require that anyone with a valid will turn it over to the probate court within a month or so of obtaining it—and if you don't, you could face civil or even criminal penalties.

For now, you probably don't need to worry about the terms of the will, though of course you want to read them if you don't already know how the property was left. If you have questions about language in the will—not at all unusual—take a look at Chapter 6, which is devoted to deciphering wills.

D. Find Other Documents That Leave Property

Always keep in mind that these days much valuable property is likely to pass outside the will. So you need to put your hands on the documents that serve as will substitutes: trust documents, bank forms that designate payable-on-death beneficiaries for bank accounts, beneficiary designations for retirement accounts, and so on. This section tells you what to look for.

1. Living Trusts

If the deceased person had a living trust, you'll probably come across the trust document as you look for the will, in a file folder or desk drawer. It will probably be titled "Declaration of Trust," "Instrument of Trust," or "Revocable Living Trust of _____ ." Like a will, a trust document is of the utmost importance—it may transfer most or all of the deceased person's property. Unlike a will, however, you don't deposit it with the probate court. So keep it in a very safe place. (Living trusts are discussed in Chapter 19.)

2. Beneficiary Designations

Without ever using a will or living trust, people can name beneficiaries to inherit many kinds of property, including bank accounts, retirement plans, cars, and stocks. These designations are made on a variety of forms provided by the bank, state motor vehicle department, or other institution that's in charge of making the ownership transfer (or keeping records of such transfers) when the original owner dies.

Transfer procedures are discussed later, in Chapter 16. This section tells you only what papers to look for.

a. Bank Accounts

To make a bank account (or certificate of deposit) a payable-on-death or POD account, the account owner must have signed and given to the financial institution a form naming the POD beneficiary. You may find a copy of that form with the deceased person's important papers. Account statements are other evidence; they should identify the account owner and POD beneficiary something like this: "Melvin S. Jones, POD Cheyenne A. Jones."

b. IRAs, 401(k)s, and Other Retirement Plans

Almost everyone names a beneficiary for individual retirement accounts and 401(k) plans. Look on the quarterly statements or in any documents the account owner received when the account was opened. If it's an employer-sponsored plan (a 401(k), for example), you can ask the employer to look up the records.

c. Savings Bonds

Owners of U.S. savings bonds can designate a payable-on-death beneficiary for the bonds, so the beneficiary inherits them without probate. Check the bonds themselves.

d. Securities

In all but a few states, people who own stocks and bonds can name transfer-on-death beneficiaries to inherit them. This is called registering the securities in beneficiary form. Statements from brokers should identify the TOD beneficiary, if any.

Most people own securities in brokerage accounts; the accounts themselves will be registered in TOD form. If someone had actual stock certificates, the certificates themselves should specify the TOD beneficiary.

e. Vehicles

A few states—California, Connecticut, Kansas, Missouri, and Ohio—allow residents to register their vehicles in transfer-on-death (TOD) form. If the deceased person lived in one of these states, check the car's registration document to see whether it names a TOD beneficiary, who inherits the car at the owner's death.

3. Joint Ownership Deeds

Gather all deeds to real estate that the deceased person owned. Each deed should state how the property was owned. If the property was owned with another person in any of the following ways, its fate won't be affected by the will, and it won't have to go through probate:

- joint tenancy with right of survivorship

- tenancy by the entirety, or

- community property with right of survivorship.

The last two methods are for married couples only. (With these exceptions: In Hawaii and

Vermont, same-sex couples who have registered with the state may own property together in tenancy by the entirety. California registered domestic partners will be able to own community property as of January 1, 2005.)

If you know that the person owned real estate but can't find the deed, you should be able to get a copy from the land records office in the county where the property is located.

4. Other Joint Ownership Documents

Couples and family members sometimes own property other than real estate jointly, in a way that avoids probate. For example, many married couples own cars and bank accounts as joint tenants or as tenants by the entirety. So keep an eye out for title documents that identify jointly owned assets. (More about this in Chapter 8, which explains how to inventory the deceased person's property.)

5. Marital Property Agreements

In Alaska, Idaho, Texas, Washington, or Wisconsin, look for a "Community Property Agreement" or "Marital Property Agreement." In these states, a married couple can sign an agreement that determines what happens to some or all of their property at death. Typically, couples declare all of their property to be community property and leave it to the survivor when one spouse dies.

In Alaska and Wisconsin, couples can use a community property agreement to name a beneficiary to inherit the property at the *second* spouse's death. (In Washington, there is confusion about whether or not spouses can do this. Some legal experts think it's allowed, but courts have not explicitly said so.) After one spouse dies, however, the survivor can amend the agreement to change who inherits his or her property, unless the agreement expressly forbids it.

For more about these agreements, see Chapter 14.

6. Prenuptial Agreements

Especially if the deceased person married more than once, you may turn up a prenuptial agreement—a contract about property management and ownership, signed by the deceased person and his or her spouse before their marriage. Prenuptial agreements don't actually leave property like a will does. But in some of them, spouses promise how they're going to leave their property at death. If a spouse didn't follow through on the promise, the survivor may want to press the issue in court. If that happens, you'll need a lawyer.

7. Transfer-on-Death Deeds

In Arizona, Kansas, Missouri, New Mexico, and Ohio, property owners can leave their real estate with a special kind of deed that is effective only at death. If you see such a deed, which should be clearly titled "T.O.D.," "Transfer on Death," or "Beneficiary" deed, hang on to it.

To be effective, a transfer-on-death deed must clearly state that the transfer is not to take effect until the owner's death. And like any deed, it must be properly signed, and it must be recorded (filed) with the property

records office in the county in which the real estate is located. Arizona's beneficiary deed form is shown below.

TRANSFER-ON-DEATH DEED (ARIZONA)

Beneficiary Deed

I, Mildred J. Cox, hereby convey to Jennifer L. Richardson, effective on my death, the following described real property: [legal description of real estate]

Mildred J. Cox

_____
Signature of Grantor

_____
Date
(acknowledgment by notary public)

No other kind of deed can transfer property at death. For example, say the deceased person signed a regular deed and then locked it in a drawer, hoping it would be found at death and transfer the property then. No luck; the deed is ineffective.

If you find a transfer-on-death deed for property in any other state, get legal advice. The states listed above have statutes that specifically authorize transfer-on-death deeds. In states without such statutes, courts have disagreed about whether or not beneficiary deeds are valid. If you find one of these deeds, see a lawyer who can research the latest law in your state.

E. Send Notifications of the Death

You'll need to notify various people and institutions of the death. You can use a simple letter like the one below. Looking through the deceased person's mail can help you determine who should be notified.

Cancel appointments. Check the deceased person's kitchen calendar or datebook and cancel appointments, such as doctor or dentists visits, that the deceased person made.

NOTIFICATION OF DEATH: SAMPLE LETTER

July 5, 20xx
Susan Watkins, DDS
3532 South Street, Suite 400
Walnut Creek, CA 94596

Re: Kathleen Laura Smith, Deceased
Date of death: June 2, 20xx
Age at death: 84
Last address: 392 Washington Court,
Montgomery, OR 97547

This is to notify you of the death of Kathleen Laura Smith. Please update your records accordingly.

Thank you.

Sincerely,

Jeremy M. Smith
465 Laurel Street
Martinez, CA 94552
(510) 555-1234

BUSINESSES AND AGENCIES TO NOTIFY

Banks

Charities the person donated to

Credit card companies

Doctors and other health care providers who may not know of the death

Former employers

Insurance companies

Landlord

Membership organizations (alumni associations and social groups, for example)

Newspaper and magazine subscription offices

Pension payers

Post Office

Social groups

Social Security Administration

State health/welfare department, if the deceased person (or a previously deceased spouse) received benefits

Veterans Affairs Department

Volunteer groups (for example, a soup kitchen where the deceased person volunteered)

1. Credit Card Issuers

Unless you're the surviving spouse and had a joint account, cut up credit cards that belonged to the deceased person and return them to the issuing bank with a notice of the death. You shouldn't need to send a certified copy of the death certificate, but you may want to include a photocopy of one.

If you're canceling a card, it won't hurt to ask the credit card issuer to do two things:

• refund part of any annual fee (if any) already paid, since the card won't be used, and

• cancel or at least reduce the remaining balance, if it isn't too large. If the alternative looks like no payment, the card issuer may be willing to make a deal, especially with a surviving spouse.

If you're the surviving spouse, and the credit card account is a joint one, contact the issuer and ask to have the account changed into your name alone. You may need to provide a certified copy of the death certificate.

⚠ **Watch for automatic billing.** If the credit card is billed automatically for certain regular costs—utilities or subscriptions, for example—don't cancel it unless you either want to stop paying those debts or you make other arrangements to have them paid.

2. Social Security Administration

As soon as you can, call the Social Security Administration's toll-free number, 800-772-1213, to notify the agency of the death.

If the deceased person was receiving monthly Social Security payments, the payment for the month of death must be returned. It doesn't matter on which day of the month the person died—the whole amount must go back.

EXAMPLE 1: *Lola dies on August 30. Her Social Security check for August is sent on September 3. That check (and any that come later) must be returned to the Social Security Administration.*

EXAMPLE 2: *Lyle dies on September 2. His Social Security check for August is sent on September 3. That check does not have to be returned.*

Most Social Security payments are now deposited directly into recipients' bank accounts. If the check was automatically deposited into a bank account, direct the bank to return the funds to the SSA.

RETURNING DIRECTLY DEPOSITED SOCIAL SECURITY CHECK: SAMPLE COVER LETTER

July 5, 20xx
Great Northern Bank
9341 East Drive, Suite 100
Walnut Creek, CA 94596

Re: Kathleen Laura Smith, Deceased
Account Number: 03338-03489
Date of death: June 2, 20xx
Age at death: 84
Last address: 392 Washington Court,
Montgomery, OR 97547

On July 3, 20xx, a Social Security
benefits check in the amount of
$642.20 was deposited directly to the
account of Kathleen Laura Smith.
Please return these funds to the Social
Security Administration, as required by
federal law.

To acknowledge your receipt of this
letter, please sign the enclosed copy
and return it to me in the enclosed
stamped, self-addressed envelope.

Thank you.

Sincerely,

Jeremy M. Smith
465 Laurel Street
Martinez, CA 94552
(510) 555-1234

Receipt acknowledged by:

Name _____

Title _____

Date _____

If the person got a monthly check in the mail, do not cash or deposit the check for the month in which the death occurred. You must return the check to the local office of the SSA.

To find the nearest Social Security office, check the phone book's federal government listings, call the SSA's toll-free number, or go to the SSA website at www.ssa.gov. On the site, you can enter your zip code and get the address and phone number of the closest office.

Some SSA staffers recommend that you deliver the check in person to the local office, rather than entrusting it to the mail. If you decide to mail it, you may want to pay a little extra to send it by registered mail. Either way, ask for a receipt. A sample cover letter is shown below.

RETURNING SOCIAL SECURITY CHECK: SAMPLE COVER LETTER

June 21, 20xx
Social Security Administration
1111 Civic Drive, Suite 180
Walnut Creek, CA 94596

Re: Kathleen Laura Smith, Deceased
Date of death: June 2, 20xx
Age at death: 84
Last address: 392 Washington Court,
Montgomery, OR 97547

Enclosed is the Social Security benefits check payable to Kathleen Laura Smith for the month of June, 20xx.

I'm also enclosing a copy of this letter, to serve as a receipt. Please sign it and return it to me in the enclosed stamped, self-addressed envelope.

Thank you.

Sincerely,

Jeremy M. Smith
465 Laurel Street
Martinez, CA 94552
(510) 555-1234

Receipt acknowledged by:

Name _____

Title _____

Date _____

3. Post Office

If the deceased person lived alone, contact the post office and have mail forwarded to you, so you won't miss anything important. Keep close tabs on all checks, statements, bills, and other items you receive; they may help you track down assets you didn't know about, or warn you of expenses on the horizon.

EXAMPLE: *While going through his late mother's bills, Trevor finds a statement from the American Association of Retired People (AARP), having something to do with the payment of medical expenses. Having just paid several thousand dollars of medical bills for his mom's last illness—expenses that Medicare didn't cover—he immediately calls the number on the bottom of the statement. He is pleasantly surprised to learn that his mother had had an AARP supplemental medical insurance policy, which covers all of what Medicare hadn't paid.*

To get the mail forwarded, submit a change of address card to the post office closest to where the deceased person lived. You can pick up a form from any post office. Or go to the post office website at www.usps.gov, where you'll find a form that you can print out or submit online.

If you use a paper form, write "DECEASED" across the top of the card and attach a copy of the death certificate when you turn it in. The post office may ask to see evidence of your authority; if so, you can produce a copy of the will that names you executor, the living trust that names you as trustee, or, later, your authorization from the probate court.

Be aware that some mail, marked for personal delivery only, may not be forwarded. Generally, items such as driver's licenses, credit cards, and government checks are returned to the sender.

Be sure only one person submits a change-of-address form. Before you make a forwarding request to the post office, make sure no other surviving family member has done so.

4. Utilities and Other Services

If the deceased person lived alone, you'll probably want to cancel various services that are no longer needed, such as:

- phone

- cell phone

- cable TV, and

- Internet access.

Don't cut off the electricity, gas (for heating in cold climates), trash collection, or water (for lawn maintenance and cleaning). When the house or condo is sold or a rental unit is turned over to the landlord, the new occupant can transfer the accounts into his or her name.

5. Landlord

If the deceased person was a renter, you'll probably want to promptly send the landlord a notice that you're terminating the lease or rental agreement. Most people work out moving arrangements with the landlord and don't need to worry about exactly what their legal rights and obligations are with respect to the property.

But if you're not sure about how much rent the estate is liable for, or when the landlord can tell you to have everything packed up and moved out, you'll want to first check the lease or rental agreement. Most of them don't say what happens in the event of a tenant's death, but you should check just in case.

If the agreement doesn't cover the situation, you can find your answer in your state's laws. In some states, a month-to-month rental agreement ends as soon as the landlord is notified of the death, ending the obligation to pay rent. You would have until the end of the paid-up rental period to get the deceased person's things moved out.

EXAMPLE: *Muriel rents her apartment under a month-to-month rental agreement. Her rent is due on the first of the month. She dies on October 5, and her son notifies the landlord of her death on October 6. Her tenancy ends on October 31.*

In some other states, you are required to give the landlord 30 days' notice of termination. Under the circumstances, though, you can probably get the landlord to agree to a shorter period if you want to clear out the unit and stop paying rent sooner than that. This is especially likely, of course, if the landlord has another tenant ready to move in.

If the deceased person had signed a lease for a certain period of time, you should still give the landlord notice that you're terminating the lease. Generally, the death does not terminate the lease. As a result, the estate is obligated to pay rent through the end of the lease term—but the landlord is legally required to try to find a replacement tenant. As soon as a new tenant moves in and starts paying rent, the estate's obligation to pay rent stops.

Don't forget to ask for the security deposit. The landlord must return the security deposit (minus allowable deductions for damage) promptly. Just how long depends on state law. You can find your state's rules on Nolo's website's at www.nolo.com or in *Every Tenant's Legal Guide*, by Janet Portman and Marcia Stewart (Nolo).

6. Membership Organizations

You'll want to notify organizations to which the deceased person belonged, so they can adjust their records.

Look for a chance to get a few dollars back. Organizations may be willing to refund dues and fees paid in advance. For example if the deceased person paid a $1,000 for club dues for the next year the day before he died, you might write to the club and see if you can get some or all of the money back.

7. Charities and Other Organizations the Deceased Person Supported

You're likely to keep getting fundraising appeals and junk mail addressed to the deceased person for quite a while, until his or her name disappears from mailing lists. To get the process started, notify charities, political organizations, schools, and any other entities the deceased person donated to during life.

F. Keep Property Secure

As mentioned earlier, it's your responsibility to make sure that the deceased person's property remains safe until it can be transferred to the people who inherit it. Take the following precautions right away. Chapter 9 discusses further steps to take.

Too much mail. Now that my late mother's mail is coming to us, we're getting all her junk mail, too. I've written "Deceased. Return to Sender" on so many envelopes that I wish I had gotten a stamp when this all started. I haven't gotten around to trying to get her off marketing lists, but I know that wouldn't solve the problem because many of the fundraising letters are from organizations she happily contributed to during her lifetime.

1. Vehicles

If a vehicle was owned in joint tenancy, the surviving owner automatically owns it and can take possession immediately. (How the new owner can get title transferred into his or her name alone is discussed in Chapter 13.) Park other vehicles in a safe place—not on the street—until you transfer them to the new owners. Collect extra keys and put them away.

2. Real Estate

If no one is living in a house or other real estate the deceased person owned, you need to protect it until it's sold or turned over to the inheritor. If there's a regular gardener or lawnmower, keep him or her coming. Put lights on a timer, enlist the help of neighbors to keep an eye out, and consider arranging for a reliable housesitter. If there's a vacation home somewhere, hire someone for a modest monthly fee to keep an eye on it and alert you to any problems or maintenance needs.

If the deceased person owned rental property, take the short-term steps necessary to keep the landlording business running smoothly. If tenants pay rent directly, let them know what's happened and give them your contact information (address and phone number) so they can keep paying rent and let you know about problems or concerns.

G. Sort Through Personal Belongings

Although you'll need to go through the deceased person's things right away to look for financial and legal documents, don't think that you need to clean out everything immediately.

Many people sort through things gradually. Even if you must clear out a house or apartment quickly, it may be easier, for practical and emotional reasons, to box up memorabilia and personal belongings and let them sit for a while. You and others close to the deceased person can go through them a few weeks or months later.

Although family fights over possessions get the most media attention, in many families, the real problem turns out to be how to dispose of lots of belongings that nobody really wants. If the job is too much for you and other family members, consider hiring a salvage company.

Go slowly. When my grandmother died, we lost $500 because my grandfather threw out an envelope from her dresser without looking in it. I'd seen it in her drawer, but never thought my grandfather would toss an envelope before looking inside.

For a fee, it will send in a team of workers to take everything. It will pay you for valuable assets—but the cost of carting away the things that don't have much (or any) resale value usually equals or exceeds that amount.

If there are some valuable items—good china or antiques, for example—a consignment store may take them. The key is to find an honest and knowledgeable store; you might want to ask a real estate broker who has worked with estate sales.

Another way to handle unwanted assets is to donate them to a charity in a way the deceased person would approve of. For example, nice clothes might go to an organization that helps homeless people find jobs; books could be donated to a library.

What to do with it all? I'd always heard about family members fighting over objects. But in my family, nobody wanted most of the things our parents left behind. Of course there were treasures, like postcards and letters from 50 years ago when our parents were courting. But my brother and I threw out dozens of old driver's licenses, passports and bridge club membership certificates, boxes full of recipes, and piles of ancient cancelled checks. We both had come from a distance, so there wasn't a lot of time to deliberate. We went through file cabinets and desks full of stuff in two days and saved about four accordion files—twice as much as we really wanted—full of things before getting on the plane to go home.

CHAPTER 5

Claiming Life Insurance, Social Security, and Other Benefits

f immediate family members depended on the deceased person for financial support, they may be hard-pressed to pay for living expenses soon after the death. Even if the estate contains valuable assets, survivors may not know how to put their hands on enough cash for urgent, ongoing expenses such as the mortgage and credit card payments. (This is especially true if credit cards were in the deceased person's name.)

In fact, knowledgeable survivors can usually get access to many sources of cash without much trouble. As the executor, you'll want to be able to help them clear any bureaucratic hurdles they encounter.

Even if survivors don't have a pressing need for cash, it usually makes sense to get the ball rolling on collecting money they have coming to them from outside sources, including life insurance proceeds, Social Security benefits, union benefits, and the like. This chapter explains the process.

It might surprise some people, but receiving payments shortly after a loved one's death can feel like a very mixed blessing. Family members may need the money—and of course the deceased person wanted them to have it—but "profiting" from the death can cause feelings of discomfort or even guilt. If you find yourself in this situation, or if you are helping someone who is, try to keep in mind that these benefits,

which are probably not large, were set up precisely as an imperfect and small way to help people who have suffered a great loss. At a time when emotional concerns are paramount, these payments can at least help survivors avoid spending precious energy worrying about financial matters.

Other sources of cash. Survivors can often tap bank accounts and credit cards for cash easily and quickly. See Chapter 12.

A. Life Insurance and Annuity Proceeds

Payments from life insurance policies and many types of annuities can provide quick and welcome income for surviving family members after a death, especially an unexpected one.

An insurance policy or annuity is a contract between the company that sold it and the person who bought it. As a result, the proceeds don't go through probate, and the executor isn't in charge of them. It's common for the policy beneficiary, not the executor, to deal with the insurance company and collect the benefits directly. Of course, you may be a beneficiary yourself. But even if you're not, you may be called upon to help financially unsophisticated beneficiaries claim the payments they're entitled to.

HOW TO FIND INSURANCE POLICIES

If you haven't had any luck finding an insurance policy in the usual places (file cabinets, desk drawers, and so on), here are some other ways to track it down.

Look through cancelled checks. Even if you find a ten-year-old check to an insurance company, contact the company. The policy could still be in force.

Ask former employers and any union to which the person belonged. Some companies and unions provide free group life insurance coverage for employees and members; family members may not be aware of the policies.

1. Life Insurance

Life insurance can be a very important source of cash for surviving family members. The beneficiary will probably want to get the claim process started as soon as possible.

a. Types of Policies

To understand what the beneficiary can expect, you'll need to know what kind of policy you're dealing with. There are many varieties of life insurance, and different companies use different terms to describe them. If you're not sure what kind of policy you're dealing with, ask the agent or read up on it on the insurance company's website.

Here are the types you're most likely to run into.

Term insurance is the simplest type of life insurance. It provides insurance protection for a specified period of time—perhaps a year, or ten or 20 years. If the policyholder dies during the term, the company pays a death benefit to the policy beneficiary. If the policyholder is still living at the end of the term, the policy simply ends unless it's renewed. A term insurance policy has no cash (surrender) value.

Whole life insurance differs from term insurance in several ways. For starters, the premiums are much higher. The company invests part of the premiums to build a cash value. During their lives, policy owners can borrow against the cash value and in some instances, withdraw part of it, though doing so reduces the death benefit and cash value of the policy. At the policyholder's death, the company pays the beneficiary the death benefit.

Whole life insurance can provide protection for the policyholder's entire lifetime, as long as premiums are paid. But with some policies, protection lasts only until the policyholder reaches a certain age; then, the company pays the policy owner the cash value of the policy. (And usually, the company tries to sell the policyholder another kind of policy, often an annuity.)

Universal life insurance is a variation of whole life insurance. It allows the policy owner to change the death benefit from time to time and vary the amount or timing of premium payments.

CREDIT OR MORTGAGE INSURANCE BENEFITS

If the deceased person had credit insurance (to pay off credit card balances or, sometimes, amounts owing on major purchases such as furniture) or mortgage insurance (to pay off a mortgage), be sure to take advantage of it. Keep in mind that the policy proceeds are earmarked for the particular debt; you can't use them for other expenses.

b.   Is the Policy Still in Force?

Obviously, if the policy expired before the policyholder died, the named beneficiaries aren't entitled to any proceeds. So you need to see whether or not the policy was still in force.

Term insurance. If the deceased person died during the original term listed in the policy and had paid all the premiums due, then the beneficiary is entitled to collect the policy proceeds. If the original term ended before the death, call the company to see whether the insurance was renewed and the term extended.

"Convertible" term insurance can be exchanged for a whole life policy. If you find an old term policy with this feature, ask whether the policyholder ever converted it into another kind of policy.

Whole life or universal life insurance. If premiums were paid, the policy should still be in effect. If it looks like the policy has expired, call the company to see whether it was renewed or converted to another type of policy.

c.   Who's the Beneficiary?

To find out who the beneficiary of an insurance policy is, look at the policy—it will tell you. It may list both a primary (first-choice) beneficiary and an alternate. The alternate beneficiary (sometimes called the secondary or contingent beneficiary) is entitled to the policy proceeds only if the primary beneficiary has died.

Some policies, called "survivorship" policies, insure two people—commonly, a husband and wife. The policy provides benefits to the survivor when the first spouse dies. It doesn't matter who dies first.

If any beneficiary is under age 18, an adult will have to take charge of the money. If the policyholder named someone (on the form provided by the insurance company) to serve as custodian or trustee for the money, it can be turned over to that person with a minimum of fuss. If not, you may need to get the probate court to appoint a guardian before the company will release the proceeds. (See Chapter 10.)

EXAMPLE: *Elliott named his young daughter Ashley as the alternate beneficiary of his life insurance policy. So that there would be an adult in charge of the money if she inherits while still a minor, he named the beneficiary (on the insurance company form) this way: "Eliza Roberts, as custodian for Ashley Strakan under the New Jersey Uniform Transfers to Minors Act."*

IF AN EX-SPOUSE IS NAMED AS BENEFICIARY

If the deceased person named his or her spouse as beneficiary and later divorced but didn't change the designation, then who gets the policy proceeds depends on two factors.

The first is state law. Many states provide that if a couple divorces, any beneficiary designations they made to each other are automatically revoked. This usually includes life insurance policy beneficiary designations. The second factor is federal law, which comes into play only if the deceased person's employer provided the life insurance policy. Federal law (the Employee Retirement Income Security Act, or ERISA) provides a uniform national standard for determining who is the beneficiary of employer-provided life insurance policies (and retirement plans such as 401(k) plans). Under ERISA, which preempts (overrules) state law, the plan administrator must give proceeds to the beneficiary named in plan documents—and not try to figure out who is entitled to proceeds under an individual state's law. That means an ex-spouse would legally be entitled to get the proceeds, even if state law says the beneficiary designation was revoked by the divorce. (Egelhoff v. Egelhoff, 532 U.S. 141 (2001).)

If an ex-spouse makes a claim, you'll want to see a lawyer to sort it all out.

d. How Much the Company Will Pay

How much beneficiaries receive depends on the type of policy and, for some kinds of policies, whether the policyholder borrowed against it.

As mentioned earlier, term life insurance pays the face value of the policy if the insured dies within the term of the insurance.

EXAMPLE: *Ann buys a ten-year $25,000 term life policy and keeps it in force by paying premiums every year. Ann dies in the ninth year. The company will pay Ann's beneficiary $25,000.*

Whole life or universal life insurance also pays the face value of the policy at the policyholder's death. (The only exception would be if the policyholder had borrowed against the value of the policy.) But with these types of insurance, the beneficiaries may also be entitled to dividends earned by the policy. The estate should also be reimbursed for unused premiums paid before the death. For example, if the deceased person paid a year's premium in February and died in June, the prorated premium for June until the next February should be refunded. Finally, the company may be obligated to pay interest on the policy proceeds from the date of death until the payment is received.

Accidental death may trigger a larger payment. It's common for policies to provide for a larger payment if the deceased person dies as a result of an accident. For example, a policy may pay double the face value if the death was caused by a train, car, or plane mishap. To find out, read the policy or ask an agent for the company.

Proceeds may be paid in a lump sum or in installments. The beneficiaries' choices (usually called "settlement options") depend on the company's rules. Some companies offer half a dozen plans—for example, you may be able to choose equal payment over a set number of years or periodic payments calculated to last the rest of your life. A beneficiary who's eager to invest the money will want to take the lump sum to try to maximize return. Someone who's less comfortable with the idea of investing a large sum may prefer to take spread-out payments. Beneficiaries who have questions about what plan makes the most financial sense for them should talk to a financial advisor.

If the proceeds exceed a certain amount, some companies automatically open an interest-paying money market account for the beneficiary and deposit the proceeds into the account. The beneficiary may find this convenient; if not, he or she can withdraw the funds and close the account at any time.

e. Claiming Benefits

First, a policy beneficiary should contact the insurance company's local agent or check the company's website. Some companies ask beneficiaries to start by sending in a form that merely reports the death; they then provide the beneficiary with a packet of forms and instructions explaining how to proceed.

Generally, a beneficiary can apply for the proceeds simply by filling out the insurance company's claim form (or forms) and submitting it to the company along with a certified copy of the death certificate. (Chapter 4 explains how to get certified copies of the death certificate.)

If more than one adult beneficiary was named, each should submit a claim form. The company will pay each one the share he or she is entitled to. If the policyholder spelled out how much each beneficiary should get—for example, "50% to Esther Lightner, 25% to Thomas Lightner, and 25% to Matthew Lightner," then that's how the money will be divided. If no shares were specified, each beneficiary will get an equal share.

If the primary beneficiary died before the policyholder did, then the alternate beneficiary can claim the proceeds. An alternate will need to submit the death certificate of the primary beneficiary in addition to the death certificate of the policyholder.

EXAMPLE: *Maxine named her husband as the primary beneficiary of her life insurance policy, and her daughter Chelsea as the alternate beneficiary. By the time of Maxine's death, her husband has already passed away. So Chelsea fills out the forms to claim the policy proceeds. To show the company she's entitled to the money, she provides copies of the death certificates of both her parents.*

The company may also instruct you to send the policy itself. If you do, be sure to make a photocopy first. If you can't find the policy but know there is one, you may need to fill out the company's "Lost Policy" form.

Many companies say they try to send money within a week or two. It may take longer if the policy was a group policy or if the policy was bought recently. If the policy was fewer than two years old, the company may conduct a routine investigation before paying the proceeds.

2. Annuities

Annuities, like life insurance policies, are contracts with insurance companies. Usually, annuities provide retirement income to the policy owner, but under certain circumstances they can result in payments to a beneficiary. People buy individual policies or may get them as part of their employment. The chief benefit of an annuity is that unlike most other non-retirement plan investments, the earnings are not taxed until they are distributed. (Just how annuity payments are taxed is complicated—usually, part of each payment is taxable income and part isn't.)

When the annuity owner (annuitant) dies, benefits may be available to a beneficiary the owner named. The benefits depend on what kind of annuity the deceased person owned. If the policy was a "life-only" annuity, then no one receives anything after the owner's death. But if the annuity contract guaranteed payments for a certain amount of time, and the annuity owner died before the term ended, the beneficiary will receive the rest of the payments.

a. Types of Annuities

Here is a quick look at the two basic kinds of annuities.

Fixed annuities. A fixed annuity is like a certificate of deposit, except the money is deposited with an insurance company. Funds earn a preset rate of interest for a designated period of time, such as one, three, or five years. If the owner dies before that time is up, the beneficiary he or she named is entitled to the accumulated value (principal and interest) of the annuity.

Variable annuities. Variable annuities are more like tax-deferred mutual funds. Investors put money into a pool of stocks and bonds, which the insurance company manages (or hires an investment company to manage). The annuity owner's account (and the amount of the annuity payments) can go up or down in value, depending on the success of the investments.

b. Who's the Beneficiary?

Like an insurance policy, an annuity policy will tell you who the beneficiary is. It may list both a primary (first-choice) beneficiary and an alternate. The alternate beneficiary (sometimes called the secondary or contingent beneficiary) is entitled to benefits only if the primary beneficiary has died.

If any beneficiary is under age 18, an adult will have to take charge of the money. If the policyholder named someone (in the policy documents provided by the company) to serve as custodian or trustee for the money, it can be turned over to that person with a minimum of fuss. If not, the probate court may need to appoint a guardian before the company will release the proceeds. (See Chapter 10.)

c. How Much the Company Will Pay

If the annuity has a death benefit (not all do, remember), typically the insurance company guarantees that when the owner dies, the beneficiary will receive the greater of:

- the accumulated value of the annuity, including earnings, or

- the amount originally invested in the annuity, less distributions.

This means that even if the value of the annuity has gone down, the beneficiary will still get the amount that was invested.

EXAMPLE: *Harriet buys an annuity and deposits $100,000 into a stock account. At her death, she hasn't received any payments, but the account's value has fallen to $90,000. Her husband, the beneficiary, receives $100,000.*

d. Claiming Benefits

To claim the benefits after the policy owner dies, the beneficiary should request a claim form from the insurance company that issued the annuity. The beneficiary will need to submit a certified copy of the death certificate with the claim form. An alternate beneficiary who makes a claim must also submit the death certificate of the primary beneficiary.

B. Social Security Benefits

As part of helping surviving family members collect benefits that are easy to claim and quick to be paid, applying for Social Security benefits should be near the top of your list.

1. One-Time Death Benefit

If the deceased person had enough Social Security work credits, the Social Security Administration (SSA) makes a one-time lump sum payment, currently a modest $255, to the surviving spouse or dependent children. (You get credits by working and paying Social Security taxes; anyone who worked for at least ten years qualifies. Someone who worked less may also qualify, depending on his or her age at death; the younger the age at death, the less work is needed.)

This payment is in addition to ongoing survivors benefits to which the spouse or children may be entitled. (See Section 2, next.)

The spouse receives the payment if the couple was living together at the time of death. If they were living apart, a spouse who was eligible for Social Security benefits on the deceased spouse's earnings record is entitled to the payment.

If there is no surviving spouse, the payment goes to the children (split equally among them) who were eligible for benefits based on the parent's earnings record.

To apply, the beneficiary should go to the local Social Security office. The staff can help with the paperwork and explain what information and documents—a certified copy of the death certificate, for example—are needed. It's helpful to call and make an appointment before visiting, to avoid the long lines that sometimes clog these chronically understaffed offices. To find the closest office, check the government listings in the phone book, use the "How to Find Your Local Office" service on the SSA website at www.ssa.gov, or call the SSA, toll-free, at 800-772-1213.

2. Monthly Survivors Benefits

Far more important than the one-time death benefit discussed just above are monthly benefits, based on the deceased person's earnings, to which family members may be entitled. You don't have to be of retirement age to receive benefits: dependent children, surviving spouses, and even some ex-spouses may be eligible. The more quickly survivors apply for these benefits, the better, because some of them are not retroactive.

Applicants can start the application process over the telephone (800-772-1213) or online at www.ssa.gov, which may speed things up, but they won't be able to complete the process without a face-to-face meeting with a staffer at an SSA office. Again, making an appointment before the trip will probably save time.

More help with Social Security benefits. *Social Security, Medicare & Government Pensions*, by Joseph Matthews with Dorothy Matthews-Berman (Nolo), explains survivors benefits in careful detail.

Social Security Survivors Benefits, a free booklet published by the SSA, is also helpful. You can get a copy online at www.ssa.gov or by calling the SSA at 800-772-1213.

a.   The Surviving Spouse

How a surviving spouse goes about claiming benefits depends on the spouse's circumstances. A surviving spouse who is already receiving Social Security benefits based on the deceased person's earnings just needs to report the death to the SSA at 800-772-1213. The SSA will change his or her monthly benefits to survivors benefits.

If, however, the surviving spouse is not already getting benefits or is receiving benefits based on his or her own earnings record, he or she will need to apply for survivors benefits. If

the spouse is already getting benefits, the SSA will check to see whether or not the survivors benefit would be higher.

If the surviving spouse must apply, eligibility will depend on the survivor's age and family circumstances. Benefits are given to any surviving spouse who:

- takes care of the deceased person's child who is under 16 or disabled (this is commonly called the "mother's benefit" or "father's benefit")

- is 60 or over, or

- is 50 or older who becomes disabled within seven years of the worker's death or within seven years after the mother's or father's benefit ends.

b.   Former Spouses

Generally, divorced spouses are eligible for benefits under the same rules as surviving spouses, if the marriage lasted at least ten years and the divorced spouse does not remarry before age 60. If, however, the ex-spouse is taking care of the deceased person's young or disabled children, it doesn't matter how long the marriage lasted.

These benefits don't affect the benefits paid to other surviving family members.

c.   Dependent Children

Unmarried children of the deceased person are eligible for benefits if:

- They are 17 or younger (or up to age 19 if they are attending high school full time). Grandchildren and stepchildren may also be eligible, under certain circumstances.

- They are disabled, no matter what their age, and became disabled before age 22.

If children are already receiving benefits, the SSA will change the benefits to survivors benefits after the family notifies the SSA of the death.

d. Dependent Parents

Parents who depended on the deceased worker for at least half of their support and who are at least 62 are also eligible for benefits.

C. Pensions

The deceased person may have been entitled to pension benefits from a private company, government agency, or union. Some pensions end at death, but many provide for payments to a surviving spouse or dependent children.

As you go through the deceased person's papers, you may find documents that alert you to a pension—or a record of payments deposited directly into the person's bank account.

If you turn up a pension, you can find out about what (if any) benefits survivors are entitled to. They may receive a part of the payments the person would have received, and maybe only for a few years. (Pensions for government employees, however, are often generous when it comes to survivors benefits.) It all depends on the terms of the particular plan and choices the deceased person may have made years ago. It may be worthwhile to

dig up the paperwork to check the history of the elections the deceased person made, to make sure survivors are getting what they're supposed to—plenty of mistakes are made in this world.

Retirement plans and IRAs. Chapter 15 discusses how inheritors can collect the funds from IRAs, 401(k), and other retirement plans, which are subject to their own special rules.

D. Veterans Benefits

Most veterans' families are not entitled to any monetary benefits. But here are a few programs that may provide some help, and some information about how to apply.

Most veterans are eligible for flags and grave markers. Many veterans also qualify for burial in a national cemetery. See Chapter 3.

1. Dependency and Indemnity Compensation

A veteran's surviving spouse (and any children under age 18) may be entitled to payments if the deceased veteran:

- died while in the service

- died from a service-related disability, or

- received or was entitled to receive VA compensation for a service-related disability that was considered totally disabling for a certain period of time.

2. Wartime Service Pension

A veteran's surviving spouse or unmarried child whose annual income is under certain very low limits may qualify for a pension at the veteran's death. The veteran must have:

- been discharged from service under other than dishonorable conditions, and

- served 90 days or more of active duty with at least one day during wartime; or, if he or she enlisted after September 7, 1980, at least 24 months or the full period for which the person was called to active duty.

3. Burial Allowance

In limited circumstances, survivors may be eligible for reimbursement of some costs paid for a veteran's burial or funeral. They may be entitled to the burial allowance if any of the following are true. The veteran:

- died because of a service-related disability

- was receiving a VA pension or compensation at the time of death

- was entitled to receive a VA pension or compensation but decided not to reduce his or her military retirement or disability pay, or

- died in a VA hospital or while in a nursing home under VA contract.

In addition, the expenses must not have been reimbursed by another source—for example, another government agency or the veteran's employer. Also, the veteran must have been discharged under conditions other than dishonorable.

4. Applying for Veterans Benefits

To apply for benefits, an applicant will need copies of the veteran's discharge papers, marriage certificate, and other basic information. For more information, contact the U.S. Department of Veterans Affairs at 800-827-1000 or visit its website at www.va.gov.

More help with veterans benefits. *Social Security, Medicare & Government Pensions*, by Joseph Matthews, with Dorothy Matthews-Berman (Nolo), discusses benefits available to veterans' survivors.

E. Wages Owed the Deceased Person

If the person was working up until the time of death and left a surviving spouse, the spouse can probably claim and promptly receive the final amount due from the employer. If there is no surviving spouse, a child or other relative may be able to claim the money. (If there is more than one sibling, they should act together.)

The amount due always includes the value of any unused vacation days. (You may, however, have to remind the employer of this.) Depending on company policy, it may also include pay for unused sick days. Also ask about unpaid bonuses, commissions, and reimbursement for expenses.

It's often wise to send a letter to the deceased person's former employer to ask about unpaid wages and commissions, bonuses, reimbursement for unpaid expenses, pensions, group life insurance, retirement funds, stock ownership, or medical benefits. Simply provide the name, Social Security number, date of death, and dates of employment (if you know them), and ask for any information the employer has on these benefits.

To find out where to send the letter, call the employer and ask for the name of the person who handles such matters. In most places, it's the company's director of human resources or personnel manager.

1. Special State Procedures

Some states have laws setting out a specific procedure that a surviving spouse (and sometimes other immediate family members) can use to be paid the deceased person's wages. Commonly, all the spouse needs to do is prepare a short affidavit (sworn statement), sign it in front of a notary public, and submit it to the employer. A sample affidavit is shown below.

The affidavit must commonly say that the person submitting it is the surviving spouse and that no probate proceeding has been started. Most of these laws impose a cap of a few hundred or thousand dollars on the amount that can be collected in this informal

way. To find out your state's limit (if any), you can look for your state's statute. (Chapter 22 discusses how to look up statutes online.) If you don't know your state's specific rule, you can still ask for whatever was owed to the deceased person. The employer may be familiar with the law and know how much can be released directly to you.

Most large employers have seen this kind of form. Smaller businesses, which might pay a surviving spouse the money even without a formal request, will probably be reassured by it.

Help for California readers. *How to Probate an Estate in California*, by Julia Nissley (Nolo), contains a form a surviving spouse can use in California to claim up to $5,000 in wages due the deceased person.

SAMPLE AFFIDAVIT FOR COLLECTING WAGES

Affidavit for Collection of Compensation Owed Deceased Spouse

I, the undersigned, state as follows:

1. [Name of deceased spouse], the decedent, died on [date], at [city and state].

2. I am the surviving spouse of the decedent.

3. No proceeding for the administration of the decedent's estate is pending or has been conducted in any jurisdiction.

4. State law [insert the citation to your state's statute if you know it] requires that earnings of the decedent, including compensation for unused vacation, up to $[amount allowed by your state law, if you know it—otherwise, just delete this whole phrase], be paid promptly to the surviving spouse.

5. I request that I be paid any compensation owed by you for personal services of the decedent, including compensation for unused vacation, not to exceed $[amount allowed by statute, if you know it—otherwise just ask for it all].

6. I declare under penalty of perjury of the laws of [your state] that the foregoing is true and correct.

_____
[surviving spouse's signature]

Date _____

[notarization]

---

2. Small Estate Affidavit Procedure

If the estate qualifies as a "small estate" under state law, there's another way to collect wages owed to the deceased person. The surviving spouse (or another inheritor, if the deceased person wasn't married), can claim unpaid compensation with a simple affidavit. It's the same procedure beneficiaries can use to claim other kinds of property without probate. The process is discussed in Chapter 17.

F. The Family Allowance

In the increasingly unusual event that the estate goes through regular probate, dependent family members can ask the probate court for a "family allowance." This is primarily cash that is quickly released from the estate (and is not available to creditors) to help with short-term living expenses. The amount available depends on state law, and generally ranges from a few thousand dollars to several tens of thousands. (Surviving spouses are also typically given other property or rights as part of the allowance—for example, the right to live in the family home rent-free for six months after the death, or a family furnishings worth up to $2,000, or the family car. For most spouses, who inherit most or everything, this isn't particularly important.)

Years ago, when most family assets were subject to a lengthy court probate proceeding and few people had credit cards, it was common to ask the court for a family allowance to pay bills until the estate could be sorted out. But today, most families have some sources of money not subject to probate (a joint bank account, for example) that are accessible quickly, and credit cards allow people to put off paying some bills. So there is usually less need to request this money.

If dependents do need the court to release money from the estate as a family allowance, you'll have to make a formal request to the probate court. It shouldn't be a difficult process—the court may even have a form you can use. Regular probate is discussed in Chapter 18.

G. Other Possible Benefits and Claims

Family members may be entitled to some other death benefits, depending on the circumstances of the deceased relative's life, health, and employment. Some of these are easy to overlook, so run down the list and see if any of them might apply to your situation.

1. Workers' Compensation

If the death occurred on the job or because of a work-related injury or illness, family members who depended on the deceased person for support will likely qualify for workers' compensation death benefits. Every state has its own workers' compensation program. Because large sums of money may be involved, you'll almost certainly want to see a lawyer with experience in this area.

If the deceased person had already been receiving workers' compensation payments because of a work-related injury, contact the insurance company that paid the benefits and make sure all benefits due the deceased person are paid. Again, you may want to consult a knowledgeable lawyer.

Help for California readers. *Take Charge of Your Workers' Compensation Claim* (California), by Christopher Ball (Nolo), explains the process for Californians.

2. State Disability Benefits

If the deceased person was receiving disability benefits from the state, notify the state agency in charge of the benefits. (Chapter 4 contains a general letter you can use.) Make sure all payments were made up to the date of death.

3. Federal Employment Benefits

If the deceased person worked for the federal government, benefits may be available to the family or to a beneficiary the employee named. Contact the agency the person worked for.

4. Railroad Retirement Act Benefits

If the person worked for a railroad and was covered by the federal Railroad Retirement Act, survivors may be eligible for benefits. For information, contact the closest Railroad Retirement Board or check out the website at www.rrb.gov.

5. Unions

Some unions provide death benefits, but this practice is becoming rarer. (And, as mentioned earlier, some unions provide life insurance.)

Family members should contact the local to which the deceased person belonged and ask whether or not any benefits are available.

6. Benefits From Health Insurance

Some health insurance policies offer limited coverage for funeral expenses. To find out, call the deceased person's health insurance provider or, if the policy was obtained through a job or membership in an organization, contact the person in charge of administering the program there.

Surviving family members may also be entitled to some benefits from the deceased person's insurance plan. You'll need to contact the insurance provider to find out whether or not this is true in your case.

7. Lawsuits for Wrongful Death

If the deceased person was killed intentionally or in an accident, survivors may be able to get sizable compensation to help make up the lost income the deceased person would have provided to the family. To get this compensation, survivors must file what's called a "wrongful death" lawsuit. Family members may win such a lawsuit if the death was caused by, for example, an incompetent doctor, a careless driver, someone committing a crime, or a defective product such as a tire that blew out on a highway.

Losing a loved one under any of these circumstances is exceptionally painful, and probably the last thing family members want to think about is a lawsuit. But lawsuits must be filed within a certain period after the death, and it can be important to gather evidence right away. So if you think a lawsuit may be justified, you should talk to an experienced personal injury lawyer as soon as you feel able. ■

Taking Care of the Estate

CHAPTER 6

Making Sense of the Will

In novels and movies, when anxious family members gather in a somber office to hear an even more somber lawyer read the terms of a will, it's a moment of high drama. In real life, it's usually considerably less tense. One reason is that today much valuable property, including retirement accounts, insurance policies, many bank accounts and securities, and property held in living trusts, doesn't pass under the terms of a will.

Even when a will does dispose of significant amounts of property, there may be little drama, because you and other inheritors may already know exactly what it provides. But the will may contain surprises or, at the very least, some language that's hard to understand. This chapter explains how to figure out exactly what the will means.

If there's no will. If despite your best efforts, you can't find a will, and will substitutes such as trusts and beneficiary designations don't fill in all the blanks, state law will dictate who inherits. See Chapter 7.

A. Does the Will Appear Valid?

Before you start deciphering the language of the will, take a moment to arrive at a tentative conclusion about the document's validity. The final word on validity will be issued by the probate court, if you go through formal probate proceedings. But it's good to be confident that the will is a legally binding

document before you begin following its instructions.

That said, it's also important to understand that:

- Family changes—for example, the will-maker's divorce or marriage—can have dramatic legal effects on the terms of a valid will. (See Section D, below.)

- No will can dispose of property that's held in joint tenancy, or in a living trust, or for which a beneficiary has been named in another binding document. (Except in Washington state; see Section D, below.)

- Even a will that that's properly signed and witnessed may be open to challenge—for example, on the ground that the will-maker didn't have the mental capacity, perhaps because of Alzheimer's or another illness, to make a valid will. (See Chapter 18.)

1. Basic Requirements

Generally, to be legally binding a will must meet three requirements, all intended to protect against fraud or forgery. It must be:

- in writing

- signed and dated by the person who made it, and

- signed by witnesses.

If a will seems to have been properly signed and witnessed, chances are all is well. You have no responsibility to investigate the circumstances of the will's signing unless someone suggests that there is a problem.

The major exception to these rules is that in about half the states, a handwritten, unwitnessed, but signed will is valid, if it's clear that it really was intended to be a will. See Section 3, below.

a. Writing

These days, most wills are generated on a computer and printed out; older wills were generally typewritten. It's permissible, however, for a will to be entirely handwritten as long as the signature and witnessing requirements (discussed below) are met.

What is troublesome, legally, is a mix of machine-generated printing and handwriting. For example, if something on a typed document is crossed out or added by hand, it's impossible to tell whether or not the change was made before or after the document was signed—or even who made it.

Handle it yourself, if possible. A minor handwritten change, or one that all inheritors agree to—for example, a note added to an existing will after a grandchild is born, leaving the new baby $1,000—is not likely to be a problem. The inheritors can probably figure out a way to honor the wish, even though they are not legally bound to do so. But if the change is major and may cause disagreement—for example, removing a beneficiary entirely—see a lawyer.

b. Signature and Date

The person who wrote the will (the "testator") must have signed and dated it at the end of the document. The signature does not have to be notarized. It's common, but not legally required, for the person to also have initialed each numbered page of the will.

ELECTRONIC OR VIDEOTAPED WILLS

Nevada is the only state that accepts electronic signatures for wills. This technology is not widespread, however, and it's exceedingly unlikely that you'll run into it. A will that was simply composed on a computer but not printed out and signed is not valid under any state's law. Similarly, a videotaped statement is not a valid will.

---

c. Witnesses

As a protection against fraud, every state requires that witnesses, as well as the will-maker, sign the will.

If the witnessing requirements were not met, the probate court judge will decide whether or not to admit the will to probate. Keep in mind that although judges take these rules quite seriously, they don't want a technical mistake to frustrate a will-maker's obvious intentions. So if no one is arguing about the validity of a will, but there was a failure to comply with witnessing laws, generally a judge will look for ways to get around the problem.

EXAMPLE: *A lawyer who prepared wills for a married couple forgot to sign the wife's will as a* *witness. He discovered the mistake after her death, and signed the will then. A court ruled that the will was valid because the lawyer had watched the will-maker sign her will, and state law did not require him to sign it at the same time. (Estate of Eugene, 104 Cal. App. 4th 907 (2002).)*

(1) Number of Witnesses

In most states, "at least two competent witnesses" must have signed the will for it to be valid. Vermont requires at least three.

In most states, the witnesses must have together watched the testator sign the will, and then signed it themselves; in others, it's enough if the will-maker told them his own signature was valid and asked them to sign later. The witnesses don't need to have read the will, but need to have known that the document they watched being signed was a will.

At the end of the will, you should find a statement something like this one:

We hereby certify that in our presence on the date written above CYNTHIA B. GONZALES signed the foregoing instrument and declared it to be her Last Will and Testament and that at her request in her presence and in the presence of each other we have signed our names below as witnesses.

Richard E. Garcia residing at 548 Founder Street, Reno, Nevada

Ramona S. Curry residing at 91 Margaret Avenue, Reno, Nevada

It's also common for witnesses to sign a longer statement and have their signatures notarized. This is called a self-proving affidavit; it makes proving the will's validity in court a simpler process. (Section B16, below, discusses these affidavits.)

(2) Age of Witnesses

The general rule is that witnesses must be legal adults—that is, 18 years or older. If a will was signed by the required two witnesses, but one of them was not yet 18, the will is invalid.

EXAMPLE: *A document purporting to be an Arkansas woman's will was signed by two people: one adult and a 14-year-old girl. When the will was challenged, the court ruled that the document was not a valid will because state law clearly requires at least two adult witnesses. (Norton v. Hinson, 989 S.W.2d 535, 337 Ark. 487 (1999).)*

(3) Witnesses Who Inherit Under the Will

In most states, someone who stands to inherit property under a will may not be a witness to it. In these states, if a beneficiary does sign the will as a witness, and there aren't enough other "disinterested" witnesses, the general rule is that the gift to the witness is cancelled. The rest of the will remains valid.

For example, in Massachusetts, if a beneficiary—or a beneficiary's spouse—serves as a witness, then the gift to the witness is void. (Mass. Gen. Laws Ann. § 191.2.)

Other states soften this rule somewhat. For example, New York law provides that if a beneficiary is also a witness, then the gift to that person is void. If, however, the beneficiary would have been entitled to inherit under state law if there had been no will, the beneficiary does get some of the bequest, up to the amount he or she would have gotten had there not been a will. (N.Y. Est., Powers & Trusts Law § 3-3.2.) Illinois has a law that is similar, but even broader; it applies if a beneficiary's spouse was a witness. (755 Ill. Comp. Stat. Ann. § 5/4-6.)

If you face this situation, you'll need to look up your state's law on witnesses. For guidance on finding what you need, see Chapter 22.

(4) Notaries as Witnesses

Wills don't need to be notarized. (By contrast, self-proving affidavits attached to wills, discussed above and in Section B16, below, do need to be notarized.) But some people get wills notarized anyway. Usually, if there's a dispute over witnessing, the notary public counts as a competent witness. For example, if only one person signed as a witness (or one witness was disqualified), but the will was notarized, the notary would be counted as the second witness.

(5) Lawyers as Witnesses

Normally, it's not a problem if the attorney who drafted the will also serves as a witness. This is true even if the attorney is appointed executor and so stands to benefit—by collecting fees for his or her work as executor—from the will.

2. Out-of-State Wills

You may find a will that was signed in a different state from the one in which the person was living when he or she died. In that situation, generally the will's validity is judged under the old state's laws. In other words, if the will was valid under the laws of the state where it was signed, the new state will accept it as valid.

3. Handwritten Wills

If you find a handwritten will that was signed in front of witnesses, the will is considered a regular will and is treated just like a typed one.

You may, however, find a handwritten will that was not signed by witnesses. It's not common, but especially if people are acting at the last minute, they sometimes simply write down their instructions, sign the piece of paper with no witnesses present, and hope for the best. Such "holographic" wills are legal in about half the states if they are signed and all important provisions are in the writer's handwriting. Some states require that they also be dated. (Each state's rule is summarized in the appendix.)

Even in many states that don't allow holographic wills, a will that was a valid holographic will when it was made in another state will be considered valid.

EXAMPLE: *Helen makes a holographic will while she's living in Oklahoma, which allows them. She later moves to Alabama but doesn't get around to making a new will before her death. The will would be accepted by an Alabama probate court because it was valid under Oklahoma law when Helen made it.*

Holographic wills provide fertile ground for arguments. Is that really the deceased person's handwriting? Was he or she of sound mind when writing it? Did he or she really intend it to be a will? And if so, was the purpose to revoke a previous witnessed will or add to it? Is it actually signed? For example, in one case, a court ruled that a woman's instructions for the disposition of her property, written in a notebook, weren't signed because her name appeared only in the front of the notebook, not at the end. (*Kidd v. Gunter*, 551 S.E.2d 646 (Va. 2001).)

See a lawyer if arguments are in the air. If the deceased person lived in a state that recognizes holographic wills, and all close family members agree that the will is valid, you should have little problem carrying out its terms whether or not regular probate is required. However, if a handwritten will creates controversy or hard feelings among likely inheritors, and especially if it disposes of very valuable assets, see a lawyer for advice as to whether or not it's likely to stand up to a challenge.

4. Lists of Property Referred to in the Will

In the absence of a will, or sometimes in addition to one, you may find typed or handwritten notes that direct who is to inherit certain items of the deceased person's property. Even though these documents don't qualify as valid holographic wills, they may be legally binding documents. (And even if they aren't, you may want to follow their instructions.) At the least, don't throw them out.

About half the states allow will-makers to refer to such a document (usually called a memorandum) to dispose of tangible items of personal property—that is, things like jewelry, books, or furniture. (Every state's rule is listed in the appendix.) By law, generally these lists cannot control what happens to the deceased person's money or other intangible assets. Utah law, which is typical, says "a will may refer to a written statement or list to dispose of items of tangible personal property not otherwise specifically disposed of by the will, other than money... ." The statute goes on to say that the person must hand-write or sign the document. If there is more than one such document, and they conflict, the most recent one is honored.

Why would someone make such a memorandum instead of spelling everything out in the will? Mainly because it's much less trouble than going back and changing a will; a memorandum doesn't have to be signed and witnessed like a will.

For the memorandum to have any effect, the will must refer to it. Otherwise, there's little reason to think that the person expected the document to be legally binding—perhaps he or she was just working out different possibilities on paper.

5. More Than One Will

It's common for people to make several wills over their lifetimes, changing the terms as they marry, divorce, have children, suffer the death of a spouse, or acquire different assets. If the deceased person didn't get around to destroying old wills, you may find more than one.

The general rule is that the most recent will supersedes the earlier ones. In fact, it's standard for a will to include a statement revoking all previous wills and codicils. Here's an example:

I, Arnold A. Kleinfeldt, a resident and citizen of Benton County, Missouri, being of sound mind and disposing memory, do hereby make, publish, and declare this instrument to be my last will and testament, hereby revoking any and all wills and codicils by me at any time heretofore made.

Even if a will doesn't expressly revoke previous wills, it may revoke them simply because it contradicts them. If a more recent will is inconsistent with an earlier one, the law generally follows the most recent wishes.

Even if you're pretty sure that an old will has been superseded by a newer one, hang on to the old document. If the later one (or part of it) turns out to be invalid for some reason, you may need the old one.

A later will that doesn't revoke or seriously contradict a former one could even be seen to be a codicil. (Codicils are discussed in Chapter 4, Section C2.) In that case, both documents would be considered together. If you're not sure, see a lawyer.

EXAMPLE: *On January 1, Bill makes a will disposing of a long list of property. On March 1, he makes another will listing just two items not covered in the previous one. Later he tells his son that he intended to supplement the first will, not revoke it. Especially if all the heirs agree, the second will could be considered a codicil to the first.*

B. Reading the Will

Now it's time to read the will. Not an out-loud reading to assembled family members—just a private read-through for you, so you get a feeling for what's there.

Although more and more wills use relatively clear language, many of them are still written in a stilted, old-fashioned style and larded with legal terms. Fortunately, once you define the jargon, the underlying meaning usually isn't that complicated.

This section lists common clauses you may find in the will and explains what they mean. As you read through the will, you may want to make a worksheet modeled on the "Summary of the Will" worksheet below. That will give you a quick reference sheet if you (or others) later have questions about the will's terms.

TERMS YOU MAY FIND IN THE WILL

Here are some of the jargon-y terms you may run across as you read the will. This is far from a complete list, so if you don't find a term here, check the glossary.

Bequeath: To leave at death; another word for "give."

Bequest: A gift of an item of personal property left at death.

Bond: A kind of insurance policy that protects inheritors against loss caused by the executor.

Devise: A gift of real estate left at death. Also a verb meaning to give at death.

Devisee: Someone who inherits real estate through a will.

Executrix: A female executor. Most wills these days simply use "executor," whether the person is a man or woman.

Failed or lapsed gift: A gift made in a will that cannot be given to the intended recipient because that person has not survived the will-maker and the will does not state what should happen to the gift.

Heir: Someone who inherits property under state law if there's no valid will.

Issue: Direct descendants, including children, grandchildren, and so on. Brothers, sisters, parents, and other relatives are not issue.

Legacy: A gift of personal property left at death.

Legatee: Someone who inherits personal property.

Per capita: A way of dividing property among the descendants of a deceased heir or beneficiary. (See Chapter 7.)

Per stirpes: See "right of representation."

Personal property: Everything but real property.

Personal representative: Another name for executor.

Real property: Land and things permanently attached to it, such as houses.

Residue or residuary estate: All property subject to a will that isn't given away specifically in the will.

Right of representation: A way of dividing property among the descendants of a deceased heir or beneficiary. (See Chapter 7.)

Seized of: Having possession of.

Testamentary: Having to do with a will.

Testator: Person who writes a will. ("Testatrix" is the old-fashioned term for a female will-writer.)

SUMMARY OF THE WILL

Executor
_____
_____
_____

Alternate(s)
_____
_____

Bond required? _____

Specific gifts

Gift	Recipient(s)	Alternate(s)
_____	_____	_____
_____	_____	_____
_____	_____	_____
	_____	_____

General gifts

Amount	Recipient(s)	Alternate(s)
_____	_____	_____
_____	_____	_____
_____	_____	_____

Residuary estate

Recipient(s)	Alternate(s)
_____	_____
_____	_____
_____	_____

Children's guardian

	Name	Address	Phone
Primary:	_____	_____	_____
Alternate:	_____	_____	_____

Trusts
Beneficiary_____ Trustee _____

Other provisions _____
_____

Date _____

Witnesses

Name	Address	Phone
_____	_____	_____
_____	_____	_____

Self-proving affidavit? _____

1. Personal Declarations

It's common for wills to begin with some basic information about the will-maker's family: the spouse's name if the person is married, and the names of any children or grandchildren. This is to make it clear what's meant by future references in the will to terms such as "my children" or "my wife." These statements are also included to show that the person made the will with these close family members in mind. So, for example, if the person lists a child but doesn't leave any property to that child, it's obvious that the will-maker did not unintentionally overlook the child. (A child who is not mentioned may have the right to claim part of the estate. See Section D, below.)

2. Nomination of the Executor

Obviously, the provision naming an executor—called a personal representative in many states—is crucial. Did the person in fact name you as executor? The paragraph naming the executor often comes near the end of the will. In addition to naming you, it will probably also name one or more alternates, who would take over if you were to decline or resign.

Here's an example:

I hereby nominate, constitute, and appoint my beloved wife, Keiko Tanaka, to act as the Executor of this my Last Will and Testament. In the event that my beloved wife Keiko Tanaka shall predecease me or chooses not to act for any reason, I nominate and appoint Richard Kawamoto, Elliott Nagai, and Miranda Whitley, in the order named, to act in her place and stead.

Some wills do not definitively state who is to serve as executor. For example, some people leave the choice up to their children, like this:

I nominate as executors ("executor") of this will those of my children who are competent and willing to act.

In that case, the children must decide among themselves who is to serve as executor. They may elect one person, or some or all of them may share the job as coexecutors.

If the person who made the will named his or her spouse as executor and later divorced, the law in most states automatically revokes the nomination. The alternate executor, if one is named in the will, would serve instead. See Section D, below.

If the will doesn't name an executor (very rare) or if no one named in the will can serve, the court will appoint someone, just as it would if there were no will. The person chosen is sometimes called the "administrator with will annexed" or "administrator CTA."

PROBLEMS WITH APPOINTMENT OF THE EXECUTOR

A probate court will honor a deceased person's choice of executor unless there's a very good reason not to.

What might such a reason be? To begin with, an executor must be a United States resident who is at least 18 years old; that's not usually a problem. Only a few states (see the appendix) forbid out-of-state executors.

In some states, an executor must also be of good moral character or at least never have been convicted of a serious crime. But it's doubtful that a court will examine someone's moral fitness unless a dissatisfied relative raises the issue.

3. The Executor's Bond

Most wills state, either in the clause that names the executor or separately, that the executor is not required to post a bond. A bond is simply an insurance policy that protects the estate if the executor steals or recklessly squanders estate funds. If the will says no bond is necessary, you won't have to buy one, and the estate will save some money. Chapter 18 discusses bonds in more detail.

4. Specific Gifts

A "specific gift" clause leaves specific items of property to specific beneficiaries, like this:

FOURTH:

(a) I give and bequeath to Anastasia Kern, should she survive me, all funds in my savings account, #48-9877A at First National Bank, Cincinnati, Ohio.

(b) I give and bequeath all of my personal effects and clothing to Matthew Porter, or if he should predecease me, then to James Hernandez.

Many wills contain no specific gifts. They simply leave everything to one person, or to several people to share equally.

Others make some specific gifts and then leave everything else to one or more other beneficiaries. For example, a will might leave some favorite books or antiques to the will-maker's nephew Tom, and the rest of the property to his children in equal shares.

Here's another specific gift clause—a rather unusual (but legal) one—which leaves it up to the executor, a trusted friend, to distribute personal effects:

I bequeath all of my personal effects, clothing, and books to my Executor hereinafter named, it being my desire that he distribute these, in his sole discretion, among my friends, colleagues, and those to whom I am devoted.

You may come across bits of unfamiliar legal jargon in a specific gift clause, like this one:

I give to my issue who survive me, by right of representation, all my jewelry, clothing, household furniture and furnishings, automobiles, and other articles of tangible personal property not disposed of in any other manner.

"Issue" means direct descendants: children, grandchildren, and so on. The phrase "by right of representation" means, basically, that if a beneficiary dies before the will-maker does, that beneficiary's offspring inherit his or her share. (A will may also direct that descendants inherit "per capita," which means—to oversimplify—that everyone who inherits in place of a deceased beneficiary gets an equal share.) Figuring out exactly how to apply these terms in practice can be very tricky. If you run into them, see Chapter 7.

⚠ Watch out for gifts to groups of people. If the will leaves gifts to groups of people such as "my children," who aren't named individually, see Section C, below.

a. Gifts of "Personal Effects" or "Personal Property"

People commonly lump not-so-valuable items together in their wills, using terms such as "personal effects" or "furnishings." If one person or a group of beneficiaries inherits everything, you won't have to worry about exactly which items belong in this category. But if one beneficiary gets "personal effects" and another gets "furniture and books," for example, you'll need to sort the deceased person's property into the right categories.

It may help you if you understand that courts commonly define the term personal effects fairly narrowly, to mean items that someone wears or carries, or that have some "intimate relation" to the person. One court, for example, ruled that cars did not pass under a will provision leaving "personal effects and household goods and furnishings." (*Matter of Estate of Roddy*, 784 P.2d 841, Colo. App. (1989).)

The term "personal property," on the other hand, is usually interpreted more broadly and given its standard legal meaning, which is all property that isn't real estate. For example, a Georgia court ruled that the term included all investment funds and accounts that the will-maker owned. Before reaching this conclusion, the court heard evidence from the lawyer who had drafted the will; she testified that the will-maker had told her he wanted to leave everything but his real estate to his domestic partner. (*Delbello v. Bilyeu*, 274 Ga. 776, 560 S.E.2d 3 (2002).)

b. Conditional Gifts

It's rare (thank goodness), but sometimes people leave property subject to certain conditions. For example, a will might say, "I give $10,000 to Sue Ellen Murphy if she goes to college" or "I bequeath $10,000 to William Murphy if he stops smoking."

These conditional or contingent gifts can be nightmares for an executor. How long should the executor wait before concluding that Sue Ellen isn't going to college or that Bill has kicked the habit? Does taking a night class at the local community college entitle Sue Ellen to her money? Can Bill claim his if he goes cold turkey for six months? If Sue Ellen doesn't get the money, who does? You get the idea.

If you run into such a provision, your best bet is probably to get all the beneficiaries together and explain the situation. If everyone can agree on how best to fulfill the will-maker's wishes, a probate judge will probably go along with your decision.

c.   Property a Will Can't Touch

A will has no effect on property that goes directly to a beneficiary or co-owner outside the will. Property may pass outside the will for one of many reasons. The most common are that the deceased person named a beneficiary for it (a retirement account, for example) or that state law provides that the surviving spouse or other close relative can claim the property (for example, the family residence).

Here are some common examples of property that passes outside the will:

- life insurance proceeds

- property held in joint tenancy or tenancy by the entirety, or as community property with right of survivorship

- property held in trust—most commonly, a living trust set up to avoid probate or estate tax

- funds in a retirement account for which a beneficiary has been named

- funds in a payable-on-death (POD) bank account

- stocks or other securities held in a transfer-on-death (TOD) account

- property covered by a written agreement between the deceased person and his or her spouse, setting out who inherits the property (Alaska, Idaho, Washington, or Wisconsin only).

If a will tries to leave this property to someone, the provision simply has no effect.

EXCEPTION FOR WASHINGTON RESIDENTS

Washington is the only state that allows people to use their wills to change the beneficiaries of certain kinds of property that usually pass outside of the will. Under the state's "superwill" statute, state residents can use their wills to name beneficiaries for:

- property held in a revocable living trust

- payable-on-death bank accounts

- individual retirement accounts, or

- joint tenancy bank accounts.

The property does not, however, go through probate.

Basically, the property goes to the beneficiary named most recently. So if someone set up one of these probate-avoidance devices and then later used his or her will to name a beneficiary for the item, it would go to the person named in the will. However, if the person then named a different beneficiary—for example, by updating the paperwork for a payable-on-death bank account—the money would go to that beneficiary. (Wash. Rev. Code § 11.11.020.)

---

5.   Specific Gifts Listed in Another Document

In some states it's legal for people to refer, in their wills, to another document that lists tangible items of property and who is to inherit them. (See Section A, above.) If the deceased person used such a list, you'll find something like this in the will:

I leave my personal property in accordance with a memorandum signed by me or in my handwriting, which I intend to leave at my death.

The memorandum (which may take the form of a letter or list) may be with the will, or you may find it among other papers. If it's validly prepared under your state's law, you'll need to treat the document as part of the will and follow its instructions.

As mentioned, it's common for people to make written or sometimes deathbed additions to their wills—even if state law *doesn't* allow it. As long as inheritors agree, it's fine to respect such added instructions.

6. Gifts of Money

A gift of a certain amount of money, without a specified source, is called a "general" bequest or legacy. Here's an example:

I give and bequeath to Charles and May Chao, or to the survivor of them, or if they should both predecease me, then to their daughter, Sara Chao, the sum of $10,000.00, it being my wish that such sum be used for the education of Sara Chao.

The executor cannot satisfy such a gift with funds that have been specifically left to another beneficiary—for example, a specific bank account that was left to someone else. The money must come, if possible, from cash that's part of the "residuary estate"—basically, any property the will doesn't specifically mention. If there's not enough cash in the residuary to make all the monetary gifts in the will, the executor gets cash by selling property from the residuary estate if possible. The executor would not sell property that was specifically left to another beneficiary. (Chapter 18 discusses these issues.)

If the beneficiary doesn't actually receive the money for an excessively long time after the death, the estate may have to pay interest on the amount. For example, in Georgia, the law requires that interest be paid beginning 12 months after the death. (Ga. Code Ann. § 53-4-61.) The will may, however, state that no interest need be paid.

7. Gift of the Residuary Estate

After specific and general gifts (if any) are listed, a will usually directs who should inherit the "residue" of the estate—that is, whatever's left after the other gifts are made.

Here's an example of a residuary clause:

I give the rest and residue of my estate to my beloved husband, Jonathan R. Gretly, or if he does not survive me, in equal shares to my children, Samantha Gretly-March and Louis M. Gretly.

The residue may also include property that was specifically left to someone, but for some reason couldn't be given—for example, an item that was left to someone who died before the will-maker did (and for which no alternate beneficiary was named). What happens to such gifts depends on the language of the residuary clause and on state laws about "lapsed" gifts. (See Section D5, below.)

The residuary estate does not contain nonprobate property. As discussed earlier, a will has no effect on property that's owned in joint tenancy, held in a living trust, or for which a beneficiary has been named in another binding document.

If the will makes no specific gifts at all—a common situation—then the residuary clause disposes of everything that's subject to the will. For example, this short paragraph serves to dispose of all of the will-writer's property:

I give, devise, and bequeath all of my property of which I die possessed, both real and personal, wheresoever it may be, to my beloved wife, Camille D'Antonio, for her to have and to use as she may see fit for her best interest.

Note that the clause doesn't use the words "residuary estate." It simply leaves all the willmaker's property.

⚠ Watch out for gifts to groups of people. If the will leaves gifts to groups such as "my children," who aren't named individually, it may not be easy to tell who's included in the group. See Section C, below.

8. Children's Guardians

If the deceased person left children under 18, and there is no surviving parent able to raise them, you need to look for a will clause that names a "personal guardian" for the children. This is the person who will raise the children. If one parent has died but a surviving parent is able to care for the child, you don't need to concern yourself with this part of the will.

If a guardian is needed, the probate court will appoint the person the deceased parent named, unless the court finds a serious problem with that person. If relatives engage in a court battle over who will be the guardian, it's not your fight—the court will make a decision, based on the best interests of the child.

Here's an example of a will clause nominating a personal guardian:

If Merilee Mathis does not survive me, I hereby nominate and appoint Carla Walton Reuther as the personal guardian of Kayla Mathis, if she is then a minor.

The will may also name a "property guardian" for the children. This person—who, in many cases, is also the personal guardian—will be responsible for managing the property the child inherits unless the will specifies another arrangement. (Children's issues are discussed in Chapter 10.)

9. Trusts

You may find in the will a clause that sets up a trust to take effect at the will-maker's death. A trust is an arrangement under which one person controls and manages property for another. Trusts created in wills are called testamentary trusts.

The most common kind of testamentary trust is one that a parent sets up for young children, so that if the parents die while the children are still young, someone (called the trustee) will manage the property they inherit until the children are older. Here's a clause creating a "family pot trust," a kind of trust many parents use when they have more than one minor child close in age:

If my husband does not survive me, I leave my estate to my two children, Madison Rose Moore and Jeremy Logan Moore, in equal shares. All property I leave to Madison Rose Moore and Jeremy Logan Moore shall be held in a trust. I nominate Angela C. McBride to serve as trustee of the trust. If Angela C. McBride is unable or unwilling to serve as trustee, I nominate Louis Ferrer to serve in her place.

Wills generally go on to set out the terms of the trust: how long it is to last, what the money can be used for, how the trustee should make decisions about spending money for each child, and so on. The trustee is the person in charge of managing and distributing the trust assets. If you are trustee of a children's trust, you'll need to scrutinize the terms of the trust to know what is required of you. (Chapter 20 is devoted to handling a child's trust.)

10. Custodianships for Minors

Another way parents (and grandparents) leave property to children is to make gifts under a law called the Uniform Transfers to Minors Act (UTMA), which has been adopted in every state but South Carolina and Vermont. So if the will leaves any property to young beneficiaries, you may find a clause that looks something like this:

I leave $10,000 to my son Raymond Kieshner, as custodian for my granddaughter Mia Elaine Kieshner, under the Iowa Uniform Transfers to Minors Act.

This means that the money will be owned by the granddaughter, but is to be managed for her by her father. He is the "custodian" of the money. The UTMA gives an UTMA custodian management rights and responsibilities, much like the trustee of a trust. Under Iowa law, the custodianship will end when Mia turns 21. In a few states, UTMA custodianships end when the beneficiary turns 18; in some other states, the giver may specify that the custodianship last as late as age 25. (Chapter 10 contains more on this, and the appendix lists every state's rule.)

The will may also contain a general clause that says that any money inherited by a certain beneficiary should go to the custodian under the state UTMA. So if the gifts to young beneficiaries don't state who is to handle the money, be on the lookout for a clause like this one:

If Mia Elaine Kieshner inherits property under this will, that property shall go to Raymond Kieshner, as custodian under the Iowa Uniform Transfers to Minors Act.

11. Pour-Over Clause

If the person who wrote the will also created a separate living trust to avoid probate, the will may contain what's called a "pour-over" clause, directing that some or all assets passing under the will be automatically put into ("poured over" to) the trust.

Here is a pour-over clause:

I give all my residuary estate, being all real and personal property, wherever situated, to which I may have any interest at the time of my death not otherwise effectively disposed of, but not including any property over which I have a power of appointment, to the trustee under a trust agreement dated January 5, 20xx, to be added to the trust property and held and distributed in accordance with the terms of that agreement and any amendments made pursuant to its terms before my death.

Because the assets are disposed of by the will, they still must go through probate if the estate is large enough to require it. But often, people who create a pour-over will intend to use it only for "leftovers"—property they didn't get around to transferring to the trust, so the value of the property is low and regular probate isn't necessary. (Chapter 17 discusses the simplified probate procedures available in these circumstances.) In any case, as executor, you'll transfer them into the trust instead of to individuals. Then the successor trustee of the trust will distribute them according to the terms of the trust document. (Chapter 19 discusses the process of wrapping up a living trust.)

12. Payment of Debts and Taxes

An important part of the executor's job is to pay the estate's debts.

a. What the Estate Pays For

Typical estate debts are expenses of the last illness, funeral costs, and taxes. You must pay these debts from estate assets. But debts that are attached to a specific asset accompany that asset to the beneficiary. For example, if someone inherits a house, they inherit the mortgage as well unless the will instructs the estate to pay it.

b. Which Assets to Use

The will may tell you whether you are supposed to use a specific source of funds to pay the estate's debts, or to pay them out of the general asset pool. Many wills, however, don't say a word about how debts and taxes are to be paid, or include only a brief statement like this, urging you to pay valid debts promptly:

I direct my Executor to pay all of my just debts, funeral expenses, and testamentary charges as soon after my death as can conveniently be done.

If there's not enough money in the estate to pay all the debts, state law will determine which debts you should pay. (See Chapter 9.) If there is enough money, and the will doesn't tell you which assets to use to pay debts, it's up to you. Executors commonly use money in bank or money market accounts that weren't specifically left to any beneficiaries or take pro rata shares from the specific beneficiaries.

If the will does give instructions, it's likely to direct you to pay debts or taxes from the residuary estate. That's what this clause does:

I direct that all succession, estate, or inheritance taxes which may be levied against my estate and/ or against any legacies and/or devises hereinafter set forth shall be paid out of my residuary estate.

If debts are relatively small, everything goes smoothly. But this kind of clause can end up having unintended and unwelcome consequences if the estate has unforeseen expenses. That's because the residuary beneficiary is commonly the big beneficiary—the person the deceased wanted to receive the lion's share of the estate. But if large debts eat away at the residuary estate, the person who was supposed to be the major beneficiary may not be left with as much as the will-writer hoped. Unfortunately, as executor, there's nothing you can do about that; you are obligated to follow the will's instructions.

13. No-Contest Clause

Some wills contain a tough-sounding provision, called a no-contest clause, designed to discourage beneficiaries from challenging (contesting) the will in court. The clause states that if a beneficiary sues, trying to throw out all or part of a will, that person gets nothing.

Here's what a no-contest clause looks like:

If any beneficiary under this will contests this will or any of its provisions, any share or interest in my estate given to the contesting beneficiary under this will is revoked and shall be disposed of as if that contesting beneficiary had not survived me.

Most of these clauses have more bark than bite. First of all, will contests are rare. And even if someone does sue, some states don't enforce no-contest provisions at all. Those that allow them usually don't enforce them against members of the immediate family. And, of course, if someone successfully challenges the will, the no-contest clause will be thrown out along with the rest of the document. (Will contests are discussed in Chapter 18.)

14. Simultaneous Death

If you face the very unusual situation of simultaneous deaths—that is, the deceased person and his or her spouse or other beneficiary died at the same time—check the will to see whether it contains a simultaneous death clause. Otherwise, you can ignore this issue.

Basically, this clause sets out who gets what if deaths were simultaneous or so close in time that it's impossible to know who died first. Generally, the clause says that the will-maker is deemed to have survived the other person, so that property does not pass to that person. The point is to make sure the property passes under the deceased person's will, not the deceased beneficiary's.

EXAMPLE: *Horace and his wife Thelma die together in a car accident. Horace's will leaves everything to Thelma, but states that if they die simultaneously, Horace is deemed to have outlived her. Thelma's will says that everything goes to Horace or, if he dies before she does, to her son by a prior marriage.*

Because of this clause, there is no need to try to determine who in fact actually died first—and no opportunity for Thelma's son to argue that Thelma outlived Horace and so inherited his property. Thelma (her estate, actually) inherits nothing. The property she would have inherited goes instead to the alternate beneficiary Horace named in his will.

If the will doesn't have a simultaneous death clause, state law determines what happens in this situation. (See Section D5, below.)

15. Other Clauses

It's unlikely, but you may run into some oddball provisions that you don't know quite what to do with. Here are a couple of examples.

a. Unenforceable Provisions

A will provision that promotes illegal behavior can't be enforced.

EXAMPLE: *The will of a Maryland doctor who died in 1963 left assets to be held in trust, providing income for several persons as long as they lived. When the last one died, the trust assets were to go to the Keswick Home, "with the request that said Home use the estate ... for the acquisition or construction of a new building ... to house white patients who need physical rehabilitation. If not acceptable to the Keswick Home, then this bequest shall go to the University of Maryland Hospital."*

When the trust was due to be dissolved, in 1998, the court ruled that although the Keswick Home "will not and cannot" enforce the racially discriminatory part of the bequest, it could accept the money and simply disregard the word "white." (*Home for Incurables of Baltimore City v. University of Maryland Medical System Corp.*, 369 Md. 67, 797 A.2d 746 (Ct. App. 2002).)

b. Provisions You Want to Contest

Even if a will provision isn't illegal, it may be repugnant to you and other beneficiaries. For example, a well-meaning pet owner might include in her will a provision ordering the executor to have her healthy dog humanely destroyed at her death, because she doesn't think it could find a good home and doesn't want it to end up in an animal shelter. When that happened in real life in San Francisco, a lawsuit resulted, and eventually the animal was taken by the San Francisco SPCA and guaranteed a good home for life. The court allowed this result, even though it contradicted the clear terms of the will, because the pet owner's obvious concern had been for the welfare of her pet. She had ordered the euthanasia only because she was unaware of a good alternative.

16. Self-Proving Affidavit

Attached to many wills is a separate document called a self-proving affidavit. This is a sworn, notarized statement, signed by all or some of the people who witnessed the signing of the will. A self-proving affidavit looks something like this, though the exact wording may vary:

SAMPLE SELF-PROVING AFFIDAVIT

On the date indicated below, FREDERICK L. KATZWEIGER declared to us, the undersigned, that this instrument, consisting of twelve (12) pages, including the page signed by us as witnesses, was the testator's Will and requested us to act as witnesses to it. The testator thereupon signed this Will in our presence, all of us being present at the same time. We now, at the testator's request, in the testator's presence and in the presence of each other, subscribe our names as witnesses.

It is our belief that the testator is of sound mind and memory and is under no constraint or undue influence whatsoever.

We declare under penalty of perjury that the foregoing is true and correct and that this declaration was executed on July 28, 1994, at Los Angeles, California.

David A. Zellner, 5998 24th Avenue, Venice, CA 90291

Elizabeth R. Thurman, 213 Cerrito Street, Los Angeles, CA 92910

[*notary public's seal and signature*]

The affidavit isn't required by law, but it makes probate easier. That's because without a self-proving affidavit, one or more witnesses may have to testify in court (or file sworn written statements) about the authenticity of the will-maker's signature and the circumstances under which the will was signed. But if an affidavit is signed by enough witnesses (usually the same number as required for the will) and attached to the will, it's considered proof enough in many states. The witnesses don't have to show up in court unless someone questions the authenticity of the will or claims that the person making the will was incompetent. That can be a boon to an executor, because it can be difficult to locate the witnesses many years after a will was signed.

C. Gifts to Groups of People

It's common for wills to contain provisions that leave property "to my children" or "to my grandchildren." It probably all seems clear enough to the person who's writing the will. But when it comes time to interpret the will, these kinds of terms can cause confusion (or worse, family fights). For example, what if the deceased person gave up a child for adoption many years ago—is that child considered one of "my children"? Or if a member of the group has died, who gets his share?

If beneficiaries are listed by name, it's probably not a group gift. For example, a gift to "my sisters, Eloise Neff and Evelyn Penchava," is not a group gift. You wouldn't need to worry about what was meant by the term "sisters."

If you run into a group gift (or "class gift," as lawyers put it) and aren't sure who's included, it's your job—or the court's job, if there is a dispute or the estate is going through probate—to discern what the deceased person intended. Generally, you must look only to the language of the will itself, not any extraneous information you may have, for answers. This section explains how to start.

If inheritors can't agree, see a lawyer. Sadly, there are lots of lawsuits over who should be included in group gifts. If you have a question about the will, get a lawyer to explain how your state's rules apply to your situation.

1. What "Children" or "Issue" Means

If it's unclear what the will-writer meant, then it's time to turn to your state's legal presumptions about what these terms mean.

For starters, "children" and "issue," when used in a will, generally amount to the same thing: someone's direct descendants.

EXAMPLE: *In his will, Bernie leaves his property equally to "my issue." He has three living children and none who are deceased, so your job as executor is simply to transfer the property to the three children.*

The rest of this section discusses problems you may run into. Scan the list; if none applies to you, you can move on.

a. Children Adopted by the Will-Maker

Generally, a child formally adopted into a family shares in any gifts made by will to the "children" or "issue" of an adoptive parent. So if a parent's will leaves a gift to "my children," the group includes adopted children unless the will says otherwise.

EXAMPLE: *Harriet leaves her entire estate "to my sister Angelina's children." Angelina's adopted son inherits along with his siblings, who are Angelina's biological children.*

b. The Will-Maker's Stepchildren

Gifts to "children" don't generally include stepchildren unless the will indicates otherwise. This rule varies from state to state, however. (A stepchild who is legally adopted by a stepparent is no longer a stepchild—he or she is an adopted child and treated just like a biological child.)

A court trying to determine meaning always looks at what the will-maker appears to have intended.

EXAMPLE: *A North Dakota woman's will described a child from her husband's first marriage as "our son." A court ruled that this showed that she intended to treat her husband's child as her child for purposes of leaving her property at death. (Davis v. Neshem, 1998 N.D. 57, 574 N.W.2d 883 (1998).)*

FOSTER CHILDREN

Foster children—children placed by a government agency with another family for temporary care—also do not normally inherit as "children" of the foster parents. They can, of course, inherit like anyone else if they're named individually.

c. Children the Will-Maker Gave Up for Adoption

If you're distributing property to the will-maker's children, you may not even think about (or know about) children the will-maker gave up for adoption. But if such children exist, they may have a significant effect on how you divvy up the property.

(1) Children Adopted by Unrelated Adults

The general rule is that when children are adopted by unrelated adults, all legal links to their biological parents are cut. The biological parents no longer have any rights or obligations toward the child, and the child has no right to inherit from the biological parents. Along with this goes the conclusion that if a parent who has given up a child for adoption leaves a bequest to "my children," the adopted-out child is not included.

EXAMPLE: *A young woman gives birth to a child, who is adopted by another family. Years later, the woman's will leaves everything to "my children." The adopted-out child is not a member of the group.*

(2) Children Adopted by Relatives or Stepparents

The result can be very different, however, if a child of the will-maker was adopted by a close relative. Some states treat the child as being part of an inheriting group of "children" under certain circumstances. Some don't.

For example, in California, a child who is adopted by a stepparent keeps the right to inherit from *both* biological parents under certain circumstances. (Cal. Prob. Code § 6451.) The child is still considered the child of the parent who gave up the child if:

- the natural parent and the child ever lived together as parent and child, or

- the natural parent was married to or living with the other natural parent when the child was conceived but died before the child's birth.

You may need expert help to sort things out. The laws that control these issues are complicated. You may want to look up your state's statutes online (see Chapter 22), but see a lawyer if you have questions or if relatives are fighting.

d. Children Born Outside Marriage

If you're distributing property to a group of children, what should you do if a child born outside marriage turns up and expects to be included? The answer depends on your state's law—and because laws in this area are changing, you will probably want to consult a lawyer for a specific and up-to-date opinion.

In most states, the words "children" or "issue" in a will do not include children born outside marriage, unless the will showed an intention to include them.

In a fair number of states, however, such children are now included in the group unless the will specifically excludes them. For example, under New York law, a will gift to "children" or "issue" now includes children born outside marriage. (N.Y. Est., Pow. & Trusts Law § 2-1.3.)

In the 15 states that have adopted the set of laws known as the Uniform Probate Code, it depends on who made the will:

- **Gifts from a parent.** If a parent leaves a gift to "my children," the group includes children born outside marriage unless the will indicates otherwise.

- **Gifts from someone other than the parent.** If someone else (for example, a grandparent) leaves property to a group of children, children born outside marriage are not included, unless while they were minors they lived with the natural parent or other close relative.

STATES THAT HAVE ADOPTED THE UNIFORM PROBATE CODE

Alaska	Idaho	New Mexico
Arizona	Maine	North Dakota
Colorado	Minnesota	South Carolina
Florida	Montana	South Dakota
Hawaii	Nebraska	Utah

One other twist: If a will uses the phrase "lawful issue," that language generally excludes children born outside marriage. But as always, a court looks first at the will-maker's intent, and if that isn't helpful, turns to the rules and presumptions of state law.

e.   Half-Siblings

A gift to "my sisters and brothers" includes half-siblings. It does not include sisters- or brothers-in-law.

2.   Group Members Born After the Will Is Made

The main reason people make gifts to groups, instead of just naming the individuals they want to inherit, is in case the group gets larger or smaller. To take a common example, a grandfather who leaves a gift to "my grandchildren" is likely anticipating that more grandchildren may be born or adopted before his death; he wants to be sure they are included. If he simply named Laurel and Lola, his current grandkids, he would need to make a new will every time another was born. (This was a bigger concern before wills became computer-generated, when updating was more trouble.)

The general rule is that members of a group who are born after the will is made but while the will-maker is still alive are considered part of the group. (In a few states, however, the birth of a child revokes a prior will; see Section D, below.)

EXAMPLE: *Ellen's will leaves $100,000 to "the children of my brother, Harold Betkis." When Ellen writes her will, Harold has two children; at her death, he has three. All three share the money.*

3. Group Members Born After the Will-Maker's Death

People who aren't born until after the will-maker has died are not usually included in the group, unless the will-maker clearly intended them to be.

EXAMPLE: *Leroy's will leaves $100,000 "to be divided equally among the surviving children of my sister Darlene." When Leroy signs the will, Darlene has one child. Before Leroy's death, she has another. When Leroy dies, the money is split between Darlene's two children. When Darlene gives birth to another child a year later, the third child is not considered part of the original group specified in the will and doesn't inherit anything from Leroy.*

The practical reason for cutting off membership in the group at the will-maker's death is that if you didn't, distribution of the property could be postponed indefinitely.

It follows that if the will states that the gift is not to be given until some particular date after the death, however, new beneficiaries who fit the group description—for example, "my grandchildren"—may be able to squeeze into the group. But the exact rules depend on how your state's law has developed over the years.

EXAMPLE: *Cole's will leaves $500,000 to be shared equally among "my grandchildren." His will provides that the money is to be kept in trust for each grandchild until that child reaches age 21. At his death, he has three young grandchildren; in the next two years, two more are born. Because these last two grandchildren are born before the oldest grandchild reaches 21—the point at which the*

trust money must be divided—they would, under the law of most states, get a share.

One exception to this rule is that a child conceived before a parent's death but born after the death inherits as do children born during the parent's life. The law sometimes refers to such children as "posthumous" children.

Rapidly advancing reproductive technology has added a previously impossible twist to the idea of the posthumous child: a child who was not yet conceived when his or her father died. If sperm or embryos are frozen before the father's death and used later to begin a pregnancy, a child may be born to a father who has been dead for years.

The complications from this new development have already made it to the courts in a handful of cases, and the legal system is slowly moving to catch up to the medical reality. If you face this very unusual situation, you'll want to consult a lawyer.

4. Deceased Group Members

Generally, if a member of a group dies before the will-maker does, the gift does not go to the deceased beneficiary's own heirs, but instead to the surviving members of the group, unless the will provides otherwise.

EXAMPLE: *Anthony leaves real estate to "my brothers and sisters." He doesn't name any alternate beneficiaries. When he signs his will, he has two brothers and two sisters still living. At his death, however, one brother has died, leaving two daughters of his own. The surviving brother and* *sisters inherit the real estate; Anthony's nieces, the children of his deceased brother, do not get a share.*

This general rule has been modified in some states. In these states, laws called "anti-lapse statutes" apply when a will beneficiary who is a close relative dies after the will is made. They are based on the assumption that the person who made the gift would want the deceased beneficiary's children to have their parent's share. If the will makes no provision for an alternate beneficiary, then the deceased beneficiary's own survivors inherit.

EXAMPLE: *Let's start with the same facts as in the last example: Anthony leaves real estate to "my brothers and sisters." When he signs his will, he has two brothers and two sisters still living; at his death, however, one brother has died, leaving two daughters of his own. If the anti-lapse law in Anthony's state applies to group gifts, then these girls (Anthony's nieces) inherit what would have been their father's share of the property.*

Anti-lapse rules are complicated. If you don't know what the will-maker intended and cannot figure out who should inherit a group gift, talk to a lawyer who's well-versed in the statutes and court decisions of your state.

D. Events That May Affect the Terms of the Will

It's not always enough, unfortunately, to read the provisions of a will and follow them to the letter. Big external events—for example, the will-maker's divorce, a beneficiary's death, or the sale of property—may significantly affect how you distribute property under the will.

This section tells you which events to look for. If you find yourself dealing with any of these situations, you may want the help of an experienced lawyer.

1. The Will-Maker Got Divorced

In most states, if someone gets divorced after making a will, any gifts that will makes to the former spouse (and in some states, to relatives of the former spouse, if they aren't also related to the will-maker) are automatically revoked. The divorce may also revoke appointment of the ex-spouse to serve as executor of the will. The rest of the will is still valid.

If the will you're working with leaves gifts to the deceased person's ex-spouse, and your state's law voids these gifts, you should proceed as if the former spouse had not survived the will-maker. The property left to the former spouse will go to the alternate beneficiary named in the will, or if there's no alternate, to the residuary beneficiary.

If the death occurred while the couple was seeking a divorce but still married, in most states these laws have no effect on the will—even though that's probably not what the deceased person would have wanted. If the couple were permanently separated, however, that might be enough to revoke the will.

If an ex-spouse is mad, see a lawyer. If you're dealing with an ex-spouse who claims a right to inherit, you'd be wise to get an opinion from an experienced lawyer.

2. The Will-Maker Got Married

In just a few states, marriage or the birth of a child also revokes a prior will, unless it's clear that the will was written in anticipation of the event. (This is the rule, for example, in Georgia; Ga. Code Ann. §§ 53-4-49, 53-4-46.) Even without such a law, the result envisioned by the will might change dramatically if the new spouse claims the share of the estate allowed by state law. (See Section 3, next.)

3. The Spouse Wants More

By law, every state makes some effort to ensure that a surviving spouse doesn't end up with an unfairly small share of the couple's property. As a result, a person making a will can't completely disinherit a spouse against the spouse's wishes, no matter what the will says. (A spouse can give up his or her rights in a waiver or prenuptial agreement, however.)

Homestead rights. In addition to the spousal protection laws discussed in this section, some states give surviving spouses rights to the couple's residence, or "homestead," even if there's a will provision to the contrary. See Chapter 12.

States protect surviving spouses in three different ways:

- **Traditional spousal share.** In most states, a spouse who didn't inherit much under the will can go to court and claim a substantial portion of the deceased spouse's estate.

- **Share of the augmented estate.** In some states, a surviving spouse can claim a share of the couple's combined property.

- **Community property.** In nine states, laws protect spouses by giving them ownership of half the couple's property before death.

Each of these methods is discussed below, and each state's system is listed in the appendix.

Most spouses are satisfied with the way the will is written and don't rock the boat. Even if the will doesn't leave them much, they may have inherited other assets (retirement accounts or jointly owned real estate, for example) outside of the will. Or they may already own plenty of property and approve of the deceased spouse's plan to leave the lion's share of his or her assets directly to others—for example, their children.

Spouses need help to assert their rights. If you are the surviving spouse and are considering claiming the share allowed you by law, you'll want to get some expert help both with making the decision and with actually making your claim in court. See a lawyer who is familiar with your state's laws and can guide you to the best course for your particular situation.

a. Traditional Spousal Share

In most states, a surviving spouse can claim about one-third to one-half of the deceased spouse's property. The spouse's share is called the statutory or elective share.

A warning, however: State laws vary dramatically. For example, instead of a fixed share, the spouse might be entitled to:

- a life estate in the deceased spouse's real estate (this means the right to use it for the rest of his or her life)

- a certain percentage of the deceased spouse's property or a fixed dollar amount, whichever is greater, or

- the amount he or she would have gotten if there had been no will—which, depending on whether or not there are children, is typically 50% to 100% of the assets.

Generally, the surviving spouse gets a share of all the deceased spouse's property, whether or not it goes through probate. So the surviving spouse can still get a share of assets such as stocks registered in transfer-on-death form, bank accounts left to a payable-on-death beneficiary, or an IRA.

To claim the statutory share, the surviving spouse must go to probate court. This process is commonly called "taking against the will." It's not the same as a will contest, which is a lawsuit in which the person bringing the suit must prove that the will is defective in some way. Instead, it amounts to the surviving spouse saying, "Hey, state law guarantees me a certain percentage of our property no matter what the will says, and I want it."

The survivor has a certain amount of time—in most states, about one to nine months after probate court proceedings begin—to decide whether or not to claim the statutory share. If the deadline is missed, so is the chance to take the share.

If a spouse asserts a valid claim, where does the money come from? After all, everything was probably left to someone else. The statutes give executors some guidance. Commonly, the spouse's share comes first from the residuary estate and finally, if necessary, from property left as specific gifts.

b. The "Augmented Estate"

To protect survivors whose spouses gave away substantial assets before death or left them to others in ways that do not require probate, these states give the surviving spouse the option of claiming a share of what lawyers call the "augmented estate." Once you cut through the jargon, this amounts to putting nearly everything *both* spouses owned in one pot and letting the surviving spouse take a good-sized portion, up to 50% in long-term marriages. (The augmented estate concept comes from the Uniform Probate Code, parts of which have been adopted by many states. See Section C1, above.)

Figuring out exactly what belongs in the augmented estate can be complicated. But basically, it includes:

- the property that goes through probate, less debts

- the value of property that goes to others at the deceased spouse's death, such as life insurance proceeds and money in a payable-on-death bank account.

- the value of large gifts given away by the deceased spouse during the two years before death, and

- all the surviving spouse's property, including anything inherited from the deceased spouse, the survivor's share of joint tenancy property, and other property with the right of survivorship.

In many of these states, how large a share the surviving spouse can claim depends on how long the couple was married. A marriage of just a year entitles the survivor to 20%; those who had been wed at least ten years get 50%.

c. Community Property States

In community property states, spouses own most property 50-50 *before* one of them dies. (Common exceptions are property acquired by one spouse before marriage or received by one spouse by gift or inheritance.) Because ownership is shared equally, a surviving spouse is assured of holding on to at least half of the couple's property.

EXAMPLE: *Jose and Marena, a married couple living in California, buy a house with money Marena earned while married. The house is their community property.*

Idaho, Washington, and Wisconsin also allow surviving spouses to claim a share of property that isn't covered by community property rules, either because it was acquired before community property rules took effect in the state or it was acquired when one or both spouses lived in another state. (Idaho Code § 15-2-201; Wash. Rev. Code § 26.16.220; Wis. Stat. Ann. § 861.02.) And in California, if the will was made before the marriage, and the spouse wasn't adequately provided for outside the will, the spouse can claim all the deceased spouse's community property and up to half of the separate property. (Cal. Fam. Code § 125.)

4. A Child Wants More

Unlike spouses, children have no automatic right to inherit. A parent can explicitly disinherit a child, or simply not leave the child any property. For example, someone who has grown, well-off children from a prior marriage and little ones from a current marriage might not leave the older offspring anything through a will.

If, however, it looks like a child was unintentionally omitted from a will (the legal term is "pretermitted"), a judge can give that child a share of the deceased parent's property. This issue crops up when the will was made before the child was born or adopted, and the parent simply didn't get around to making a new will including the new child. The law assumes that the parent would not have wanted the new child left out and, accordingly, gives that child a share.

EXAMPLE: *By the time William and Betsy get around to making their wills, they have two children. After their third child arrives, they don't* *think to update their wills. When William dies unexpectedly, the last child may be entitled to a share of her father's estate even though she's not mentioned in the will.*

Some states give the overlooked child the same amount of property he or she would have received had there been no will. Although states vary on how this is figured, it is typical to give half to the surviving spouse and divide the other half among the children.

The precise rules that apply in this unusual situation are set out in each state's laws. Your state may impose important restrictions on the general rule. For example, in some states, a child born after the will was signed doesn't get anything if the deceased parent had any other children when the will was signed but didn't leave them anything, either. (For example, see Ariz. Rev. Stat. § 14-3902; Cal. Prob. Code §§ 21620 and following.) Again, state law is trying to guess the parent's wishes; if the parent didn't leave property to the other children, preferring the other parent to handle it, then he probably wouldn't have wanted property to go directly to a younger child, either.

If you have a problem, you may want to look up your state's law and also see a lawyer. (Chapters 22 and 23 discuss lawyers and legal research.)

5. Beneficiaries Have Died

If the will leaves property to someone who died before the will-maker did, or soon after, you must figure out who inherits the property. Sometimes the will tells you; in other cases, you must look to your state's law.

If the gift was made to a group of people who are not individually named in the will but identified by their relationship to the will-maker—for example, "my children," special rules apply when one group member dies. (See Section C, above.)

a. Survivorship Requirements

Many wills state that beneficiaries cannot inherit unless they live for a specific amount of time after the will-maker dies. This time is called a "survivorship period," and commonly ranges from about five to 60 days. Here is a will clause that contains a 30-day survivorship requirement:

I give all my personal and household effects, such as jewelry, clothing, automobiles, furniture, furnishings, silver, books, and pictures, to my husband, Eugene Banks, if he survives me for thirty days or, if he does not so survive me, to such of my children who survive me for thirty days.

Sometimes the survivorship requirement is in a separate clause that applies to all beneficiaries named in the will, like this:

A beneficiary must survive me for 45 days to receive property under this will. As used in this will, the phrase "survive me" means to be alive or in existence as an organization on the 45th day after my death.

If the will doesn't impose a survivorship requirement, state law may. In some states, including all the states that have adopted the Uniform Probate Code (listed in Section C1, above), all wills are subject to a five-day survivorship period.

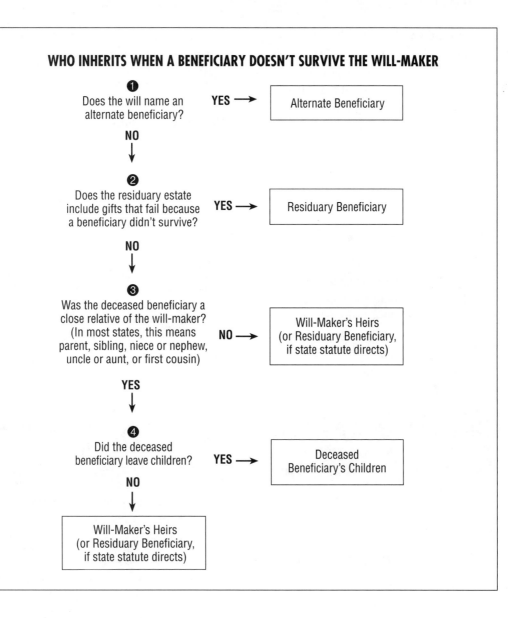

WHO INHERITS WHEN A BENEFICIARY DOESN'T SURVIVE THE WILL-MAKER

❶
Does the will name an
alternate beneficiary?   **YES** → Alternate Beneficiary

NO
↓

❷
Does the residuary estate
include gifts that fail because   **YES** → Residuary Beneficiary
a beneficiary didn't survive?

NO
↓

❸
Was the deceased beneficiary a
close relative of the will-maker?
(In most states, this means   **NO** → Will-Maker's Heirs
parent, sibling, niece or nephew,   (or Residuary Beneficiary,
uncle or aunt, or first cousin)   if state statute directs)

YES
↓

❹
Did the deceased
beneficiary leave children?   **YES** → Deceased
                                        Beneficiary's Children

NO
↓

Will-Maker's Heirs
(or Residuary Beneficiary,
if state statute directs)

If neither the will nor state law imposes a survivorship period, then surviving even an hour longer than the will-maker is enough to inherit. In that case, you would turn the property over to the deceased beneficiary's estate, and it would go to the beneficiary's own heirs or will beneficiaries.

If, however, the will-maker and the beneficiary appear to have died simultaneously, special rules apply. See Section B14, above.

b. Alternates Named in the Will

If the will names alternates for the beneficiaries, it's clear what happens to property if the first-choice recipient doesn't meet the survivorship requirement: The alternate gets it. (Though even this can get a bit murky when gifts are left to a group of people; see Section C4, above.) Here's a typical clause that names an alternate beneficiary:

I leave my interest in the house at 332 Brookhaven Drive, Atlanta, Georgia to my wife, Delores Brown or, if she does not survive me, to my daughter Jessica Brown and my son Andrew Brown in equal shares.

If the alternate also died before the will-maker did, see Subsection c, next.

c. If There's No Alternate Beneficiary

If the will does not name an alternate, or the alternate has died, you have something called a "lapsed" or "failed" gift. Depending on state law and how the will is written, the property will go to either:

- the residuary beneficiary named in the will

- the primary beneficiary's descendants, under your state's "anti-lapse" law, or

- the deceased person's heirs under state law, as if there were no will.

The residuary beneficiary. Some wills clearly state that lapsed gifts become part of the residuary estate (residue). If so, then the gift passes through the residuary clause.

EXAMPLE: *Eric's will contains a clause that says, "My residuary estate includes all property I own at my death that is subject to this will and that does not pass under a specific bequest, including lapsed or failed gifts." Eric's will leaves his house to his two grown children, Ashley and Anna, but does not name alternate beneficiaries for them. Anna dies before he does. At Eric's death, the half-interest in the house that would have gone to Anna passes instead to the residuary beneficiary named in the will.*

It's important to realize that many wills do *not* define the residuary estate this way. In that situation, if the alternate beneficiary is not available (or none was named), look to see whether or not your state's anti-lapse law applies.

The beneficiary's descendants. Every state (except Louisiana) has an "anti-lapse" law, which tries to guess what the will-maker would have wanted when a will gift to a relative fails. Unless the will named an alternate beneficiary, anti-lapse laws generally give property to the children of the deceased beneficiary.

EXAMPLE: *Belinda's will leaves her residuary estate to her sister Roxanne and her brother Martin. The will also provides that "if either one of them shall* *predecease me, then I leave my residuary estate to the other surviving brother or sister." As it turns out, they both die before Belinda does. Roxanne had no children; Martin leaves two.*

Without the state's anti-lapse statute, the gift would pass under the state's "intestate succession" law—in other words, just as if Belinda had made no will at all. But because the anti-lapse law applies, the property goes to Martin's two children.

Anti-lapse laws commonly apply only if the deceased beneficiary:

- was either the will-maker's grandparent or a direct descendant of a grandparent (parent, sibling, niece or nephew, uncle or aunt, first cousin, and so forth), and

- left children of his or her own.

These laws almost never apply to a beneficiary who isn't related by blood to the will-maker. (In Arizona, though, they do apply to stepchildren. Ariz. Rev. Stat. § 14-2706.) That means spouses are not covered.

EXAMPLE 1: *Darlene's will leaves everything to her husband and doesn't name an alternate beneficiary. Darlene's husband dies before Darlene does. At Darlene's death, the anti-lapse statute does not apply; that means his two children from a previous marriage do not inherit the estate. Instead, it goes to Darlene's heirs as determined by state law.*

EXAMPLE 2: *In her will, Rose leaves her car "to my good friend Erin Graham." The will doesn't name an alternate beneficiary for the car. Erin dies before Rose does, but Rose doesn't get around to updating her will. At Rose's death, because Erin is*

not a close relative covered by the anti-lapse statute, the car passes not to Erin's children but under the residuary clause of Rose's will.

If you conclude that a deceased beneficiary's children should inherit in place of their parent, you next face the sometimes thorny question of how to divvy up the parent's share.

EXAMPLE: *Lester leaves property equally to his three children, Dennis, David, and Tanya. His will doesn't name alternates for them. Tanya dies before Lester does, leaving two children of her own, Tiffany and Stephanie. Under some states' laws, the girls would split their mother's one-third share; under others', the property would be evenly divided among the four beneficiaries, one-fourth to each girl and to each surviving son, Dennis and David.*

Get expert help figuring out who gets what. Every state has rules about this process, and they can be complicated. If you are in doubt and especially if family members raise questions, you'll want to consult a lawyer who has expertise in handling such situations.

If the anti-lapse statute doesn't apply because the beneficiary was not a blood relative covered by the statute, the statute may state that the gift goes into the residuary estate. (For example, see Connecticut's statute at Conn. Gen. Stat. § 45a-442.) Otherwise, the gift will go to the will-maker's heirs, as described next.

The will-maker's heirs. If the will doesn't tell you who should receive some or all of the property of a deceased beneficiary, and your state's anti-lapse statute doesn't apply because the deceased beneficiary wasn't a close blood relative of the will-maker, the property will pass under state intestate succession laws, just as if there were no will. (Chapter 7 explains how to figure out who inherits.)

d. Residuary Gifts

If the will named more than one residuary beneficiary, and one of them died before the will-maker did, in most (but not all) states, the surviving residuary beneficiaries inherit the deceased beneficiary's share unless the will directs otherwise. (The residuary beneficiary, remember, inherits everything that passes under the will but isn't specifically left to another beneficiary.)

EXAMPLE: *Laura leaves her residuary estate to her three sons, Michael, Andrew, and Conor. She doesn't name alternates for them. Michael dies, leaving a child of his own, before Laura does. Under most states' rules, Laura's two surviving sons inherit the entire residuary estate. Michael's child does not get a share.*

6. The Lawyer Who Drafted the Will Inherits Property

Lawyers figure in an embarrassing (for the profession) number of cases involving inappropriate gifts from elderly and infirm clients. These gifts may be void under the law of your state. For example, in Texas, any gift to an attorney who drafted the will is void unless the client and lawyer were related. (Tex. Prob. Code § 58b.) Some states disallow only substantial gifts.

Even if state law doesn't expressly make such a gift ineffective, a bequest to a lawyer always raises a red flag. The lawyer may have exerted undue influence over the will-maker, making it possible to have the probate court void the gift if the executor or a family member protests. (See Chapter 18.)

7. Property Has Been Given Away or Sold

A long time may pass between the time a will is signed and the death of the person who signed it. As a result, by the time death occurs, the person may own a very different collection of property. For example, a will-maker may have sold a house and moved into an apartment, traded in an old car for a new one, and taken money out of stocks and put it into CDs.

But an outdated will may still leave the house, the old car, and the stocks to family members and friends—who may be expecting to inherit something. Whether or not they will be disappointed depends on what your state law says.

a. Uniform Probate Code States

In states that have adopted the set of laws called the Uniform Probate Code (listed in Section C1, above), it's presumed that if someone makes a will and then sells, gives away, or loses property, he or she still wants the named beneficiary to get something. So the UPC includes these general rules:

- If the will-maker acquired another item as a replacement for the old one—a new car for an old one, for example—the beneficiary is entitled to the replacement.

- If the item was sold or destroyed, and some or all of the proceeds (from the sale or from an insurance policy) have not yet been collected, the beneficiary gets those unpaid proceeds, plus cash if necessary to give the beneficiary the value of the item.

- If an item that was left specifically to a beneficiary is no longer in the estate, the beneficiary is entitled to a sum of money equal to the value of the gift—unless there's evidence that the will-maker wanted a different outcome.

- If the item was sold or destroyed while someone else had legal authority over the will-maker's property, then the beneficiary has a right to money in an amount equal to the insurance proceeds or net sale price. The most common situation is when an attorney-in-fact or conservator has taken over management of an incapacitated person's affairs. The beneficiary has this right even if the money has already been received and mixed with the will-maker's other assets. But the right goes away if the will-maker lived for at least a year after a court determined he or she was incapacitated.

As you can see, combing through these rules can be tiring—and arguing about them in court even worse. Far better to get the beneficiaries to simply agree about what to do in such an instance than to involve lawyers and courts in the haggling.

b. Other States

Unless a state has adopted a law to the contrary, the rule is harsh but simple: A specific gift simply fails if the will-maker no longer owns the item at death. The would-be beneficiary gets nothing. (This phenomenon is called "ademption.")

Just about the only wrinkle in this rule is that if an item merely "changed its form" after the will was signed, the beneficiary is entitled to the new manifestation. So if the will-maker sold a piece of land in exchange for a promissory note, the person who was originally slated to inherit the land might get the promissory note instead. But courts have been inconsistent when it comes to applying this rule, which is a little fuzzy to start with.

As always, your job (and the probate court's, if necessary) is to carry out the intent of the person who made the will. The will probably won't say anything about what should happen, but if all the beneficiaries agree that the will-maker would have wanted the beneficiary to get something, you can work it out.

EXAMPLE: *Laurence's will, made in 2002, left his 1998 Ford Taurus to his nephew Carlos Figueroa. But when Laurence dies in 2008, he's long since traded in the Ford for a Toyota Camry. Legally, Carlos doesn't have much of an argument, because the will doesn't leave him "the automobile I own at my death" or otherwise state that Laurence wants to be sure Carlos inherits something. But if all the beneficiaries agree that Laurence would have wanted Carlos to get the Camry, the uncertainty is solved and everybody's happy.*

If people don't agree, and a disappointed beneficiary presses a claim in court, it's not likely to be successful.

EXAMPLE: *A Texas woman's will left certain real estate to her niece and nephew. After she signed the will, she sold part of the real estate. The Texas Supreme Court ruled that the niece and nephew were not entitled to the proceeds of the sale. The rule may be harsh, the court said, but it's well established in state law and can easily be avoided by including proper language in the will. In other words, the lawyer who drafted the will should have written it differently if his client wanted a different result. (San Antonio Area Foundation v. Lang, 35 S.W.3d 636 (Tex. 2000).)*

If, however, the court does decide that the will-maker intended the beneficiary to get something, and the item mentioned in the will was disposed of shortly before death, the beneficiary may receive the proceeds (if it was sold) or a different item (if it was exchanged for something else).

⚠️ **There are exceptions to the rule.** As mentioned, states can carve out limited exceptions to the general rule. For example, in California, if the deceased person had a conservator (someone appointed by a court to handle the person's affairs because he or she couldn't), and the conservator sold property that had been specifically left to someone, the beneficiary is entitled to the proceeds of the sale. (Cal. Prob. Code § 21134.)

8. Beneficiaries Have Already Gotten Their Inheritance

Beneficiaries aren't supposed to get a double share. So if the will-maker, while still alive, gives them their inheritances, the beneficiaries aren't supposed to later inherit under the will, too. But how to know whether or not the will-maker meant a lifetime gift to take the place of a will provision? Harder yet, how to prove it?

In general, the law presumes that a lifetime gift is not meant to replace a will provision. If, however, there is clear evidence to the contrary—for example, a written statement—this presumption can be overcome. Once again, it's not something you want to fight about in court. Much better to get beneficiaries to agree to a fair solution.

9. The Will-Maker Gave You Different Instructions

As you go through the deceased person's papers, you may find notes or lists that seem to set out intended beneficiaries. Or the deceased person may have given you oral instructions that supplement or even contradict his or her will. What should you do?

Unlike a will, these notes, lists, and oral requests are probably not legally binding. (In some states, however, memos that leave personal property and are referred to in the will are a legal part of the will; see Section B5, above.) But it's always possible that the inheritors under the formal, witnessed will may decide to honor the deceased person's wishes.

EXAMPLE: *Nancy's son Jeff finds her will, dated two years before her death, in which she divides all property among her three children. Paper-clipped to the will is a note in Nancy's handwriting that says, "Jeff—Will you, Gina, and Sally please see that my nurse and companion Andrea receives my bedroom furniture, to thank her for caring for me. –Mom."*

This note is not legally binding, because it wasn't signed and witnessed like a will, or (if Nancy's state allows it) referred to in Nancy's will. But Nancy's children would be typical if they felt that the note placed a moral obligation on them. ■

CHAPTER 7

If There's No Will

If you've concluded that the deceased person—like many Americans—didn't leave a will, you'll have to look elsewhere for your marching orders.

Keep in mind that lots of assets aren't passed by will anyway. Some common examples include:

- life insurance proceeds

- real estate, bank accounts, and other assets held in joint tenancy, tenancy by the entirety, or community property with right of survivorship

- property held in a living trust

- funds in an IRA, 401(k), or other retirement plan account for which a beneficiary has been named

- funds in a payable-on-death (POD) bank account, and

- stocks or other securities held in a transfer-on-death (TOD) account.

To find out who inherits these kinds of property, you'll need to locate the documents in which the co-ownership or beneficiary designation was established—for example, a Declaration of Trust, a joint tenancy deed, or a life insurance policy. (Chapter 8 explains what to look for.)

To find out who inherits other assets—generally, solely owned property for which no beneficiary has been formally named, such as a house owned by a widow—you need to consult state law. Every state has "intestate succession" laws that parcel out property to the deceased person's closest relatives—even if the result may not be exactly what he or she would have wanted.

A. Who's in Charge

When there is no will to name an executor, you must turn to state law, which provides a list of people who are eligible to fill the role. Generally the person is called an "administrator," not an executor. Some states, however, call anyone who's in charge of an estate the "personal representative," whether the person was nominated in a will or is appointed by the probate court in the absence of a will.

If a probate court proceeding is necessary, the court will choose someone based on the priority list set out in state law. Most states make the surviving spouse, if any, the first choice. (In California, Hawaii, and Vermont, a surviving domestic partner is treated like a spouse if the couple registered with the state.) If there is no spouse, or he or she declines to serve, adult children are usually next on the list. Or the court may simply appoint the closest relative who stands to inherit something. (The theory is that someone who hopes to receive property from the estate is likely to manage it prudently.) The judge must appoint the person with the highest priority under the law unless the person turns down the job or is disqualified for some reason—for example, because he isn't old enough or has a conflict of interest.

If the estate does not go through probate (because all property can be transferred without it), no court will be involved, and no administrator will be appointed. Even if you are not formally given authority by the court, however, you and surviving family members can use the priority lists as a guide for choosing someone to informally take charge of things.

HOW COURTS CHOOSE ADMINISTRATORS: TWO EXAMPLES

California has a typical approach, except that it treats domestic partners—unmarried couples who have registered with the state—just like surviving spouses for this purpose. (Cal. Prob. Code § 8461.) Here is California's priority list:

1. Surviving spouse or domestic partner
2. Children
3. Grandchildren
4. Other issue (great-grandchildren and other direct descendants)
5. Parents
6. Brothers and sisters
7. Issue of brothers and sisters (nieces and nephews, and their children)
8. Grandparents
9. Issue of grandparents (uncles, aunts, and their children)
10. Children of a predeceased spouse or domestic partner
11. Other issue of a predeceased spouse or domestic partner
12. Other next of kin
13. Parents of a predeceased spouse or domestic partner
14. Issue of parents of a predeceased spouse or domestic partner
15. Conservator or guardian of the estate
16. Public administrator (someone the court pays to administer estates when no one else is available)
17. Creditors
18. Any other person.

Georgia, on the other hand, doesn't go into so much detail; it simply allows the heirs (the people who will inherit the property under state law) to choose someone unanimously. (Ga. Code Ann. § 53-6-20.) If they can't, the judge appoints someone, using this short list of preferences:

1. The surviving spouse, unless an action for divorce or separate maintenance was pending between the couple
2. One or more other heirs, or the person the majority of them chooses
3. Any other eligible person
4. Any creditor of the estate
5. The county administrator.

B. Who Gets What: The Basic Rules

Every state has laws that direct what happens to property when someone dies without a valid will, and the property was not left in some other way (such as a living trust). The idea behind these intestate succession laws is to do what the deceased person would have wanted; whether or not the state hits the mark in an individual situation depends, of course, on the circumstances.

1. How State Laws Work

Generally, only spouses and blood relatives inherit under intestate succession laws; unmarried partners, friends, and charities get nothing. The only exception is that in California, Hawaii, and Vermont, a surviving domestic partner is treated like a spouse for purposes of inheritance, if the couple registered with the state. (New Jersey's domestic partnership law does not treat registered domestic partners like spouses when it comes to inheritance, but as this book goes to press, Massachusetts appears poised to allow same-sex couples to undergo a civil union and get the same rights as married couples.)

If the deceased person was married, commonly the surviving spouse gets the largest share. If there are no children, the surviving spouse often receives all the property. If there are also surviving children, in most states they share the property with the surviving spouse. More distant relatives inherit only if there is no surviving spouse or children. In the rare event

that no relatives at all can be found, the state takes the assets.

To get an idea of how intestate succession works, take a look at New York's inheritance rules, below. (N.Y. Est. Powers & Trusts Law § 4-1.1.) The table may look intimidating—but remember that only a bit of it applies to any one family. Just read down the first column until you find your family situation, and then you'll quickly get a good idea of who would inherit.

WHO INHERITS IF THERE'S NO WILL: NEW YORK

Surviving Family	Who Gets What
Spouse, but no children, grandchildren, or other direct descendants	Spouse gets everything
No spouse, but children or other direct descendants	Children share the property*
Spouse and children	Spouse gets $50,000 plus half of the property that goes through probate. The children share the other half.*
No spouse or children, but both parents	Each parent gets half (though a parent who failed to provide for the child up to age 21 may not get anything)
No spouse or children, but one parent	Parent gets everything
No spouse, children, or parents, but siblings	Siblings divide everything**
No spouse, children, parents, or siblings, but nieces or nephews	Nieces or nephews divide everything
No spouse, children, parents, siblings, nieces, or nephews	Half goes to next of kin on mother's side, half to next of kin on father's side

*   If a child is deceased, his or her children also get a share.
** If a sibling is deceased, his or her children also get a share.

In the nine "community property" states, the task is made more complicated because married people own two legally distinct types of property, separate and community. (To greatly oversimplify, community property is what either spouse acquires while married, except for gifts and inheritances. Separate property is everything else.) Depending on the family makeup, the different kinds of property may go to different heirs.

COMMUNITY PROPERTY STATES

Alaska*	Arizona
California	Idaho
Louisiana**	Nevada
New Mexico	Texas
Washington	Wisconsin***

*Married couples can create community property with a written agreement.
**This book doesn't cover Louisiana law.
***Wisconsin's system of property ownership is like that of community property states, but it is called "marital property."

California's rules are shown below. For purposes of inheritance, a surviving registered domestic partner is treated just like a surviving spouse.

WHO INHERITS IF THERE'S NO WILL: CALIFORNIA

Surviving Family	Separate Property	Community Property
Spouse, but no children, grandchildren, or other direct descendants, parent, or sibling	Spouse gets everything	Spouse gets all
Spouse, no children (or other direct descendants), but parent	Spouse gets half, parent gets half	Spouse gets all
Spouse and one child	Spouse gets half, child gets half**	Spouse gets all
Spouse and more than one child	Spouse gets one-third, children share two-thirds**	Spouse gets all
Spouse, no children or other direct descendants, no parent, but sibling	Spouse gets half, siblings get half**	Spouse gets all
No spouse or children, but parents	Parents get everything*	No community property
No spouse, but children or other direct descendants	Children share everything**	
No spouse, children, or parents, but siblings	Siblings (including half-siblings) get everything**	
No spouse, children, parents, or siblings, but grandparents or their descendants	Grandparents (or their descendants) divide everything	
No spouse, children, parents, grandparents, or descendants of children, parents or grandparents, but descendants of predeceased spouse	Descendants of predeceased spouse divide everything	
No spouse, children, parents, grandparents, or descendants of children, parents or grandparents, or descendants of predeceased spouse	Next of kin	

* But if deceased person's spouse died within prior 15 years, property attributable to that spouse goes to certain of his or her close relatives.

** Children of a deceased member of the group (except for surviving spouse's children) also get a share.

2. Finding Your State's Rules

If you need to know the exact rules that apply to your situation, you must find out exactly what your state's intestate succession law says. Start with the page for your state in the appendix, which lists your state's statute. You can look up the statute online, for free. (Chapter 22 tells you how.) Reading it should give you a pretty detailed picture. But because legal language can be confusing, and courts may have weighed in on what terms mean, you may also want to consult a lawyer who's familiar with the rules and can help you apply them to your family situation.

Once you've got a preliminary list of the heirs, you may want to note their names and addresses on a worksheet like the one below. It may be handy for you to refer to, to give to a lawyer you work with, or to use when you're filling out court documents if you go through probate.

C. Understanding Key Terms

Intestate succession laws are full of references to groups of people such as "children" and "issue." You may think you know just what "children" means—but don't be too sure until you check your state's laws. It's not always obvious. This section explains some of the terms you're likely to run into.

Lawyers speak this language. If you need help deciphering the intestate succession laws of your state, get help from an experienced lawyer who can research how courts in your state have interpreted troublesome terms and explain everything to you in plain English.

HEIRS

Name & Address	Relationship	Phone	Email
Phyllis Chesterman 443 Sunbird Drive Phoenix, AZ 83222	Surviving spouse	(432) 555-1234	phyllis142@yahoo.com
Carl Chesterman 49382 Wabash Avenue Chicago, IL 61299	Child	(316) 555-8977 (H) (316) 555-9987 (W)	chess@hotmail.com
Amanda Grudzelonik 3219 Elm Street Prospect Heights, IL 61633	Child	(308) 555-9123 (H) (319) 555-4575 (cell)	mandyg@yahoo.com
Janine Chesterman 987 Bridge Street, Apt. A Arlington, VA 23432	Child	(431) 555-3847 (H) (343) 555-3422 (W)	jcenterprises@chesterman.com

1. Spouse

To qualify as a surviving spouse, the survivor must have been legally married to the deceased person at the time of death. Usually, it's clear who is and isn't married. But not always.

Legal separation or pending divorce. What if the couple had separated before one spouse died, or if one person had begun divorce proceedings? A judge may have to rule on whether or not the surviving member of the couple is considered a surviving spouse for purposes of inheritance. In some cases, judges have ruled that if a court had issued a decree of legal separation before the death, the survivor did not inherit as a surviving spouse. Other courts might stick to the literal language of a state statute and conclude that unless there has been a final divorce decree, the couple was still husband and wife. If you run into this situation, lawyers will no doubt become involved; you, as executor, can leave it to the judge to decide.

Common-law marriage. A few states allow common-law marriages—that is, in these places, a man and a woman who never went through a marriage ceremony can be considered legally married under certain circumstances. Just living together for a certain number of years does not create a common-law marriage. The couple must intend to be married and present themselves to the world as married.

If someone claims status as a surviving spouse but cannot produce the marriage license to prove it, a judge will have to decide, based on all the circumstances of the relationship, whether or not there was in fact a common-law marriage. Even if your state does not allow the creation of common-law marriages, a judge might treat as valid a common-law marriage that was created in another state.

STATES THAT ALLOW COMMON-LAW MARRIAGE

Alabama	New Hampshire[3]
Colorado	Ohio[4]
District of Columbia	Oklahoma
Georgia[1]	Pennsylvania[5]
Idaho[2]	Rhode Island
Iowa	South Carolina
Kansas	Texas
Montana	Utah

[1] If created before 1997.
[2] If created before 1996.
[3] For inheritance purposes only.
[4] If created before October 10, 1991.
[5] But under a 2003 court ruling, no new common-law marriages can be created in Pennsylvania. (*PNC Bank Corp. v. Workers' Compensation Appeal Board (Stamos)*, 831 A.2d 1269 (Pa. Cmwlth. 2003).)

2. Children and Issue

The simple term "children" can mean different things to different people—and under different laws, as discussed below. Many state statutes use the term "issue" to describe who should inherit in the absence of a will. In this context, issue means direct descendants of the deceased person—children, grandchildren, and so on.

a. Children Adopted by the Deceased Person

In all states, in the absence of a will or other estate plan, legally adopted children inherit from their adoptive parents just as biological children do.

b. The Deceased Person's Stepchildren

Most states do not include stepchildren—that is, children of the spouse of the deceased person who were never legally adopted by the deceased person—in their definition of children for purposes of inheritance. In other words, stepchildren generally don't inherit from their stepparent unless they are named in a will or some other document such as a beneficiary designation form for a retirement account.

In a few states, however, it may depend on the circumstances of the relationship. In California, for example, if the deceased person had a relationship with the stepchild that began when the child was young and contin-ued throughout the parent's life, and there is evidence that the parent would have adopted the child except for a legal barrier (for ex-ample, the biological parent wouldn't consent), the stepchild has the same inheritance rights as a child. (Cal. Prob. Code § 6454.)

If you face this question, the easiest solu-tion—as always—is to have the heirs agree on what to do. If, for example, everyone agrees that the deceased person would have wanted the stepchild to inherit, there's no problem. Heirs can divide property any way they want.

FOSTER CHILDREN

Foster children—children placed by a government agency with another family for temporary care—also do not normally inherit as "children" of the foster parents. However, California applies the same rules to foster children as it does to stepchildren. If you are uncertain about a foster child's rights and concerned about an argument in court, consult a lawyer.

c. Children Adopted by an Unrelated Adult or Family

In most states, giving a child up for adoption to an unrelated adult or family severs the legal tie between the child and the birth parents. The child can no longer inherit from the birth parents under intestate succession laws, and the parents can no longer inherit from the child.

EXAMPLE: *An unmarried teenager puts her baby up for adoption. For inheritance purposes, the baby would be considered a child of his adoptive parents, but not of his biological mother or father.*

d. Children Adopted by a Stepparent

A child who is adopted by a stepparent may still inherit from the biological parents; it depends on state law.

EXAMPLE: *Paul and Inez, a Minnesota couple, divorce when their daughter Deborah is just a baby. Later, Inez marries Vincent, who adopts Deborah. If Paul, Inez, or Vincent dies without a will, Deborah will be considered a child of each parent under Minnesota law.*

This rule can also be important if the stepparent adoption takes place after the death of the biological parent.

EXAMPLE: *Samantha's husband Jerry is killed in an accident. Several years later she remarries, and her new husband legally adopts her son Dylan. Jerry's father (Dylan's grandfather) dies a few years later, without leaving a will. Dylan is entitled to inherit from his grandfather under his state's intestate succession laws.*

Usually, the law of the state where the deceased person died, and in effect at the time of death, applies to the situation.

EXAMPLE: *George, a resident of Alabama, married and divorced twice. He had a son from each marriage. Both ex-wives moved to another state and remarried, and both of their new husbands adopted the child from the previous marriage. When George died without a will, the sons claimed part of their biological father's estate. The Supreme Court of Alabama ruled that children adopted by their stepfathers had the right to inherit from their biological father under Alabama law. (Raley v. Spikes, 614 So. 2d 1017 (Ala. 1993).)*

e. Children Born After the Parent's Death

A child conceived before a parent's death but born after the death inherits under intestate succession laws just as do children born during the parent's life. The law sometimes refers to such children as "posthumous" children.

Rapidly advancing reproductive technology has added a previously impossible twist to the idea of the posthumous child: a child who was not yet conceived when his or her father died.

If sperm or embryos are frozen before the father's death and used later to begin a pregnancy, a child may be born to a father who has been dead for years.

If the deceased father's property has already been distributed, there won't be anything for the new child to collect, even if he or she is included in the intestate succession laws' definition of issue. But the question may be important for other reasons; for example, the mother may want the baby to qualify for certain benefits that come only with status as legal issue of the deceased father.

The complications from this new development have already made it to the courts in a handful of cases, and the legal system is slowly moving to catch up to the medical reality. Courts appear ready to grant some of these children status as "issue" under the intestate succession laws, but it takes some work to get to that conclusion.

EXAMPLE: *In 1995, a Massachusetts woman gave birth to twins who had been conceived through artificial insemination using her late husband's sperm. The couple had stored the sperm when the husband had been diagnosed with leukemia and was told treatment might leave him sterile.*

The court ruled that in certain circumstances, a posthumously conceived child may be considered "issue" under the state's intestacy statute. The surviving parent must show that there is a genetic relationship between the child and the deceased parent and that the deceased person "affirmatively consented to posthumous conception and to the support of any resulting child." (Woodward v. Commissioner of Social Security, 435 Mass. 536, 760 N.E.2d 257 (2002).)

Another court, however, has ruled that under similar circumstances, a child cannot inherit as a child under Arizona's intestate succession law. The court excluded a child conceived after the father's death because the state intestate succession law includes only children who were "in gestation" at the time of the father's death. (*Gillett-Netting v. Barnhart,* 231 F. Supp. 2d 961 (D. Ariz. 2002).)

f. Children Born Outside Marriage

A child born to unmarried parents always inherits from his or her biological mother, unless an unrelated family adopts the child. That's because it's clear who the mother is.

Determining paternity can be more difficult. If the parents were never married, usually the child must show some kind of proof to inherit from the father. Depending on the state, acceptable proof might be:

- a written statement of paternity from the father

- evidence that the father acknowledged that the child was his (commonly, by living with the child at least for a while and treating him or her as his own)

- a court order declaring paternity, or

- evidence that the parents went through a marriage ceremony that for some reason did not result in a legal marriage—for example, one of the persons was married to someone else.

3. Brothers and Sisters

If an intestate succession law includes the deceased person's "sisters and brothers" or "siblings" as heirs, this group generally includes half-siblings.

EXAMPLE: *Jackson dies without leaving a surviving spouse or children. Under his state's law, his brothers and sisters are his heirs, entitled to inherit his property. This group includes his sister Jennifer and his brother Jason. It also includes his half-sister June, who was born to his father and a new wife after Jackson's mother and father divorced.*

The term siblings may even include half-siblings who were adopted out of the family.

D. If an Heir Has Died

Obviously, an heir who has died can't inherit. But if the heir was a close relative, such as a child of the deceased person, his or her offspring may be entitled to take some or all of what their parent would have received. Figuring out whether this is the case can be tricky, but it's essential that you do so before distributing assets.

1. Survivorship Requirements

To inherit under intestate succession laws, an heir may have to survive a certain amount of time after the deceased person. In a good number of states, the required period is 120 hours, or five days. This ensures that someone who dies at about the same time as the deceased person doesn't inherit property, which would immediately go to his or her own heirs or beneficiaries. (The statute is guessing that most people wouldn't want that result.)

EXAMPLE: *Dirk and his son Eric are injured together in an accident. Dirk dies the next day, without leaving a will. Eric dies two days later.*

Dirk's property will pass to his widow and his surviving children, in the shares set out by state law. Eric's estate will not inherit. (If Eric left children of his own, however, they may be entitled to a share of Dirk's property directly; see Section 2, below.)

In some states, however, an heir need only outlive the deceased person by any period of time—theoretically, one second would do.

Many states have adopted a law (the Uniform Simultaneous Death Act) that says for purposes of inheritance, each person is treated as if he had survived the other. That prevents a person's assets from going to someone who lives only a few minutes or hours longer, and then being passed to that person's heirs. Instead, the assets go to the deceased person's own heirs.

EXAMPLE: *Dirk and his son Eric are both killed in a car accident. No one knows who died first. Dirk's executor proceeds as if Dirk lived longer, which means that Eric inherits nothing from him. Similarly, Eric's executor proceeds as if Eric outlived Dirk, which means that Dirk inherits nothing from Eric.*

Disputes over this issue are rare. If you think one is coming, look up your state's law on simultaneous death (see Chapter 22) or consult a lawyer who's familiar with your state's rules.

2. Rights of a Deceased Heir's Descendants

Intestacy laws often provide that if one of a group of heirs has died, his or her children inherit their parent's share. In other words, they take the place of the parent.

EXAMPLE: *Lucas dies without a will. One of his two daughters, Hillary, died before he did, leaving two children of her own. These two grandchildren inherit the portion of Lucas's estate that their mother would have inherited if she were still alive.*

This concept, called the "right of representation," is pretty straightforward—at least in theory. Children stand in the place of ("represent") their deceased parent when it comes to inheritance. If an heir and all of his children are deceased, grandchildren may even be entitled to inherit in the heir's place.

But figuring out exactly how the children (or even grandchildren) of a deceased heir inherit is not always easy. States define representation in at least three different ways.

One method used by many states is to divide the inheritance into shares, one share for each member of the generation closest to the deceased person. Then you take the shares of any deceased members of that generation, combine them, and divide them equally among the survivors in the next generation. Thoroughly confused? A diagram may make this easier to grasp:

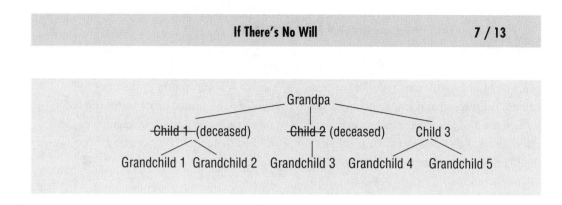

Step 1. Even though Child 1 and Child 2 are deceased, Grandpa's property is divided into three shares, one for each child.

Step 2. Child 3, the only living child, gets a one-third share. His children, Grandchildren 4 and 5, get nothing.

Step 3. The other two-thirds is divided equally among the three children of Child 1 and Child 2, so each gets a two-ninths share.

Another common method is to give each set of grandchildren their deceased parent's share. Using this scheme, the situation in the preceding example yields a different result.

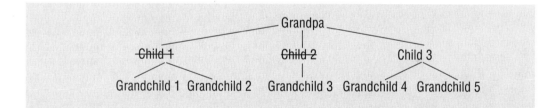

Step 1. Again, Grandpa's property is divided into three shares, one for each child.

Step 2. Child 3 gets his one-third share, and his children get nothing.

Step 3. Another one-third share is split between the children of Child 1 (so Grandchildren 1 and 2 each get one-sixth), and the last third goes to the child of Child 2.

These rules are tricky. If you need to figure out who inherits in a situation like this, talk to a lawyer who's knowledgeable about the intestate succession law of your state.

E. Taking Care of Minor Children

Parents of young children who make a will typically name someone to serve as the personal guardian of their children. In the very unusual event that both parents died before the children were grown, a judge would appoint their choice to serve as guardian and raise the children. But if a guardian is needed and there's no will, how does a judge know whom to appoint?

In that situation, someone must go to probate court (even if there is no probate proceeding, the same court generally handles guardianship cases) and ask the court to select a guardian. The judge must gather as much information as possible about the children, their family circumstances, and the deceased parents' wishes, and try to make a good decision. The primary rule is that the judge must always act in the best interests of the children. (Chapter 10 discusses getting a court to appoint a guardian for children.) ∎

CHAPTER 8

Taking Inventory

Now you're ready to begin a very important job: figuring out what the deceased person owned and owed. To help you reorganize your information, this chapter contains an inventory form for you to fill in.

Why take a formal inventory? For one thing, as executor (or trustee) it's your legal responsibility to take care of the assets until you distribute them to the new owners. And you also need to know what the deceased person left before you can determine whether or not you'll need to conduct regular probate court proceedings.

This chapter also helps you start estimating what each item of property is worth. You'll need to know these values for tax purposes and to see whether or not the estate qualifies for your state's simplified "small estate" probate procedures. And if the estate goes through probate, you'll probably have to supply the court with reliable estimates of each major asset's value.

Finally, you'll finish filling in the inventory form by recording how each asset was owned—for example, whether it was owned alone, in joint tenancy with someone else, or as community property with a spouse. That affects both who inherits it and how you can later transfer it to them.

You may need to do some follow-up work to fill in all the blanks in the inventory form, but if the estate contains only simple, ordinary assets—bank accounts, real estate, vehicles— you should make progress quickly.

Step 1: Look for Assets

If you had some time to prepare before the person died, you may already have a good idea of what's in the estate. Even so, assets may have been overlooked or only recently acquired. It's your responsibility to do a little digging.

Keep in mind that there really may be money under the mattress. A surprising number of people, especially older people, squirrel away cash or other valuables in some unlikely spots. It may be worth your while to check places such as mattresses, old shoeboxes, and maybe even the freezer. Talk to family members or old friends the deceased person may have confided in. If you find a few items and suspect more are secreted somewhere, you'd better look in the sugar canister.

To locate financial assets such as stocks, bank accounts, and insurance policies, look for the documents that concern them. Check for bills, tax returns, investment records, and monthly or quarterly statements from brokers, banks, and mutual funds.

Start by going through a desk or other main bill-paying spot and any nearby file cabinets. Probably the most fruitful places to look for evidence of property are the deceased person's checkbook and credit card statements. (And remember that some people no longer use a paper checkbook—their records are on their computer.) Go through them carefully. Keep an eye out for payments for:

- insurance premiums

- car registration

- real estate expenses such as property tax, mortgages, and utilities (evidence of property you may not already know about)

- income taxes (including any quarterly estimated payments)

- contributions to retirement or investment accounts

- storage unit rental

- contributions to charity, and

- safe deposit box rental.

The checkbook may also show deposits of income from employment, rental property, business interests, or investments.

Recent income tax returns are also very useful, because they show interest, dividend, and employment income and should give you a good picture of what investments the deceased person owned. All of this information will be crucial when it's time to file the final tax returns for the deceased person, because you must document income and expenses. (Chapter 11 discusses taxes.)

As you go through tax returns for the past few years, keep an eye out for what comes and goes. If one year's return shows income from an investment but the next one's doesn't, find out what happened. The investment may have been sold—but maybe not. Millions of dollars worth of stocks end up unclaimed by the people who should inherit them.

As you plow through paper, don't overlook online records. First, check email if you can—and remember that many people have more than one email account. Some bills and statements may come only through email.

You may also need to dig up passwords to get access to online accounts—for example, access to brokerage account records may be only through a password-protected website. If you don't have passwords and can't get to these records, you'll have to contact the companies, explain the situation, and supply some proof that you're entitled to act on behalf of the deceased person.

If you find it, file it. While you're at it, take note of dues, subscriptions, and legal and medical documents. You may need all of them later, and there's no sense in going through everything twice. (Chapter 4 discusses setting up a simple filing system.)

What's that behind the lawnmower? Only one person knew my mother had stashed $20,000 worth of jewelry in the garage. I never would have known it was missing. I knew that Mom had a pile of jewelry, but I couldn't have said exactly what she owned. We'd never discussed it.

If you have access to it, check the deceased person's safe deposit box. (Chapter 4 discusses access to safe deposit boxes.) It may contain valuables or documents (deeds, contracts, bonds) that will alert you to valuable property.

Find out what you're missing. If you know Uncle Harry was a partner in a business, kept a boat, and owned a golf club membership that can be sold to the next member, but you can't find the relevant records, then you need to cast a wider net. Start by talking to relatives, friends, and colleagues.

FINDING ASSETS

Asset	Documents to Look For
Annuity	Policy document, premium statements (paper or email), cancelled checks
Bank account, CD	Account statements, checkbook, passbook, and evidence of online banking
Boat	Title and registration documents
Small business interests	Stock certificates, shareholder agreements, limited liability company member agreements, partnership agreements, contracts or franchise agreements; trademark registration issued by U.S. Patent & Trademark Office
Copyright	Contract, registration documents issued by U.S. Copyright Office (copyrights no longer have to be registered, but it's still common)
Debt owed to the deceased	Promissory note
Life insurance	Premium statements (paper or email), cancelled checks
Limited partnership investment interest	Statements from partnership
Money market fund	Statements (paper or email) from broker (possibly the same statement that lists securities)
Motor vehicle	Title or registration document (might be in the vehicle)
Patent	Patent issued by U.S. Patent & Trademark Office
Precious metals	Statement from company from which metals were bought; more rarely, actual coins or ingots
Real estate	Deed, divorce settlement agreement, prenuptial agreement, property tax statements, mortgage statements, checks from tenants
Retirement account	Statements (paper or email) from account custodian
Royalties	Contracts
Stocks or bonds	Mutual fund or brokerage account statements (paper or email); rarely, stock mutual funds certificates or bonds themselves
Stock options	Option papers issued by company

Step 2: Make a List of Assets

If the deceased person's estate ends up going through probate, you'll have to file an inventory with the court. But even if you don't, a written list of assets will help as you manage, and eventually distribute, the property. You may want to use the form below or something similar to summarize the results of your inventory.

List all the property the deceased person owned, even if you're sure it can be transferred to the new owners without probate. Also be sure to include property that was owned jointly with someone else. For now, you just want an inventory that is as complete as you can make it. Later, you can estimate value and determine how you're going to transfer each asset to its new owners—through regular or informal probate, or by using an out-of-court procedure.

When it comes to items of small value (financial or emotional), you'll probably find that it makes sense to group them. You don't need to list every book, pot, and pan separately.

ASSETS

	Date-of-death value	Value of deceased person's share	How title held*	Probate?
Real estate 1547 Oak Street, Peoria, Il (single-family residence), owned with Allen Smith	$180,000	$90,000	JT	No
Cash accounts Checking acct. #88999-24567 at First Bank of Illinois, POD Jennifer Smith	$3,200	$3,200	S, POD	No
Savings acct.#5578 at First Bank of Illinois	$10,500	$10,500	S	Yes?
Stocks, bonds, and mutual funds ABC Mutual Fund Acct. #55-4423432, owned with Allen Smith	$85,800	$42,900	JT	No
Life insurance and annuities Global Ins. Co., Policy #88499B-1, Allen Smith, beneficiary	$100,000	$100,000	S	No
Retirement accounts IRA, at International Fund Management Co., Acct. # G4433212, Allen Smith, beneficiary	$32,000	$32,000	S	No
Wages or benefits				
Business interests				
Limited partnerships				
Vehicles Chrysler PT Cruiser, owned with Allen Smith	$7,000	$3,500	JT	No
Other assets Diamond wedding ring Household furnishings and personal effects	$1,000 $2,000	$1,000 $2,000	S JT	
Total assets		$285,100		

* Abbreviations:

S: Solely owned	CP: community property	TBE: tenancy by the entirety	JT: joint tenancy
TIC: tenancy in common	P: partnership	T: held in trust	POD: payable-on-death
CP WROS: community property with right of survivorship			

DEBTS

Debt	Amount	Creditor	Date next payment due
Car loan	$2,000	Bank of the Midwest	June 1, 20xx
Visa	$1,700	First Mutual Bank	June 15, 20xx
Total debts	$3,700		
Total net value of estate	$281,400		

1. Real Estate

Real estate (called "real property" by lawyers) is land and things permanently attached to land, including buildings, fences, and trees.

Condominiums, vacation cabins, time-shares, rental property, commercial property, mobile homes that are permanently attached to lots, farmland, and, in some states, things like permanent dock spaces and landing rights are classified as real estate. Some long-term property leases—for example, those for a term of ten years or more—may also qualify as real estate under your state's law. In any case, this is a good place to list such things, because chances are they are valuable.

For purposes of the inventory, all you need to put down is the property address and a brief description, such as "single-family residence," "condo," or "vacation cottage."

If the deceased person owned shares in a real estate investment trust (REIT), that interest isn't considered real estate. List it under "stocks, bonds, and mutual funds" below.

2. Cash and Bank Accounts

Here, list not only currency that was in the deceased person's possession, but all kinds of items or accounts that are basically cash, including traveler's checks, certificates of deposit, and checking and savings accounts.

For all cash accounts, put down the bank or other financial institution, the account number, and the balance at the date of death. If you don't know the exact balance—or perhaps you're not even sure whether or not an account is still open—you can check with the bank later.

Before the bank will release this information to you, however, you'll need to show that you're entitled to it. If you go through regular probate, you can produce the document issued by the probate court (usually called your "Letters") that appoints you as executor. If you don't have court authorization, you can probably get the information you need by presenting the bank with a copy of the death certificate and a sworn statement (affidavit) you've signed, stating that no probate proceedings have begun or are expected and that you are distributing the deceased person's assets.

AFFIDAVIT OF ASSUMPTION OF DUTIES

I, Katherine Krellmer Segal, of legal age, being duly sworn, declare:

Samuel P. Krellmer, the decedent, died on February 22, 20xx, as shown by the certified copy of the death certificate attached to this document.

At his death, the decedent was a resident of Contra Costa County, California. His last address was 392 Washington Court, Walnut Creek, CA 94547.

No application or petition for the appointment of an executor is pending or has been granted in any jurisdiction.

Under the terms of decedent's will, I am the sole beneficiary and have assumed responsibility for distributing the assets in his estate.

Katherine Krellmer Segal
Date: *March 11, 20xx*

[*notarization*]

3. Stocks, Bonds, and Mutual Funds

List retirement accounts separately. In this section, stick to nonretirement accounts. There's another space on the inventory form to enter retirement accounts, which may contain securities.

Most people who own stocks, bonds, mutual fund shares, or shares in a real estate invest-

ment trust (REIT) don't actually have the stock or bond certificates in their possession. (You may, however, find certificates tucked away in a safe deposit box.) Instead, they have documents that prove their ownership. Commonly, these are monthly or quarterly statements from brokers or mutual fund companies.

Some people get statements from the individual companies in which they own stock and from individual mutual funds. Other folks receive one statement that tracks all their holdings—for example, they may have money in five different mutual funds and three stocks, but have a consolidated statement through a company that serves both as a broker and mutual fund company, such as Charles Schwab, Vanguard, or Fidelity. In that case, a copy of the latest statement will serve as a complete inventory.

Investing basics. Depending on how the stocks and bonds were owned, you may be able to turn them over to the people who inherit them without needing to manage or even fully understand these investments. But if you want or need to learn more, there's a wealth of plain-English information online. For example, the Motley Fool website, www.fool .com, offers a good introduction to investing.

a. Stocks

On the inventory form, list the number of shares of stock owned, the corporation that issued them, and what exchange (New York Stock Exchange or NASDAQ) the stock is traded on. If the stock isn't common stock (most is), note what kind it is—for example, preferred stock, warrants, or put and call options.

b. Mutual Funds

List the name of each fund (remember that lots of companies offer many different funds), the number of shares of each fund, and the address of the company that manages it.

c. Bonds

A bond is basically a promise to repay a loan. You lend a company or government $1,000; it promises to pay you back the $1,000 at a certain date, and to pay you interest (usually, every six months) until then. There are a few kinds of bonds you're likely to run into:

- **U.S. government bonds (treasuries).** These include Treasury notes, bills, and bonds, and also notes indexed for inflation. Some treasuries mature in three months, others in 30 years. The U.S. government guarantees these bonds, and the income from them is not subject to state or local taxes. Some government agencies and federally chartered corporations, such as the Federal National Mortgage Association (Fannie Mae) and the Federal Home Loan Mortgage Corporation (Freddie Mac), also sell bonds backed by the federal government.

- **Tax-free municipal bonds.** State and local governments sell their own bonds, too, commonly called munis. If the bonds are from the bondholders' state, any income that he or she receives is not subject to federal income tax.

- **Corporate bonds.** Big companies also raise money by selling bonds. Most individual middle-income investors buy shares in bond funds issued by mutual fund companies, rather than buying bonds directly from corporations.

- **U.S. savings bonds.** These bonds, of course, are an investment in the federal government.

When you're listing bonds, record the total gross face amount (for example, $10,000), the name of the company or government that issued them, the interest (coupon) rate, and the maturity date. For U.S. savings bonds, record the face amount, issue date, and serial number.

4. Life Insurance

Here, list life insurance policies the deceased person owned. Put down the name of the company, the policy number, the name of the insured person, and the beneficiary.

The beneficiary will probably take care of collecting the policy proceeds, which will not need to go through probate. If you think any beneficiaries might not know about the money they're entitled to, be sure to notify them. They'll need the insurance policy documents, but it won't hurt for you to keep a copy. You'll need to include the amount of the proceeds if you add up the total value of the estate for estate tax purposes.

 Check ownership of the policies. It's possible that the insured person didn't actually own a policy insuring his or her life. Some people, especially if they're concerned that their estates may owe federal estate tax, give away ownership of life insurance policies, usually to the beneficiary or to a special trust. If the deceased person didn't own the policy, the proceeds aren't included in his or her estate, and you don't have to list the policy in your inventory. If you're not sure who owned the policy, contact the insurance company.

5. Retirement Accounts

List all retirement accounts—IRAs, Roth IRAs, 401(k) or 403(b) plans, Keogh accounts, and so on—and the amount in each at the date of death. Put down the account number and the name of the account custodian (the company that administers the account).

Keep a copy of the most recent statement you can find. You may need the information it contains to establish a date-of-death value for the account.

6. Wages or Benefits From Employers

If the deceased person was working until shortly before death, the employer may owe the estate unpaid wages, compensation for accrued vacation time, commissions, or death benefits. For purposes of the inventory form, estimate the amounts you expect are due and list their source, or if you can't even guess at the amount, call the employer and ask. Usually, employers pay these amounts directly to the surviving spouse or children. (See Chapter 5 for information on claiming wages.)

7. Small Business Interests

Did the deceased person own a small business, either alone or with others? If so, list it on your inventory. Note the name of the business and also its legal form: sole proprietorship, corporation, limited liability company, or partnership.

Unless the business was operated as a sole proprietorship, you'll need to find out how ownership was shared. You may find papers—tax returns, partnership agreements, articles of incorporation, shareholder agreements, limited liability corporation documents, or others—that will tell you. Or you can contact the other owners for information.

STOCK OPTIONS

If the deceased person received stock options from an employer, they may be valuable assets. (An option gives you the right to buy company stock at a fixed price.) If you find documents that grant options, read them carefully to find out whether or not:

- the option can be exercised at death
- the option plan allows close family members to exercise them at death, and
- there is a time limit on the exercise.

If you can't find the answers in the option documents, ask the employer.

8. Limited Partnerships

A limited partnership is a kind of investment in a business venture. Investors, called limited partners, do not make day-to-day business decisions and do not have personal liability for business debts. (Other partners, called general partners, do.) A statement from the partnership should tell you the value of the deceased person's investment.

9. Vehicles

List any cars or other motor vehicles (motor-cycles, boats, planes, and the like) the deceased person owned. Include the make, model, and year.

10. Everything Else

If the deceased person owned some valuable assets that don't fit neatly into the categories already discussed, list them here.

a. Intangible Assets

Don't overlook what may be valuable legal rights—for example, to collect a debt from someone. The deceased person may have owned a patent, giving him or her the legal right to protect an invention from use by others. Perhaps he or she owned a copyright on a book and so had the right to receive royalties from its sales and to collect money from anyone who copied it without permission. You need to include these assets in your inventory.

PROPERTY MANAGED FOR SOMEONE ELSE

You may find bank or brokerage statements for property that the deceased person did not actually own, but managed for someone else. For example, the deceased person may have had power of attorney—that is, the legal authority to act for someone else—over the assets of a disabled spouse or friend. Or the deceased person may have managed property for someone too young to handle it alone. Here's what to look for:

- Accounts the deceased person managed for a child under the state's Uniform Transfers to Minors Act (UTMA). These will say something like "Tiffany Rogers, Robert K. Vleck Custodian Ohio UTMA."
- Account statements that identify the deceased person as a "POA," "agent," "attorney-in-fact," or "AIF."

These assets are not part of the deceased person's estate, and you don't need to include them in your inventory. But if you know who is responsible for taking over for the deceased person, you should notify that person of the death.

These assets aren't things you can touch (that's why they're known as intangible assets), but they usually have documents that serve as evidence of their existence. Some fairly common examples include:

- payments or royalties due the deceased person under a contract with a publisher or other business

- copyrights

- patents

- court judgments (from a successful lawsuit), and

- promissory notes (representing money owed to the deceased person).

b.   Tangible Assets

Finally, list any other significant tangible items—that is, physical objects such as furniture, art, tools, jewelry, heirlooms, and computers. You don't need to catalog every teacup, but don't overlook items that are valuable for either financial or emotional reasons. You can lump not-so-valuable things together—for example, "books and CDs," "clothing," or even "household furnishings and personal effects."

COMMON KINDS OF VALUABLE TANGIBLE PROPERTY

Animals	Collectibles
Antiques	Computers and
Appliances	related equipment
Art	Electronic equipment
Books	Exercise equipment
CDs, records, tapes	Furniture
Cameras	Jewelry
Camping equipment	Musical instruments
China, crystal, silver	Rugs
Clothing with resale	Sports equipment
value	Tools
Coins, stamps	

Step 3: Estimate the Value

How important is it to calculate the precise value of the deceased person's property? It depends. A sole beneficiary who inherits everything (or almost everything), without probate may not care about a precise valuation, as long as it's clear that the estate isn't large enough to owe state or federal estate taxes. In almost every other situation, however, you'll need a solid valuation. Here is why:

The estate might qualify for simplified "small estate" probate procedures. If at least some assets look like they're headed toward probate, you'll want to check out your state's small estate rules. Every state offers a streamlined summary probate process for small estates. What qualifies as a small estate, however, is different in every state. You'll need to know the estate's value to determine whether or not it's eligible. (The rules are explained in Chapter 17.)

The probate court requires it. If you file a probate court case, the court will require an inventory and appraisal of all the estate assets.

The estate might owe federal estate tax. If the value of all the assets looks like it's close to the federal estate tax threshold ($1.5 million in 2004), you need a reliable valuation. You may need to file a federal estate tax return. Even if you don't file a return because you decide the estate isn't worth that much, you may need some proof to back up your decision if the IRS challenges it.

The estate might owe state estate tax. Many states don't assess their own estate tax. But in some states, an estate that isn't large enough to pay federal estate tax may still owe estate tax to the state. (See Chapter 11.)

Beneficiaries will want to know. If the estate is to be divided among several beneficiaries, they may want to know what items are worth so they can be sure the division is fair. And if there isn't enough to satisfy all the bequests the deceased person made by will, valuing assets becomes even more important.

Beneficiaries need to know the new tax basis of valuable assets. Whoever inherits property gets a new tax basis in that property: the market value at the date of death. The new owner needs to know this new basis to figure tax liability later, when the property is sold. (Chapter 11 discusses this issue.)

Lean toward the high side. When getting assets appraised, you'll want to get as high a value as can be reasonably defended, as long as the total value of the estate doesn't go so high that estate taxes are due. A higher value now means a higher basis for the new owner, which translates into lower capital gains taxes later.

1. Real Estate

How do you know how much real estate is worth? One surefire way to find out is to quickly put it on the open market and sell it. And in some cases, that's just what inheritors may want to do. But if the estate is going through probate, you may need to notify beneficiaries and possibly even get court approval before selling real estate.

Short of actually selling it, the easiest way to get an estimate for a house, condominium, or residential lot is to ask two or three local real estate agents to walk through the property and give you a figure, in writing. If they know about recent sales of comparable properties in the neighborhood and whether the market is hot or cold, taking the average of their figures should give you a reasonable result.

You may, however, want a formal appraisal from a licensed real estate appraiser. You'll probably need an appraisal if the real estate is commercial property or income-producing residential property such as a duplex or apartment building. Such assets are harder to value accurately than most residential units, for which there are lots of comparable sales.

To find a licensed appraiser, ask a local real estate agent, mortgage broker, or bank to recommend someone. Expect to pay at least several hundred dollars for a residential appraisal, and more for an appraisal of commercial property.

However you decide to proceed, don't procrastinate too long. Real estate markets can change quickly, and you need the date-of-death value. It's hard for anyone to reliably estimate that later.

Consider the source. Valuing real estate is always a somewhat subjective exercise. A good real estate agent will give you a realistic estimate, to avoid getting your expectations too high. But an agent who hopes to be hired to sell the property might romance you with a high estimate. Appraisers, on the other hand, have no reason to inflate a valuation.

2. Stocks and Bonds

You'll need a date-of-death value for stocks and bonds. How to get it depends on the kind of security you have.

a. Publicly Traded Stocks

The easiest way to get a date-of-death value is to ask the brokerage firm that managed the deceased person's investments. Another is to get pricing data for the day of death from a newspaper (the *Wall Street Journal* publishes daily stock prices) or website. If you go this route, you need to calculate the average of the lowest and highest prices the security sold for on the date of death.

EXAMPLE: *Florence owned 100 shares of General Industries stock. On the day she died, shares of General Industries sold on the stock exchange for a low of $45.80 and a high of $47.20. To get the mean price, add the high and low price and divide by two:*

45.80
+47.20
93.00 divided by 2 = 46.50

Because Florence owned 100 shares, the total date-of-death value is $4,650.

If the death occurred on a day when the stock market was closed, take the average of the sales prices on the trading days immediately before and after the date of death.

COMPLICATED SECURITIES

Most people own common stock. But if the stock was preferred stock or some other more complicated creature such as warrants or put and call options, you'll need to find out more from the company. For example, with preferred stock you'll need to know the nature of the preference. Preferred stockholders get paid first (ahead of those who own common stock) when dividends are handed out—or when a company's assets are divvied up in bankruptcy. Also, some preferred stock can be traded in for (more) shares of common stock; this is called "convertible" preferred stock.

b. Mutual Funds

You can get a date-of-death value of the deceased person's holdings from the fund company.

c. Bonds

Your best bet is probably to contact the company or broker from which the bonds were bought, and ask for help. To do it yourself, take the average of the lowest and highest selling price on the date of death, just as you would for stocks. Then add any accrued interest that was due but not yet paid by the date of death. To calculate the amount of accrued interest, multiply the daily interest rate by the number of days between the last payment and the date of death.

d. Stocks That Aren't Publicly Traded

If the estate contains stock that isn't publicly traded, ask the company how much it's worth. Unless some of the stock has been sold recently, an appraisal may be necessary.

3. Life Insurance and Annuities

You need to estimate the value of all policies the deceased person owned, no matter whose life was insured.

a. Policies on the Deceased Person's Life

The value of a life insurance policy the deceased person owned on his or her own life is the amount the policy will pay to the beneficiary. Include it on your inventory even though you probably won't be in charge of collecting the money for the policy beneficiary. (The beneficiary can collect the policy proceeds directly; they don't need to go through probate.) The amount of the proceeds is counted when it comes time to determine whether or not the estate is big enough to owe estate tax.

b. Policies on Someone Else's Life

If the deceased person owned a policy insuring the life of a spouse or someone else, the value of the policy is not the amount of the proceeds (which won't be paid now), but the "cash value" of the policy itself. Generally, that value is only a few thousand dollars—much less than the amount of the eventual proceeds.

To ascertain the cash value of the policy as of the date of death, ask the insurance company.

c. Annuities

Contact the insurance company that sold the annuity and ask for a date-of-death valuation. (Some annuities don't have any value remaining after death; see Chapter 5.)

4. Businesses

Putting a value on the deceased person's interest in a small business is a job for a professional. Contact an appraiser who knows how to value both the tangible and intangible assets of a business. To find an appraiser, ask a lawyer who specializes in small business matters or an accountant who does a lot of work with small businesses.

Look for a buy-sell agreement. If there are other co-owners, find out whether or not they all signed a buy-sell agreement. Sometimes these agreements put a value on the business, in advance, for estate tax purposes.

5. Limited Partnerships

What a limited partnership is worth depends on what the deceased owner was entitled to under the particular agreement. You can ask the partnership to put a value on the deceased person's interest (in writing, if at all possible), or hire a CPA to do it.

6. Vehicles

To get a value for a run-of-the-mill used car, check the *Kelley Blue Book*, available in libraries or online at http://kbb.com. If the car is unusual—an antique or classic—get an appraisal from an expert.

Step 4: Add Up Debts

You can't figure out the value of the estate until you know what the deceased person owed. So after you've made a list of assets, it's time to add up the debts.

COMMON DEBTS

Car loans
Credit cards
Expenses of administering the estate: lawyer, appraiser, or court fees
Expenses of last illness
Funeral, burial, or cremation costs
Loans from friends or relatives
Mortgages
Utilities

For purposes of an estate, there are basically two kinds of debts:

- those that are attached to (secured by) a specific asset—for example, a car loan or real estate mortgage, and

- those that aren't—for example, a credit card balance.

As executor, you'll handle the two kinds of debts differently. Debts that are linked to a specific piece of property generally go to the new owner, along with the property. So someone who inherits a house gets the mortgage balance and property tax bill along with it. Other debts are paid from the estate. (See Chapter 9 for more on paying bills while you're administering the estate.)

When you list a debt, record the amount, the name of the creditor, and the date the next payment is due.

Credit card companies may cancel at least some debt. It's worth asking. (See Chapter 4, Section E1.)

Step 5: Determine How Title Was Held

To know who inherits the property and whether or not it needs to go through probate, you must know how the property was owned. Generally, only property that the deceased person owned alone has to go through probate. Most assets that were owned with someone else, held in a living trust, or for which the person had named a pay-on-death beneficiary, can be transferred to their new owners without probate. All that is discussed later, in Chapter 12. Here, just figure out how the asset was owned and note the type of ownership on the inventory form.

1. Ways Property Can Be Owned

For each asset, you need to know whether the deceased person owned it alone or together with someone else. And if it was owned with someone else, you need to determine how the co-owners held title: in joint tenancy, as community property, or in some other way. The kinds of ownership you're most likely to run into are listed below.

When you're looking at title documents, you may also run across a "POD" or "TOD" notation—for example, a bank account held in the name of "Doris Tutwiler, POD William G.

Tutwiler." This is very important—it means that the asset has a "payable-on-death" or "transfer-on-death" beneficiary, who automatically inherits the property when the owner dies. How to handle these assets is discussed in Chapter 16. For now, just note the beneficiary's name on the inventory form in the "how title held" column.

2. Solely Owned or Not?

Sometimes it's easy to know who owned an asset, and sometimes it's not.

Usually, the answer can be found by looking at the title document, if there is one. For example, for real estate, the deed should tell you who owned the property.

Even if the title document shows that the deceased person owned the property alone, however, state laws and private agreements may give someone else—in most cases, a

HOW WAS TITLE HELD?

Type of Property Ownership	Abbreviation
Solely owned	S
Co-owned	
Joint tenancy	JT
Tenancy by the entirety*	TBE
Community property*	CP
Community property with right of survivorship	CP WROS
Tenancy in common	TIC
Partnership (business)	P
Held in trust	T

* Available only to married couples (or registered domestic partners) in some states.

spouse—ownership rights. Ownership can be affected by:

- community property laws, which give spouses half ownership of most property in some states (see Section 3e, below)

- a prenuptial agreement

- a community property agreement (often called a spousal property agreement) between the deceased person and his or her spouse, and

- a living-together agreement (if the deceased person was a partner in an unmarried relationship).

3. Property Owned With Someone Else

If you've determined that the deceased person owned property with someone else, next you need to find out exactly how they shared ownership of the asset.

If there is a title document to the property—for example, the deed to real estate or the title slip for a car—look there first. It should tell you.

Much property, of course, has no title document—after all, there's no deed to a dining room table. Questions about ownership are unlikely to crop up, but if they do—for example, if the deceased person was living with someone, or a relative claims to have only lent an item to the deceased person—you may need to hunt up receipts or talk to people who know the item's history.

Each of the major ways to hold title to co-owned property is discussed next.

a. Joint Tenancy

Joint tenancy is probably the most common way for people to own property together. When one joint owner dies, the property automatically passes to the surviving co-owner(s), without probate. Couples often own many big-ticket items—real estate, cars, bank accounts, and stocks—in joint tenancy.

Each co-owner owns an equal share of the property. For example, if there are three co-owners, each one owns a one-third interest.

To see whether or not property was held in joint tenancy, check the deed or other title document. Usually you'll find something like this:

"Maeve J. Nester and Colleen A. Sullivan, as joint tenants with right of survivorship,"

"Arnold Smith and Heather Smith JT,"

"Benjamin Grigov and Margaret Grigov, in joint tenancy," or

"Joseph R. Breitland and Oliver H. Breitland, in joint tenancy WROS."

It's not always this clear, however. For example, say you're trying to determine whether or not a car owned by a married couple was joint tenancy property. In some states (California and Connecticut, for example), using "or" between the names of the husband and wife creates a joint tenancy. So a car title that lists "Chester Longfellow or Madeline Longfellow" as owners creates a joint tenancy, meaning that when Chester or Madeline dies, the survivor automatically owns the car alone. If instead it said "Chester Longfellow and Madeline Longfellow," ownership would be a tenancy in common (and the car would not automatically pass without probate). In Arizona, the way to create a joint tenancy with right of survivorship is to join the names of the owners with "and/or." And in Kentucky, any car owned by a husband and wife is a joint tenancy unless the title document states otherwise. (Ky. Rev. Stat. Ann. § 186A.035.)

If you're not sure whether or not something was owned in joint tenancy, get help. If you're puzzling over a car title, check with the state motor vehicles department. For other assets, you'll probably want to ask a lawyer.

b. Tenancy by the Entirety

When to look for this kind of ownership. Tenancy by the entirety is an option only for married couples in the states listed below (or, in Hawaii or Vermont, for unmarried couples who have registered with the state). If the deceased person wasn't eligible, you can skip this discussion.

STATES WHERE TENANCY BY THE ENTIRETY IS AVAILABLE

Alaska**	Missouri
Arkansas	New Jersey
Connecticut	New York**
Delaware**	North Carolina**
District of Columbia	Ohio*
Florida**	Oklahoma
Hawaii	Oregon**
Illinois**	Pennsylvania
Indiana**	Rhode Island**
Kentucky**	Tennessee
Maryland	Utah**
Massachusetts	Vermont
Michigan	Virginia
Mississippi	Wyoming

*Only for real estate, if created before April 4, 1985.

**For real estate only.

In many states, married couples opt to own property in tenancy by the entirety, a sort of joint tenancy for married couples. Property held this way automatically goes to the surviving spouse, without probate, when the first spouse dies.

To see whether or not a married person's property was held in tenancy by the entirety, look on the real estate deed or other title document. You may find something like this:

"Shawn L. Smithfield and LaToya A. Smithfield, as tenants by the entirety," or

"Anthony Renaud and Nora Jane Renaud, in tenancy by the entirety."

In some states, however, even if the title doesn't mention tenancy by the entirety, the law presumes that a married couple holds their property (or real estate, at least) as tenants by the entirety unless some other kind of ownership is specified. The law is not always clear on this. If you have a question about it, ask a knowledgeable lawyer.

UNMARRIED COUPLES

In Hawaii and Vermont, unmarried couples who have registered with the state as reciprocal beneficiaries (Hawaii) or gone through a civil union ceremony (Vermont) can also own property as tenancy by the entirety.

c. Tenancy in Common

If the title document merely names the co-owners without mentioning the form of title, they probably owned the property as "tenants in common."

Tenancy in common has no right of survivorship—that is, when one owner dies, the survivor doesn't automatically own the property. The share of the property owned by the deceased person passes under his or her will or trust, or under intestate succession laws.

People use tenancy in common when they want to own property together but don't want the survivor to inherit when the first owner dies. For example, two brothers might buy some farmland together, or business partners might buy a building for their company.

If the co-owners were married, different rules may apply. State law may provide that if no form of title is mentioned, married couples hold the property in joint tenancy or as tenants by the entirety (see Subsections a and b, above). See a lawyer for advice if you're unsure.

d. Community Property With Right of Survivorship

When to look for this kind of ownership. Read this section if the deceased person was married and lived or owned real estate in Alaska, Arizona, California, Nevada, or Wisconsin. Otherwise, you can safely skip it.

Some community property states allow married couples to take title to property as "community property with right of survivorship" or "survivorship community property." If property is held in this way, the deed or other title document will describe the ownership something like this:

"Jeremy N. Serkov and Kathryn A. Serkov, as community property with right of survivorship."

If a couple held title this way, the surviving spouse automatically owns the whole asset when the first spouse dies, even if there's a will provision to the contrary. No probate is necessary to transfer title into the name of the surviving spouse.

e.　Community Property

When to look for this kind of ownership.
Community property exists only in the states listed below. Unless the deceased person was married and lived or owned real estate in one of them, you can safely skip this section.

COMMUNITY PROPERTY STATES

Alaska*	Nevada
Arizona	New Mexico
California	Texas
Idaho	Washington
Louisiana	Wisconsin**

*Alaska couples can create community property by a written agreement.
**Wisconsin's system of property ownership is basically like that of community property states, but it is called "marital property" there.

Married couples in community property states sometimes take title, especially to real estate, as "community property" or "as husband and wife." But even if they don't, or if the property doesn't have a title document, the property may legally be community property.

No matter how a married couple holds title to their property—for example, as joint tenants—it may be community property if the law of the state says it is. Even property owned in the name of just one spouse may be community property.

Community property belongs to both spouses equally. If, as is common, the surviving spouse inherits the deceased spouse's half, it can generally be transferred with a simplified probate court procedure instead of formal probate. (Chapter 14 discusses this.)

If you get stuck, get expert help. As you'll see, trying to determine what's community property and what's not can be bewildering. If you aren't sure of your conclusions and think family members might object to them, see a lawyer. It will be worth it.

Some particularly dicey areas:

- businesses that began as one spouse's separate property, especially if the other spouse worked in the business

- separate property to which substantial improvements were made with community funds (or the other way around).

(1) General Rules

In community property states, the general rule is that husbands and wives own, in equal shares, almost anything either of them earns or acquires while they're married. For example, each spouse's wages are the community property of both. Things bought with those wages are also community property.

The big exceptions to the general rule are property that just one spouse receives as a gift or inheritance; such items are that spouse's "separate property." Property one spouse owned before the marriage is also separate property, unless during the marriage it becomes thoroughly mixed up with community property. (The legal term for this is "commingling.") In long-term marriages, there is usually little or no separate property dating from before the couple married.

These rules are very important when you're trying to figure out who inherits what property, and how to transfer it to those new owners. Each spouse is free to leave his or her half of the couple's community property to anyone—for example, through a will. If the spouse doesn't leave the property to another person, however, it automatically goes to the surviving spouse. And several community property states offer a simplified transfer procedure for community property that goes to the surviving spouse.

COMMUNITY VS. SEPARATE PROPERTY: SOME EXAMPLES

Property	Separate or Community?	Why
A computer the husband inherited during marriage	His separate property	Property inherited by one spouse alone is separate property
A car the wife owned before	Her separate property	Property owned by one spouse before marriage is separate property
A boat, owned and registered in the husband's name, which he bought during the marriage with his wages	Community property	It was bought with community property (income earned during the marriage)
The family home, which the deed states that both spouses own as joint tenants and which was bought with the husband's wages	Community property	It was bought with community property (income earned during the marriage)
A video camera the wife received as a gift	Her separate property	Gifts made to one spouse are that spouse's separate property
$10,000, inherited by the wife 20 years ago and deposited into a checking account owned and used by both spouses	Community property	The $10,000 (which was the wife's separate property) has become so mixed with community property funds that it has become community property
A brokerage account, owned in joint tenancy, set up by a married couple in New York before they moved to California	Quasi-community property (treated just like community property; see Subsection 4, below)	It would have been community property had the couple lived in California when they acquired it
Proceeds of a life insurance policy, naming the wife's mother as beneficiary, that was paid for with community property funds	Community property	Community funds were used to pay for the premiums, so the proceeds are also community property
Pension payments stemming from work done while the employee was married	Community property	The pension is compensation for the work done, just like wages

(2) Agreements Between Spouses

Spouses are free, while both are alive, to make their own rules about what is community property and what is separate. For example, a couple might decide that they want their house, bought with community property funds, not to be community property. To make that decision legal and binding, they would need to sign an agreement spelling it out.

In some states (Washington, for example), it's become common for spouses to sign agreements that turn all of their property into community property when the first spouse dies. If you discover that the deceased person signed such an agreement, you should follow its terms with respect to its classification of property.

STATES THAT AUTHORIZE COMMUNITY PROPERTY AGREEMENTS

Alaska	Wisconsin
Idaho	Texas
Washington	

In some states, these community property agreements can even control what happens to the property at the second spouse's death. In Alaska and Wisconsin, this is clearly allowed. In Washington state, however, there is confusion about whether or not spouses can agree that a third party will inherit community property after the second spouse's death. If you run into such an agreement, see a lawyer.

What if a will tries to leave community property in a way that contradicts a community property agreement? The agreement prevails. Because these agreements are binding contracts, neither spouse can revoke them alone. (The one important exception is that in Alaska, after one spouse dies, the survivor can amend the agreement to change who inherits his or her property.)

If the deceased person signed a community property agreement, it is probably still in effect unless the spouses:

- agreed to cancel ("rescind") the agreement

- divorced, or

- separated permanently.

These rules change as courts rule on specific cases. If you aren't sure whether or not a community property agreement signed by the deceased person is still in effect, see a lawyer.

(3) Property That's Mixed Together

Property often starts out as one spouse's separate property but gets hopelessly mixed with the couple's jointly owned property. When that happens, it's considered community property. For marriages of more than ten years, most property is probably community property because of commingling rules, unless the spouses carefully kept it separate.

EXAMPLE: *Adrian owns a small house when he marries Ashley. They soon sell the house and use the proceeds, along with community property* *funds and some of Ashley's own money, to buy a bigger home. Over the years they improve and add on to the house. Because it would be nearly impossible to figure out what proportion of the house's current value is attributable to the original contributions from Adrian and Ashley, the house is considered community property.*

(4) Property Acquired in Another State or Before Marital Property Laws Took Effect

Four community property states—California, Idaho, Washington, and Wisconsin—have special rules that apply if a married couple acquires property that wasn't community property at the time, but would be considered community property under current law.

In California, Idaho, and Washington, this means property acquired in a state that doesn't follow the comunity property system. If property that the couple acquired when they lived in another state would have been community property had it been acquired in the community property state, it is termed "quasi-community property." It is treated just like community property when one of the couple dies.

EXAMPLE: *Jason and Arabella live in Indiana, where they marry and live for several years. Then they head west to California, bringing with them the money they've saved from their earnings. That money is now community property, because it would have been community property if they had earned it in California.*

In Wisconsin, such property is called "deferred marital property." This label applies

to property either acquired out of state or acquired in Wisconsin before the state's marital property laws (which operate like community property laws) took effect in 1986. When one spouse dies, the survivor is entitled to half the value of the couple's combined deferred marital property. If, however, the survivor has inherited property worth that amount from the deceased spouse, he or she cannot claim any more. (Wis. Stat. § 861.02.)

EXAMPLE: *Clara and Herbert have lived in Wisconsin all their lives; they married in 1965. In 1970, Herbert bought a vacation cabin with money he had earned during the marriage. Because the cabin would be marital property if it had been bought after 1986, it is considered deferred marital property. It's worth $50,000. Clara owns $20,000 of deferred marital property herself.*

At Herbert's death, Clara can claim half of the total value of the couple's deferred marital property, or $35,000. But if she has already inherited at least that much from Herbert, she isn't eligible to claim any more.

4. Property Held in a Living Trust

These days, many people create simple revocable trusts to hold property. These "living trusts" are designed to avoid probate for the assets held in the trust. The people who create such trusts (called grantors, settlers, or trustors) serve as trustees as long as they're alive, meaning they keep complete control over trust property.

If the deceased person held property in such a trust, include the trust property in your inventory, even though it won't go through probate. You'll need to know its value (at least an approximate figure) to determine whether or not the estate will have to file a federal estate tax return.

If you are the successor trustee of the trust—that is, the person who takes over the trust after the deceased person's death—then you'll be in charge of transferring all the trust property to its new owners.

To know whether or not property was held in trust, you need to look at two documents:

- the trust document (sometimes called an instrument or declaration of trust), which created the trust, and

- the paper that transferred ownership of the particular item to the trustee.

The trust document itself will tell you the terms of the trust, the identities of the beneficiaries, and other information—things that will be extremely important to you later on. But for now, concern yourself only with the property held in the trust. Start by looking for a list of property (usually called a "schedule") attached to the trust document.

Even if an item is listed on a trust document schedule of property, it still may not be actually held in trust. For an item to pass under the terms of the trust, it must be formally owned by the trustee. Look for a document showing title held in the name of the trustee—for example, a deed showing the owner of real estate is "John S. Andreeson,

trustee of the John S. Andreeson Living Trust" or a brokerage account titled "John S. Andreeson, Trustee UTD June 4, 20xx." (UTD stands for "under trust dated.")

EXAMPLE: *Millie sets up a basic probate-avoidance living trust, naming herself as trustee. On the property schedule attached to the trust document, she lists her house and several other items. But she never gets around to signing a deed transferring the house from herself as an individual to herself as trustee of the trust. The house does not pass under the terms of the trust—meaning it may have to go through probate.*

For items that have formal title documents, you must find a document transferring title to the name of the trustee. For example, ownership of real estate must be transferred by a deed.

COMMON KINDS OF TITLE DOCUMENTS

Item	Title Document
Real estate	Deed
Bank account	Bank document
Car	Title/registration papers
Insurance policy	Insurance company form

A lawyer may be able to help get property into a living trust even after death. In some states (California, for example), courts will allow property that wasn't formally transferred into the trust to pass under the trust, if it was listed in the trust document. But to get this result, you must file a request with the court, showing that the person who set up the trust intended the property to be held in trust. Going this route may or may not be worth the time and expense, compared with simply transferring the property through probate.

If an item doesn't have a title document—for example, household furnishings—it's usually enough if the items are simply listed in the trust document or property schedules. Sometimes, though, people create and sign a transfer document that resembles a bill of sale. Such a transfer document is required by law in some places, including New York. (N.Y. Est. Powers & Trusts Law § 7-1.18.) ■

CHAPTER 9

Managing Assets and Paying Bills

If you're an executor or a trustee, your most basic obligation is to take good care of the property in the estate or trust until you turn it over to its new owners.

For physical items, this means you must prevent damage, see that that they stay in good repair, and keep them adequately insured. For intangible assets—money and investments—you must take reasonable steps to avoid declines in value, which means you must keep an eye on how they're doing and shift investments if prudent. You'll also have to use assets to pay the deceased person's valid debts.

What you'll need to do to manage property (and how long you'll need to do it) depends in large part on whether you're handling an estate or a trust. Property in a simple living trust can be transferred to trust beneficiaries right away, without probate proceedings, and you may not have to take many of the steps outlined in this chapter. But even if assets must go through probate, your obligations shouldn't last more than a six months to a year. In short, you won't need to work out a complicated investment strategy or maintain vehicles or real estate over the long term.

This chapter outlines some steps you should take to fulfill your duty to manage the property and pay the debts of the deceased person—for however long that responsibility lasts.

More information on managing a long-term trust. If you're the trustee of a bypass (AB) trust or a child's trust, which may last for years, see Chapter 21 (bypass trusts) or Chapter 20 (trusts for children) for more details on your duties.

A. Your Legal Duties

As executor, you have control over someone else's money and property—and as a result, the law imposes a very high standard of behavior on you. (The legal term for this is a "fiduciary duty.") In other words, you have both great authority and great responsibility. You must always make decisions about estate property with the best interests of the estate's creditors and beneficiaries in mind.

In legal terms, you must be honest, prudent, loyal, and impartial. This section gives some commonsense ways to live up to those requirements when you're handling estate property.

If you live up to these duties but the estate suffers a loss—for example, you invest estate assets carefully but they still decline in value—you have done nothing wrong, and you will suffer no adverse consequences. But if you violate your duties, beneficiaries or creditors can go to court and seek to void (cancel) actions that you've taken. The court may also remove you as executor and put someone else in your place. You will be required to reimburse the estate for any losses caused by your recklessness or dishonesty.

IF YOU'RE SERVING WITH A CORPORATE COTRUSTEE

If you're a cotrustee with a trust company or bank, take advantage of its staff's expertise. You should be able to get help with investment decisions, accounting, tax returns and planning, real estate, small businesses, and record keeping. The institution may also offer some useful services you might not have thought of—for example, a bank might lock away valuables in its vault without charging the estate an extra fee.

People at the financial institution should be thoroughly familiar with your state's rules about permissible investments of estate property. They may even have their own investment vehicles; many states let corporate fiduciaries create their own funds in which assets can be invested, allowing executors to diversify the estate's investments without increasing risk to an unacceptable level.

1. Put the Estate First

The key to avoiding personal liability while serving as an executor is to stay away from any action from which you personally profit. Instead, you must act in the interests of the creditors and beneficiaries.

You may never, for example, sell yourself estate property. You should sell an asset only when doing so is in the best interests of the estate, and if you do sell an asset, your job is to get the highest price. If you're the buyer, too, then obviously you have a conflict of interest.

You also should never lend yourself money from the estate. Even if you know you'll pay back the loan quickly—even if you do in fact pay back the loan quickly, with interest—it is strictly forbidden.

Similarly, you may not make a deal that benefits someone to whom you are closely related—your spouse, children, or other very close relatives (or their spouses). The law treats these deals just the same as ones that involve you directly.

If you are entitled to pay yourself for serving as executor, document exactly what the payments are for and be prepared to explain why the amounts are justified by the amount of work you've put in.

2. Keep Estate Assets Separate From Your Own

It's never okay to mix estate assets with your own. All income generated by estate property should go into the estate checking account (see Section C, below), not your personal account.

3. Be Fair to All Beneficiaries

If more than one person inherits property, you must be impartial in your dealings with them.

Being impartial does not mean treating each beneficiary exactly the same. But there is room for charges of favoritism if you give one beneficiary his property more quickly than another without a good reason, or violate one beneficiary's privacy by discussing confidential matters with another.

To prevent challenges from unhappy beneficiaries, you will want to do two things. First, have good reasons for any distribution you make, and second, write down those reasons. (For more about distributing money to or for the beneficiaries, see Chapter 18.)

4. Don't Take Risks

When it comes to managing property and investments, you must act with prudence, which means reasonable skill and caution. The emphasis is on caution: You should be careful with estate money and absolutely stay away from risky investments. Your job is to not lose money. Even if you would invest your own money aggressively, you must apply a more cautious standard to estate money. You should not try to produce the most possible gain—that strategy entails unacceptable risks. (For more on how to manage cash, stocks, and other investments in the estate, see Section E, below.)

5. Follow the Will's Instructions

A typical will doesn't contain a lot of specific orders. Instead, it grants you, as executor, a long list of powers. For example, you'll probably have authority to hire lawyers and other experts, to pay debts, to sell property, and so on.

But if the will does contain any instructions, you must follow them. For example, if it directs you to sell stocks as soon as possible, you must do so—even if you think the price might improve if you were to wait a month or two. If, however, you think that following the will's directions would definitely cause an unnecessary loss to the estate, you can ask the probate court for permission to chart a different course.

B. Keeping Good Records

Wrapping up an estate involves a million details, and it's impossible to remember everything. Keeping careful records both of financial matters and of decisions you make will make your life much easier.

Just how detailed you need to be depends on your particular circumstances, both financial and familial. If you're the only beneficiary or you are in a small, close-knit family and you aren't worried about arguments and second-guessing, then don't worry about an elaborate system of formal record keeping. But if you think someone may be looking over your shoulder just waiting to criticize, take more pains to be thorough.

You probably have a good idea of what financial records to keep. Obviously, you need complete checkbook entries for checks written and amounts deposited. (See Section C, below.) If you can't fit enough information in the check register, use a ledger book or a simple computer program.

Keep all documents relating to the sale or distribution of assets—for example, bids, bills of sale, and receipts. It's also important to keep copies of all correspondence with banks, insurance companies, government agencies, other institutions, and beneficiaries.

Especially if you do something that may spark disagreement or resentment among beneficiaries, be sure to document it. For example, if you decide you must turn down a beneficiary's request for an early distribution of money, write yourself a little memo and put it in your files. Include exactly what the beneficiary wanted, when you discussed it, how you arrived at your decision, and how you communicated that decision to the beneficiary. Memories fade, and it may help family relationships if you have written evidence of what's gone on, created at the time the events occurred.

Getting your system up and running. For more on setting up a record-keeping system, see Chapter 4.

SOME PAPERS TO KEEP

- Bills
- Correspondence about the estate or trust (letters to and from beneficiaries, for example)
- Tax returns
- Check registers
- Canceled checks (if the bank provides them)
- Anything from the IRS
- Insurance policies
- Receipts from recipients of trust money
- Reports to beneficiaries
- Statements from all accounts

If you pay yourself, keep extra-good records. If you use estate or trust funds to compensate yourself for serving as executor or trustee, write down the amounts, dates, and why each payment is justified.

C. Setting Up an Estate or Trust Bank Account

Once you have been appointed executor by the probate court or taken on the job of trustee, you'll probably want to open a bank account in the name of the estate or trust. Usually, an account for an estate is registered this way, or something similar: "Estate of Gerald S. Smith, Deceased, Pamela S. Smith, executor."

Watch the fees. If you incur bank fees because of your own carelessness—an overdraft charge, for example—you'll be personally responsible.

1. What Kind of Account to Open

You'll want an account that allows you to write checks, so you can pay the deceased person's final bills and court costs and eventually distribute monetary gifts to beneficiaries. Which kind of account is right for you depends on your circumstances.

During a typical probate, which lasts less than a year, a basic checking account will work. You can deposit any estate income into it and use the funds to pay debts and expenses. Especially if a significant amount of money is involved, try to find an account that pays at least a small amount of interest.

For a simple living trust, which you'll wind up in a few weeks or a few months, you may not even need to open a separate account. There may already be a bank account in the deceased person's name as trustee of the trust. If so, you should be able to take over its control by virtue of your authority as the new trustee.

If the trust will last for years, as may be the case with AB or children's trusts, you'll definitely need an account for the trust. A checking account might work, but it may be a better idea to set up a single account that can handle both investments and cash. For example, investment companies such as Fidelity, Charles Schwab, Vanguard, and others offer combined brokerage and cash accounts that let you write checks. Everything shows up on one statement, which greatly simplifies your record keeping. The deceased person may even have one of these accounts already—in which case you can reregister the account in your name as trustee. (See Chapters 20 and 21.)

Don't open an out-of-state account. If you live in a different state than the deceased person did, you may be tempted to open an estate account close to you instead of where the person lived. Don't do it. If the estate earns income in your state, you may have to file a state tax return for that state, too.

2. Getting a Taxpayer ID Number From the IRS

You'll need a taxpayer ID number to open any bank or investment account, because the estate or trust is itself a taxpayer. To get an ID number, fill out and send to the IRS a simple form with a confusing title: IRS Form SS-4, *Application for Employer Identification Number*. Obviously, you're not an employer, but nevertheless this is the form you need. You can get a copy from Social Security offices, post offices, or the IRS website at www.irs.gov. After you send in the form, you should get your ID number (EIN) back in about four weeks. You can also file the form electronically through the IRS website.

To get the number more quickly, fill in the form and then call the IRS. (Phone numbers are listed on the back of the form.) It will assign a number over the phone that you can use immediately. You'll still need to write that number on the SS-4 form and mail or fax it to the IRS.

3. Using the Account

Once you've opened the account, transfer the funds from all the deceased person's bank accounts to it. (But don't touch payable-on-death accounts, which go directly to the named POD beneficiary and are not part of the estate, or joint tenancy accounts, which belong to the surviving joint owner.) Also deposit all income you receive on behalf of the deceased person or that is generated by estate assets—stock dividends or rental income from an apartment building, for example.

You can use the money you deposit to pay debts, taxes, and expenses of administration—such as probate court filing fees, and lawyer or other professional fees. How to handle those issues is discussed in Chapters 11 and 18.

Of course, you must keep good records of every transaction. When you deposit money, note the amount, date, and source in the checkbook. (If there's not enough room, keep a separate ledger on paper or computer.) When you write a check, put down the amount, date, recipient's name, and purpose.

If extra money—more than you'll need for expenses over the next few months—starts piling up in the account, you should probably transfer the surplus to a federally insured interest-bearing account or safe investments such as short-term government obligations. (Section E, below discusses your duty to stay away from investments that are at all risky.) Any new accounts you open should, of course, be held in the name of the estate or trust.

Never mix personal and estate funds. If you ever find it absolutely necessary to pay expenses with personal funds and then reimburse yourself from estate or trust assets, keep meticulous records. For example, say you find yourself at the court clerk's office without the estate checkbook and need to pay a fee. If you write a check from your personal account, be sure to get a receipt and put it in your files. And when you reimburse yourself from the estate account, note exactly why.

D. Keeping Tangible Assets Safe

What you need to do to keep estate or trust property safe depends on the kind of property—and people—you're dealing with. Again, if you're the only beneficiary, or there are just a few and you all get along, you can be a little more relaxed. But if you're handling a large estate with lots of beneficiaries, you'll need to be more businesslike.

Different assets require different security measures. Obviously, you take care of an art collection differently than you do a boat or a vacation home. The important thing is to take prompt, appropriate steps to protect the property, whatever it is.

Rent space if you really need it. You must take good care of physical objects—don't store an antique upholstered chair in a musty garage, for example. If you've got a houseful of physical objects that you need to secure, you may decide that you need to keep renting the deceased person's apartment to keep its contents safe, or rent a secure storage space. Either way, you can pay reasonable costs from estate assets.

1. The Deceased Person's Residence

If no one is living in a house or other real estate the deceased person owned, you need to maintain and protect it until it's sold or turned over to the inheritor.

IF THE DECEASED PERSON RENTED

If the deceased person was a tenant, notify the landlord promptly. (See Chapter 4.) Until the rental property is cleared out, however, you should take the precautions discussed in this section.

REAL ESTATE ESSENTIALS

☐ Pay property taxes
☐ Keep insurance in force
☐ Maintain the property
☐ Make mortgage payments
☐ Pay utility bills

Especially if probate is involved, taking care of real estate may entail significant expense to the estate. For example, depending on when bills and taxes were last paid, you may need to pay for homeowner's insurance, local property taxes and special assessments, utilities, and the mortgage. You also have a legal responsibility to keep the property in reasonably good shape—for example, it's your job to get a leaky roof repaired so the interior won't be damaged.

In addition, think about day-to-day security issues. If there's a regular gardening or lawnmowing service, keep it coming so the house looks lived-in. Put lights on a timer. Enlist the help of neighbors to watch for problems, and consider arranging for a housesitter. If you suspect that an untrustworthy person (even a relative) has keys to the property, you may want to change the locks.

If there's a vacation home somewhere, hire someone for a modest monthly fee to keep an eye on it and alert you to any problems or maintenance needs.

2. Rental Real Estate Owned by the Deceased Person

If the deceased person owned rental property, it's up to you to take steps to keep the landlording business running smoothly in the short term. If there's a property manager, take advantage of that arrangement. If tenants pay rent directly (not to a resident manager or management service), let them know what's happened and give them your address and phone number so they can keep the rent checks coming and let you know about problems or concerns.

If a tenant stops paying rent or violates other important terms of the lease, you should quickly begin the process of ending the tenancy—and evicting the tenant, if necessary. It's important to keep cash coming in, given that you must pay the mortgage, insurance, and other expenses associated with the property. If you must evict a tenant, you may need to consult a local lawyer who's familiar with the process.

Like running any business, it's no easy job to manage rental property, even on an interim basis. That's why you should do all you can to turn the property over to its eventual inheritor as quickly as legally possible or, if called for under the will or trust, sell it and distribute the proceeds.

3. Vehicles

If the estate includes vehicles, you'll need to keep insurance coverage up to date, and make loan payments if the cars aren't paid for, until they can be transferred to their new owners. You'll also have to keep vehicles parked in a secure place and if necessary, take care of routine maintenance.

It's usually smart to get vehicles out of an estate quickly. For starters, they're expensive to insure and maintain. And their value usually decreases constantly. If a beneficiary is happy to take possession of a car—and assume the related costs along with it—so much the better. And if nobody wants the car, it's to everyone's advantage to sell it before its value slips a little more.

Many states make it simple to transfer cars to the people who inherit them; you can contact your state's motor vehicles agency for information. (See Chapter 12.) And even if the estate goes through probate, you may be able to sell a car or give it to beneficiaries early. (See Chapter 18.)

4. Small Things

It's easy to lose track of watches, jewelry, and other small valuables. So put them in a small container, tape it shut securely, and label it across the tape. If possible, have someone with you when you secure these items, and sign and date the container. Then store it all in a secure place.

5. Cash

If you find a wad of cash when you're cleaning out the deceased person's house or apartment, deposit it in the estate checking account if you've opened one. If not, count the money, put it in an envelope, seal it, and write the amount across the flap—all in the presence of a witness, if possible. Then sign and date the envelope, and have the witness do the same. Finally, place the money in a safe place and let others in the family know you have done so. Don't deposit it in your own account—it's never okay to mix your property and the deceased person's.

E. Managing Cash Accounts and Investments

As mentioned above, your job is to preserve estate assets for the inheritors and creditors, not to make a killing on Wall Street. Be conservative.

1. Bank Accounts

If the deceased person had several bank accounts, close them and consolidate the funds into the account you open for the estate. (See Section C, above.) Your appointment as executor gives you the authority to do this. (Again, you don't have authority over payable-on-death accounts, which belong to the POD beneficiary without probate, or joint tenancy accounts, which belong to the surviving joint owner.)

⚠️ **Check for automatic payments before closing accounts.** Many people have arranged to have their regular monthly bills—for such things as utilities, mortgages, phone service, and credit cards—paid by automatic deductions from their bank accounts. Don't close an account without making other arrangements to pay these bills.

2. Securities

It's often best to simply leave stocks and bonds in the deceased person's name until you transfer them to the people who inherit them. You probably won't be managing the assets for more than a few months, anyway. Especially if the deceased person was a reasonably conservative and knowledgeable investor, don't worry about small daily ups and downs in value—after all, you are just sticking with the deceased person's plan.

If, however, the portfolio contains volatile stocks, you will want to sell them and put the proceeds in the estate bank account (see Section H, below) or into very safe investments, such as government bonds or insured bank accounts. Common sense should tell you that investing in small businesses or most individual stocks is too risky.

Your state's law, in fact, may restrict you to government bonds or to accounts insured by the FDIC. For example, unless the court allows otherwise, executors in Pennsylvania can invest estate funds only in:

- Federal or Pennsylvania obligations (bonds)

- an interest-bearing and FDIC-insured bank account (if there are any restrictions on withdrawal, they cannot last more than one year)

- an FDIC-insured savings account of a bank or savings and loan, or

- if the executor is a corporation (a trust company, for example), a money market mutual fund affiliated with the corporate executor.

(Pa. Stat. Ann., tit. 20, § 3316.)

If you receive dividend checks or checks for interest on bonds, deposit them into the estate bank account.

💡 **Resist all that free advice you get.** If you're in charge of a good-sized estate, you may get unsolicited investment advice from stockbrokers, financial advisors, and family members. Ignore them and stick to safe, conservative investments.

F. Paying Claims and Debts

As executor or trustee, it's your job to see that legitimate debts are paid from the deceased person's assets. You are not personally liable for the debts, unless you are the surviving spouse and state law makes you responsible. (See Section 5, below.) But if you're the surviving spouse, you probably don't have any new responsibilities—what were joint bills simply become your bills, and you pay them as you and your late spouse always did. For example, you'll keep paying the mortgage, utility bills, medical insurance premiums, credit card bills, and so on.

Don't overlook insurance that covers specific kinds of debts. Health insurance may cover the expenses of the deceased person's last illness. And if the deceased person was covered by credit or mortgage life insurance, be sure to take advantage of the policy proceeds to pay off credit cards or a mortgage. (Chapter 5 discusses claiming insurance policy proceeds.)

Trustees: Be cautious. If you're handling a simple living trust, you could probably transfer all the property within a few weeks. But you won't want to do that before you've paid all the bills, unless you are the only inheritor, you expect only routine bills, and you can simply pay them yourself as they come in. (See Chapter 19 for more on paying bills when you're the trustee of a simple living trust.)

1. Debts You Don't Need to Pay

In most cases, the biggest debts don't need to be paid off. Mortgages and car loans, for example, stay with the property that secures them—which means that whoever inherits the property also inherits the debt.

2. Formal and Informal Claims

You'll hear from creditors in one of two ways: informally or formally.

Most creditors' claims will be of the informal variety, just ordinary bills sent to the deceased person and forwarded to you as executor. The deceased person's will, trust, or state law gives you authority to go ahead and pay these bills without any formal process. (Or, if the deceased person had authorized automatic deductions from a bank account to pay regular bills each month, the bills may keep getting paid without any action on your part until you close the account.)

If the estate goes through probate, creditors have a certain period of time in which to file formal claims with the court. The deadline is usually a few months after creditors are notified of the death. (Chapter 18 discusses how you are required to notify creditors of their right to make claims; you must notify them either individually or by a legal notice published in the local newspaper.)

Information on taxes. Some of the biggest checks you may have to write are to the IRS and your state's revenue agency, for taxes. Chapter 11 discusses tax issues.

3. How to Pay Claims

When you pay a debt on behalf of the deceased person, use the estate checking account (or, if you're a trustee, an account held in the trust). Keep a record of all payments. (See Section B, above.)

4. If There Isn't Enough Cash

Even large estates may not contain a lot of liquid assets—that is, cash or assets than can be easily converted to cash, such as stocks. But you'll need cash to pay the bills, so you'll want to figure out, at least roughly, the total amount of the bills you expect to come in. Use the list below to help you.

If it looks like there aren't enough liquid assets to cover the debts, you'll have to consider selling assets to get the cash you need. And of course you should not distribute any property to beneficiaries unless you are positive that there will be enough left over for all debts and taxes.

POSSIBLE EXPENSES

- Expenses of the last illness

- Funeral costs

- Family allowance (court-ordered amount paid to the immediate family from estate funds, to help with living expenses)

- Ordinary bills (last credit card bills, for example)

- Income taxes (state and federal)

- Probate costs (lawyer, appraiser, CPA, court fees, and so on)

- Real estate expenses (mortgage, insurance, property tax, maintenance, repairs)

- Expenses of other assets (insurance, maintenance, storage—of vehicles, valuables, and so on)

- Estate taxes (state and federal—but most estates aren't large enough to owe these taxes)

---

5. If There Aren't Enough Assets

If the estate doesn't contain enough assets to pay all the debts, state law provides a priority list. High-priority debts—usually funeral expenses, the family allowance, lawyers' fees, court costs, and executor's fees—are paid in full, to the extent possible. Lower priority creditors, such as credit card issuers, may simply be out of luck.

a. Property That Creditors Can't Go After

Some property is legally out of creditors' reach. In many states, immediate family members are entitled to a "homestead" allowance (a certain amount of equity in the family home) and to a family allowance (a certain amount of cash or personal belongings in the estate). Creditors cannot grab property that's protected by state law in this way.

EXAMPLE: *When Noreen's husband died, he left her his half-interest in their house. Under the homestead law of her state, creditors cannot take the first $50,000 of Noreen's equity in the house. So even if creditors sued her, won, and forced the sale of the house, Noreen could keep $50,000 of her equity.*

Sometimes there are exceptions—for example, a homestead exemption may not apply if the creditor is the state, seeking reimbursement for medical services given to the deceased person.

Another protection, in some states, is that property that was held in joint tenancy may not be liable for the debts owed solely by the deceased person. This depends on state law.

EXAMPLE: *Bernie owed some business debts when he died. The debts were in his name alone, and under the law of his state his wife was not automatically liable for these debts. Bernie and his wife Brenda owned their house in joint tenancy, so when he died, Brenda automatically became the sole owner. Under the law of their state, creditors cannot go after the house for payment of Bernie's individual debts.*

b. Priority for Paying Debts

Every state's priority list is a little different, but to give you an idea of how these systems work, here is how claims are paid under Texas law.

TEXAS: PRIORITY OF CLAIMS

As an example of how states prioritize debts when there isn't enough money to go around, here is a summary of the order in which Texas executors are to pay claims:

a. Funeral expenses and expenses of last illness up to $5,000

b. Allowances made to the surviving spouse and children

c. Expenses of administration and the preservation and management of the estate

d. Other claims in the order of their classification. (Tex. Prob. Code § 320.)

There are eight classes of claims:

1. Funeral expenses and expenses of last sickness in a reasonable amount up to $15,000

2. Expenses of administration

3. Claims secured by liens (legal claims tied to specific assets), including tax liens, to the extent they can be paid out of the security (property to which the lien is attached) alone

4. Delinquent child support

5. Certain taxes (including penalties and interest) due to the state

6. Cost of confinement set by the Texas Department of Criminal Justice

7. Repayment of certain medical assistance payments made by the state for the deceased person

8. All other claims. (Tex. Prob. Code § 322.)

If there isn't enough to pay all the claims in one class, the creditors in that class are paid on a prorated basis.

If it looks like there are going to be more claims than money to pay them, see a probate lawyer. Although you may be reluctant to add another expense, you need detailed advice about property that your state may exempt from creditors' claims and what debts should be paid first.

6. Your Personal Obligation to Pay Debts

Executors often wonder whether they are personally responsible for the estate's debts. The answer is usually no. But there are two exceptions:

- If you caused the estate to lose money through your carelessness or dishonesty, you are personally responsible. (See Chapter 2.)

- If you are the surviving spouse, you may be responsible, depending on the circumstances.

A surviving spouse's responsibility depends both on the particular debt and the laws of the state. If the spouses incurred the debt together—for example, a mortgage on a jointly owned house or a joint credit card—then the surviving spouse is legally responsible for the entire debt if the estate does not have enough funds to pay it.

If the deceased spouse incurred the debt alone, then the surviving spouse's obligation depends on state law and the way property was owned. Property the surviving spouse owns alone does not usually have to be used to pay off debts the deceased spouse incurred alone. And property the couple owned in tenancy by the entirety (a method of holding title available to married couples in many states) automatically belongs to the survivor when one spouse dies. In most states, it does not have to be used to pay debts of the deceased person, except debts for which the property was pledged as security—for example, the mortgage.

EXAMPLE: *Joyce and her husband Don hold title to the house they own together as "tenants by the entirety." Don also owns his own business; Joyce is not a co-owner. When Don dies, he leaves behind several business debts.*

Because the house was owned in tenancy by the entirety, two things happen at Don's death. First, Joyce, as the surviving co-owner, automatically owns it (without probate). Second, the business creditors cannot go after the house for payment of the business debts, which Don incurred alone.

Joint tenancy property may get such protection, but it depends on state law. Generally, the half of the property that belonged to the deceased person must be used to pay debts.

In community property states, property that was community property, belonging to both spouses, must normally be used to pay creditors of the deceased spouse. But a surviving spouse's separate property is not subject to creditors' claims. (Chapter 8 discusses these methods of ownership and lists the states where they are available.)

Get help with these questions. As you can see, it's not always easy to sort out a surviving spouse's obligations. If you're not sure, and a significant amount of money is involved, see a lawyer.

G. Giving Property to Beneficiaries

If you're winding up a simple living trust or handling a small estate, you can probably quickly give the property to the beneficiary who inherits it. If you're taking the estate through probate, however, you may run into some restrictions—it depends on your state law and your authority under the will. (See the discussion of probate for small estates in Chapter 17 and regular probate in Chapter 18.)

At the very least, be sure that you keep control of the process of handing out assets and that people don't start helping themselves. As discussed in Chapter 3, you cannot let relatives or friends—even perfectly well-meaning ones—simply walk away with property that belonged to the deceased person. Even if they swear the item was promised to them, just say no—or at least "not yet."

If they pressure you, assert your authority as executor and explain that you have a responsibility to keep things as they are until you are legally permitted to distribute property. Make it clear that people will get everything that was left to them—just not this minute. It may make people feel better to know that no one else is getting anything now, either. If necessary, have a family meeting to explain your legal duty to do things according to the book.

H. Selling Property

As mentioned earlier, you may want to get rid of some estate or trust property quickly, or you may need to sell assets to raise cash. How easy it is to do either of these things depends on whether or not you're going through probate.

If you're wrapping up a simple living trust, there should be no problem with selling assets—you just have to be sure that you have enough property left to pay debts and taxes, and then you can transfer everything else to the inheritors. If you're going through probate, however, there will be rules about what you can do and when.

1. Why to Sell Property

There are a few common situations in which you'll want to sell or give away assets.

Property is going down in value. If certain assets are falling in value or are expensive to maintain, you'll want to sell them quickly to minimize losses. Cars and boats are common examples, because their value decreases over time, and it costs money to insure, store, and maintain them. The same is true if the deceased person owned a farm or business that no longer needs certain valuable equipment—if you don't sell it quickly, you'll just end up paying for insurance and upkeep until you eventually do sell it for less.

Investments are too volatile. You shouldn't keep risky investments; sell them and put the money in something safe. (See Section E, above.)

You need cash to pay the deceased person's debts. When you add up the major expenses for which the estate is responsible (see Section F, above), you may find that although the estate contains considerable valuable property, there isn't enough cash to cover the bills.

Beneficiaries don't want to share ownership. If two or more beneficiaries have been left an asset to share, they may want you to sell it and divide the proceeds among them. For example, two children might not want to own fractional shares of their parents' house or cars, and might prefer you to handle the sale. (The best approach, though, is usually to transfer the asset to the inheritors and let them sell it.)

2. How to Sell Property

If you're the only beneficiary, selling estate property shouldn't be a problem; there's no one to complain about it if you carefully account for the proceeds and use them to pay valid debts. But if other beneficiaries are involved, and you want to sell estate property during a regular or small estate probate proceeding, here are some of the issues you may have to consider:

- Does the will tell you which assets to sell if you need to raise cash to pay debts?

- If the will doesn't give you any guid-ance, does state law? For example, it may say that you must first sell assets that were not specifically left to a beneficiary. (To get the specific rules in your state, you'll need to research the law or ask a lawyer; see Chapter 22.)

- Do you have authority to sell, or do you need to get prior permission from the probate court? If you're using "small estate" procedures (see Chapter 17) or conducting a regular probate with power to proceed under the Independent Administration of Estates Act (see Chapter 18), you probably don't need court approval or supervision to sell property.

- If the property was specifically left to someone, you should get that beneficiary's written permission to sell it—or if that's impossible, a probate court order authorizing you to make the sale.

- Even if you don't need court permission, you may need to notify (in writing) all interested parties before you sell, to give them a chance to object. This is espe-cially likely if you want to sell real estate.

I. Handling a Business

If the deceased person owned a business, or a part-interest in one, your responsibilities are greatly increased. You will probably need expert help to assess the value of the business and, unless you're already involved in running it, to operate it even for the short term.

Most executors have no interest or expertise in running a business owned by the deceased person. You'll either want to sell it promptly (or if it was co-owned, sell the deceased person's interest in it) or turn it over to whoever inherits it as quickly as possible. (If a good manager is already in place, you may be able to increase that person's compensation in exchange for taking on extra responsibilities.) Either way, you'll probably have to assume ultimate responsibility for its operation in the meantime.

If the deceased person owned the business with other people, you will have to work closely with them. Start by looking for any agreements among the owners that direct what is to happen when one co-owner dies. Look for anything called a co-ownership, management, shareholders', members', partnership or buy-out (buy-sell) agreement. Often, such an agreement gives a surviving co-owner the right to buy the deceased person's share, either from the estate or the inheritor. Many agreements also contain a method for appraising the business and making buyout payments.

Get a hard-eyed accountant to help you value the business and strike a good deal with co-owners. A well-intentioned but inexperienced executor can get fleeced.

1. Sole Proprietorship

If the business was a sole proprietorship, owned entirely by the deceased person, your threshold question is whether to close the business immediately or to keep operating it until you can turn it over to inheritors. The deceased person's will may instruct you; if it doesn't, you'll have to decide what's in the best interests of the estate and beneficiaries. Do what you can, of course, to follow the wishes of the deceased person—did he or she expect the business to be sold, or harbor a deep desire to see it continue? Also consider the feelings of the beneficiary. If you know that the inheritor will quickly sell the business, there is probably no point in doing the work it takes to keep it going.

Your ultimate duty is to the beneficiaries and creditors of the estate. If you don't think you can make a profit by continuing the business, then obviously you should close it. And if the estate needs cash to pay debts or taxes, you may need to sell the business (or at least its valuable assets) to raise the necessary liquid assets—even if you'd prefer to keep it operating.

If you are already active in the business, you'll know how to run it during probate proceedings. But if not, you'll have a long list of things to do. Three of the most important are:

- keeping a good manager or, if the deceased person ran the business alone, finding one

- understanding how money flows in and out of the business, so you'll be able to spot trouble coming if receipts go down or expenses go up, and

- making sure all business taxes (especially payroll taxes, if the business has employees) are paid on time.

If the business produces a lot of income, you'll want to consult a lawyer.

2. Partnership

If the business was a partnership, the death of one partner dissolves the partnership unless a partnership agreement provides to the contrary. An agreement may, for example, state that the partnership may continue, but that the surviving partners can buy the deceased partner's share at a certain price or after an appraisal establishes a value.

If the partnership does dissolve, the surviving partners are responsible for winding up the partnership's affairs. They must give you, as executor, the deceased person's remaining share, along with an accounting.

3. Limited Liability Company

The LLC's operating agreement or a separate buy-sell agreement should dictate what can happen when a member-owner dies. For example, it may spell out who can buy the member's share of the business (other LLC members or outsiders), at what price, and on what payment terms. In some states, surviving members must vote on whether or not to continue the LLC. If they don't want to go forward, the LLC will be dissolved, and the surviving members must deliver the deceased partner's share of the company assets to you.

4. Closely Held Corporation

When one co-owner of a privately owned corporation dies, his or her shares may be left to a beneficiary in a will or trust. But until ownership of the stock is formally transferred, you, as executor, may have to make decisions in place of the deceased owner.

Despite what the will or trust says, the stock may not even pass to the beneficiary. A shareholders' agreement (buy-sell agreement) may give the surviving co-owners certain rights. For example, the surviving shareholders may be entitled to buy the deceased owner's stock at an agreed-upon price.

You may want to sell the deceased person's shares of the corporation, but find that you can't—obviously there is no public market for shares of a small privately held corporation. In that case, you and the other owners might explore selling or liquidating the business. If there is no shareholders' agreement and the other shareholders are uncooperative, you'll have to look to the corporation's bylaws or to state law to determine how to proceed.

Get help sorting out the documents. If you are confused by apparently contradictory language in a will or trust, and a shareholders' agreement, immediately see a lawyer specializing in estate problems. ∎

CHAPTER 10

Caring for Children and Their Property

A death that comes at the end of a long and good life can be a great loss for those left behind, but it's one that most people know almost instinctively how to deal with, given time to grieve. But when a young or middle-aged person dies and leaves young children, there are a multitude of other emotions and concerns, some of them sure to be quite painful. The most pressing issue is likely to be arranging for the children's immediate care.

Questions that are less emotional, but still complicated, can come up when a young person inherits property. The law requires that there must almost always be an adult in charge of it—but who, and how does that person get legal authority? And if the person who's raising the child doesn't control the child's property, how will the two work together for the child's benefit?

This chapter discusses some of the legal and practical issues that may arise when a death leaves young children without parents, or when a young person inherits a substantial amount of property.

A. Immediate Concerns

As executor, you are in charge of carrying out the terms of the deceased person's will. Unless both parents are unavailable and the will names you as the deceased person's choice for personal guardian, you have no legal responsibility to personally care for young children. But because you are almost surely a close relative or friend, you may well find yourself helping to work out the details of their care.

Unless the death was sudden and unexpected, the deceased parent probably arranged for someone to care for his or her young children. Even before the death, a close relative or friend may have already stepped in and begun providing care. If no plans were made, relatives, friends, or neighbors usually step forward quickly to care for children in an emergency. All should keep in mind that having just one or two people who devote themselves to the children at this traumatic time—rather than shuttling them from person to person—can make things easier on the children.

Steer people in the right direction if necessary. In almost all families, people pull together at a time of grief; disagreements about custody of a child, if any, typically arise later. But if you sense conflict brewing, check the deceased parent's will to see who it names as the child's personal guardian. Then let people know what the deceased parent thought best for the child—and encourage them to honor that wish.

In the days and weeks just after the death, legal arrangements about child custody and property are not paramount. The child just needs someone to assume responsibility for daycare or school, health care, sports, piano lessons, and all the other ordinary, day-to-day parts of childhood. Teachers, doctors, and other people will likely be understanding about legal formalities until the new guardian has time to get authority from a court.

LETTING CHILDREN ATTEND A PARENT'S FUNERAL

Relatives sometimes keep young children away from a parent's funeral or memorial service. They act from the best of motives: an attempt to spare the children an experience that will cause them pain or that they will not understand. But what is best for the child?

There is no one right answer for all families. But generally, attending an event that honors a parent and marks his or her passing can help children in much the same way it helps adults. It may make it easier for the child to talk about or ask questions about the death; it may help the child say goodbye and accept that the parent is really not coming back. And it may forestall future resentment. A child who is not allowed to attend a parent's funeral may later feel unfairly deprived of the chance to participate in an event of intense emotion and significance.

Information for grieving children and families. The Barr-Harris Children's Grief Center website, www.barrharris.org, offers information you may find helpful and contains links to related websites. You can also contact the center at 122 S. Michigan Avenue, Suite 1300, Chicago, IL 60603, 312-922-7474.

B. Raising a Child

A personal guardian takes the place (however imperfectly) of a parent. A guardian provides basic needs—food, shelter, schooling, and health care—and ideally, offers plenty of those other essentials, love and guidance.

Usually, the personal guardian is chosen by the deceased parent and named in the parent's will. If there's no will, or if it doesn't name someone, a court will choose the guardian.

Typically, the personal guardian also handles financial matters for the child. That arrangement isn't legally required, however. The deceased parent's will or trust, or a court, may name another adult to manage property the child inherits. This is particularly likely if the deceased person left a large estate and thought the personal guardian wasn't financially experienced enough to manage it. (See Section C, below.)

KINDS OF GUARDIANS

You may hear the term "guardian" used in at least two different ways:

Personal guardian: The person who has been appointed by a court to raise a child, including making decisions about the child's physical, medical, and educational needs. Sometimes this person is called the "guardian of the person."

Property guardian: Someone who is given authority by a court to manage a child's property. The property guardian may also be called the "guardian of the estate." (Property guardians are discussed in Section C, below.)

One or both of these guardians may be needed in any given situation. Often, but not always, the same person fills both roles.

1. Is a Personal Guardian Necessary?

Only if a child has been orphaned—left without any parent able to raise him or her—must a court appoint someone to serve as the child's legal guardian.

a. If There's a Surviving Parent

If a child has one surviving parent, normally that parent takes over child-rearing responsibilities. This is true even if the deceased parent's will names someone else to serve as guardian or expresses a wish that the surviving parent not take custody of the child.

EXAMPLE: *Brian and Natalie divorced three years ago, and Brian took primary custody of their two children. In his will, Brian named his sister as his choice for a personal guardian for the children if one were ever needed.*

When Brian dies in an accident, Natalie is awarded custody of the children over the objections of Brian's sister and other family members, who believe Natalie has never been a good mother.

Exceptions to this general rule are made only if the court concludes that there is some compelling reason to give custody of the child to someone other than the surviving parent. For example, a parent who is in jail, has failed to support or contact the child for a long time, or has a serious drug problem, would not be a suitable parent. But a person doesn't lose parental rights just because he or she is poor, ill, or unpopular with other family members.

b. If Another Adult Takes Over Informally

Some adults raise children (often their grandchildren) without getting a formal guardianship. Eventually, though, they will probably run into problems enrolling the child in school, consenting to nonemergency medical care, or getting government benefits for the child. These problems can be solved by going to court and getting legal authority to raise the child.

2. How to Get a Guardian Appointed

A guardianship proceeding involves going to court and asking to be appointed as a child's personal guardian. It's usually an uncontested proceeding, with few court appearances. How long it takes to file all the paperwork and get a decision from the judge depends on the court, but it shouldn't take more than a few months.

To start the process, the person who wants to be guardian—usually, the person nominated in the deceased parent's will or a close relative if there's no will—files a request with a local court. In most places, the court that handles probate—for example, the Superior Court or the Surrogate's Court—handles guardianships as well. You may be able to get fill-in-the-blanks forms and instructions from the court, either on paper or from the court's website.

There will be a fee for filing the request form; the amount varies from court to court. A prospective guardian who can't afford to pay it can ask that the fee be waived. Most courts have a procedure to follow, requiring the person asking for a fee waiver to show proof that paying the fee would be a hardship.

When appointing a guardian, the court gives substantial weight to the deceased person's wishes, but its duty is to determine what is in the best interests of the child. To this end, the court will probably dispatch a social worker to perform a home study of the prospective guardian. That process will involve home visits from the social worker and interviews with the prospective guardian, other family members, and the child, too, if he or she is old enough. The investigator then makes a recommendation to the judge.

As part of the process, the court may require that relatives be notified of the pending request and may hold a brief court hearing. The hearing will probably be a formality unless a relative contests the guardianship request for some reason.

Help for California readers. *The Guardianship Book for California: How to Become a Child's Legal Guardian*, by Lisa Goldoftas and David Brown (Nolo), contains all the forms and instructions necessary to get a legal guardianship in California without a lawyer.

3. Who Serves as Guardian

If the deceased parent didn't indicate a preference for who should serve as personal guardian, or if the person nominated in the will can't serve, the judge must pick someone. Courts generally like to pick blood relatives, but of course circumstances affect these decisions. The court must always act in the best interests of the child.

EXAMPLE: *Sandra, a single mother, dies after a long illness, leaving behind her eight-year-old son Ryan. Not having a lot of property, Sandra didn't make a will, and so there's no record of her choosing anyone to be Ryan's personal guardian.*

Ryan's father left the family long ago and has had almost no contact with them since; no one is even sure where he lives now. Sandra's sister Barbara lives nearby, but has three young children of her own. During Sandra's illness, Ryan spent a lot of time with the family's next-door neighbors, a couple named Terri and Dave, who have two teenage children. The whole family grew to love Ryan, he's comfortable with them, and Terri and Dave are willing to become his guardians.

Sandra's sister is at first reluctant to think of Ryan living with people who aren't part of the family. She and Sandra didn't spend much time discussing what would happen to Ryan, because the subject always seemed too painful to Sandra. Although Barbara can hardly imagine taking on another child—especially a child dealing with the trauma of losing the only parent he's ever really known—she feels that it's her duty to take him in.

But by spending time with Terri and Dave, Barbara sees how much they genuinely care about Ryan. She also sees that they have the time and resources to devote to him. Eventually, after talking to Ryan about it, she concludes that Ryan would be better off living with Terri, Dave, and their children. Everyone agrees that Barbara and her family should continue to be a big part of Ryan's life, but that Terri and Dave should have legal guardianship. The court, after conducting its own inquiry into the situation, agrees.

If there's no obvious candidate to be the personal guardian, concerned family members should get together and discuss the matter. After all, relatives and close friends should know—better than a judge who is a stranger to the family—what would be best for the children.

Don't forget to take the child's wishes into account. Children who are 14 or older can actually challenge a judge's decision on their own, but even younger children should be consulted by both family members and the judge. If family members and the child agree on a guardian, there should be no reason for a judge not to go along with the consensus.

If, however, not everyone can agree about who should be appointed as guardian, it's always best to try to work out a solution out of court. A neutral mediator who is trained to help people solve such problems can be a big help; the court should be able to recommend someone. But if you can't work something out, you'll definitely need a lawyer to help you ensure the best result for the child.

4. Court Supervision of the Guardian

The court supervises the guardian for as long as the guardianship lasts, but the amount of court involvement varies greatly depending on the situation and state law. The guardian may, for example, be required to file periodic reports with a court showing how much money was received for the child and how it was spent. Any funds the guardian receives for the child must, of course, be used for that child's benefit. There may be a limit on

expenditures that can be made without court approval—so, for example, if the guardian wants to use some of child's money for an expensive computer or two weeks at a pricey summer camp, advance court approval may be required.

If the guardian moves, he or she will probably be required to notify the court. Moving a child out of state generally requires prior court permission.

Except for these requirements, a guardian is treated much like a parent when it comes to day-to-day matters. In other words, no one will be looking over the guardian's shoulder unless a serious problem—trouble at school, criminal behavior, or something along those lines—crops up.

5. When the Guardianship Ends

Ordinarily, a guardianship continues until the child reaches legal adulthood—age 18 in most states. A judge could decide to end a guardianship sooner, if it appeared that it were no longer necessary, but that would be unusual. A guardianship would also end if the child became "emancipated"—that is, attained the legal status of an adult before age 18. That happens most often when a minor gets married or joins the military.

A personal guardian who wants to step down from the post for some reason must notify the court. The guardianship appointment process will then start over again, and the judge will choose another family member or friend to take over.

C. Managing a Child's Property

If any children younger than 18 inherit a significant amount of property from an estate or trust you're handling, you must turn that property over to the adult who has the legal authority and responsibility to watch over it. That adult may or may not be the child's parent.

1. Is an Adult Property Manager Necessary?

Minor children—those under age 18—can own money and other property. But if they own very much, the law requires that an adult manage it for them.

When is formal management needed? It depends on state law and on your particular situation. If a minor inherits less than a few thousand dollars, most states allow the parents to take charge of it without any court supervision or formal appointment. And if the young person inherits tangible objects—for example, a set of china or some heirlooms—then usually the parents simply take possession of the items, and there is no need for ongoing management. But if a minor inherits property that has title (ownership) documents—land, bank accounts, or stocks, for instance—then the adult in charge of that property must have authorization from a will, trust, or court. The institutions or agencies that safeguard property records or keep custody of the property—title companies, banks, and brokers, for example—will insist on it.

2. Kinds of Property Managers

To find out whether an adult already has legal authority to control a minor beneficiary's property, look at the document that left the property—the will, trust, or life insurance policy, for example. The person who left the property to the child will likely have arranged for someone to manage it.

Check the document to see whether it appoints someone as:

- a "custodian" under a state law called the Uniform Transfers to Minors Act (it will read something like this: "I leave $10,000 to Theresa Smith, as custodian for Allison J. Raske under the Wisconsin Uniform Transfers to Minors Act"), or

- the trustee of a child's trust.

If a custodian or trustee has been appointed, that person can take control of the property the child inherits and manage it in the child's best interests. If not, you, as executor, may be able to appoint a custodian yourself or you may need to get a court to appoint someone to take responsibility for the inherited property. A court-appointed property manager is commonly called a property guardian or guardian of the estate.

This section discusses these three ways—as custodian, trustee, or property guardian—in which an adult can exercise legal authority over a minor's money.

WHO HAS AUTHORITY OVER PROPERTY A YOUNG PERSON INHERITS

Title	Appointed by:	Legal authority comes from:
Custodian	Deceased person (in will, trust, or life insurance policy) or executor	Uniform Transfers to Minors Act, as enacted by state
Trustee	Deceased person (in will, trust, or life insurance policy)	Trust document
Property guardian	Court (but may have been named in the deceased person's will)	State law

3. General Legal Duties of the Property Manager

Custodians, trustees, and property guardians basically all have the same legal responsibilities. They must always manage and spend a child's property honestly and prudently, and in the best interest of the young person. They must keep good records, accounting for all money that is invested or spent. Sound familiar? It's much like being an executor— you're in charge of someone else's money and must be extremely careful with it.

The adult's specific duties and powers are set out by state law or in the document that grants the legal authority. For custodians and property guardians, it's state law; for trustees, the trust document itself. When a property manager's authority expires (under the terms of a trust document or state law), the manager must turn over what's left to the beneficiary. Usually, management lasts until the beneficiary reaches an age from 18 to 35.

Especially if the amount of property being managed is large or if the management lasts several years, the manager will probably want help from a tax professional or investment adviser. As long as the expense is reasonable and appropriate, the bills can be paid from the child's property.

EXAMPLE: *Susan has been appointed both the personal guardian and property guardian of her friend's daughter Alicia. Susan feels comfortable raising Alicia, but isn't so sure about how to invest the considerable sum of money Alicia inherited when her mother died. Susan also worries that Alicia's grandparents don't trust her money management skills; they've hinted more than once that it might be best for them to take over.*

Susan consults an investment adviser who doesn't sell investment products and so can give her objective advice on how to invest Alicia's money safely and use it to pay for Alicia's expenses. The adviser's recommendations, given in a short written report, also reassure Alicia's grandparents that their granddaughter's inheritance is in safe hands.

4. Custodians Under the UTMA

When it comes to managing property for a young person, a custodianship is an extremely useful alternative to a trust.

a. General Features of a Custodianship

Custodians get their authority from a law called the Uniform Transfers to Minors Act (UTMA), which has been adopted by every state but South Carolina and Vermont.

Someone who serves as an UTMA custodian has the right to collect, hold, manage, invest, and reinvest the young person's property. The custodian must act honestly and prudently, and can spend as much of the property "as the custodian considers advisable for the use and benefit of the minor." None of these actions require a court's approval. The custodian must, however, keep good records so that tax returns can be filed on the minor's behalf.

A separate custodianship must be set up for each child. In other words, a custodian cannot pool assets and manage them for two children. And there can be only one custodian for one child; cocustodians aren't allowed. Courts do not appoint or supervise a custodian.

b. Custodians Named by the Deceased Person

Many grandparents and parents who leave money to children in a will or trust, or through a life insurance policy, name a custodian to manage the property for the minor beneficiary.

The custodianship lasts until the child reaches the age specified by state law—21 in most states. In a number of states, however,

people leaving property to minors have some flexibility about the ending date and can specify any age from 18 to 25. If no age is specified, then in most states the custodianship ends at the youngest age in the allowed range. For example, a custodianship under the Pennsylvania UTMA lasts until the minor turns 21 unless the person who left the property specified a later age, up to 25. (You can find your state's rule in the appendix.)

EXAMPLE: *George leaves property to his grandson Jeremy, appointing Jeremy's mother as custodian. Georges's will reads: "All property left in this will to Jeremy Robertson shall be given to Jean Whitmeer as custodian under the Tennessee Uniform Transfers to Minors Act until Jeremy reaches age 25."*

When the custodianship ends, the custodian gives any remaining money to the beneficiary, who is now legally old enough to control it without help.

c. Custodians Named by the Executor

Even if the deceased person didn't name a custodian under the UTMA, it may not be too late. If you need to transfer property to a minor, but there is no custodian or trustee, the UTMA gives you, as executor, the power to appoint a custodian. It's in many ways preferable to going to court and getting a property manager appointed.

In most states, the UTMA gives an executor authority to transfer a minor's property to an adult or trust company as custodian if there is no will, or if the will or trust does not authorize it. (It can't, however, be done if the will actually forbids it—something that's exceedingly unlikely.) The executor must consider the action to be in the best interest of the minor, and if the property is worth more than a certain amount—$10,000 in most states—the probate court must approve the transfer. Each state's rule is summarized in the appendix.

When an executor appoints a custodian, many states provide that the custodianship ends when the minor reaches legal adulthood (the "age of majority"). In most states, that's 18. A custodianship commonly lasts longer when the deceased person appointed the custodian. (See Subsection a, just above.)

5. Trustees of Children's Trusts

A trust for children can be set up in a will or as part of a living trust. People usually use trusts if they're leaving a young beneficiary a lot of money or other property and want management to continue longer than is allowed under the UTMA. The trustee manages the property for the child or children, following the terms of the trust document.

Information for trustees. Chapter 20 is devoted entirely to the topic of serving as trustee of a child's trust.

6. Property Guardians and Other Court-Ordered Solutions

If no management was set up for the property that children inherit—for example, if there was no will, and a child inherits under state law—

and you can't appoint a custodian under the UTMA, then you'll need to ask the probate court to prescribe some kind of management.

Usually, the court will appoint someone to serve as a property guardian for the child. In some states this person is called a "conservator" or a "guardian of the estate." As mentioned above, a court-appointed property guardian has the same basic duties as a custodian or trustee. The big difference is that the guardian must regularly report to the court on how the child's assets have been managed and spent.

There may, however, be other options:

- In some states (California, for one), the probate court has power to appoint a custodian under the UTMA (see Section 4, above) instead of a property guardian. (See Cal. Prob. Code § 3413.) This makes life much simpler for the person managing the property, because he or she won't have to keep reporting to the court about how assets are managed and spent for the child.

- The court may also direct that funds inherited by a child—for example, the proceeds of a life insurance policy—be placed in a "blocked" account at a bank. An adult is given limited authority over the funds and may withdraw them only with prior court permission.

Wills sometimes nominate someone to serve as property guardian. When the court chooses a property guardian or custodian, it will honor the deceased person's preference, if it is known, unless there is a good reason not to.

In most cases, the same person who serves as a child's personal guardian also manages property, either because the deceased parent chose the same person for both functions or because the court appoints the same person. But sometimes it's sensible to have two different people doing what are two very different jobs. (Section D, below, discusses what can happen when personal guardians clash with property managers.)

Typically, a property guardianship or other court-ordered arrangement lasts until the child reaches 18 or the assets are used up for the child's benefit. The guardian can then make a final accounting, distribute what's left of the property to the child, and ask the court to be released from his or her responsibilities.

D. Personal and Practical Issues

It is never easy to take over rearing a child who has been left without parents, but guardians draw upon sometimes unexpectedly large reservoirs of love, patience, and strength to do it. And although meeting the legal standards for managing a child's property can be exacting and time consuming, that can be done, too, with honest effort and perhaps some expert help.

The most stubborn problems often come from another direction: family members. Whether it's the child's schooling, religion, diet, friends, or after-school activities, everyone is likely to have an opinion. And most people would agree that up to a point, that can be good. Whether or not you believe that it takes a village to raise a child, no one can or should

raise a child in isolation. A network of concerned relatives and friends can be a wonderful thing.

But it can also grow oppressive. For instance, if you're in charge of a child's inheritance, you may come to believe that there just isn't enough money to provide everything the child needs. In that case, you make the best decisions you can. (If the money is in a trust, the trust document may give you some direction on how to set priorities.) Other relatives, not as familiar with the financial realities as you are, may not understand the difficulties or may second-guess your decisions. They may even tell the child you should be managing things differently.

There is no simple fix for these problems. One of the trickiest parts of being an executor is handling volatile emotional issues, and this is doubly true when children are involved. Tact, patience, and a willingness to really listen may turn out to be more valuable than any financial skills you possess. You may want to call on a family member everyone trusts and respects as an informal mediator to help you arrive at a workable solution.

Friction is especially likely to occur when one person has custody of a child and another controls the purse strings. It's crucial that the two adults work together well, always keeping the best interests of the child in the forefront. But that's sometimes easier said than done. It's a good idea if the two people meet regularly, first to map out a long-term plan (possibly with the help of a financial adviser) and then to check in with each other and see how it's working.

EXAMPLE: *Andrea is the personal guardian for her nephew Zachary, and her brother Peter is the custodian of Zachary's property. Peter is a cautious, skilled investor, and Andrea has no complaints about his management of the assets. But ever since he was cool to her requests for money to send Zachary to a summer camp that's a little pricey but seems perfectly suited to Zach's needs, she's beginning to suspect he's just plain cheap. Peter, for his part, worries that unless he puts the brakes on Andrea's spending, she'll burn through Zach's money before he reaches college age.*

Peter and Andrea decide to meet for a long talk at a restaurant, away from Zach and other family members. Andrea explains that she's trying hard to give Zach, who is struggling to adjust to the loss of his parents, confidence by finding him the ideal summer camp. Peter listens and then tells Andrea about his own concerns; he knows that Zach's parents would want him to have money enough to choose the right college when the time comes.

Talking face to face helps calm the resentments that had begun to build up. Both Andrea and Peter are reminded that they have the same goal: to do what's best for Zach. They end up agreeing on a budget for camps and other activities and decide that Andrea will discuss some alternatives with Zach before making a final decision about summer plans. And they agree to meet regularly to discuss little problems before they grow into big ones. ■

CHAPTER 11

Taxes

Death and taxes, the two great certainties of life (according to Benjamin Franklin), are often linked in our minds. But fortunately, tax problems are seldom a major concern after a death, and your job as executor probably won't entail any novel or complicated tax issues. Beneficiaries shouldn't run into any serious questions, either.

This chapter discusses the main issues and points the way to more help.

A. Overview

Before getting into the nitty-gritty of income and estate taxes, here's a quick look at the big picture.

1. Who Is Responsible for Filing Tax Returns

If the probate court appoints you executor, you are responsible for filing tax returns and paying tax bills on time.

If there's no official executor, whoever has taken responsibility for the deceased person's property is responsible for taxes, too. Usually, that's a relative who stands to inherit property or a friend who's agreed to wind up the deceased person's affairs.

If all the deceased person's property was left in trust, and there's no probate, taxes are the responsibility of the trustee. If there is both a trust and a will, the successor trustee and the executor should work together. The trust document may give instructions—for example, it may direct the trustee to pay certain amounts for certain taxes if the executor makes a request in writing.

2. Returns You May Need to File

The table below lists all the possible tax returns you might have to file. But don't get discouraged—it's unlikely that you'll actually need to file more than a few. Keep in mind, too, that expert tax help is readily available and can be paid for with estate assets.

Most executors must file income tax returns for the year in which the deceased person died. If the estate goes through probate and during that time receives income, you'll also need to file an income tax return for the estate itself.

Only if the estate is very large—more than $1.5 million for deaths in 2004—will you need to file a federal estate tax return. Whether or not a state estate tax return will be necessary depends on state law, but generally only large estates must file.

TAX RETURNS YOU MAY NEED TO FILE

Kind of Return	Required If:	Due Date
Final federal income tax return (for last months of the deceased person's life)	The deceased person received at least a minimum amount of income (set by federal law) in the last calendar year of life	April 15 of the year following the death
Final state income tax return (for last months of the deceased person's life)	The deceased person received at least a minimum amount of income (set by state law) in the last calendar year of life	April 15 of the year following the death
Federal income tax return for the estate	The estate receives more than a minimum amount of income (set by federal law)	April 15 (for previous calendar year)*
State income tax return for the estate	The estate receives more than a minimum amount of income (set by state law)	April 15 (for previous calendar year)*
Federal income tax return for a trust	There's a trust that receives at least a minimum amount of income (set by federal law)	April 15 (for previous calendar year)*
State income tax return for a trust	There's a trust that receives at least a minimum amount of income (set by state law)	Depends on state law
State inheritance tax returns	The state imposes inheritance tax (these returns are filed by those who inherit, not by the estate)	Depends on state law
Federal estate tax return	The amount of property left is very large	Nine months after death
State estate tax return	A federal estate tax return is required, OR the state imposes its own estate tax	Nine months after death

*Or, if the estate or trust chooses to use a noncalendar tax year, the 15th day of the fourth month after the end of the trust's taxable year.

Getting tax forms. You can get quick access to tax forms for all states and the federal government at the Federation of Tax Administrators' website, at www.taxadmin.org. You can also get IRS forms on the IRS site, www.irs.gov, or by calling 800-TAX-FORM (800-829-3676).

3. Where Does the Money Come From?

The money to pay taxes comes from what the deceased person left. You aren't responsible for paying the deceased person's taxes, unless you are the surviving spouse and you share responsibility for them. You may, however, incur personal liability if you don't fulfill your duty to file necessary returns on time and pay the tax due from estate funds, as discussed in the next section.

4. Your Personal Liability

If you don't file required tax returns or pay what's due, your neglect could cost you, in the form of penalties and interest. If you hire professionals to prepare the returns, you still have this personal responsibility; if the pros are late, it's your fault for not supervising them well enough.

Tax debts take priority over just about all other debts of the estate. So rule number one (and two and three, for that matter) is never pay significant amounts to other creditors or give estate property to beneficiaries unless you're sure the estate will have enough left to pay any tax due. If the estate comes up short, you could be personally liable for the tax bill, up to the amount you distributed to other creditors or beneficiaries. (Of course, you'll need to pay some routine bills such as utilities and mortgages, just to take care of the estate property—see Chapter 9.)

EXAMPLE 1: *Katherine is the executor of her mother's estate. She pays several large debts of the estate and hands out a large sum to an inheritor— and months later, is unpleasantly surprised to find that there isn't enough money left in the estate to pay her mother's final income tax bill. Because Katherine distributed more than the amount of the bill, she must now pay it out of her own pocket.*

EXAMPLE 2: *Bob is the executor of his aunt's estate. He forgets to file his aunt's last income tax return, and as a result is personally liable for the interest and penalties charged by the IRS. Paying the interest and penalties takes a sizeable chunk out of the money he inherits from his aunt.*

AVOIDING PERSONAL LIABILITY FOR ESTATE TAX

Fewer than 2% of estates owe federal estate tax. But if you think estate tax may be due, you can ask the IRS to tell you the amount. If you make this request before filing the estate tax return, the IRS must notify you within nine months after the return is filed. Once you pay the bill, you're off the hook. (IRC § 2204(a).)

---

5. Paying Taxes on Your Compensation

If you accept compensation for acting as an executor or trustee, you must include the amount as part of your own gross income at tax time. People who inherit much or all of the estate anyway commonly waive their right to take fees from the estate. (See Chapter 2, Section B.)

B. The Deceased Person's Income Tax: Form 1040

As the executor, it's your job to file the deceased person's final income tax returns for the year of death. You must file both state and federal (and local, if required) returns. If a joint return is filed, the surviving spouse shares this responsibility. (IRC § 6013(a).) Of course, the executor is often the surviving spouse.

If the deceased person regularly got help from a tax preparer, that person may be of invaluable help to you, too. So when you look through the deceased person's records, pay attention to the name of any tax service, lawyer, or accountant.

Missing tax returns. If you discover that the deceased person didn't file returns for previous years—not uncommon in cases of long illness—the job of filling in those gaps also falls to you. If you find yourself in this situation, get help from a tax professional.

More information. See IRS Publication 559, *Survivors, Executors, and Administrators.*

1. Is a Return Required?

If the deceased person received little income in his or her last year, you don't have to file income tax returns. The table below shows the cutoff amounts for federal income tax returns. These figures are adjusted annually. You can get the current amounts from the IRS website (www.irs.gov) and the your state's taxing authority. (The appendix lists the website of every state's tax agency.)

Gross income usually includes money, goods, and property the deceased person received from, for example, a job, pension, investments, disability payments, and IRAs and retirement plans (except Roth IRAs). For people with larger incomes, a portion of Social Security may also be taxable. Gross income also includes gross receipts from self-employment, minus the cost of goods sold. In other words, everything that was income before death is still considered income.

WHEN A FEDERAL INCOME TAX RETURN IS REQUIRED (2003)

Filing status	Age	Gross income was at least
Single	Under 65	$7,800
	65 or older	$8,950
Head of household	Under 65	$10,050
	65 or older	$11,200
Married filing jointly	Under 65 (both spouses)	$15,600
	65 or older (one spouse)	$16,550
	65 or older (both spouses)	$17,500
Married filing separately	Any age	$3,050
Qualifying widow(er) with dependent child	Under 65	$12,550
	65 or older	$13,500

(Source: IRS Publication 501)

Even if a return isn't required, file one anyway if a refund is coming. A refund may be due if tax was withheld from salaries, pensions, or annuities that the deceased person received.

TAXATION OF SOCIAL SECURITY BENEFITS

Whether Social Security benefits are taxable depends on the recipient's total income and marital status.

Generally, if Social Security benefits were the deceased person's only income, they are not taxable. If the deceased person received other income as well, use the worksheet in the Form 1040 instruction book to find out how much, if any, of the Social Security income is taxable.

For a quick computation, add one-half of the Social Security benefits to all other income, including tax-exempt interest. If this amount is more than the "base amount" for the appropriate filing status, a part of the benefits is taxable. The base amounts for the 2003 tax year are:

- $25,000 for single, head of household, or qualifying widow/widower with a dependent child
- $25,000 for married individuals filing separately who did not live with their spouses at any time during the year
- $32,000 for married couples filing jointly
- $0 for married individuals filing separately who lived together at any time during the year.

For more information, see IRS Publication 915, *Social Security and Equivalent Railroad Retirement Benefits*.

---

2. Special Rules for Surviving Spouses

As you might expect, some special rules apply to surviving spouses.

a. Filing a Joint Return

A surviving spouse has the option of filing a joint tax return for the year of the deceased spouse's death, unless the spouse remarries during that year. In that case, file a "married filing separately" return for the deceased taxpayer.

b. Tax Benefits for Surviving Spouses

If you are a surviving spouse and have a dependent child, you may get an income tax break for two tax years after the death of your spouse. If you qualify for a special filing status, called "qualifying widow(er)," you can pay the tax rate that usually applies only to married couples. The result may be a smaller tax bill.

To be eligible, you must meet all of these requirements:

- You must have been entitled to file a joint return with your spouse for the year of death (whether or not you actually did).

- You must not have remarried before the end of the current tax year.

- You must have a child, stepchild, or foster child who qualifies as your dependent for the tax year.

- You must provide more than half the cost of maintaining your home, which is the child's principal residence.

3. When the Income Tax Return Is Due

You'll need to file an income tax return for the year in which the person died. That's called the final tax return, and it's due when it would have been due if the deceased person were still alive—for most people, on April 15.

EXAMPLE: *Albert dies in September 2004. His executor must file only a 2004 income tax return for him, due April 15, 2005.*

If when the person died, he or she hadn't yet filed a tax return for the year before the death, you'll have to file that tax return as well.

EXAMPLE: *Julia dies in March 2005, before filing her tax return for 2004. Her executor, Harold, must file a 2004 return for Julia by April 15, 2005. A year later, he must file a 2005 return for Julia, reporting the income she received during the few months she lived that year.*

4. What Forms to Use

A federal income tax return for a deceased person is filed on the familiar Form 1040. After you enter the taxpayer's name, write "Deceased" and the date of death. The IRS also asks you to write DECEASED and the date of death across the top of the form; some people recommend using a red pen to make sure it isn't overlooked. If you're the surviving spouse and are filing a joint return, also write the name of your deceased spouse at the top.

Signing the form. If you're the executor, sign the form yourself, in your capacity as estate representative.

EXAMPLE: *Janice signs her father's final tax return "Janice Wyzynski, Executor of the Estate of Ambrose Polenka, Deceased."*

If you're the surviving spouse and file a joint return, sign it yourself, adding after your signature the words "filing as surviving spouse." If you're not the executor, and one is appointed before the return is due, have him or her sign too.

What if there is no surviving spouse, and no executor has been appointed by the court? In that case, whoever has taken charge of the deceased person's property signs the return as "personal representative."

5. Claiming a Refund

If you're the surviving spouse filing a joint return, there's no extra paperwork involved in claiming a refund. Anyone else filing a return on behalf of a deceased person must file additional documents.

INCOME TAX RETURNS: DUE DATES

Date of death	Return for:	Due date
Before April 15	Previous calendar year Year of death	April 15 of year of death April 15 of year following death
After April 15	Year of death	April 15 of year following death

- If you're the court-appointed executor, you'll need to attach a copy of the court document that authorizes you to act. (This may be called your "Letters Testamentary," "Letters of Administration," or something similar, depending on the state.) A copy of the will that appointed you executor is not enough.

- If you don't have official court authorization to represent the estate, you must file IRS Form 1310, *Statement of Person Claiming Refund Due a Deceased Taxpayer*, along with the return.

6. Special Rules for Final Tax Returns

In general, the same federal tax rules apply to a return for a deceased person as apply to a living taxpayer. The same items are income, the same deductions are allowed, and the same credits may be claimed. Here are just a few rules that answer common questions:

- The personal exemption may be claimed in full, unless someone else claimed the deceased person as a dependent.

- The full standard deduction may be claimed, if deductions are not itemized.

- The full credit for the elderly or the disabled may be taken if the deceased person was 65 or older or had retired by the end of the tax year on permanent and total disability.

- Qualifying medical expenses may be claimed as a deduction either on the final income tax return or, if a federal estate tax return is filed, on that return. (They cannot be deducted on the estate's income tax return, discussed in Section C, below.) Because estate tax rates are higher than personal income tax rates, it usually saves money to take the deduction on the estate tax return if you have the option.

If the deceased person was self-employed, you'll probably need to pay federal self-employment tax (reported on Schedule SE of Form 1040) in addition to regular income tax. Self-employment tax is due if the deceased person earned $400 or more (2003 figure) from self-employment.

C. The Estate's Income Tax: Form 1041

The final income tax return you file on behalf of a deceased person covers the person's income up until the day of death. But after that, income may still arrive—for example, interest on a bank account or rents from a building the deceased person owned.

The IRS calls any income the deceased person would have received, had he or she lived, "income in respect of the decedent." It may belong to the estate or to beneficiaries who receive it.

Income received by the estate must be reported on what is called a "fiduciary" income tax return (IRS Form 1041). This return covers the period from the date of death until all the property is transferred to its new owners. After the new owners have the property, it's their responsibility to report and pay tax on any income it produces. (See Section H, below.)

More information. IRS Publication 559, *Survivors, Executors, and Administrators,* contains a wealth of helpful information and sample forms. You can get it online at www.irs.gov.

1. Is a Fiduciary Return Required?

If the estate has more than $600 of annual gross income (2003 figure), you must file a fiduciary income tax return.

You probably won't have to file a Form 1041 unless the estate trudges through regular probate proceedings. That's because in most states, probate takes at least six months. During that time, assets in the estate may generate taxable income that will pile up in the estate.

If, on the other hand, all the assets can be transferred to beneficiaries promptly, outside of probate, you probably won't need to file an income tax return for the estate. So if the deceased person held property in a living trust, in joint tenancy, or any other way that avoids probate, you may be able to avoid the need to file a tax return. The property can be transferred quickly, and its new owners will receive, and pay tax on, any income the assets produce.

EXAMPLE: *When Morrie dies, virtually everything of value he owns is held in joint tenancy with his wife Gloria: their house, car, and bank accounts. Gloria automatically owns everything at his death. She will take care of the paperwork that transfers these assets into her name alone, and report any*

income they produce (such as interest from the bank accounts) on her own income tax return. She doesn't need to file an income tax return for Morrie's estate.

If the estate does go through probate, you'll need to allocate income between the deceased person's income tax return and the estate's tax return. It's not always easy. That's because people or institutions— for example, banks that pay interest on CDs—don't switch over to paying the estate the instant someone dies. Until the payor is notified of the death and gets the estate's taxpayer ID number (see Section 2, below), it can't make payments to the estate.

That means that at the end of the year, when you're trying to figure out how much the deceased person received and how much the estate received, you can't rely on the forms provided by the payors. These forms—W-2's, Form 1099s, and others—cover the whole calendar year, and will probably include payments made both while the person was alive and after death.

Notify payors of the death and give them the estate's taxpayer ID number as soon as possible. With luck, you'll get the payor to issue two end-of-year forms, one showing payments to the deceased person and one to the estate.

If you're the surviving spouse, you may also need to split certain kinds of income between yourself and the estate. Form 1041 is only for the estate's income. Unlike a final personal income tax return, there's no such thing as a joint Form 1041.

EXAMPLE: *Elizabeth's husband Max dies in May. They own several bank accounts and pieces of real estate together. Some of them are held in joint tenancy, which means that Elizabeth owns them immediately upon Max's death. The income they produce is now Elizabeth's; it doesn't go to the estate and so doesn't need to be reported on the estate's tax return.*

One of their shared accounts, however, is held as "tenants in common." That means it doesn't pass automatically to Elizabeth outside of probate; Max actually used his will to leave his half to his son from a previous marriage. (Elizabeth still owns her half-share.) During probate, before the account is formally transferred to the son, the income that's reported on the bank's monthly statement must be split between Max's estate and Elizabeth.

You might want help. If you're handling an estate that will go through probate and has diverse income streams, you'll probably want to hire a tax expert—an accountant or lawyer—to help with allocations and the like.

COMMON KINDS OF ESTATE INCOME

interest
dividends
rent
royalties
profit from the sale of assets (capital gains)
income from a business or trust

---

2. Getting an ID Number for the Estate

Before you can file the estate's tax return, you need to apply for a taxpayer ID number, commonly called an EIN, for the estate. Basically, it's the equivalent of a Social Security number for an individual, and you'll need it for tax returns you file on behalf of the estate. If you don't use it on the tax return, you'll be subject to a penalty. You *cannot* use the deceased person's Social Security number.

If you opened an estate bank account, you probably already have a taxpayer ID number. If you need information on how to get one, see Chapter 9, Section C.

3. Notifying the IRS That You're in Charge

When you start acting in a fiduciary capacity for an estate, you must notify the IRS. You do that by filing IRS Form 56, *Notice Concerning Fiduciary Relationship*. It's a simple form.

Before you can file it, you'll need the estate's taxpayer ID number, discussed just above. Send it to the same IRS office where you file tax returns for the deceased person and the estate.

You also use Form 56 to notify the IRS when you stop acting on behalf of the estate—that is, if you quit and somebody else takes over, or when the property has all been distributed.

4. Completing the Return

The income tax return for an estate is much like the income tax return for an individual. There are some differences, however, in the deductions and credits you can claim. A few common deductions are set out below.

DEDUCTIONS ON THE ESTATE'S INCOME TAX RETURN

You can deduct	You *cannot* deduct
• $600 exemption (all estates) • Expenses of administering the estate • Losses on the sale of an estate asset	• Medical or dental expenses of the deceased person* • Funeral expenses

* Can be deducted on the deceased person's individual income tax return, if they're paid within one year of death.

Every estate gets a $600 exemption. You can also deduct the routine expenses the estate has incurred—for example, the fees of lawyers or accountants, the cost of supplies, or taxes paid on real estate.

5. When the Return Is Due

The fiduciary tax return is generally due on April 15 for the previous calendar year, just like an income tax return for an individual.

EXAMPLE 1: *Jacob dies on June 1, 2004, but his bank accounts and mutual funds keep generating interest and dividends. His widow Theresa immediately inherits some of these accounts, without probate, because she and Jacob held them as joint tenants. The income from these accounts doesn't go to the estate, but instead to her. Income from the accounts that were solely owned by Jacob, however, goes to Jacob's estate after his death.*

Theresa, who is the executor, finishes distributing all of his property to the beneficiaries on December 15, 2004. On April 15, 2005, she files two federal income tax returns:

- *2004 final joint income tax return for Jacob and Theresa (Form 1040), covering all of 2004 (although Jacob died in the middle of the year, the return covers the whole calendar year), and*

- *2004 income tax return for Jacob's estate (Form 1041), covering the period from June 1 (the date of death) through December 15, 2004, the day the estate was closed.*

If the estate is open for more than one tax year, the first fiduciary tax return is called the initial return, and the last one the final return.

EXAMPLE 2: *Esther dies on February 20, 2005. Her son Alex, the executor, wraps up the estate in just over a year, on March 1, 2006. Alex must file two estate income tax returns:*

- *2005 income tax return for Esther's estate (Form 1041), covering the period from her death on February 20, 2005 through December 31, 2005. This is called the initial return. It's due on April 15, 2006.*

- *2006 income tax return for Esther's estate (Form 1041), covering the period from January 1, 2006 through March 1, 2006. This is the final return and is due on April 15, 2007.*

You don't have to pay taxes based on the calendar year, although most people do. If you wish, you may choose a "fiscal year"—another

12-month period—when you file the estate's first Form 1041.

6. Who Pays the Tax

If tax is due with the initial fiduciary tax return, or any subsequent returns except the final one, you pay it out of estate assets. (The will may direct which assets to use.)

Things usually work differently with the final fiduciary income tax return—which, if the estate is open only one calendar year, will be the only fiduciary return. You, as executor, couldn't pay any tax due—the estate's assets have already been transferred to the beneficiaries. So on that return, all income is passed through to the beneficiaries. You must prepare, for each beneficiary, an IRS Form K-1 (Form 1041): *Beneficiary's Share of Income, Deductions, Credits, Etc.* The beneficiaries report the income on their own personal income tax returns and pay any tax due on it.

A tax professional can help you sort it out. If these tax matters are more of a challenge than you want to take on, it's a good time to get some expert help. A tax expert can probably prepare these forms in a fraction of the time it would take you, and may even come up with enough savings to cover the fee.

7. Estimated Tax Payments

Just like an individual, an estate may be required to make quarterly estimated tax payments. These payments are required if the estate is open so long that it has a tax year that ends two or more years after the date of death. Unless the estate you're handling gets badly tangled in probate, this two-year rule shouldn't affect you. If you must make estimated payments on behalf of the estate, use IRS Form 1041-ES.

8. State Income Taxes

Most states also require estates to pay state income taxes if they receive at least a certain amount of income. Check with your state's taxing authority for the current rules.

D. Income Tax on Trusts

If you're in charge of a trust set up by the deceased person, you may have more tax concerns to deal with. It all depends on the kind of trust. The most common kind of trust—a revocable living trust designed to avoid probate—does not create any tax issues. Most other kinds of trusts, including trusts for children, do.

1. Simple Living Trusts

If you're the trustee of a simple living trust (a revocable trust designed only to avoid probate, without any tax-saving features to complicate it), you probably won't need to file an income tax return for the trust. That's because you can likely distribute trust property to the beneficiaries quickly after the death of the person who created the trust (called the grantor, settler, or trustor). After all the trust property has been transferred to its new owners, the trust ceases to exist. If the new owners receive income from the trust assets they've inherited, they'll report it on their personal income tax returns.

2. Ongoing Trusts

If a trust exists long enough to receive at least $600 in annual income, the trustee must get a federal taxpayer ID number (EIN) and file a fiduciary income tax return (IRS Form 1041) for the trust. (IRC §§ 6012(a)(4),(b)(4).) The process is much the same as filing a fiduciary return for an estate, which is discussed in Section C, above.

Common kinds of trusts that may fit this description include trusts set up to manage property left to minor children and AB (bypass) trusts, set up by married couples to reduce or eliminate federal estate taxes. (With an AB trust, the bypass trust is the taxpaying entity.)

You may also need to pay quarterly estimated taxes. (IRC § 6654.) Certain trusts, however, can choose to be considered part of the estate for income tax purposes, so no separate income tax return is necessary. (IRC § 645.)

If you're the trustee of anything but a simple living trust, get expert help. Many tax issues affect the trust and the beneficiaries. Talk to a lawyer who handles trust administration or a CPA who has experience in administering trusts.

E. Federal Estate Tax

Luckily for executors, most estates don't need to file a federal estate tax return (IRS Form 706), because only large estates—currently, those worth more than $1.5 million—are subject to this tax. In a few years, the tax may even disappear entirely. But there is considerable uncertainty about its future, because Congress is likely to revisit the issue soon, and there are very strong opinions on both sides.

Don't go it alone. If you are in charge of a large estate, you will need expert help with estate taxes from an experienced lawyer, accountant, or both.

1. Who Needs to File

It's not always easy to know whether or not a federal estate tax return is required. Here are some guidelines to help you figure it out.

a. General Rules

The executor must file a federal estate tax return if the gross estate, on the date of death, exceeds a certain amount. (What constitutes the "gross estate" for tax purposes is discussed later in this section.) These amounts, which are scheduled to keep going up for the rest of this decade, are listed below.

THE FEDERAL ESTATE TAX THRESHOLD

Year of death	Estate tax return must be filed if gross value of the estate exceeds:
2002 or 2003	$1 million
2004 or 2005	$1.5 million
2006, 2007, or 2008	$2 million
2009	$3.5 million
2010	*estate tax repealed*
2011	$1 million unless Congress extends repeal

Some estates must file estate tax returns but won't actually owe any tax, because deductions will put them below the tax threshold. But even if you're sure that the estate won't owe tax, you must still file a return if the estate's gross value exceeds the threshold. For example, no estate tax is due on any amount of property left to a spouse who is a U.S. citizen; it all passes tax-free. So if the deceased person was married and left $2 million to her husband, her estate won't owe any tax. (More on this important rule a little later.) But you must file an estate tax return anyway.

EXAMPLE: *Jorge has a gross estate valued at $1.7 million when he dies in 2004. A federal estate tax return must be filed because the value of the estate is over $1.5 million, the estate tax threshold for that year.*

However, Jorge's executor claims deductions for debts (a mortgage, car payments, and money owed to a family member), taxes due, last illness and funeral expenses, and administration expenses (for example, attorneys' and accountants' fees and court costs). They bring the value of his net estate below $1.5 million, so no tax is due.

SPECIAL RULES FOR FAMILY BUSINESSES

Estates that contain family businesses can qualify for an additional exemption from estate tax, bringing the total that can pass tax-free to $1.3 million. (For federal tax purposes, this benefit became superfluous in 2004, when the individual estate tax exemption rose to $1.5 million, but it may still be important in some states that impose their own estate tax and follow this rule.) To qualify for this advantageous tax treatment, the business must meet a long list of requirements. Among them:

- The business must make up more than half of the value of the estate.

- The deceased owner must have participated in the business for several years before death.

- The business must be left to family members or long-term employees.

If the new owners leave the business within ten years, they will be required to pay back some or all of the tax savings.

If you think the estate you're handling qualifies for this special tax treatment, see a lawyer who has experience with the complicated rules.

The gross value of the estate includes all types of property owned by the decedent, from CDs and shoes to stocks, vehicles, retirement accounts, and real estate. Also count the deceased person's share of joint tenancy property, death benefits, and assets held in a living trust. And you must add in the proceeds of any life insurance policies or annuities the deceased person owned, and, if you're in a community property state, the deceased person's half-share of any community property.

b. Common Questions

Just what did the deceased person own, for tax purposes? It's not always clear. Here are the rules for a couple of kinds of property you may have questions about.

Joint tenancy property. If the deceased person bought joint tenancy property with someone else—commonly a spouse—then each person owned half the property. At the death of one owner, the value of a half-interest in the property is included in the estate for tax purposes.

EXAMPLE: *Margie and Tom bought their house together and hold title to it in joint tenancy. When Tom dies, Margie automatically owns the house, without probate. Half the value of the house is included in Tom's estate for tax purposes.*

The situation is different if the property was wholly owned by one person first and then put into joint tenancy later. Many people do this to avoid probate. For example, an elderly parent may add a son or daughter to the deed to the family house as a joint tenant. In such cases,

federal tax law requires that the entire value of the joint tenancy property be included in the estate of the first owner, for estate tax purposes, if the others acquired their interests for less than full value.

EXAMPLE: *Estelle, a widow in her 80s, signs a deed transferring ownership of her house to herself and her grown daughter, Sarah, as joint tenants. This means Estelle and Sarah each own a half-interest in the property. But when Estelle dies, the entire value of the property (not just Estelle's half) is included in her estate for federal estate tax purposes.*

Life insurance proceeds. It's easy to overlook life insurance proceeds when you're adding up the value of the gross estate. If the deceased person owned the policy, or if the estate is the policy beneficiary (uncommon), the deceased person's taxable estate includes the proceeds of the policy.

EXAMPLE: *Eugenia owns a life insurance policy on her life; her son is the beneficiary. When Eugenia dies, he receives the proceeds, which are counted as part of Eugenia's taxable estate.*

The deceased person may, however, have transferred ownership of the policy to someone else precisely so the policy proceeds would not be included in the taxable estate.

EXAMPLE: *Ralph buys an insurance policy on his life and names his wife as the beneficiary. He then transfers ownership of the policy to his wife. He no longer makes premium payments, and he no longer has the power to change the beneficiary or otherwise affect the policy. When he dies, the proceeds are not included in his taxable estate.*

To keep policy proceeds out of the taxable estate, the original owner must give up any control over the policy. If someone keeps the power to change beneficiaries, revoke an assignment, obtain a loan against the cash value, pledge the policy for a loan, or surrender or cancel the policy, then that person has what are called "incidents of ownership." As a result, the policy proceeds will be included in the taxable estate even if someone else technically owned the policy.

c. If You're Not Sure Whether You Need to File

If you think the estate's value is close to, but below, the threshold amount, you may want to get an appraisal from a qualified outsider.

Whether or not you'll need to get some estate assets appraised may depend in part on the kind of assets the deceased person owned. Securities, for example, can be valued with certainty; it's easy to find out exactly what they were selling for on the date of death. Assigning a value to real estate or a small business, on the other hand, is much less precise. If the estate you're dealing with contains assets that don't have a readily ascertainable value, it's a good idea to get a professional opinion before making decisions about estate taxes. You'll need it if you decide not to file and that decision is ever challenged.

EXAMPLE: *Ruth dies in 2005, leaving the bulk of her property to her brother Robert, who is also her executor. Most of the property is held in a simple probate-avoiding living trust or owned in joint tenancy, and so can be transferred quickly outside of probate. Only securities valued at $120,000 and miscellaneous personal property of little value are not held in the living trust or in another way that avoids probate.*

Robert, after taking inventory of Ruth's entire estate, thinks it has a gross value of about $1.3 million. If that's correct, he won't need to file a federal estate tax return, because the amount is below the $1.5 million estate tax threshold. But because most of the value of the estate is real estate, he hires a professional appraiser. That will give him a solid estimate on which to base his decision whether or not to file.

Look into alternate valuation dates. The gross value of estate property can be assessed as of the date of death or as of six months later. Obviously, you'll want to choose whichever date gives the overall estate a lower value for tax purposes. The difference can be substantial if assets—stocks, for example—drop or rise sharply in value soon after death. (Chapter 8 discusses inventorying and appraising estate assets.)

2. The Filing Deadline

A federal estate tax return is due nine months after the date of death.

If you can't make that deadline, you can ask for a six-month extension, using IRS Form 4768. The IRS will automatically grant your request if you make it before the original due date.

An extension lets you off the hook only for filing the return. You still have to pay any tax due by the original deadline. To minimize penalties and interest, make your best estimate of the amount owed and send it in. You can get an extension of time to pay only if you can show that it's impossible, or nearly so, to pay on time. The usual extension is a year, but the IRS sometimes allows longer periods. If a small business makes up a large part of the estate, you may get to pay the bill in installments. (The IRS recognizes that a business may be high in value but low in cash available to pay taxes.)

If you don't pay the tax on time, penalties and interest will quickly be added to the amount the estate owes. The penalty mounts up at the rate of 5% for each month, up to a maximum of 25%. That's in addition to interest.

3. Can You Do It Yourself?

The estate tax return is long and detailed, and completing it requires making many complex choices that can have serious financial consequences. Given that you won't be filing a return unless the deceased person left at least $1.5 million worth of property, you're best off hiring professional help.

Read along. Even if you don't prepare the return yourself, you may want to look at the IRS booklet, *Instructions for Form 706*, which will help you understand what the tax return requires.

4. Estimating the Tax Owed

Even if the estate's gross value is above the estate tax threshold, meaning a return must be filed, the estate may not owe any tax. That's because a wide array of deductions and credits can reduce or eliminate it. This section helps you arrive at a rough estimate of what the estate may owe.

a. Common Deductions

Here is an overview of the most common deductions.

The marital deduction. The most important deduction for married couples is the "unlimited marital deduction." In plain English, it means that property left to a spouse, regardless of amount, is not taxed. The only restriction on this rule is that the spouse who inherits the property must be a U.S. citizen. (The citizenship of the deceased spouse doesn't matter.) Amounts left to noncitizen spouses do not qualify for any marital deduction.

Charitable gifts. The value of any property left to a tax-exempt charity can be deducted from the gross taxable estate. Tax-exempt status is granted by the IRS to religious and educational groups. If you don't know whether or not a beneficiary qualifies, ask for proof.

Other deductions. Deductions are also allowed for:

- expenses of administering the estate (appraisals and court costs, for example)

- expenses of the deceased person's last illness (these can be deducted either here or on the deceased person's final income tax return, but not both)

- funeral expenses, and

- debts (mortgages, income taxes, credit card balances, and so on).

After these deductions are subtracted from the gross estate, the result is called the "net estate."

b. Taxable Gifts

After you've subtracted allowable deductions, you may need to add some amounts to the net estate. You add back in any taxable gifts the deceased person made while alive. That gets you the "taxable estate"—the figure on which the estate tax is based.

The overwhelming majority of lifetime gifts are exempt from tax, including:

- gifts of less than $11,000 per recipient per year ($10,000 for gifts made before 2002)

- gifts of any amount to spouses who are U.S. citizens

- gifts to spouses who are not U.S. citizens, up to $114,000 per year (before 2004, the limit was $100,000 to $112,000, depending on the year)

- gifts of any amount made in direct payment of someone's medical bills or tuition.

A gift was taxable only if it did not fall into any of these exempt categories. In that case, a federal gift tax return should have been filed.

Gift tax is not usually paid until death. Gift and estate tax are really one tax (the "unified gift and estate tax"), applied both to large gifts during life and large amounts left at death. (This is supposed to change after 2010, but it's really impossible to know what the law will be like then.)

Taxable gifts are tricky. If the deceased person made taxable gifts during his or her lifetime, that's another reason to talk to a tax expert. You can't just add gifts back into the gross estate, because tax rates depend on the size of the gifts.

c. The Estimated Tax

If you want to estimate how much tax the estate will owe, use the worksheet and tax tables below.

ESTIMATING THE TAXABLE ESTATE

Gross value of estate	$ _____
Property left to U.S. citizen spouse	– _____
Property left to tax-exempt charities	– _____
Expenses of last illness	– _____
Funeral expenses	– _____
Expenses of estate administration	– _____
Debts and taxes	– _____
Net value of estate	$ _____
Taxable gifts made during life	+ _____
Taxable estate	$ _____

If you arrive at a "taxable estate" of less than $1.5 million, the estate should not owe tax—but remember that you're just making a rough estimate here. See an accountant or lawyer for a definitive answer.

If you think the estate will be liable for tax, use the tables below to estimate the tax due. There are two steps:

Step 1. Figure the tentative tax. Use the "Estate Tax Bill" table below. Don't be scared by this amount; you'll get to subtract a big credit in Step 2.

THE ESTATE TAX BILL

If the taxable estate is:	The tentative tax (before subtracting the tax credit) will be:
$1 to $1.25 million	$345,800 plus 41% of amount over $1 million
$1.25 to $1.5 million	$448,300 plus 43% of amount over $1.25 million
$1.5 to $2 million	$555,800 plus 45% of amount over $1.5 million
$2 to $2.5 million	$780,000 plus 48%* of amount over $2 million
$2.5 to $3 million	$1,025,800 plus 48%* of amount over $2.5 million
more than $3 million	$1,290,800 plus 48%* of amount over $3 million

*The maximum marginal rate goes down to 47% in 2005, 46% in 2006, and 45% in 2007.

Step 2. Subtract the tax credit. On the table below, find the estate tax credit for the year of death. The tax credit for 2004 is equal to the amount of tax on $1.5 million—which is why everyone who dies in that year can leave up to $1.5 million free of estate tax.

THE UNIFIED GIFT/ESTATE TAX CREDIT

Year of Death	Estate Tax Credit	Equal to Tax on
2002 or 2003	$345,800	$1 million
2004 or 2005	$555,800	$1.5 million

ESTIMATING ESTATE TAX DUE

Tentative tax	$ _____
Personal gift/estate tax credit	− _____
Total tax	_____

The answer you get will be the total estate tax the estate owes.

EXAMPLE: *Edward, a widower, dies in 2004 with a gross estate of $2 million. He leaves $50,000 to charity and the rest to his son and daughter, in equal shares. Because Edward left most of his property in a living trust, the estate avoids probate, and assets are quickly distributed with no unusual expenses.*

Here is how Edward's daughter, his executor, estimates the estate taxes that will have to come out of the estate before she and her brother can take their inheritance.

ESTIMATING EDWARD'S TAXABLE ESTATE

Gross value of estate	$	2,000,000
Property left to spouse	–	0
Property left to tax-exempt charities	–	50,000
Expenses of last illness	–	5,000
Funeral expenses	–	5,000
Expenses of estate administration	–	2,000
Debts and taxes	–	8,000
Net value of estate	$	1,930,000
Taxable gifts made during life	+	0
Taxable estate	$	1,930,000

ESTIMATING EDWARD'S ESTATE TAX DUE

Tentative tax	$	749,300
Personal gift/estate tax credit	–	555,800
Total tax	$	193,500

5. Paying the Federal Tax

As executor, it's your job to come up with enough money from the estate to pay the taxes. But which assets should you use?

The will may give you some direction here. It's common, for example, for wills to instruct the executor to pay taxes from the "residue" of the estate—that is, property that isn't earmarked for a specific beneficiary. (The residue or residuary estate is discussed in Chapter 6.) An unusually organized person might have even set aside a liquid account or taken out an extra life insurance policy and designated it for payment of taxes.

If there is no will, or it doesn't mention estate taxes, the tax usually comes from each beneficiary, in proportion to what each inherits. (This is called a pro rata share.) An accountant can figure out the numbers. If each person has been left cash or liquid assets, such as marketable securities, accomplishing this is easy—just reduce each person's take proportionately.

If there isn't enough cash to pay the taxes, you may have to sell estate property to raise the necessary funds.

6. Gift Tax Returns

If the deceased person made any taxable gifts before death, a federal gift tax return should have been filed. Generally, gifts worth more than $11,000 ($10,000 before 2002) given to one recipient in a calendar year are taxable.

But people often overlook filing a gift tax return when making a large gift, such as giving a child money to make a down payment on a house; that's one reason the IRS frequently audits estate tax returns. If you discover that taxable gifts were made but not reported, you'll need to file a gift tax return now, along with the estate tax return.

EXAMPLE: *Before she died, Frieda gave a half-interest in her small retail business to her daughter, Gretchen. It never occurred to either of them to file a federal gift tax return. But the business was worth $300,000, making the gift to Gretchen worth $150,000. Gift tax would be assessed on this transfer, eating up some of the gift/estate tax credit available when Frieda's estate tax return is filed. (Still, the estate would owe estate tax only if all the credit were used up; most estates are too small to owe estate tax.) (See Section 1, above.)*

7. Other Estate Tax Concerns for the Executor

Estates large enough to owe federal estate tax often have built-in complications, making expert help a must. Here are a few examples:

- There is an AB (sometimes called "credit shelter") trust. The trustee is responsible for splitting the AB trust into Trust A and Trust B, in a way that maximizes overall tax savings. (See Chapter 21.)

- There is a QTIP or QDOT trust. These trusts are designed to postpone estate taxes until the death of the second spouse. You will have to decide whether or not it makes financial sense to put the trust into effect (this is called making the "QTIP election"). Making the election is just a matter of checking a box on the estate tax return.

- The deceased person left more than a total of $1.5 million to beneficiaries more than one generation away, usually grandchildren. In this case, the estate may owe what's called "generation-skipping transfer tax," which is calculated on the estate tax return.

8. Working With a Tax Expert

As stressed above, preparing a federal estate tax return isn't a job for an amateur unless you have the time and energy to get up to speed on a very complicated subject. The help of an experienced lawyer or accountant is well worth the cost now (a professional may find deductions you would overlook, saving you money), and it may be a godsend later if the tax return is audited—as estate tax returns commonly are.

That said, you'll still be doing a lot of work to help get the return filed. You'll need to gather and give your tax expert important information, including:

- an appraisal of the estate assets, including professional appraisals for hard-to-value items such as real estate, art, and jewelry (see Chapter 8)

- a report of debts left by the deceased person

- records of expenses of administering estate property

- names and Social Security numbers of beneficiaries, and

- a list of tax-exempt charitable gifts.

Help your tax preparer do a good job by turning over necessary information as soon as possible. Keep in close contact with the tax adviser, and keep track of deadlines. Remember that, as executor, it's your responsibility to make sure tax matters are handled on time.

It also falls to you, the executor, to sign the actual estate tax return. You sign "under penalty of perjury," which means that you are swearing that to the best of your knowledge, the tax return is complete and accurate. Before you sign, go over the return carefully and make sure all assets are accounted for.

Tax returns affect each other. If you hire an expert to help you file an estate tax return, but plan on doing the estate's income tax return yourself, be sure to discuss your strategy with the tax pro you hire. For example, some deductions can be taken on either return, but not both. If an estate tax return must be filed, but there are enough deductions

to make the estate owe no estate tax, you'll want to use some of the "surplus" deductions on the estate's income tax return. You and the estate tax return preparer each need to know what the other is doing.

F. State Inheritance and Estate Taxes

Because of recent changes in federal and state tax laws, it's becoming more likely that an estate will have to pay a separate estate tax to a state where the deceased person lived or owned real estate. In most cases, though, the state tax amount will not be huge.

There are three kinds of state taxes you may need to know about:

- **Pick-up taxes,** which are due only if the estate owes federal estate tax and can be taken as a credit on the federal estate tax return (which means they do not increase the total tax bill)

- **State estate taxes,** which may affect estates that aren't large enough to owe federal estate tax, and

- **Inheritance taxes,** which are imposed not on the estate but on the people who inherit the property.

These laws are in flux. If there's a chance the estate may owe state estate tax, see a tax lawyer who can bring you up to date on this rapidly changing area of the law.

1. Pick-Up Taxes

Until 2005, all states can collect part of what
an estate pays to the federal government in
federal estate taxes. This is called a "pick-up"
or "sop" tax. If the estate is large enough to
owe federal taxes, you simply pay a portion of
that amount to the state. You must file a state
estate tax return, but the state doesn't add any
additional tax. Put another way, the state takes
the money from the feds, not the estate.

The percentage that the states collect has
shrunk over the last few years, because of
federal tax legislation enacted in 2001. (The
law doesn't affect the total amount that an
estate must pay, only the split between the
state and federal treasuries.) As of 2005, the
states' share goes down to zero.

2. State Estate Taxes

Almost 20 states now impose their own estate
taxes, and more may join the list soon. State
estate taxes are levied on the estate property
itself, just as the federal estate tax is. The estate
may owe tax to a state if the deceased person
lived there or owned real estate there.

States used to simply take a share of any
federal estate tax paid (see Section 1, above).
But because states can't claim as big a share of
federal estate tax revenue as they used to (and
as of 2005, they'll get nothing), they have
begun to impose their own estate taxes to
make up for the lost revenue. These state taxes
are no longer connected to the federal system.
As a result, estates may have to pay state tax
even if they aren't large enough to pay federal
estate tax.

In states that do add an estate tax, only large
estates will be taxed (though each state can set
its own threshold), and the rates are usually
not high enough to take a huge bite out of an
estate. Some states—for example, Arizona,
California, and Florida—are unlikely to enact a
state estate tax, because it would require a
constitutional amendment.

⚠ **Even a tax-saving trust may not save you
from taxes.** Even if the deceased person
used a trust designed to eliminate federal estate
taxes, such as an AB or marital life estate trust,
the estate may owe tax to the state. That's
because the deceased person's trust may hold
an amount of property that exceeds the state's
threshold for state estate tax, even though it's
below the federal estate tax threshold.

EXAMPLE: *Roy and his wife Ann, who are Rhode
Island residents, make an AB trust. At Roy's death,
his share of the couple's property is $800,000.
That amount goes in Trust B, the deceased spouse's
bypass trust. Because Roy's estate is under the
federal estate tax threshold, it does not owe federal
estate tax. It will, however, owe Rhode Island
estate tax, because that state no longer just
imposes a pick-up estate tax; it currently taxes
estates of $675,000 or more.*

3. State Inheritance Taxes

About a dozen states impose what are called
inheritance taxes. The entire estate is not taxed;
instead, beneficiaries must pay tax based on
what they inherit. They may owe inheritance

tax even if they inherit a relatively modest amount of property.

The tax rate is based on how much beneficiaries inherit and on their relationship to the deceased person. Spouses and children generally pay low rates or nothing at all, but more distant relatives or friends are subject to higher rates. For example, Connecticut doesn't tax money left to a surviving spouse, but children must pay 3% to 8% of what they inherit, on amounts over $50,000.

Although it is the legal responsibility of the beneficiaries to pay the inheritance tax, you, as executor, will probably be involved. For example, the will may direct that estate funds be used to pay the inheritance tax. In that case, you would pay the tax from those funds and transfer the property to the beneficiaries free from any tax obligation. And if there is a formal probate proceeding, the judge may insist on seeing proof that all inheritance taxes have been paid before the estate can be closed.

If the property doesn't pass through probate—for example, joint tenancy property that is automatically inherited by the surviving owner—the beneficiary generally pays any tax due.

⚠️ **Watch out for long-ago deaths.** Even if a state does not now impose inheritance or estate taxes, it might have at some time. And if you are dealing with the estate of someone who died when the tax was in effect, you may need to pay some tax. One common occurrence is to find that real estate, usually the family home, is still held in joint tenancy with the decedent's predeceased spouse. If the first spouse died many years ago, while a now-repealed state inheritance or estate tax was in effect, tax may be due. To find out, talk to an accountant or lawyer.

WHICH STATE'S TAXES APPLY?

If the deceased person owned property in more than one state, the estate may owe some kind of death tax to more than one state. Here are the basic rules:

- The state where the deceased person lived can tax all of his or her personal property (that's everything but real estate), plus any real estate situated in that state.

- If the deceased person owned real estate in another state, that state can tax it.

Sometimes it's not clear where the deceased person lived, for tax purposes. For example, a New Yorker may have a second home in Florida and spend much of the year there. New York imposes a state estate tax, but Florida doesn't, so determining the person's legal residence can have important financial consequences.

If you're not sure about the person's residence, try to determine which state the person considered his or her permanent home. Where did the person work, vote, register cars, and pay taxes? If the answer isn't clear, and you're concerned about estate taxes, see a lawyer.

G. Other Taxes

Income and estate taxes are the biggies for executors. But don't forget some other kinds of taxes, too.

1. Real Estate

If the estate contains real estate, you may need to pay property tax that comes due while you're in charge of the property. (Managing real estate is discussed in Chapter 9.)

2. Business

If you are in charge of a small business, you'll need to pay a whole set of business taxes. The most important of these are payroll taxes, which are due quarterly. If you fail to see that they are made, you could be personally liable for the tax plus penalties. The business will probably also owe estimated income taxes.

If the business has a bookkeeper or payroll service that can continue to make all necessary tax payments, great. Just keep an eye out to make sure they are paid. If the deceased person handled the payments without help, you'll probably want to get expert help fast.

H. Beneficiaries and Taxes

Executors are commonly beneficiaries as well. This section discusses some issues you may face if you inherit property or receive income that would have gone to the deceased person. This information may also help you answer questions from other beneficiaries.

1. Income Owed to the Deceased Person

Sometimes, a beneficiary receives money that would have gone to the decedent if he or she had lived. Such money is called income "in respect of the decedent." In that case, the beneficiary must pay tax on the money.

EXAMPLE: *Shortly before he died, Garrett did some work for his neighbor Bess. He didn't receive the final payment before his death, and Bess doesn't get around to paying off the balance until after the probate is over and the estate is closed. So she pays Rose, his widow, instead. That money is income that Rose must report on her personal income tax return.*

If Bess had paid the money while the estate was open, it would have been the estate's income. Rose would have reported it on the estate's income tax return. (See Section C, above.)

2. Income Tax on Inherited Property

The general rule is that beneficiaries do not owe income tax on money or property they inherit. For example, someone who inherits $50,000 in cash doesn't have to report it as income on a personal tax return.

That said, there are—of course—a few exceptions.

a. Money Inherited From Retirement Accounts

As you probably know, someone who sets up an IRA or participates in a 401(k) plan generally names a beneficiary (or more than one) for it. If there's any money left when the person dies, it goes directly to the beneficiary. This process avoids probate—but not taxes. Whether or not the beneficiary owes income taxes on the inherited money depends on how the IRA was set up, how contributions were made, and who inherits the cash.

Traditional IRAs and 401(k) plans. Some or all of the money a beneficiary inherits from a traditional IRA or 401(k) or 403(b) plan is taxable. Basically, if the contributions the deceased person made to the account were tax-deductible (as most are), then the money is taxed when it's withdrawn. If some nondeductible contributions were made (if, for example, in one year the deceased person's contributions to an IRA exceeded the limit on tax-deductible contributions), they (and income attributable to them) are not taxable. You'll need IRS Form 8606—and probably some help from the IRS or a tax professional—to make the calculations.

Surviving spouses can defer the tax by rolling over the account into a retirement account of their own and leaving the money in it. Other beneficiaries can ease the tax bite by taking the money out over several years. (Chapter 15 discusses the rules.)

Roth IRAs. Rules are different for Roth IRAs. When a beneficiary withdraws money the account owner contributed, it's never taxed, because the contributions were made with money that had already been taxed. The money these contributions generate is also not taxed, if it has been in the account for at least five years. (For more about Roth IRAs, see Chapter 15 and IRS Publication 590.)

Help with tax issues. *IRAs, 401(k)s & Other Retirement Plans: Taking Your Money Out*, by Twila Slesnick and John C. Suttle (Nolo), explains beneficiaries' options.

b. Life Insurance Proceeds

The beneficiary of a life insurance policy does not have to pay tax on the policy proceeds if they're paid in a lump sum. But if the money is paid in installments, with interest, part of each payment is taxed.

EXAMPLE: *Tricia is the beneficiary of her father's $300,000 life insurance policy. If she takes the whole $300,000 at once, she won't owe a penny of income tax on it.*

If, however, she chooses instead to accept the insurance company's offer of a total of $400,000 in ten annual payments of $40,000 each, she must pay tax on everything over $300,000. She calculates the tax-free portion of each annual payment as follows: $300,000 divided by ten payments = $30,000 per year. The $10,000 over that amount is taxable as interest income.

c. Property Subject to Estate or Inheritance Tax

Inheritance or estate taxes may also take a bite out of a beneficiary's inheritance.

If the estate is large enough to owe federal or state estate tax, (see Sections E and F, above), the estate tax is supposed to be paid before beneficiaries get their inheritance. Unless the deceased person specified otherwise in a will or trust, a percentage of the value of every gift is subtracted to pay the tax. The result is the same as if all the beneficiaries had received their property and then chipped in to pay their share of the estate tax.

EXAMPLE: *When Aaron dies, he leaves $1.5 million worth of property to Mark and $500,000 to Jeremy. Because Mark inherits 75% of the property, his inheritance will be reduced by an amount equal to 75% of the federal estate tax due. The other 25% of the tax due will come out of Jeremy's share. The executor will pay the tax before giving Mark and Jeremy their inheritances.*

And, as discussed above, some states impose an inheritance tax directly on the people who inherit. (See Section F, above.)

3. Tax Basis of Inherited Property

Every item of property, from your car and house to your securities and easy chair, has what is called a "tax basis." That's the amount you use to calculate taxable gain or loss if you sell the item. Tax basis is usually important only for property that's likely to go up in value, allowing you to sell it at a profit—forget about the car and easy chair. When you inherit property, special rules apply to determining your basis.

More information. IRS Publication 551, *Basis of Assets*, can tell you more about tax basis. You can find it online at www.irs.gov or order a copy from the IRS at 800-829-3676.

a. How to Figure Tax Basis

Generally, your tax basis is the amount you paid for the property.

EXAMPLE: *Laura buys a house for $100,000. Her tax basis is $100,000. If she sells the house for $150,000, her taxable gain is $50,000.*

And now for some good tax news. When property is left at death, the new owner's tax basis is the value of the property as of the date of death. This is called the "stepped-up basis" rule.

EXAMPLE: *Balbina inherits a house from her father. When her father bought the house, he paid $100,000 for it, so his tax basis was $100,000. But at his death, it was worth $150,000, so Balbina's tax basis is $150,000.*

This rule is important because it gives many inheritors a tax break. It means that if the value of the property went up after the deceased person acquired it but before that person's death, the inheritor does not have to pay tax on that gain.

EXAMPLE: *Balbina sells the house for $150,000 soon after inheriting it. She has no taxable gain.*

b. Special Rules for Community Property

COMMUNITY PROPERTY STATES

Alaska*	Nevada
Arizona	New Mexico
California	Texas
Idaho	Washington
Louisiana	Wisconsin

*Married couples can create community property by agreement.

In community property states, stepped-up basis rules give many surviving spouses a big tax benefit. While both spouses are alive, they each own a half-interest in community property—that is, property acquired during the marriage. But when one spouse dies and the other inherits the deceased spouse's half of the community property, *both* halves get a stepped-up basis.

EXAMPLE: *Jonathan and Marie live in Washington, a community property state. All their large assets are community property. Jonathan dies first, and Marie inherits everything, including stock they bought years ago for $100,000 that is worth $300,000 at Jonathan's death. Although Marie already owned a half-interest in the stock and inherits only the other half-interest, the basis of all the stock is stepped-up to the date-of-death value, $300,000.*

If Jonathan and Marie had sold the stock shortly before Jonathan's death, they would have had to report a taxable gain of $200,000. But if Marie sells the stock shortly after Jonathan's death, she will have no taxable gain.

Many couples own property that legally qualifies as community property, but isn't held as community property—that is, the title document doesn't explicitly say community property. For example, they may have bought a house with community property funds, but taken title to it in joint tenancy. In that case, to get the stepped-up tax basis, the surviving spouse will have to prove to the IRS that the property was community property.

EXAMPLE: *Jeanette and Frank bought their California home with community property funds, and legally, it is community property. But the deed that gave them title to the house states that they own it in joint tenancy. After one spouse dies, the survivor will need to show the IRS—for example, by evidence of what money was used to buy the house—that the house was in fact community property.*

> **⚠ For large estates, tax basis rules for inherited property may be changing.**
> Current federal law states that when the federal estate tax is abolished in 2010, no more than $1.3 million of each deceased person's property will qualify for a stepped-up basis. It will be up to the executor to pick which property gets it. Congress, however, will almost certainly take another look at the estate tax system before 2010. Right now, it's impossible to predict whether the basis rules will actually change in this way.

I. Typical Situations

Here are a few typical situations executors may face, and the tax issues involved in each.

1. Everything Left to Surviving Spouse

Celeste, a resident of Florida, died on October 14, 2004, at the age of 66. Her gross estate was worth $300,000; it consisted mainly of her one-half interest in a condo she owned with her husband, Len, who is 68. They had no children. Her estate did not require probate, because all of her property was held in joint ownership with Len or in other ways that avoided probate, and passed outright to Len.

From January 1, 2004 to October 14, 2004 (the date of Celeste's death), Celeste and Len received interest and dividend income of $20,000. Half of that income ($10,000) belonged to Celeste. They also each received Social Security payments.

Len was responsible for filing final income tax returns, both state and federal, for Celeste for the period January 1, 2004 to October 14, 2004. They were due by April 15, 2005. He decided to file a joint return, because that provided the more advantageous tax treatment.

Because Celeste's estate was far below the federal estate tax threshold for her year of death ($1.5 million), no federal estate tax return was required. Florida does not impose a separate estate tax, so there was no additional state estate tax to pay.

Fiduciary income tax returns were also not required, because Celeste's estate did not require probate and no legal representative was appointed. Len will report any future income he receives from assets in Celeste's estate on his own personal income tax returns.

Type of Return	Required?	Why	Due Date
2004 federal income tax return (for last months of Celeste's life)	yes	Celeste had enough income to require it.	April 15, 2005
2004 state income tax return (for last months of Celeste's life)	yes	Celeste had enough income to require it.	April 15, 2005
Federal income tax return for the estate	no	There was no probate.	
State income tax return for the estate	no	There was no probate.	
Federal estate tax return	no	Estate wasn't big enough.	
State estate tax return	no	Federal estate tax return wasn't required, and Florida doesn't impose its own estate tax.	
Federal trust income tax return	no	There was no trust.	
State trust income tax return	no	There was no trust.	
Inheritance tax return	no	Florida does not impose this tax.	

2. Everything to Adult Children

Louise, a California widow, died on July 1, 2004. Her will left everything to her four children.

Because Louise owned the house in her own name and had not set up a living trust to pass it without probate at her death, the children were required to begin a probate court proceeding. The funds in the IRA passed directly to the children without probate, as did the bank accounts, which Louise had registered in payable-on-death (POD) form. Similarly, because she had registered her brokerage account in transfer-on-death (TOD) form, naming her children as equal beneficiaries, probate was not needed for the account.

LOUISE'S ASSETS	
House	$ 400,000
Brokerage account	$50,000
IRA	$15,000
Bank accounts	$30,000
Total	$495,000

Type of Return	Required?	Why	Due Date
2004 federal income tax return (for last months of Louise's life)	yes	Louise had enough income to require it.	April 15, 2005
2004 state income tax return (for last months of Louise's life)	yes	Louise had enough income to require it.	April 15, 2005
Federal income tax return for the estate	no	Although there was probate, the estate did not receive enough income to require a tax return.	
State income tax return for the estate	no	Although there was probate, the estate did not receive enough income to require a tax return.	
Federal estate tax return	no	Estate wasn't big enough.	
State estate tax return	no	Federal estate tax return wasn't required, and California doesn't impose its own estate tax.	
Federal trust income tax return	no	There was no trust.	
State trust income tax return	no	There was no trust.	
Inheritance tax return	no	California does not impose this tax.	

3. A Large Estate

William, a well-off bachelor, died on February 15, 2004 in his home state of New York. He left this property:

ASSET	VALUE
House (appraised by an independent appraiser)	$600,000
Vacation cottage	$250,000
Artwork	$150,000
Stock (listed on the New York stock exchange)	$350,000
Life insurance	$300,000
Car	$20,000
Bank account	$30,000
Total	**$1.7 million**

Because William owned much of his property in his own name alone, and hadn't created a living trust or used other probate-avoidance devices, probate court proceedings were required for his estate. The probate court appointed his brother Jack as executor, as William had instructed in his will. The probate was closed on December 17, 2004.

Because the amount of the gross estate exceeded the federal estate tax exemption for 2004 ($1.5 million), Jack had to file a federal estate tax return for the estate. The estate was also large enough to require a New York estate tax return.

Deductions from the estate amounted to $40,000:

Outstanding debts	$15,000
Income taxes due	$15,000
Last illness and funeral expenses	$10,000
Total	**$40,000**

After subtracting these deductions, the taxable estate was $1,660,000.

William had received a total of $10,000 from his employment, along with dividends and interest, for the period January 1, 2004 to February 15, 2004 (the date of death). William hadn't yet filed his income tax returns for 2003 when he died.

Type of Return	Required?	Why	Due Date
Federal income tax returns (for 2003 and the part of 2004 during which William was alive)	yes	William had enough income to require it.	April 15, 2004 (for 2003) April 15, 2005 (for part of 2004)
State income tax returns (for 2003 and the part of 2004 during which William was alive)	yes	William had enough income to require it.	April 15, 2005 (for 2003) April 15, 2005 (for part of 2004)
Federal income tax return for the estate (for period after death until assets distributed to beneficiaries)	yes	There was regular probate, and the estate received enough income.	April 15, 2005 (for February 16 to December 17, 2004)
State income tax return for the estate (for period after death until assets distributed to beneficiaries)	yes	There was regular probate, and the estate received enough income.	April 15, 2005 (for February 16 to December 17, 2004)
Federal estate tax return	yes	Gross estate exceeded exempt amount of $1.5 million.	November 15, 2004 (nine months after death)
State estate tax return	yes	Gross estate exceeded exempt amount of $1.5 million.	November 15, 2004 (nine months after death)
Federal trust income tax return	no	There was no trust.	
State trust income tax return	no	There was no trust.	
Inheritance tax return	no	New York does not impose this tax.	

4. Large Estate With Trust

Georgette and Leon had been married for 25 years when Leon died on November 20, 2004. His one-half interest in the property he and Georgette owned was worth over a million dollars.

ASSET	VALUE
House	$800,000
Rental property	$250,000
Boat	$30,000
Stocks	$200,000
Vacation home	$200,000
Cadillac	$10,000
Money market fund	$100,000
Total	$1.68 million

Leon's will named Georgette as executor and left his one-half interest in the house, car, and money market account to her. The rental property and stocks were left in trust to his three children. His estate required probate, which ended on October 17, 2005.

Georgette and Leon received income of $125,000 during the period from January 1, 2004 to November 20, 2004 (the date of Leon's death), one-half of which was attributable to Leon.

Because the gross estate was more than $1.5 million, Georgette was responsible for seeing that a federal estate tax return (Form 706) was filed nine months after Leon's death. But because most of Leon's property was left to Georgette, it passed free of estate tax under the marital deduction. As a result, the estate didn't actually owe any federal estate tax.

Type of Return	Required?	Why	Due Date
Federal income tax returns (for the part of 2004 during which Leon was alive)	yes	Leon had enough income to require it.	April 15, 2005
State income tax returns (for the part of 2004 during which Leon was alive)	yes	Leon had enough income to require it.	April 15, 2005
Federal income tax return for the estate (for period after death until assets distributed to beneficiaries)	yes	There was formal probate, and the estate received enough income.	April 15, 2005 (for November 21, 2004 to December 31, 2004) April 15, 2005 (for January 1, 2005 to October 17, 2005)
State income tax return for the estate (for period after death until assets distributed to beneficiaries)	yes	There was formal probate, and the estate received enough income.	April 15, 2005 (for November 21, 2004 to December 31, 2004) April 15, 2005 (for January 1, 2005 to October 17, 2005)
Federal estate tax return	yes	Value of the gross estate exceeded exempt amount.	August 21, 2005 (nine months after death)
State estate tax return	yes	Federal estate tax return was required.	August 21, 2005 (nine months after death)
Federal trust income tax return	yes	The trust received at least a minimum amount of income (set by federal law).	April 15 (for previous year), unless trust chooses a non-calendar tax year.
State trust income tax return	yes	The trust received more than a certain amount of income (set by state law).	April 15 (for previous year), unless trust chooses a non-calendar tax year.
Inheritance tax return	no	California does not impose this tax.	

More information on taxes. *Your Executor Duties*, by Holmes Crouch (AllYear Tax Guides), offers detailed looks at the tax returns filed after a death.　■

Transferring Property

PART 4

CHAPTER 12

Property That Doesn't Go Through Probate

When it's time to transfer the deceased person's property to its new owners, you may be able to avoid the hassle and delay of probate court proceedings altogether. (Better yet, beneficiaries may be able to handle the whole thing themselves.) Almost every estate contains at least some property that can be transferred to its new owners easily, without probate. Over the last 20 years there has been what lawyers call a "nonprobate revolution"— an explosive increase in the use of "will substitutes" that make probate unnecessary.

There are basically three means by which property can be legally transferred at death to its new owners. Here they are, from best to worst from your perspective as executor:

- **No probate.** Property goes quickly and directly to the new owner with some simple paperwork but no probate court involvement.

- **Simple probate.** If the estate is small enough, property can go through simplified probate court procedures, which take only a few weeks or months and shouldn't require a lawyer.

- **Regular probate.** This means a regular court procedure—but many states now offer an informal probate process that's much like the small estate procedures.

This chapter explains what property can pass without probate. If an asset doesn't fall into one of the exceptions to probate discussed in this chapter, then check out Chapter 17 to see whether the estate may be eligible for your state's simple probate process. If that doesn't

work, you'll have to use regular probate, discussed in Chapter 18. Generally, you're most likely to face a probate court proceeding if the deceased person wasn't married at the time of death and didn't do any probate-avoidance planning.

REASONS TO GO THROUGH PROBATE

Even if out-of-court methods are available to transfer property in the estate, you may want to file a probate court case. Here are a couple of situations in which probate may be a good idea:

- You expect large claims from creditors and want probate because it gives creditors a deadline for submitting claims; if they miss it, they're out of luck.

- Beneficiaries are fighting and may get mad at you, and you want court supervision to help protect yourself from lawsuits.

A. Common Assets That Don't Go Through Probate

In general, two kinds of property don't need to go through probate:

- property the deceased person owned with someone else in a way that gives the surviving owner automatic ownership, and

- property for which the deceased person named a beneficiary in a document other than a will.

EXAMPLE: *At her death, Ramona owned a house and bank account in joint tenancy with her husband. She also owned an individual retirement account. On a form provided by the institution that managed the IRA, she had named her husband as beneficiary. Her daughter was named as the beneficiary of a life insurance policy Ramona owned on her own life. None of Ramona's assets will have to go through probate.*

The checklist below includes common kinds of nonprobate property. Go down the list and, based on the inventory you made in Chapter 8, check the kinds of property you think the estate includes. Then read the section covering that kind of property to see whether or not you can really get by without probate.

Finally, go to the chapter listed in the table for information on transferring the property to the people who inherit it. Although this book doesn't show you exactly how to transfer property in all 50 states, it can point you in the right direction.

CHECKLIST: COMMON KINDS OF NONPROBATE PROPERTY

In estate?	Type of Property	Chapter
	Joint tenancy property	13
	Tenancy by the entirety property	13
	Community property with right of survivorship*	14
	Living trust property	19
	Real estate that qualifies as a homestead and passes automatically to the spouse or children	
	Household goods and other property that goes to immediate family members under state law	5
	Wages, salary, or commissions due the deceased person	5
	Payable-on-death bank accounts	16
	Life insurance proceeds	5
	Retirement accounts (IRAs, 401(k) plans, and others)	15
	Securities registered in transfer-on-death (beneficiary) form	16
	U.S. Savings bonds, if co-owned	13
	U.S. Savings bonds registered in payable-on-death form	16
	Vehicles registered in transfer-on-death form*	16
	Vehicles that go to immediate family members under state law	
	Pension plan distributions	5
	Real estate left in a deed that takes effect at death*	16
	Personal property in "small estates"	17

* This option is allowed in only a few states.

B. Joint Tenancy Property

Legally, when one co-owner dies, joint tenancy property automatically belongs to the surviving co-owner(s). No probate is necessary. But the new owner(s) still need to complete some simple paperwork to make it clear to the world that they own the entire property. Chapter 13 explains how.

Community property states: If an asset held in joint tenancy was owned by a married couple in a state that uses the community property system of ownership (Alaska, Arizona, California, Idaho, Nevada, New Mexico, Washington, or Wisconsin), it may also be, legally, community property. In that case, you may have a choice about how to transfer the property to the surviving spouse. The surviving joint tenant can use the general procedure for joint tenancy property. Or there may be a special procedure for community property. For example, in California there is a special (and simple) way to submit a couple of forms to get a probate court order confirming the surviving spouse as the owner. It may be advantageous, from a tax standpoint, to characterize the joint tenancy property as community property. (See Chapter 11.)

C. Tenancy by the Entirety Property

Property that married couples (or domestic partners who have registered with the state in Hawaii or Vermont) own in tenancy by the entirety is transferred like joint tenancy property, with a sworn statement signed by the surviving spouse. No probate is necessary. If the property is real estate, the document must be recorded (filed) in the county land records. (See Chapter 13.)

D. Community Property

Some community property states have procedures to make it easy for a surviving spouse to take ownership of community property when the first spouse dies. Formal probate may not be necessary.

1. Community Property With Right of Survivorship

If the deceased person and the surviving spouse held title to property as "community property with right of survivorship," the property goes to the survivor automatically, without probate. (This option is available only in a few states.) To get the property into his or her name, the surviving spouse usually just records a simple affidavit (sworn statement). Chapter 14 explains the process.

2. Property Covered by a Community Property Agreement

If the deceased person and his or her spouse signed a community property agreement, you may be able to transfer property covered by the agreement without probate.

These agreements state who gets the couple's community property when one spouse dies. No probate is necessary. Usually, spouses agree that the survivor inherits all the community property, though other arrangements are possible.

3. Other Community Property

If the community property isn't covered by the procedures discussed just above, it still may be able to go to the surviving spouse without probate. For example, in California the survivor can file a simple fill-in-the-blanks form with the probate court that asks the court to transfer community property. (Chapter 14 has details.)

E. Property Held in a Living Trust

Property held in a revocable living trust can be transferred to its new owners without probate; that's the main purpose of creating a living trust. After the person who created the trust dies, the person named in the trust document to take over as trustee (the successor trustee) can transfer trust assets directly to the trust beneficiaries. No probate is necessary. (See Chapter 19.)

As executor, you have no authority over trust property unless you are also the successor trustee.

F. Real Estate That Qualifies as a Homestead

Although the term "homestead" may conjure up images of sod houses on the prairie or log cabins in the woods, these days a homestead

just refers to the legal protections that state law gives to a person's primary residence. Every state has its own definition.

In some states, a deceased person's homestead property may automatically go to the surviving spouse or children, without probate—and despite any will provisions that try to leave it to other beneficiaries.

EXAMPLE: *Fred and Martha own a house and small farm in Minnesota. Fred has a son from a former marriage, but he and Martha have no children. Fred's interest in the house and land is covered by Minnesota's homestead law. When Fred dies, state law entitles Martha to a "life estate" in the homestead unless she's waived her right by signing an agreement; this means she can use the land and live there the rest of her life. Fred's son will inherit the land after her death, whether Martha wants him to or not. (Minn. Stat. Ann. § 524.2-402.)*

Unless family members are fighting about who gets what, it probably isn't important to identify exactly what property is a homestead under state law, and who is entitled to inherit it. Knowing what property is a homestead, however, may save the estate money, because in some states homestead property inherited by close family members is protected from creditors (except the lender who financed the house purchase).

See a lawyer if you have questions. If you're concerned about disputes among family members or claims from creditors, see a lawyer to find out exactly what state law says about your situation.

G. Property That Passes to Immediate Family by Law

Under many states' laws, household goods— items that may be important to family members but are not usually of great value to others—can go to members of the immediate family without probate.

As a practical matter, the executor often hands over these objects, following the wishes of the deceased person's will, without worrying about what the law says. But if you are concerned that family members might argue later, be sure you are legally authorized to distribute small items. Talk to a lawyer or look up your state's statutes if necessary. (See Chapters 22 and 23 for help.)

H. Salary or Wages

If an employer owed the deceased person salary or wages, the employer will generally pay the amount due directly to the surviving spouse (or children, if there is no surviving spouse). (Chapter 5 discusses how to present a request to the employer.)

I. Payable-on-Death Bank Accounts

If you've found a bank account that names a beneficiary to inherit the funds at death, the money won't have to go through probate. In fact, the beneficiary can probably claim it without any help from you. (See Chapter 16.)

Two kinds of accounts can have such a beneficiary: payable-on-death (POD) accounts, and Totten trust accounts. The signature card for a POD account usually reads like this: "Esmee Duland POD Tiffany Duland." The card for a Totten trust or revocable trust account is usually worded like this: "Mabel L. Ostrov, in trust for Harvey Stein."

The difference between the two kinds of accounts (one is based on a contract between the depositor and the bank, the other on principles of trust law) shouldn't matter to you as executor. Either way, account funds can go directly to the beneficiary without probate.

J. Life Insurance Proceeds

Proceeds of a life insurance policy on the deceased person's life go directly to the named beneficiary, without probate. The only exception is if the estate was named as the beneficiary (this is rare) or all of the named beneficiaries (both primary and alternate) have died (also rare). To learn about how the beneficiary can claim the proceeds, see Chapter 5.

K. Individual Retirement Accounts

Almost everyone names beneficiaries for their individual retirement accounts, such as IRAs and 401(k)s, on the forms provided by the account custodian. Unless the deceased person named his or her estate as the beneficiary of an account (very unlikely), the funds remaining in these accounts can go to the beneficiaries directly. (See Chapter 15.)

L. Securities Registered in Transfer-on-Death Form

Almost all states allow people to register stocks, bonds, mutual funds, and brokerage accounts in transfer-on-death (TOD) or beneficiary form. The brokerage company statements will show you who owned the stock and whether or not ownership was registered in this way.

If a TOD beneficiary was named, the securities won't have to go through probate. Instead, the beneficiaries can claim them directly. (See Chapter 16.)

M. Savings Bonds

Savings bonds can be transferred without probate if two people co-own them, or if a single owner has named a payable-on-death (POD) beneficiary.

Bonds can be registered in co-ownership or beneficiary form, but not both. No more than two people can be listed as a savings bond's owner: either two co-owners, or one owner and a POD beneficiary.

1. Co-Owned Bonds

If the deceased person owned U.S. savings bonds with another person, the surviving owner automatically inherits the bonds. No

probate is necessary. (Chapter 13 discusses how to get bonds reissued in the surviving owner's name.)

2. Bonds Registered in Beneficiary Form

U.S. savings bonds can also be registered in payable-on-death form. (The names will look something like this: "MaryAnn Levy, POD Nicole Levy.") If the owner designated a POD beneficiary for the bonds, that beneficiary inherits them without probate. (Chapter 16 discusses how to get the bonds reissued in the new owner's name.)

N. Vehicles

Lots of states, recognizing that it doesn't do anybody any good to have a car sitting around until probate is wrapped up, have come up with some way to allow cars to be quickly transferred to new owners after a death.

1. Vehicles Registered in Transfer-on-Death Form

Only a few states allow this. Only California, Connecticut, Kansas, Missouri, and Ohio currently offer this sensible form of car and boat registration.

If the registration shows a transfer-on-death (TOD) beneficiary, the vehicle does not need to go through probate. Chapter 16 discusses the transfer procedure.

2. Vehicles That Qualify for Nonprobate Transfer Under State Law

A fair number of states have simple, streamlined methods to transfer ownership of a deceased person's vehicles. Sometimes these methods are available only to the surviving spouse or only if the value of the vehicle is below a certain amount.

For details and forms, your best bet is to contact your state's motor vehicles agency. To find a link to that agency's website, look on the Response Insurance website, at www.response .com/tips_tools/great_links.asp.

You may have to do a little digging. Many state websites don't discuss transfers at death or include them in their main list of subjects. If you don't see what you're looking for right away, keep burrowing into the site. For example, try the "Forms" section and you may be rewarded with exactly the document you need.

O. Pension Plan Distributions and Other Death Benefits

If named beneficiaries are entitled to death benefits, such as pension plan distributions, the beneficiaries can claim them without probate. (See Chapter 5.)

P. Real Estate Left by a Transfer-on-Death Deed

Only a few states allow this. Transfer-on-death deeds are authorized by statute only in Arizona, Kansas, Missouri, New Mexico, and Ohio.

If you've found a valid transfer-on-death deed, the real estate won't have to go through probate; it will go directly to the named beneficiary with no further action on your part. The transfer procedure is discussed in Chapter 16.

Q. Personal Property in "Small Estates"

Probate courts, and probate lawyers, don't want to be bothered with small estates, which are more trouble than they're worth. So if the total value of the estate is small enough, most states allow the beneficiaries to claim their property without going to court. Instead, beneficiaries prepare a simple sworn statement (affidavit) and present it to whoever's got the property (for example, a bank) or to whoever is in charge of ownership records (for example, the state motor vehicles department). People can use an affidavit to collect their property whether or not there is a will. The affidavit states that the person is entitled to use the affidavit procedure and is entitled to inherit the property.

How useful the affidavit procedure is depends on your situation. It's subject to some important restrictions:

- The deceased person must have left a small estate, as defined by state law. This varies from a few hundred dollars to more than $100,000.

- Affidavits can't be used to transfer real estate except in certain circumstances in a couple of states (Texas and California).

- In most states, inheritors cannot use the affidavit procedure if regular probate court proceedings have begun.

The estate you're handling may qualify even if it doesn't seem very small. That's because when it comes to determining the value of the estate, in many states you don't count the value of certain kinds of property—for example, real estate located in another state or motor vehicles.

But most important, many states count only the value of property that goes through probate. That means that all living trust property, joint tenancy property, TOD assets, and other nonprobate property are excluded.

EXAMPLE: *Monique lives in Indiana, which restricts use of its out-of-court affidavit procedure to estates worth no more than $25,000. Monique leaves about $200,000 worth of property at her death. But the relatives who inherit her property can still use the affidavit procedure because Indiana, like a number of other states, includes only assets that* would otherwise go through probate. So property left in a living trust, payable-on-death bank account, or through another probate-avoidance technique is not counted.

Monique's estate contains:

- *her house, worth $80,000, which she transferred to a living trust to avoid probate*

- *securities, worth $40,000, that she registered in beneficiary form*

- *payable-on-death bank accounts containing $30,000*

- *a $40,000 retirement account for which she's named a beneficiary*

- *a car worth $7,500, and*

- *miscellaneous personal property and household items worth $10,000.*

Because only the $10,000 of miscellaneous items would be subject to probate, Monique has a "small estate" under Indiana law. Her inheritors can use the affidavit procedure to claim the household items (though as a practical matter, the executor will probably just hand them over without requiring any documents). They can submit an affidavit to the state motor vehicles agency to re-register ownership of the car. No probate will be necessary.

To find out whether or not your state offers an affidavit procedure, and if so whether the beneficiaries you're dealing with can use it, see your state's summary page in the appendix. ∎

CHAPTER 13

Transferring Joint Tenancy and Other Survivorship Property

Property held in joint tenancy, tenancy by the entirety, or community property with right of survivorship automatically passes to the survivor when one of the original owners dies. Real estate, bank accounts, vehicles, and investments can all pass this way.

Legally, the moment one owner dies, the survivor becomes the sole owner of the entire property. This is true even if the deceased co-owner's will tries to leave the deceased person's half to someone else. No probate is necessary to transfer ownership of the property.

But even though the survivor automatically owns the property, the world has no way of knowing that until the survivor "clears title" to the property. Generally, all the surviving owner needs to do is fill out some simple documents and take them to the local land records office. The exact procedure in your state may vary from the general process outlined here, but this chapter should give you a good idea of what's involved.

If you're an executor appointed in a will, then technically, joint tenancy property does not come under your authority. The property is not governed by the will and it's not part of the deceased person's probate estate. But as a practical matter, in many instances the executor is also a surviving joint tenant. So you may need to clear title to joint tenancy property yourself—or help a relative do it.

Transfer procedures that apply to joint tenancy generally apply to the other forms of "survivorship property" as well: tenancy by the entirety (available to married couples in many states) and community property with right of survivorship (available to married couples in a just a few states).

(Reminder: If you don't know how the co-owners held title to the property, see Chapter 8.)

A. Real Estate

Legal rules affecting real estate are always set by the state in which the real estate is located. So to transfer jointly owned real estate to the surviving co-owner, you'll have to find out the exact procedure for your locality.

The general idea, however, is the same everywhere. You need to put a document on file in the local public land records, showing that one joint owner has died and that the surviving co-owner is now the sole owner of the property.

1. Documents You Need

In some states, it's enough for the surviving joint owner simply to file (record) a certified copy of the deceased co-owner's death certificate. (Chapter 4 discusses how to get certified copies of the death certificate.) In others, the surviving co-owner must also sign and file a statement setting out the facts and explaining that he or she is now the sole owner. The statement may need to be notarized (in which case it's called an affidavit), or merely signed "under penalty of perjury," without a notary (in which case it's usually called a declaration). It never hurts to file such a statement, even if it's not the custom in your state.

The affidavit is usually called an "Affidavit—Death of Joint Tenant" or "Affidavit of Survivorship." Typically, it contains these simple elements:

- a legal description of the property (get that from the original deed)

- a statement that the property was held in joint tenancy (or in tenancy by the entirety or as survivorship community property)

- recording information (usually, a book and page number) that identifies the document that established the joint ownership (look on the deed that transferred the property to the co-owners)

- the name and date of death of the deceased owner, and

- the name of the new owner (the surviving owner).

The death certificate and affidavit establish that one co-owner has died and that the survivor now owns the property alone.

A sample affidavit for surviving spouses, from Iowa, is shown below.

Track down local documents. To find out what documents are required in your state, talk to someone at a title company or the county land records office. To see survivorship affidavits for your state, look for some that have been filed recently and are part of the public records, or go to a law library and look at real estate form books that lawyers use. (Chapter 23 discusses legal research.) And of course, you can always ask a lawyer.

AFFIDAVIT OF SURVIVING SPOUSE FOR CHANGE OF TITLE TO REAL ESTATE

STATE OF IOWA   )
) SS.
COUNTY OF MCDONALD   )

I, Emmeline A. Hardin, being first duly sworn on oath, depose and state as follows:

1. I am the surviving spouse of Joseph H. Hardin, who died on the 12th day of July, 20xx.

2. The following described real estate was owned only by Joseph H. Hardin and this Affiant, as joint tenants with full rights of survivorship at the time of Joseph H. Hardin's death:

   [*legal description of property*]

3. I hereby request that the auditor enter this information on the transfer books pursuant to section 558.66 of the Iowa Code.

_____
Emmeline A. Hardin

Subscribed and sworn to before me this
_____ day of _____, 20___.

Notary Public in and for the State of Iowa

⚠️ **You may need to meet other state or local requirements.** Before you record your documents, check with the land records office to find out whether or not additional documents are required. In California, for example, a form must be filed whenever real estate is transferred, to let the local tax assessor know that the property may need to be reassessed for property tax purposes.

2. Where to File Your Documents

Whatever documents (probably a death certificate and affidavit of survivorship) you need, file (record) them at the county land records office where the property is located. This place goes by different names in different states; it's commonly called the County Recorder or Registrar of Deeds.

Most counties charge about $10 to $15 to record the first page of a document, and a smaller amount for each additional page. You can call ahead to find out the exact amount.

You can do your filing in person or by mail. If you use the mail, be sure to include a cover letter that directs the clerk to return the originals to you, and a stamped, self-addressed envelope. If you deliver your documents in person, a clerk will stamp them with the filing information, make copies, and give you back the originals.

💡 **Go in person if you can.** That way, if there's a minor problem with your papers, a helpful clerk may explain what's wrong—and better still, how to fix it.

B. Bank Accounts

If the deceased person owned an account together in joint tenancy (or in tenancy by the entirety or as survivorship community property) with someone, the surviving co-owner can still use the money in the account after the death. The surviving co-owner, typically a surviving spouse or child, automatically owns all the money in the account, without any probate proceedings.

Getting the bank account shifted into the name of the survivor is usually pretty simple. The surviving joint tenant should take a certified copy of the death certificate to the bank, along with the checkbook or savings account passbook, if you have them. The bank will change the ownership records.

C. Securities

How you go about getting title to securities (stocks or bonds) transferred into the name of the surviving joint tenant depends on how the securities were owned. Did the owners have stock certificates, or, as is much more common, were the stocks held in a brokerage account? This section discusses both situations.

1. Brokerage Accounts, Mutual Funds, or Money Market Funds

If the deceased person owned a brokerage account or mutual fund account in joint tenancy, your best bet is to contact the brokerage company. You should be able to find a toll-free customer service number on an account statement or on the company's website.

The website may also contain forms and instructions that explain exactly what to do. For example, the Fidelity fund group website offers a downloadable form called "Change of Account Registration Form." The surviving joint tenant fills out the form, following the instructions for the situation (death of a joint tenant), and sends it to the company, along with a certified copy of the death certificate. Fidelity will reregister the account in the name of the surviving owner. Other large investment companies have similar procedures and forms with similar names such as "Transfer of Ownership" or "Change of Ownership" (Vanguard).

If the deceased person held a variety of investments in one account—an increasingly common way for people to manage their investments—then one change may do it all. If,

however, there are several different accounts, you'll have to make more changes.

It's important to know that the surviving joint tenant's signature on the forms may have to be "guaranteed" so that the company knows it is genuine. Getting a signature guaranteed is a lot like getting a signature notarized—but notarization is *not* a substitute for a guarantee. Normally, banks or brokers the surviving co-owner deals with have the power to guarantee a signature. (You don't have to get the signature guarantee at the institution that holds the funds.) The bank employee or broker, shown that the signature is genuine, will sign the document and stamp it "signature guaranteed," and you're on your way.

2. Certificates

If the deceased person possessed actual stock or bond certificates, you'll need to have them reissued in the surviving co-owner's name. Do this by sending them to the corporation's "transfer agent." You'll find the transfer agent's name and address listed on the stock or bond certificate. (If the stock isn't publicly traded, there won't be a transfer agent, so you'll have to deal directly with the company.)

You'll need to send the transfer agent these documents:

- the original stock or bond certificates

- a certified copy of the deceased co-owner's death certificate

- a stock or bond power, signed by the surviving co-owner

- an Affidavit of Residence signed by the surviving co-owner and notarized, and

- a cover letter signed by the surviving co-owner.

Here's an explanation of the last three of these documents:

The **stock power** authorizes transfer of the shares. It may be printed on the back of the stock certificates or found as a separate form available from banks or brokers (sometimes on their websites). Fill in the basic information about the surviving joint tenant (name and Social Security number), and then about the stock or bond: the number of shares, the kind of stock (common or preferred), the name of the company, and the numbers of the stock certificates (printed on the certificates). You don't need to fill in the name of the "attorney" who is appointed to transfer the securities; commonly, this person is the employee of the transfer agent who actually makes the change on the corporation's records.

The surviving co-owner's signature on the stock power must be "guaranteed" so that the transfer agent knows it is genuine. For instructions, see Section C1, just above.

IRREVOCABLE STOCK OR BOND POWER

Account Number _____

FOR VALUE RECEIVED, the undersigned does (do) hereby sell, assign, or transfer to:

_____ | **Name(s) of new owner(s) of stock (i.e., surviving joint tenant(s), surviving spouse or beneficiary)**

Social Security or Tax Identifying Number ___ **Social Security number of new owner(s)**

Number of shares _____ shares of **Type of stock (common, preferred, etc.)**

IF STOCK, COMPLETE THIS PORTION

stock of ___ **Name of company** _____

represented by Certificate(s) No. **Number of stock certificate**

inclusive, standing in the name of the undersigned on the

books of said company.

Number of bonds _____ bonds of ___ **Issuer of bond(s)** _____

IF BONDS, COMPLETE THIS PORTION

_____ in the principal amount of $___ **Face value** _____

No(s). **Number(s) of bond certificate(s)** _____

inclusive, standing in the name of the undersigned on the

books of said company.

The undersigned does (do) hereby irrevocably constitute and appoint **Leave this blank**
_____ attorney to transfer the said stock
or bond(s), as the case may be, on the books of said company, with full power of
substitution in the premises.

IMPORTANT: The signature(s) to this power must correspond with the name(s) as
written upon the face of the certificate(s) or bond(s) in every particular without alteration.

Dated: _____

Signed by surviving joint tenant, surviving spouse, executor or administrator of decedent's estate, or the beneficiary entitled in the case of small estates

Person(s) Executing This Power Sign(s) Here

_____

SIGNATURE GUARANTEED

An **Affidavit of Residence** (sometimes called an Affidavit of Domicile) is a simple document that states where the deceased person was a legal resident. The surviving co-owner signs the statement in front of a notary public. If the deceased co-owner was a resident of the state where the company issuing the stock is incorporated, a transfer tax may be due.

SAMPLE AFFIDAVIT OF RESIDENCE

I, Mary Catherine Fitzgerald, being duly sworn, depose and say:

I reside at 105 Elm Street, City of Monroe, County of Beaumont, State of North Carolina, and I am the executor of the estate of Elspeth Hannah Clausten, who died on January 1, 20xx.

At the time of death, the legal residence of decendent was the City of Springfield, County of Beaumont, and State of North Carolina, and had been the same for approximately two years.

_____

Signature of Affiant

CERTIFICATE OF ACKNOWLEDGMENT OF NOTARY PUBLIC

State of   )
) ss.
County of   )

On _____, before me, _____, a notary public in and for said state, personally appeared _____, personally known to me (or proved on the basis of satisfactory evidence) to be the person whose name is subscribed to the within instrument, and acknowledged to me that she executed the same in her authorized capacity, and that by her signature on the instrument the person, or the entity upon behalf of which the person acted, executed the instrument.

WITNESS my hand and official seal

_____

Notary Public for the State of:

[NOTARIAL SEAL]   My commission expires: _____

The **cover letter** is also signed by the surviving co-owner. It simply directs that the securities be reregistered in the name of the surviving co-owner. A sample letter, which you can adapt to your needs, is shown below.

Call ahead. Before you finalize the letter, call to make sure that the transfer agent hasn't changed since the certificates were issued.

COVER LETTER TO STOCK TRANSFER AGENT

July 19, 20xx

[*name & address of transfer agent*]

Re: Securities of Joseph H. Johnson, deceased

Enclosed are stock certificates registered in the names of Joseph H. Johnson and Adele M. Johnson.

Certificate number: A4546548
Type of security: common stock
Number of shares [*or for bonds, the face amount*]: 100
Name of company: Runaway Manufacturing, Inc.

These shares were owned in tenancy by the entirety by Joseph H. Johnson and Adele M. Johnson. Please cancel the enclosed certificates and issue new certificates in the name of the surviving spouse, Adele M. Johnson, Social Security number 123-45-6789.

I have enclosed a Stock Power, a certified copy of Mr. Johnson's death certificate, and an Affidavit of Residence.

Sincerely,

Adele M. Johnson
4444 North 27th Street
Clarkdale, Illinois 61890
(555) 555-1234

Once you've got the whole package together, send everything by registered mail and request a return receipt.

D. Vehicles

If a car or other vehicle (motorcycle, RV, or small boat) was owned in joint tenancy, tenancy by the entirety, or as survivorship community property, it should be easy to get title transferred into the name of the surviving co-owner. (If you're not sure whether or not the vehicle was owned in joint tenancy or another form of ownership with survivorship rights, see Chapter 8.)

The rules vary somewhat from state to state, but you'll need to provide:

- a copy of the death certificate (you may not need a certified copy; check your state DMV's rules)

- the vehicle's title slip, and

- its registration card.

If you can't find the title or registration, you can request duplicates from the state motor vehicles department.

You'll probably also have to fill out a simple transfer form provided by the state motor vehicles department. Depending on the state, the DMV may also require proof of insurance and proof of compliance with emission control (smog) rules.

The fee for retitling a car is usually quite low, commonly less than $25. Some states charge nothing when the transfer is necessary because of a death.

You can find a lot of state-specific information, and often forms as well, on the Internet. For a link to the website of your state's motor vehicles agency, check the Response Insurance website, at www.response.com/tips_tools/great_links.asp. Once there, look for information on registration. If you can't find what you need, call the local office and ask for guidance.

Even if the car wasn't owned jointly, your state may offer a simple way to transfer title without probate. For example, in many states, a car automatically goes to the surviving spouse (or next closest relative) unless the owner's will provides otherwise. See Chapter 12.

E. Savings Bonds

If two people are co-owners of a United States savings bond, when one owner dies the survivor automatically becomes the sole owner. The survivor can redeem the bond, have it reissued in his or her name, or just leave it.

The advantage of getting the bond reissued in the survivor's name is that the survivor can then name a beneficiary for the bond. That way, at the survivor's death, the bond will automatically pass to the person he or she named as beneficiary, without probate. During the bond owner's life, the beneficiary has no rights to the bond.

To get new bonds issued in the survivor's name, use a Treasury Department form called "Request to Reissue United States Savings Bonds." It is available at banks or online at www.publicdebt.treas.gov (go to the "Forms" section and look under "Reissue Forms"). The surviving owner must sign the form in front of someone at a bank who is an authorized "certifying officer."

If for some reason you can't get everything done at your local bank, contact a Federal Reserve Bank. You can find the closest Federal Reserve Bank online, at www.publicdebt.treas .gov/sav/savdies.htm.

F. If Title Wasn't Cleared When the First Joint Tenant Died

It's not uncommon to discover, if you're dealing with the estate of the second joint tenant to die, that title to property was never officially cleared when the first joint tenant died. In other words, official records show that the property is owned by two people—both of whom are now deceased. In that case you've got a little more work to do.

Before you can transfer the property to the person who inherits it now, you must go back and clear ownership records of the name of the first joint tenant to die. To do that, just follow the steps in this chapter as if the person had just died. Then you can go ahead with the transfer to the new owner.

EXAMPLE: *Herbert and Helen own their home in joint tenancy. When Herbert dies, Helen does nothing to clear title to the house, so in the public records, it still appears that Herbert and Helen are the owners. But the joint tenancy ended at Herbert's death; Helen is the sole owner.*

When Helen dies, the house passes to the beneficiary she named in her will. But before it can be transferred during regular probate proceedings, her executor must first clear the title, as should have been done when Herbert died. ■

CHAPTER 14

Transferring Community Property

If you are handling the affairs of your late spouse and live in a community property state, odds are good that you will be able to transfer ownership of community property to yourself without going through regular probate.

COMMUNITY PROPERTY STATES

Alaska*	Arizona
California	Idaho
Louisiana**	Nevada
New Mexico	Texas
Washington	Wisconsin***

*Married couples can create community property with a written agreement.
**This book doesn't cover Louisiana law.
***Wisconsin's system of property ownership is like that of community property states, but it is called "marital property."

Community property, remember, is property that belongs to both spouses. Even assets that are held in only one spouse's name may legally be community property. If you aren't sure whether or not a particular asset was community property, Chapter 8 can help you figure it out.

This chapter outlines each state's rules for transferring community assets to a surviving spouse.

Pending divorce. Once a couple divorces, there is no more community property. If the deceased person was in the middle of a divorce at the time of death, but it wasn't yet final, it's a good idea to see a lawyer.

A. Your Transfer Options

Every community property state has its own rules about how community property can be transferred to a surviving spouse. Here is what to look for:

- **Survivorship community property: no probate.** If you and your spouse held title to an asset as "community property with right of survivorship," you now automatically own the property. Real estate, bank accounts, vehicles, and investments can all pass this way.

- **Community property agreement: no probate.** If you and your spouse signed an agreement authorizing it, your community property can now pass to you without probate.

- **Special procedures for community property: quicker probate.** A few states offer probate shortcuts for community property.

Check the table below to see what's available in your state. If you can't take advantage of any of these shortcuts, community property is treated just like other property—which means it may have to go through probate.

OPTIONS FOR COMMUNITY PROPERTY

State	Survivorship community property	Community property agreements	Quicker probate for community property not covered by agreement
Alaska	yes	yes	
Arizona	yes		
California	yes		yes
Idaho		yes	yes
Nevada	yes		
New Mexico			yes
Texas		yes	yes
Washington		yes	
Wisconsin	yes	yes	

The rest of this chapter discusses community property agreements and the special state procedures that make transferring community property easy. If you're dealing with survivorship community property, the process of getting title in your name alone is just like clearing title to joint tenancy property; see Chapter 13 for information.

B. Community Property Agreements

In Alaska, Idaho, Texas, Washington, and Wisconsin, a married couple can sign an agreement that determines what happens to some or all of their property at death. Usually, couples declare all of their property to be community property and leave it to the survivor, without probate, when one spouse dies. The agreement functions much like a will—with the important difference that the property doesn't have to go through probate when the first spouse dies.

1. Validity of These Agreements

Different states have different rules about what makes community property agreements valid. All states require them to be in writing. They may need to be witnessed or notarized. They may also need to have been recorded (filed) in the county where the couple lived and where they owned real estate.

WAS A COMMUNITY PROPERTY AGREEMENT REVOKED?

Neither spouse can, acting alone, change or revoke a community property agreement. To revoke an agreement, generally the spouses must:

- agree to cancel (rescind) the agreement
- divorce, or
- separate permanently.

Just making a will that leaves property in a different way may not revoke the agreement.

These rules mostly come from courts, and they can change. If you have questions about the validity of a community property agreement, see a lawyer.

2. Transferring Community Property to the Surviving Spouse

When the first spouse dies, the survivor immediately owns all the property covered by the agreement. But you'll still need a document that shows that you are the sole legal owner.

Exactly what you'll need to do to get title into your name depends on the kind of asset. You'll need different documents for real estate than for bank accounts, for example. But, you'll probably need to start with at least these two documents:

- a copy of the community property agreement, and
- a certified copy of the death certificate.

Give these to whatever institution or agency controls the title documents—for example, for vehicles it's the state motor vehicles agency, for stocks and bonds it's the company's transfer agent, and for bank accounts it's the bank. For real estate, talk to the title company that issued title insurance for the property. You'll probably need to record (file) in the land records office a copy of the agreement, the death certificate, and perhaps a sworn statement that the deceased person's debts and taxes have been paid. (The agreement may have been recorded before the death; if so, the original signed agreement should be stamped with the recording information.) Some states have statutes that specifically address the steps to take; you can probably also get help from the institution or agency you're dealing with.

WHAT HAPPENS AT THE SECOND SPOUSE'S DEATH

In Alaska and Wisconsin, a community property agreement can name a beneficiary to inherit the property at the second spouse's death. (In Washington, it's not clear whether or not spouses can do this.) After one spouse dies, however, the survivor can amend the agreement to change who inherits his or her property, unless the agreement expressly forbids it.

C. State Probate Shortcuts

California, Idaho, New Mexico, and Texas offer surviving spouses relatively easy ways to transfer community property to themselves. This section outlines those abbreviated procedures.

⚠️ **Taking a probate shortcut can have a downside if you expect big debts.** When you accept your deceased spouse's half of the community property, generally you also accept liability for his or her debts. That's not a problem for most people. But if your spouse owned a business or had big tax debts from before your marriage, you may worry that large debts might surface later and that creditors could go after the property. In that case you might want to probate your spouse's estate, to take advantage of probate's cutoff of creditors' claims. (See Chapter 18.)

1. California

California offers surviving spouses two ways to take sole title of community property.

a. Affidavit for Community Real Estate

If you and your spouse explicitly held title to real estate as community property—that is, the deed says you owned it "as husband and wife" or "as community property"—then you, as surviving spouse, can use a simple sworn statement (affidavit) to get title in your name alone. The one-page affidavit gives the legal description of the property, which you can take from the deed. It states that one spouse has died and that you now own the property outright. It must be signed in front of a notary public.

You file (record) the affidavit, and a certified copy of the death certificate with the county recorder's office in the county where the property is located. These documents become part of the public record, serving to show that ownership has passed to you.

b. The Spousal Property Petition

You can use this probate shortcut to transfer any kind of property to yourself (community or separate property you inherit from your late spouse) as surviving spouse. It's useful when:

- You can't use the affidavit procedure for real estate discussed just above, because even if the real estate was in fact community property, title to it wasn't held as community property.

- You want to transfer property other than real estate.

This process still involves the probate (Superior) court, but it's simpler than a regular probate court case. To begin the process, you prepare a document called a Spousal Property Petition (a fill-in-the-blanks form, provided by the court) and file it with the court. In the form, you ask that the property be transferred to you. The court will schedule a hearing, and you'll have to mail a notice of the hearing to interested persons.

Eventually the court will issue a Spousal Property Order, transferring ownership of the property to you. If real estate is being transferred, you can record (file) the order with the recorder in the county in which the property is located, and then the public records will clearly show that title is now held in your name only.

📖 **Help for California readers.** Once again, your best bet is to check *How to Probate an Estate in California*, by Julia Nissley (Nolo). This extremely helpful book contains forms and nitty-gritty instructions on how to transfer property to a surviving spouse.

2. Idaho

Idaho offers a simple probate procedure when the surviving spouse didn't leave a will, the entire estate is community property, and the surviving spouse is the only heir. You file a simple petition with the probate court, and if the court finds that you've met these requirements, it issues an order stating that you now own everything. (Idaho Code § 15-3-301.)

One potential drawback to this method is that you become legally responsible for any claims made against your spouse's estate. With regular probate, creditors' claims are cut off after a few months—but that's not true with this procedure. For most people, this isn't an important issue, but if you worry about large claims from creditors, you should consider going through probate.

3. New Mexico

If certain conditions are met, New Mexico allows a surviving spouse to take title to the couple's residence without probate. (N.M. Stat. Ann. § 45-3-1205.) There are no other special probate shortcuts for community property.

Here are the requirements:

- The property was your principal residence (or your spouse's).

- You inherit the property by will or intestate succession (that is, under state law).

- The property was held as community property.

- The property is valued, for property tax purposes, at less than $100,000.

- No probate is necessary for other assets, and no probate proceedings have begun.

- Certain debts (funeral expenses, expenses of last illness, and your spouse's "unsecured" debts—that is, debts not attached to specific property) have been paid.

- Federal and state taxes have been paid.

To transfer the property, you prepare a written statement describing the property and stating that you have met each condition. Your signature doesn't have to be notarized, but you do sign "under penalty of perjury," which is like testifying under oath. You're swearing that your statements are true to the best of your knowledge.

You can file (record) the affidavit with the county clerk as soon as six months after the death. It must be accompanied by a certified copy of the death certificate, a copy of the deed to the property (containing the legal description), and the original will, if there is one. These documents become part of the public record, serving to show that ownership has passed to you.

4. Texas

If your spouse died without a will, and under Texas law the property you owned together as community property passes to you, the surviving spouse, then no probate is necessary. (Tex. Prob. Code § 155.) And if there is no probate, you have power to use community property to pay debts and to "wind up community affairs." (Tex. Prob. Code § 160.) If there is a will, however, probate will probably be necessary.

D. When the Second Spouse Dies

If you're dealing with the estate of the second spouse to die, you may find that title to property was never officially cleared when the first spouse died. In that case you've got a little more work to do.

Before you can transfer the property to the person who inherits it now, you must go back and clear ownership records of the name of the first spouse to die. To do that, you'll need to provide death certificates for both spouses, to show whoever controls the title documents that both are now deceased. ■

CHAPTER 15

Claiming Money in Retirement Plans

A deceased person who had some kind of retirement plan account—an IRA, 401(k), 403(b), Keogh, or SEP-IRA—almost surely named a beneficiary to inherit any funds left in the accounts after his or her death. The beneficiary can (in almost all cases) claim these funds without probate proceedings. If you're not a beneficiary, you, as executor, may not be involved at all—but as with collecting other nonprobate property, you may be called upon to help less financially sophisticated beneficiaries get their money. If for some reason there is no beneficiary—either because the deceased person didn't name one or the named person (and any named alternate) has died—you will definitely play a role, because the money will become part of the estate.

If you're the only beneficiary and want to take the cash out of the account right away, the process is easy. Contact the firm that administers the account (the name and contact information, including a website address, will be on the account statements) and ask how to proceed. Probably all you will need is a certified copy of the death certificate and proof of your own identity.

It may, however, reduce your own income taxes if you keep the money (or at least some of it) in a retirement account for a while, so you can defer taxes on the money until it's distributed to you.

This chapter covers only the basics.
Retirement plan beneficiaries face many choices, with varying tax consequences. Before

you decide how to proceed—especially if there is more than one beneficiary—consult the much more detailed discussion in *IRAs, 401(k)s & Other Retirement Plans: Taking Your Money Out*, by Twila Slesnick and John C. Suttle (Nolo). It's an extremely lucid and thorough explanation of the available distribution options.

A. Retirement Plans: The Basics

To make intelligent decisions about when and how to withdraw money you inherit from a retirement account, it is key to understand the basic rules that govern these accounts.

1. How Retirement Plans Save on Taxes

As you no doubt know, with conventional IRAs and 401(k) plans, people can put off paying some income taxes until retirement, when they expect to be in a lower tax bracket. The tax break comes because the contributions to these accounts (up to a limit) are made with pre-tax dollars (401(k) plans) or are tax-deductible (IRAs). If those contributions grow through wise investment, the growth isn't taxed until the account owner or a beneficiary withdraws funds from the account. And the money that would otherwise have gone to pay taxes can be invested for years, to help grow the account.

A relative newcomer to the retirement plan roster, the Roth IRA, also saves on taxes but operates on a different principle. The account owner must pay taxes on amounts contributed to a Roth IRA, but the money (including growth from investment) is not taxed when it's withdrawn. So if the invested money has grown, all the growth is tax-free.

2. Early Distribution Penalties

If an account holder withdraws retirement plan money before reaching age $59^1/_2$, the IRS generally assesses a 10% penalty on the amount distributed, in addition to any tax due. (There are a few significant exceptions to the rule.) Beneficiaries who inherit funds because of the account owner's death, however, do not have to pay this penalty.

EXAMPLE: *Sara, 43, inherits the funds in her father's IRA. She can take money out of the account without paying the 10% early distribution penalty.*

3. Required Minimum Distributions

The tax laws are written with the intention that retirement account money be used for retirement. Accordingly, they require account owners to withdraw at least a certain amount each year (the "required minimum distribution") typically beginning when they hit age $70^1/_2$. These rules affect how a beneficiary must withdraw funds, too, as discussed later in this chapter.

a. When They Start

Here are the basic rules on when mandatory distributions must begin:

IRA: Age $70^1/_2$.

401(k) plan: Age $70^1/_2$ or at actual retirement, whichever is later. (Self-employed people must begin withdrawals at age $70^1/_2$.)

403(b) plan (for employees of educational or religious entities): Age $70^1/_2$ or actual retirement, whichever is later.

Roth IRA: No required distributions.

b. How Much Must Be Distributed

Once required distributions start, the amount that must be taken out of the account each year depends on the life expectancy of the account owner and of the beneficiary, as shown in IRS actuarial tables. The longer the life expectancy, the smaller the required distributions.

For purposes of calculating life expectancy, the IRS assumes that the beneficiary is ten years younger than the account owner. The beneficiary's actual age is considered only if the beneficiary is the spouse and is in fact more than ten years younger than the account owner.

Again, it's important to understand that life expectancy is not based on the health of the account owner or beneficiary, but on the IRS table. Look up your age and you'll find your statistical life expectancy. (You can find the IRS tables in *IRAs, 401(k)s & Other Retirement Plans: Taking Your Money Out,* by Twila Slesnick and John C. Suttle (Nolo).)

c. Penalties

If an account owner or beneficiary doesn't make a required distribution, the law imposes an impressive 50% penalty. That means the penalty amount is half of the amount that should have been withdrawn that year.

4. How Inherited Funds Are Taxed

If you inherit money from a conventional IRA or 401(k) plan, you must pay income tax on it—something that isn't true for other property you inherit. Money from retirement plans is taxed because, as mentioned earlier, contributions to these accounts are usually tax-deductible or made with pre-tax dollars. The tax on that money, and on the income it earns after being invested, is deferred until the money is distributed from the account.

Money withdrawn from a Roth IRA, on the other hand, is generally not taxed. That's because unlike conventional IRAs, Roth IRAs are funded with after-tax money.

A. Who's the Beneficiary?

For most people, it's easy to figure out who the beneficiary is—it's whoever the deceased person named on the forms provided by the retirement plan administrator. But rarely, it may not be obvious where the money should go, as might be the case if the beneficiary didn't want the money, or a former spouse did. This section discusses a few possible complications.

1. The Beneficiary Declines the Money

Occasionally, a beneficiary doesn't need or want the money in a retirement account. For example, a widow in a high income tax bracket might prefer not to pay income tax on retirement account funds that she doesn't particularly need. If she's the primary beneficiary, she can avoid the tax by "disclaiming," or giving

up, the inheritance. It will then pass to the alternate (contingent) beneficiary named in the retirement plan documents.

The alternate beneficiary—in many instances a child or grandchild—is likely to be younger and in a lower income tax bracket. Because that beneficiary can take required distributions over many years, based on his or her life expectancy, the money in the account will continue to grow tax-free. The result will be significant tax savings.

If you think disclaiming might be a good idea, consult a tax expert or financial planner. Before you act, be sure you understand the long-term consequences of your decision.

2. The Surviving Spouse's Rights

Most people name their spouses to inherit the funds in their retirement plan accounts. But even a surviving spouse who wasn't named as the beneficiary may still have the right to claim some of the money. The rules are different in different states; here is a brief outline of them.

Solving squabbles. Lots of people name someone other than a spouse—their children, for example—as the beneficiaries for retirement plans, with the full consent of their spouse. But if a spouse and other beneficiaries are arguing about who should get the funds in a retirement account, they need to either get some help settling their competing claims—perhaps with the help of a neutral mediator—or hire lawyers (the much more expensive option).

a. IRAs

A married person who has a conventional or Roth IRA is free to designate anyone as the beneficiary. But a surviving spouse may still have the right to claim some of the money.

- If the couple lived in a community property state—Alaska (by agreement only), Arizona, California, Idaho, Louisiana, Nevada, New Mexico, Texas, Washington, or Wisconsin—the funds in the account may be community property, owned equally by each spouse. The surviving spouse could claim his or her half.

- In any other state, the surviving spouse may be able to make a claim to some of the funds if he or she wasn't left a significant share of the deceased spouse's property. Just how much a survivor can claim varies from state to state; see Chapter 6.

SPOUSES CAN CHANGE THESE RULES

If a couple signed a contract (a prenuptial agreement or a community property agreement) setting out each other's rights to property, it may address their claims to retirement plan funds. If such an agreement exists, read it carefully.

---

b. 401(k), 403(b), and Keogh Plans

Under federal law, the surviving spouse is entitled to claim all the money in the plan unless he or she signed a waiver consenting to the deceased spouse's choice of a different beneficiary. A waiver form is usually provided by the firm that administers the plan.

The waiver must have been signed while the couple was married. A prenuptial agreement signed before the marriage, in which either one of the engaged couple waived the right to the other's retirement plan, isn't enough.

3. A Former Spouse's Rights

What if someone named his or her spouse as beneficiary of a retirement account, and later the couple divorced but the account owner didn't change the beneficiary designation? Whether or not the ex-spouse still inherits the funds depends on the kind of account and on state and federal law.

See a lawyer if an ex-spouse makes a claim. In this unusual situation, expert help is called for.

a. IRAs

If the account is an IRA, what happens depends on state law. In many states, divorce automatically revokes a beneficiary designation made to a former spouse, which means that the ex-spouse is out of luck. In that situation, the alternate (contingent) beneficiary would inherit instead.

b. 401(k), 403(b), Keogh, and Pension Plans

If the money is in a 401(k) plan, pension plan, or employer-provided life insurance policy, the ex-spouse inherits if he or she is the named beneficiary. This is true even if state law says that a divorce automatically revokes such a beneficiary designation. That's because federal law (the Employee Retirement Income Security Act, or ERISA) governs these plans and requires plan administrators to distribute proceeds to the beneficiary named in plan documents—even if state law says it should go to someone else. (*Egelhoff v. Egelhoff*, 532 U.S. 141 (2001).)

C. If the Surviving Spouse Is the Beneficiary

Most married people name their spouses to inherit their retirement plan money. If you're the surviving spouse and sole beneficiary of the money in an IRA or retirement plan, you have more flexibility than other beneficiaries. This section discusses your options.

⚠ If required minimum distributions had begun before your spouse died, then you must make the required withdrawal for the year of death. After that, you can choose between rolling over the account to your own name or leaving it in your spouse's name.

1. Rolling Over the Account

Because of the tax advantages discussed below, most spouses who are sole beneficiaries choose to "roll over" the money in an IRA or 401(k) plan, turning it into their own retirement account. To do that, you need to contact the retirement account administrator and complete some paperwork.

Once the account has been rolled over, everything is just as if you were the original owner. You can name a beneficiary (or more than one) to inherit the funds at your death. Required minimum distributions will begin when you reach 70$\frac{1}{2}$, and the amounts will be based on your life expectancy as set out in IRS tables. If you remarry, required distributions will be based on the joint life expectancy of you and your new spouse, if your new spouse is more than ten years younger.

You don't have to pay income tax on money in the account until you withdraw it. Meanwhile, the funds can keep earning tax-deferred income. So not only do you get to put off paying taxes; when you withdraw money during your retirement, you'll probably be in a lower tax bracket.

⚠ Don't roll over the account if you are under age 59$\frac{1}{2}$ and want to withdraw money. As a beneficiary, you are not subject to the usual 10% early distribution penalty (before age 59$\frac{1}{2}$), meaning you can take out some or all of the funds with no penalty. But you lose that exemption if you roll over the account and it becomes your own.

EXAMPLE: *Annie is 45, with two children still at home, when her husband dies and she inherits the money in his 401(k) plan. She may need to withdraw money from the account in the next few years.*

*If she rolled over the money into her own retire-
ment account, and then withdrew some of it before
age 59½, she would have to pay the 10% early
withdrawal penalty. Instead, she leaves the money
in her late husband's account. It will continue to
earn income that won't be taxed until she withdraws it, and she can make withdrawals without
penalty.*

A rollover can happen at any time, even
years after the spouse's death. If, however, you
take early distributions (that is, distributions
made before you are 59½) and use your status
as beneficiary to avoid the usual 10% penalty
on such distributions, you may lose your right
to roll over the rest of the money in the
account. That's what the IRS has indicated in at
least one letter to an individual taxpayer.
Although such "private letter rulings" aren't
laws and don't apply to other taxpayers, they
offer insight into the position the IRS may take
in the future.

INFORMAL ROLLOVERS (IRAS ONLY)

Even without a formal rollover, you can
change an IRA (but not a 401(k), 403(b),
or other retirement plan) into your own
name if you:

- don't take a required distribution
  when you're supposed to (by December 31 of the year after death or by
  December 31 of the year the deceased
  spouse would have turned 70½), or

- make additional contributions to the
  IRA.

If you do either of these things, the IRS
treats the IRA as your own. If you do want
to roll over an IRA, however, it's better to
follow the formal rollover procedures—that
way, there will be clear records of what was
done.

2. Leaving the Account in the Deceased Spouse's Name

Your other alternative is to simply leave the
retirement account in your deceased spouse's
name. To avoid penalties, you must begin
taking required minimum distributions by the
later of:

- December 31 of the year after your
  spouse's death, or

- December 31 of the year your spouse
  would have turned 70½.

The amount of the required minimum
distributions is determined by your life
expectancy alone, as found in the IRS single
life expectancy table. If, however, you were

older than your deceased spouse, then you can use your spouse's statistical life expectancy. (This idea takes some getting used to because obviously, a deceased person doesn't have a life expectancy. It's all just statistics.)

You can and should name a beneficiary to inherit any funds left in the account at your death. If you do, you must continue to base minimum required distribution amounts on your life expectancy. You cannot base them on the joint life expectancy of you and your beneficiary.

D. If There Is One Beneficiary, Not the Spouse

If you're named as the sole beneficiary of retirement plan money, and you're not the surviving spouse, you have two choices. You can take all the money out right away and pay income tax on it, or keep the money in the account for now and begin withdrawing it more slowly. (If there is more than one beneficiary, see Section E, below.)

You must start taking money out soon, even if you're not yet 59½, but you do not have to pay early distribution penalties. You must, however, pay ordinary income tax on the money you take out of the account.

If you don't need the money right away, spreading out the withdrawals over your statistical life expectancy may be wise. First, it lets you postpone paying the income tax until you withdraw money. Second, it prevents a big influx of inherited money from bumping you into a higher income tax bracket. Third, the

money that would otherwise go for taxes can keep growing.

You cannot make tax-deductible contributions to the IRA or retirement plan account or roll it over into your own name.

Companies have forms for everything — and some good advice. Many companies that administer retirement accounts offer valuable information that can help you choose among your options—for example, a calculator to let you figure out how much money you'll have to withdraw from the account each year. And once you've made your choice, you may be able to authorize the company to carry it out just by filling in a form on its website.

1. The First Year

If the deceased person died after reaching age 70½, you must take the required minimum distribution for the calendar year of death, unless it had already been taken. (You can find out from the account administrator if you don't already know.) The amount is the amount that the account owner would have been required to take in that year.

2. The Second and Later Years

After the first year, you may withdraw the funds based on your own life expectancy. To do that, beginning in the year after the death, you use an IRS table to determine your statistical life expectancy and calculate the minimum amount that must be distributed each year by dividing the amount in the account by the life expectancy figure. (Or, if you are older than the person you're inheriting from, then you can use his or her statistically longer life expectancy to calculate required distributions.)

You use the table only once to get your life expectancy. Then, each subsequent year, you reduce this original number by one.

EXAMPLE: *Loretta is the beneficiary of her sister's IRA. The year her sister dies, Loretta takes the distribution that her sister would have been required to take. The next year, she uses the IRS table to look up her statistical life expectancy, which is 17 years. Her required minimum distribution for that year is the amount of money in the account divided by 17.*

The next year, she uses 16 years as her statistical life expectancy and bases the required minimum distribution on that figure.

⚠ **Some plans require that you withdraw all the money within five years.** Fortunately, you're not likely to run into this issue. It's a holdover from the days before the IRS relaxed its rules about distributions to inheritors.

E. If There Are Multiple Beneficiaries

If the deceased person named more than one beneficiary, things can be more complicated. This section explains the general rules.

1. Special Rules

First, you need to know about a couple of special situations involving cobeneficiaries.

a. When a Spouse Is a Cobeneficiary

Surviving spouses lose their unique options (discussed in Section C, above) if they are not sole beneficiaries. They are treated just like the other cobeneficiaries, except that a spouse still has the right to roll over inherited funds into his or her own retirement account.

b. When People and Entities Are Cobeneficiaries

IRS rules about withdrawing money from retirement plan accounts are different for people and for other beneficiaries such as charities. Generally, people can leave money in a tax-deferred account longer. But if someone names both a person and an entity as beneficiaries, the stricter rules (discussed in Section G, below) apply to both beneficiaries—which could cost the person money.

You can get around this problem, however, with a little post-death maneuvering. The IRS gives you until September 30 of the year after the account owner's death to determine who the beneficiaries are. If the charity or other entity gets its share of the account before that date, it's technically no longer a beneficiary when the September 30 deadline comes around.

EXAMPLE: *Charlie names his wife Alice and the Friends of the Springfield Library as beneficiaries of his IRA. If the charity takes its half of the money before the September 30 deadline, this leaves Alice* *as the only remaining beneficiary for purposes of calculating required minimum distributions. Because she's now the only beneficiary, she can take advantage of the more lenient distribution rules available only to spouses.*

As you can see, this practice doesn't change who gets the money in the account—you can't do that after the account owner's death. But you can take advantage of IRS rules to avoid big tax payments by inheritors.

2. Cobeneficiaries' Options

Cobeneficiaries usually can choose between splitting or sharing the account. Most prefer to split it.

a. Splitting the Account

If the retirement plan administrator allows it, and most do, multiple beneficiaries can split the account into separate ones. In that case, the standard distribution rules discussed above apply to each account. This approach is usually advantageous, because it gives beneficiaries the option of withdrawing funds based on their own life expectancies. (See Section D, above.)

⚠️ **The first year is different.** In the year that the accounts are separated, required minimum distributions must be made based on the life expectancy of the oldest beneficiary. The next year, each beneficiary can begin using his or her own life expectancy to calculate minimum required distributions.

Splitting is not always possible, however. If the plan administrator won't agree to it, beneficiaries are stuck with the rules that apply to multiple beneficiaries of one account, discussed next.

b. Sharing One Account

If you're one of several beneficiaries who must share the deceased person's account, your options depend on what the plan allows.

Five-year rule. Some plans require the beneficiaries to withdraw all the money within five years after the death. If you find yourself in this situation, there's nothing you can do to change it.

Life expectancy rule. If the plan doesn't require all the money to be distributed in five years, beneficiaries can use the IRS life expectancy table as a basis for calculating required minimum distributions, with one important twist: The distributions must be based on the life expectancy of the oldest beneficiary. If some beneficiaries are much older than others, the younger ones will have to withdraw money (and pay tax on it) more quickly than they may wish to. To calculate the required minimum distribution, look up the life expectancy of the oldest beneficiary, and divide the amount in the account by that number. Each subsequent year, reduce the original life expectancy number by one. (See Section D2, above, for an example.)

F. If a Trust Is the Beneficiary

It's not common, but some people name a trust as the beneficiary of a retirement account. If you run into that situation, the beneficiaries' options will depend on what type of trust it is.

Some kinds of trusts, including most simple living trusts designed to avoid probate, are what's known as "qualified trusts" under IRS rules. If you're dealing with a qualified trust, minimum required distributions can be calculated based on the life expectancy of the trust beneficiary. (If there's more than one trust beneficiary, though, then the rules for multiple beneficiaries apply; the account cannot be split for purposes of using different life expectances. See Section E, above.)

A surviving spouse who is the sole beneficiary of a trust may be able to formally roll over the retirement account and treat it as his or her own. (Section C, above, discusses spousal rollovers.) It depends on how the trust is structured, which means trust beneficiaries may well want some expert advice on their options.

If a trust isn't a qualified trust under IRS rules, then there is no "designated beneficiary" for the retirement account, and different rules apply. (See Section G, below.)

Get help with questions. If you need to know whether or not a trust is a qualified trust, see a lawyer who has experience with these matters.

G. If There Is No "Designated Beneficiary"

Under IRS rules, a "designated beneficiary" is a person or a qualified trust (trusts are discussed in Section F, above). Any other beneficiaries— for example, charities or corporations—are not designated beneficiaries, which means they are subject to different rules.

Here are those rules, in a nutshell:

If the death occurred before minimum distributions were required. All funds must be distributed to a nondesignated beneficiary in five years. (Obviously, required minimum distributions can't be calculated based on life expectancy— that wouldn't work for a nonhuman beneficiary.) If a person and a charity are both named as beneficiaries, both are subject to the five-year rule. (See Section E1, above, for a way you may be able to get around this rule.)

If the deceased person had already begun making minimum withdrawals. Required distributions are based on the deceased person's statistical life expectancy, calculated as of the year of death. Each year, that life expectancy figure would be reduced by one year to calculate the required payout.

H. If the Beneficiary Has Died

If the beneficiary named by the account owner died before the account owner did, then the funds will go to:

- the alternate (contingent) beneficiary, if any was named or,

- the estate, if there is no alternate beneficiary (see Section J, below).

I. If No Beneficiary Was Named

In the unlikely event the account owner never named a beneficiary, retirement funds may end up in the estate. However, it depends on the circumstances. The funds may go to someone under the law—for example, under federal law, 401(k) plan funds generally go to the surviving spouse. (See Section B2, above.)

J. If the Estate Is the Beneficiary

Few people name their estates as retirement account beneficiaries. One obvious drawback to naming the estate as the beneficiary is that the funds will probably have to go through probate. In addition, distribution rules are not generally as favorable as they are for other beneficiaries.

The deceased person's estate is not a "designated beneficiary" under IRS rules (see Section G, above). Here are the rules for distributing funds to the estate:

If the death occurred before minimum distributions were required. The account must be paid to the estate by December 31 of the fifth year following the year of death.

If the deceased person had already begun making minimum withdrawals. In this case, the funds can be withdrawn and paid to the estate based on the account owner's remaining life expectancy, calculated as of the year of death. Each year, that life expectancy would be reduced by one year to calculate the required payout.

Once funds are in the estate, they pass under the residuary clause of the will, if any, or under state intestate succession laws. ■

CHAPTER 16

Claiming Payable-on-Death Assets

These days, people leave lots of property to inheritors by using "payable-on-death" (POD) or "transfer-on-death" (TOD) designations. The owner of the property simply names a POD beneficiary on a form. Then, when the owner dies, the property doesn't have to go through probate; the named beneficiary can claim it directly.

It's common for people to name payable-on-death beneficiaries for several kinds of property, including:

- bank accounts

- stocks and bonds, either held separately or in a mutual fund or brokerage account, and

- U.S. savings bonds.

In a few states, people can name transfer-on-death beneficiaries for vehicles and even real estate. Each of these is discussed below.

IRAs and retirement plans. People name beneficiaries for individual retirement accounts and plans, too. Collecting these funds doesn't require probate, but it does involve many IRS rules. See Chapter 15.

A. If the Asset Was Co-Owned

If property is jointly owned, any POD beneficiary inherits it only after both owners have died.

EXAMPLE: *Melanie and Zachary own a bank account together in joint tenancy. They name their daughter Fiona as the POD beneficiary. When the first spouse dies, the survivor will own the account. When the second spouse dies, Fiona will inherit it.*

B. The Effect of Divorce on POD Beneficiaries

Most states have laws providing that if someone names his or her spouse as a POD beneficiary, and the couple later divorces, then the beneficiary designation is automatically canceled. These laws are based on the assumption that people who don't change the beneficiary designation of a former spouse probably meant to do so.

EXAMPLE: *Carly names her husband Bob as the POD beneficiary of her savings account. They later get divorced, but Carly doesn't get around to changing her POD beneficiary on the bank's form.*

When Carly dies, the law of her state provides that Bob does not inherit the account, even though his name is still listed in the bank's records as the POD beneficiary. Instead, the money goes to Carly's estate. It will pass under the residuary clause of her will, or if she had no will, under the terms of state law.

These state laws do not, however, affect assets that are governed by federal law, including 401(k) retirement plans, employer-provided life insurance policies, and pension plans. (These are governed by the federal

Employee Retirement Income Security Act, better known as ERISA.) The U.S. Supreme Court has ruled that under ERISA, when the plan participant dies, the plan administrator must simply pay the proceeds to the beneficiary the deceased person named. The administrator does not have to try to figure out who should get the money under a particular state's law. (*Egelhoff v. Egelhoff*, 532 U.S. 141 (2001).)

C. How Beneficiaries Can Claim Assets

The exact procedure for claiming POD assets depends on what kind of property the beneficiary inherits, but the process is always fairly similar and should be simple.

1. Bank Accounts

If the deceased person owned a bank account as a payable-on-death (POD) account (sometimes called a Totten trust), the POD beneficiary named in the bank's records can collect the money promptly, without probate. All the beneficiary needs to do is to show the bank proof of death (a certified copy of the death certificate) and personal identification.

2. U.S. Savings Bonds

The POD beneficiary of a savings bond automatically becomes the bond's sole owner when the original bond owner dies. The beneficiary can:

- do nothing with the bond

- redeem the bond by taking it to a bank or other financial institution that pays savings bonds (the beneficiary will need personal identification), or

- get the bond reissued (reregistered) in the beneficiary's name alone or with some other person.

To get a new bond showing the beneficiary as the owner, the beneficiary must complete Form 4000, *Request to Reissue United States Savings Bonds*. It's available online or from a bank.

The form comes with instructions for filling it in. As part of getting the bond reregistered, the beneficiary can add a co-owner or a POD beneficiary of his or her own. That's often a good idea.

After the form is complete, the beneficiary must sign it in front of someone who is authorized to "certify" the signature. This isn't the same as notarization. Most banks have employees who are authorized certifying officers.

Finally, the beneficiary must send the signed form, with a certified copy of the death certificate, to one of the Savings Bond Processing Sites listed on the form.

Where to get help online. Forms, instructions, and information are available at www.publicdebt.treas.gov/sav/savreiss.htm.

3. Vehicles

If you've inherited a car that was registered in TOD (beneficiary) form, you'll need to get the vehicle reregistered in your name. It should be an easy process, involving a fill-in-the-blanks form and a small fee.

You'll need to submit several documents to the state motor vehicles department, including:

- an application for the new certificate of ownership

- the old certificate, if you have it, and

- a copy of the death certificate.

After you submit these documents and pay the small fee, the state will issue a new registration.

For forms and instructions, contact your state's motor vehicles department. Try the agency's website first; you may find everything you need there.

If the car wasn't paid for at the owner's death, the new owner inherits the debt as well as the car.

4. Real Estate

In Arizona, Kansas, Missouri, New Mexico, and Ohio, owners of real estate can use what are called transfer-on-death or beneficiary deeds. To be valid and effective, the deed must have been recorded (filed) before the owner's death, with the county land records office in the county where the property is located. (The office that keeps local land records goes by different names in different states; for example, in some places it's called the county recorder, in others the register of deeds.)

The person who inherits real estate through the beneficiary deed must put something in the public land records showing that ownership has changed. Not all states' laws set out a specific procedure for the beneficiary to follow. The ones that do require the beneficiary to record two documents:

- a certified copy of the death certificate, and

- an affidavit (sworn statement, signed in front of a notary public) setting out certain information.

For example, the Ohio statute (Ohio Rev. Code Ann. § 5302.22) requires the affidavit to contain the following information:

- the name and address of each transfer-on-death beneficiary who survived the deceased owner

- the date of the deceased owner's death

- a description of the real estate, and

- the name of any TOD beneficiary who did not survive the deceased owner.

If the TOD deed named more than one beneficiary, but not all of them survived the original owner, then the surviving beneficiaries must also record certified copies of the death certificates of the deceased beneficiaries.

The fee to record these documents is usually modest, just a few dollars per page. You can call ahead to find out. ■

CHAPTER 17

Special Procedures for Small Estates

Every state has some sort of streamlined procedures for winding up "small estates"—though what qualifies as a small estate varies greatly from place to place. (In some cases, you can use small estate procedures for assets in very large estates.) These methods are simpler, quicker, and cheaper than regular probate.

Most states offer two basic kinds of transfer methods for small estates:

- simplified or summary probate, which lets you conduct a faster and easier version of regular probate, and

- an out-of-court affidavit procedure, which lets beneficiaries claim assets from whoever has possession of them by presenting a sworn statement explaining why they're entitled to the property.

This chapter explains both.

A. Are You Handling a Small Estate?

States make a summary probate or affidavit procedure available only to estates that meet a size limit set out in the state's statutes. In most states, the estate can meet this requirement in either of these circumstances:

- the estate is small to start with, or

- some of the estate passes outside probate anyway, and what's left is under the size limit.

A summary of each state's rules can be found in Sections B and C, below. This section explains how to read and understand these rules.

1. How States Define Small Estates

In most states, a small estate is one that has a value below a flat amount—say, $75,000.

Some states, however, don't specify a dollar amount as an upper limit. Instead, they grant small estate status to estates that will be used up by paying certain high-priority debts: the family allowance mandated by law for immediate family members, reasonable funeral and burial expenses, and medical costs of the last illness. The reasoning is that if there's nothing left for other creditors, there's no need for a probate court proceeding. Obviously, estates of very different size will qualify, depending on the debts of the deceased person.

Some states use both monetary and nonmonetary criteria in their definitions. Connecticut, for example, defines small estates as those that do not contain real estate and do not exceed $20,000 in value. In Georgia, an estate cannot qualify as a small estate unless there is no will.

If a state has more than one transfer procedure for small estates, it will define "small estate" separately for each process. As a result, an estate might qualify for summary probate, but not for the out-of-court affidavit procedure.

2. What Kinds of Property to Count

Even estates that contain several hundred thousand dollars worth of assets may qualify for small estate procedures. That's because when you add up the value of the estate, you can probably exclude many valuable assets.

In many states, for example, only probate assets are counted. That means you can exclude:

- property held in a living trust

- bank accounts or securities registered in payable-on-death (POD or TOD) form

- life insurance proceeds

- joint tenancy property

- tenancy by the entirety property

- retirement accounts for which a beneficiary is named, and

- community property that passes to a surviving spouse without probate.

Some states also exclude real estate or motor vehicles.

EXAMPLE 1: *Robert, a California resident, dies owning property worth almost $400,000, including:*

- *a payable-on-death bank account with $10,000 in it*

- *$20,000 worth of stocks*

- *a car worth $18,000, and*

- *a house worth $350,000, which he owns as community property with his wife and leaves to her in his will.*

The limit for "small estates" in California is only $100,000, but property that goes to a surviving spouse and vehicles aren't counted toward that limit. In addition, California doesn't count the value of nonprobate property—in Robert's case, the payable-on-death bank account that already has a named beneficiary. So only the stocks count toward the $100,000 limit, allowing Robert's estate to qualify for small estate procedures.

EXAMPLE 2: *Tina lived in Indiana, which restricts use of its small estate affidavit procedure to estates worth no more than $25,000. Her executor estimates that Tina left assets worth about $200,000 consisting of real estate, securities, a bank account, a 401(k) plan, and miscellaneous personal property. But for purposes of deciding whether or not she left a small estate that's eligible for the affidavit procedure, Indiana counts only assets that would otherwise go through probate.*

Here's how Tina's $200,000 estate breaks down:

- *her house, worth $80,000, which she held in a living trust to avoid probate*

- *securities worth $40,000, which she registered in beneficiary (TOD) form*

- *payable-on-death bank accounts containing $30,000*

- *a $40,000 401(k) account for which she had named a beneficiary, and*

- *miscellaneous personal property and household items worth $10,000.*

Under Indiana law, only the $10,000 of miscellaneous items are subject to probate. Because Tina held title to everything else in a way that would *avoid probate, it can pass directly to inheritors. As a result, Tina left a "small estate" under Indiana law. Her inheritors may use the out-of-court affidavit procedure to claim the household items, and no probate is necessary.*

3. Subtracting What's Owed on Assets

When you're trying to figure out whether or not an estate is small enough to escape regular probate, some states require you to use the market value of the property; others instruct you to subtract any amounts owed on it. It can make a huge difference, of course.

EXAMPLE: *When Agnes, a widow, dies, she is a resident of Arizona. She owns no real estate but leaves behind a car, some stocks, bank accounts, and household furnishings, with a total market value of $55,000.*

Arizona law says that her inheritors can claim the property without probate if the total value, less "liens and encumbrances," is no greater than $50,000. Because Agnes still owed $7,000 on her car when she died, that amount (a lien on the car) can be subtracted. That brings the total value of her estate down to $48,000—low enough to qualify for the small estate procedure.

B. Claiming Property With Affidavits

The affidavit (sworn statement) procedure is the simpler and faster way to go if you're dealing with a small estate. Encourage benefi-

ciaries to use it if they can. All they'll have to do to collect their property is prepare a simple statement, sign it in front of a notary public, and present it, along with a certified copy of the death certificate, to the person or institution in possession of the property.

Each state's procedure is summarized in the appendix. To use the affidavit procedure, you'll need to look up your state's statute (listed in the appendix). It's not difficult and you can do it online. (See Chapter 22 for instructions.)

STATES WITH AFFIDAVIT PROCEDURES

Alaska	Minnesota
Arizona	Montana
California	Nebraska
Colorado	Nevada
Delaware	New Mexico
District of Columbia	North Dakota
Hawaii	South Carolina
Idaho	South Dakota
Illinois	Texas
Indiana	Utah
Iowa	Virginia
Kansas	Washington
Louisiana	Wisconsin
Maine	Wyoming
Michigan	

1. Who Can Use an Affidavit

If the estate meets the state's definition of "small estate," and regular probate proceedings have not begun, generally anyone who is entitled to inherit some of the deceased person's property can use an affidavit to collect it. In a few states, however, only close relatives can use affidavits.

It doesn't matter whether or not there was a will. You can use an affidavit if you were named as a beneficiary in a will or if you inherit under state law.

EXAMPLE: *Marguerite and her brother Marvin inherit all of their mother's property when she dies without a will. Her estate is small enough to qualify for the affidavit procedure in her state. To claim the funds in their mother's bank account, Marguerite and Marvin fill out an affidavit, sign it in front of a notary, and take it (with a certified copy of the death certificate) to the bank.*

2. What Kind of Property Can Be Claimed

It's common for beneficiaries to claim bank accounts, stocks, and cars with affidavits. In most states, affidavits work for anything but real estate.

In the few states that do have an affidavit procedure for real estate, the new owner will have to file the affidavit with the probate court or the county land records office. That's because real estate ownership is always a matter of public record.

3. The Waiting Period

Most states don't allow beneficiaries to use the affidavit procedure until a month or so after the death. This is to give an executor time to begin formal probate proceedings, if necessary. If a regular probate court case is begun,

property must be distributed through that process and not through the affidavit process.

4. Preparing the Affidavit

If you or other beneficiaries want to use the affidavit procedure to claim property, the process will be easier if you can use a pre-printed, fill-in-the-blanks affidavit form. There are a few different places to look for such a form:

- **The state statute.** A few states provide fill-in-the-blanks forms in their statutes. (Check the appendix for your state's rule.)

- **The institution you'll be submitting the affidavit to.** Some banks, other financial institutions, and state motor vehicle agencies deal with this sort of transfer all the time: they may have their own affidavit forms.

If you can't get a preprinted form, you'll have to put together your own affidavit. It shouldn't be difficult; you just have to read your state statute and make sure your state-ment covers everything the statute requires. Most statutes list exactly what you need to include.

Commonly, an affidavit must state that:

- The value of the probate estate does not exceed the "small estate" limit in the statute.

- The required after-death waiting period has elapsed.

- No probate court proceedings have begun.

- The person signing the affidavit (the claimant) is entitled to the property. Although, oddly, it's not always required by statute, it's a good idea to explain why you're entitled—for example, because of the deceased person's will or under state intestate succession law.

Your state may require different or additional information. That's why you always need to read the statute itself. To see what a typical affidavit looks like, take a look at the one below, which is based on the Minnesota statute.

SAMPLE AFFIDAVIT FOR COLLECTING WAGES

Affidavit for Collection of Personal Property Under Minnesota Statutes 524.3-1201

I, the undersigned, state as follows:

1. _____, the decedent, died on _____.

2. The value of the entire probate estate, wherever located, including specifically any contents of a safe deposit box, less liens and encumbrances, does not exceed $20,000.

3. At least thirty days have elapsed since the decedent's death, as shown by the attached certified copy of the decedent's death certificate.

4. No application or petition for the appointment of a personal representative is pending or has been granted in any jurisdiction.

5. I, the undersigned, am entitled to payment or delivery, under the terms of the decedent's will, of the following property:

   _____

   _____

   _____

6. I declare that the foregoing is true and correct.

_____   _____

Signature   Date

[notarization]

If more than one person is claiming the property, all should sign the affidavit.

If you're asking for more than one item of property from one person or institution, you can list all of the items on the same affidavit. Describe the property in enough detail to make it clear what you're asking for. For example, if you're claiming a bank account, list the account number and the branch of the bank where it was opened.

CHILDREN WHO INHERIT

If someone under age 18 inherits property and wants to use an affidavit to claim it, things are a little more complicated. Minors cannot sign such an affidavit, so someone must sign on their behalf.

Who can sign? It depends on the circumstances.

- If the amount isn't large (usually less than a few thousand dollars), state law may allow the child's parent to sign the affidavit.

- If the property was left in a will, and the will names someone to be "custodian" of the property under the state's Uniform Transfers to Minors Act (discussed in Chapter 10), then the custodian can sign.

- If the child already has a court-appointed guardian, the guardian can sign.

If none of these options is available, then you may need to ask a court to appoint a guardian for the child, or you may be able to appoint a custodian yourself. See Chapter 10.

In most states, the law requires your signature on the affidavit to be notarized, meaning you must sign the affidavit in front of a notary public. In a few states, however, it's enough to declare "under penalty of perjury" that the statement is true. The statute will tell you. But even if the statute does not mandate notarization, some banks and other financial institutions insist on it anyway. So before you sign your statement, check with the company or agency that holds the assets you are trying to claim.

Help for California readers. For a tear-out California affidavit form and instructions on how to use it, see *How to Probate an Estate in California*, by Julia Nissley (Nolo).

5. How to Claim the Property

After your state's waiting period (if any) is up, the person who's entitled to inherit the property can present the affidavit to the person or institution (a bank, for example) that possesses the property or is in charge of transferring its ownership (a brokerage company, perhaps).

a. Other Documents You'll Need

Some other documents must normally accompany the affidavit, including:

- a certified copy of the death certificate

- a copy of the will (if any), if the institution insists on seeing it

- proof that the deceased person owned the property—for example, stock certificates or a bank statement—if required by the institution you're presenting the affidavit to, and

- if you're claiming stocks or bonds, the documents discussed in Subsections d and e, below.

If the affidavit appears to be truthful, the person or institution may, by law, turn over the property without fear of being sued by someone else later. The institution doesn't need to investigate whether or not the statements in the affidavit are actually true.

EXAMPLE: *In his will, Perry leaves $20,000 to Alice. A month after Perry dies, Alice goes to his bank and fills out the affidavit form she picks up there, swearing that she is entitled to the money and that the estate qualifies for the state's small estate affidavit procedure. The bank, after looking at the affidavit and a copy of Perry's death certificate, transfers $20,000 from Perry's account to her.*

b. Where to Send the Affidavit

In most states, the beneficiary needs to give the affidavit only to the entity that is holding the property. But some states require a copy to be sent to the state taxing agency, in case any state taxes are due. If the decedent received any public benefits based on financial need (welfare or medical benefits for low-income patients) another copy may need to go to the Health or Welfare Department; if there's money left in the estate, the government will want to be reimbursed for the value of the aid it provided.

c. If You Run Into Resistance

Most banks, brokers, and other entities are quite familiar with their state's affidavit process. If the paperwork is in order, they will release the assets without problems.

But if someone refuses to cooperate, just showing an unhelpful clerk a copy of the statute (readily available online or at a public law library) should melt away the opposition. If that doesn't get results, chances are a phone call or letter from a local lawyer will. And as a last resort, you could go to court—small claims court, if your state allows this kind of dispute to be resolved there—and demand that the assets be turned over.

d. Special Rules for Stocks and Bonds Held in Brokerage Accounts

If you want to claim stocks, and the deceased person held them as part of a brokerage account or owned mutual fund shares, your best bet is to contact the brokerage or mutual fund company. You should be able to find a toll-free customer service number on an account statement or on the company's website.

The website may also contain forms and instructions. For example, the Fidelity fund group website offers a downloadable form called "Change of Account Registration Form." You fill out the form, following the instructions for your situation, and send it to the company, along with the affidavit and a certified copy of the death certificate. Fidelity will reregister the account in the name of the new owner. Other large investment companies have similar procedures and forms with similar names such as "Transfer of Ownership" or "Change of Ownership."

As the new owner, you will have to provide your tax identification number (your Social Security number). And you will probably have to get your signature on the transfer document "guaranteed," which is a way to give the company proof that it is genuine. Getting a signature guaranteed is a lot like getting a signature notarized—though notarization is *not* a substitute for a guarantee. You can get a guarantee from an authorized employee of an FDIC bank, a trust company, or broker. (You do not have to get the signature guarantee at the institution you're claiming property from.) Once a bank employee or broker is satisfied that your signature is genuine, they'll sign the document and stamp it "signature guaranteed," and you're on your way.

Don't worry if a form asks for your court authorization. It's standard practice for many of these companies to ask to see the probate court papers (usually called "letters testamentary") that authorize you to act as executor of the estate. Just explain that there is not going to be any probate—remember that your affidavit states, under oath, that no probate proceedings have begun—and they should let you proceed.

e. Special Rules for Stock Certificates and Bonds

It's unusual, but sometimes people have actual stock certificates or bonds in their possession.

If this is true in the estate you're handling, you'll need to send them to the corporation's "transfer agent," along with the affidavit and some other documents. The transfer agent's name and address should be listed on the stock or bond certificate.

Stock in private businesses. If the deceased person owned stock in a privately held company (one whose stock isn't traded on a public exchange), you'll be dealing directly with the other business owners, not a transfer agent.

Send the transfer agent these documents:

- the affidavit

- the original certificates

- a certified copy of the death certificate

- a stock or bond power, signed by the new owner

- an Affidavit of Residence, signed by the new owner and notarized, and

- a cover letter signed by the new owner.

Here's an explanation of these papers:

The **stock power** is a document that authorizes transfer of the shares. It may be printed on the back of the stock certificates or found as a separate form available from banks, brokers, or many websites. (For a sample stock power, see Chapter 13.) Fill in the basic information about the new owner (name and Social Security number), and then about the stock or bond: the number of shares, the kind of stock (common or preferred), the name of the company, and the numbers of the stock certificates. You don't need to fill in the name of the "attorney" who is appointed to transfer the securities; commonly, this person is the employee of the transfer agent who actually makes the change on the corporation's records.

The new owner's signature on the stock power will have to be "guaranteed" so that the transfer agent knows it is genuine. Guaranteed signatures are discussed just above, in Subsection d.

An **Affidavit of Residence** is a simple document that states where the new owner lives. (For a sample form, see Chapter 13.) If the new owner is a resident of the state where the company is incorporated, transfer tax may be due. You can get forms from brokers or banks, or create your own. The new owner signs the statement in front of a notary public.

The **cover letter** is also signed by the new owner or owners. It simply directs that the securities be reregistered in the name of the new owner. If more than one person is inheriting, be sure to state what share each one gets. A sample letter, which you can adapt to your needs, is shown below.

COVER LETTER TO STOCK TRANSFER AGENT

July 19, 20xx

[*name & address of transfer agent*]

Re: Securities of Joseph H. Johnson, deceased

Enclosed are stock certificates registered in the name of Joseph H. Johnson.

Certificate number: A4546548
Type of security: common stock
Number of shares [*or for bonds, the face amount*]: 100
Name of company: Runaway Manufacturing, Inc.

These shares were owned in tenancy by the entirety by Joseph H. Johnson. Please cancel the enclosed certificates and issue new certificates in the name of the inheritor, Jessica M. Johnson, Social Security number 123-45-6789.

I have enclosed an Affidavit for Collection of Personal Property Under 755 Ill. Comp. Stat. 5.25-1, a Stock Power, a certified copy of Mr. Johnson's death certificate, and an Affidavit of Residence.

Sincerely,

Jessica M. Johnson
4444 North 27th Street
Clarkdale, Illinois 61890
(555) 555-1234

Once you've got the whole package together, call to make sure that the transfer agent hasn't changed since the certificates were issued. Then send everything by registered mail and request a return receipt.

C. Using Simplified Probate

If the deceased person's estate qualifies for simplified probate (called summary administration in some states), congratulations—you've avoided a full-fledged probate proceeding.

This section explains how to determine whether or not this process is available to you and gives an overview of how it works.

1. State Eligibility Rules

It's not always easy to tell whether or not you can use simplified probate. In most states, the general idea is to add up the estate's assets, subtract debts, and see whether or not the resulting figure is below the dollar limit. That sounds simple enough, but you may run into unfamiliar terms and concepts along the way— for example, "costs of administration" or "liens and encumbrances." And some states have quirky rules about what kinds of property are excluded when you add up the value of the estate. (The examples in Section A, above, may help you.)

The appendix contains a summary of each state's eligibility rules for simplified probate and a citation to the state statute that sets out the details. Start with the inventory and estimates you compiled in Chapter 8, and see

whether or not your estate has a shot at qualifying for simplified probate. If you need help, check the glossary of this book, read your state's statute (Chapter 22 explains how to find it online), or ask a lawyer for clarification.

2. How It Works: An Overview

You can use simplified probate only if you have not begun regular probate proceedings. You begin the process by filing a written request with the local probate court, asking to use the simplified procedure. (That step is discussed in Section 4, below.) If the judge agrees that the estate qualifies for simplified probate, you're on your way.

What happens next depends on state law and local court practice. Your state may require you to:

- Publish a simple notice of the death in a local newspaper.

- Give creditors and people who might inherit (under the will or state law) written notice of the death and the probate proceedings.

- If there's no will, ask the court to make a formal determination of who is entitled to inherit the assets. (That can be a good thing—it means the court, not you, will figure out who inherits under the sometimes hard-to-understand intestate succession statutes.)

All these things can probably be handled by mail; you shouldn't have to make any court appearances. After a waiting period, during which creditors can make their claims and any interested parties can object, you can pay the bills and distribute the property. If you don't have possession of some of the assets, such as a bank or investment account, you'll be able to get them as soon as you have a copy of the probate court's order authorizing the distribution.

When you've distributed all the property, you'll need to file a closing statement with the court, showing where everything went. In states where you were not required to notify creditors before distributing the property, you may need to send the closing statement to creditors, too.

What to do if someone questions your authority. When you're going through a simplified probate procedure, some states issue official documents authorizing you to proceed as executor, and some don't. If you don't have a court document but need to show someone your authority to act for the estate, generally it's enough to produce the will, which names you as executor.

3. Can You Do It Yourself?

Small estate procedures are intended to be easy to use, without a lawyer. Whether or not you need to hire a lawyer depends on how much other help you can get for free or at a reasonable cost. Your best sources of inexpensive help are:

- materials published by the court
- self-help books, and

- the probate court staff.

Some court systems provide good explanatory materials and forms, both on paper and online. And some court clerks are willing to help people along. Unfortunately, other courts leave people to figure things out themselves.

If you can't find good help where you live, you may want to get advice from an experienced lawyer or paralegal. You don't necessarily have to turn the whole process over to a professional—but having someone available as a coach, to answer questions and help smooth over any rough patches, can make a huge difference. In some situations it may be wise to involve a lawyer to reassure a concerned family member that everything has been done properly.

Even if you consult a lawyer, the overall cost of simplified probate should be less than that of regular probate. The process will be over more quickly, too.

Help for California readers. For complete instructions on handling a summary probate without a lawyer in California, see *How to Probate an Estate in California*, by Julia Nissley (Nolo).

4. Getting Started

Most states impose a waiting period of a month or two before you can start the simplified probate process. (Again, you can find this rule, and others you'll need to know, by reading your state's statute.) Once that period has passed, your first step is to get the court's permission to begin the process. Do this by filing a document (commonly called a petition or affidavit for summary probate) with the probate court in the county where the deceased person lived.

It's not always called probate court. Depending on where you live, the right court may be called probate court, orphans' court, superior court, circuit court—you get the idea. Call a likely sounding court and ask where small estates cases are handled, or check the state simplified probate statute (listed in the appendix).

a. The Petition

Some states have preprinted, fill-in-the-blanks forms for summary probate, available free from the court clerk or from a website operated by the local court or by the state.

If preprinted forms aren't an option, you'll have to prepare the necessary documents from scratch. This means you'll need to pay attention to both what information the document must contain and how the document looks.

Specific requirements vary from state to state, but in most cases the petition must:

- say that the estate qualifies as a "small estate," as state law defines that term

- list the people or organizations entitled to inherit the property

- say that no request for formal probate has been made, and

- say that all (or certain) debts and taxes have been paid.

To make sure you're including everything required by the court, check the state statute. (Again, the citation to each state's statute is in the appendix; Chapter 22 explains how to find it online or in a law library.)

Then check your local court's rules (available from the court clerk) about how documents must be prepared. Courts are often fussy about the documents they'll accept. For example, they may not accept anything that's not on numbered, letter-sized paper, and they may have rules about the amount of space that must be left at the top of the first page for the court's stamp. Try to find a good sample and copy the format.

In some states, you don't start with a special small estate form; instead, you begin just as if you were starting a regular probate proceeding. Then, after you file an inventory and appraisal of estate assets, the court will approves the simplified procedure if the estate qualifies.

b. Other Documents

You will probably also need to submit, along with the petition, a certified copy of the death certificate, the will (if there is one), and an inventory and appraisal (estimated dollar value) of all the deceased person's assets. (You've probably done a lot of the inventorying and valuing already, in Chapter 8.) You may also need to get all the beneficiaries' written consent to the simplified probate. Again, you'll have to read your state's statutes. ■

CHAPTER 18

The Regular Probate Process

Probate is the court-supervised process of gathering the deceased person's assets and distributing them to creditors and inheritors. Unless family members or creditors are fighting, however, court involvement is minimal. The typical probate is more paperwork than Perry Mason.

If you're lucky, the deceased person will have created a probate-avoidance plan, and as a result you won't need to take the estate through probate court. (Even if little probate-avoidance planning was done, you may be able to use simplified probate; Chapter 12 explains your options.) But if you do, don't fret. Probate is not usually the nightmare it's made out to be. Especially in the 16 states that have adopted the set of laws called the Uniform Probate Code (UPC), you'll probably never see the inside of a courtroom. True, the paperwork is tedious, but stick with it and you'll do fine.

In some ways, probate can even be an easy path to tread. The court has an established procedure for you to follow, and entities such as banks, title companies, and government agencies will readily accept your authority when you have written authorization from a court.

What's more, many courts are getting better about making information and forms more easily available (often online). Managed sensibly, probate probably won't be hugely expensive or drawn out.

This chapter provides a summary of the probate process and answers common questions about it. It cannot, however, show you

exactly how to shepherd an estate through your state's probate court. Probate is full of details—and probate procedures vary significantly from state to state, and even from county to county. You'll need guidance that's tailored to your location. You may get that help from the probate court, from privately published materials, or from a lawyer.

Help for California readers. The very best resource for California do-it-yourselfers is *How to Probate an Estate in California*, by Julia Nissley (Nolo). It contains all necessary forms and instructions and guides you through the entire California probate court process.

A. Common Questions About Probate

If you're wondering what to expect from probate, here are a few things you may want to know right away.

1. How Much Does Probate Cost?

It's undeniable that probate costs eat away at the value of an estate, reducing the amount that eventually gets to the people who inherit the property. Some estimates put the typical tab at 5% of the value of the estate, but for most people that's probably on the high side.

The court filing fees themselves are usually not too hefty. In roughly half the states, the initial charge is a flat fee, which ranges from about $40 to $200. In many of these states, each county sets its own fee. In the other half of the states, the court fee depends on the value of the assets that will go through probate. Generally, the fee is a few hundred dollars for an estate worth a few hundred thousand dollars.

The court fee is far from the largest expense, however. The estate must commonly pay a lawyer, an appraiser, and perhaps an accountant and tax preparer before all is said and done. You are also entitled to compensation for your work as executor, although many executors who are family members or close friends don't take any payment. (See Section 5, below.)

Lawyers either bill the estate at an hourly rate ($150 and up) for their work, charge a lump sum for handling a probate case or, in some states, take as a fee a percentage of the total value of the estate. (Chapter 23 discusses working with and paying lawyers, including how to keep costs as low as possible.)

2. Is There a Deadline for Starting Probate?

Most families want to get probate started—and finished—as soon as possible. Typically, they begin the process within two or three months after a death.

In most states there is no deadline for starting a probate proceeding. Many states require that anyone who has possession of a deceased person's will promptly turn it over to the court within a certain number of days (commonly ten or 30 days after the death), but that's not the same as beginning a probate case.

Some states, however, require that if there is a will, probate must begin within three or four years. To use the informal probate option allowed in some states (Section C, below), you must begin within three years after the death.

3. How Long Will It Take?

Because procedures vary so widely from state to state, and because your own efforts affect how quickly things move along, it's difficult to generalize about how long a typical probate takes. But in most places, a straightforward probate case can be wrapped up about six months to a year after you file the first papers and the court appoints you as executor. Of course, many factors influence the timeline, including:

- how efficiently you (and the attorney, if any) work

- whether or not beneficiaries argue about distribution of the assets

- what kinds of assets the estate contains—for example, a small business may slow things down

- whether or not there are any disputes over creditors' claims

- if there's a house, how long it takes to clear it out and sell it (if that's what beneficiaries want), and

- how complex the tax situation is—for example, if the estate is worth more than $1.5 million and a federal estate tax return is required, you're looking at a minimum of nine months.

4. Who Will the Court Name as Executor?

Probate courts try to honor will-makers' wishes whenever possible, and this is especially true when it comes to the choice of executor. (Remember that in some states, the executor is called the personal representative.) Courts appoint the person named in the will unless there are serious problems with that person— for example, the person has lied to the court, mismanaged the estate, refused to obey court orders, or appears unable to perform the executor's duties. Objections or hostility from other beneficiaries is not reason enough for the court to refuse to appoint the will-maker's chosen executor.

If there is no will, state law determines who has priority to serve as executor. (See Chapter 7.)

IF YOU AREN'T THE NAMED EXECUTOR

You don't have to be named executor in the will to begin probate. Any interested person—for example, a family member who may inherit property—can begin probate. Usually, this happens only if there is no will, or the named executor (and any alternates named by the will) can't or won't start the probate process.

5. How Much Are Executors Paid?

As executor, you are entitled to be paid a reasonable amount for the work you do on behalf of the estate. Most family members who inherit a substantial amount don't accept a fee,

however. (Compensation is discussed in Chapter 2, Section B.)

B. The Typical Probate Process

Bearing in mind that no estate is perfectly typical, here is a general outline of the probate process in the majority of states—those that do *not* use the entire Uniform Probate Code. (Almost all states have enacted bits of the UPC.)

→ If your state is listed below, read this section. If it's not, skip to Section C, below.

STATES THAT HAVE NOT ADOPTED THE ENTIRE UNIFORM PROBATE CODE

Alabama	New Hampshire
Arkansas	New Jersey
California	New York
Connecticut	North Carolina
Delaware	Ohio
District of Columbia	Oklahoma
Georgia	Oregon
Illinois	Pennsylvania
Indiana	Rhode Island
Iowa	Tennessee
Kansas	Texas
Kentucky	Vermont
Louisiana	Virginia
Maryland	Washington
Massachusetts	West Virginia
Mississippi	Wisconsin*
Missouri	Wyoming
Nevada	

*Has an informal probate proceeding that is very similar to that in UPC states.

1. Getting Started

If the deceased person's will named you as executor, or if there was no will and you're looking to take on the job, you begin the probate process by asking the court to officially make you executor. (If there's no will, in some states you'll ask to be the "administrator." Chapter 7 discusses how the court chooses someone to act for the estate in this situation.)

To make this request, you will probably need to file an application, death certificate, and the original will (if there is one and you haven't deposited it with the court already) with the local probate court. The document in which you make your request will probably be called a petition or application. It must conform to court rules and contain certain information, such as the date of death, names of surviving family members and of beneficiaries named in the will, and so on. Your court may provide a fill-in-the-blanks form; if it doesn't, you'll have to type something up from scratch. (Section F, below, discusses preparing court documents.)

If your court allows it, and many do, you can file your request for probate by mail. But you may want to go in person. It's a good way to find out what kind of help you'll be able to expect from the clerk's office.

Generally, you will conduct your probate case in the county where the deceased person was living at the time of death. This is true even if the person happened to die while outside of that county or the state. If the deceased person left a will, it probably mentions the county in which the will-maker resided.

EXAMPLE: *Geraldine's will begins with the statement, "I, Geraldine Hogan, a resident of Sutter County, California, state that this is my last will and testament . . .."*

If the deceased person lived in more than one county, you have to decide which place the person intended to be a permanent residence. For example, many older folks who've spent their lives in cold climes eagerly decamp to Florida, Arizona, or some other toasty spot every winter.

To determine which place the deceased person really considered home, look first at what the will says. (A will can't change reality—if someone made a will in Illinois and then moved to California, Illinois is no longer the state of residence. But if the person's legal residence isn't clear, the will may be evidence of what the person considered home.) Then look at other documents, such as tax returns, a driver's license, and vehicle registrations.

If the deceased person owned real estate in more than one county in the same state, you can handle it all in one probate. There's no need to conduct a separate probate proceeding in the other county.

2. The First Hearing

When you request to be appointed executor, the court will schedule a hearing to give interested parties a chance to object. Before the hearing, you'll need to tell interested people and businesses about it. That means sending formal legal notices to beneficiaries named in the will and also to heirs under state law (the people who inherit if there's no valid will).

You'll also send notices to creditors you know about, and publish a legal notice in a local newspaper to alert any others you don't know about. You don't have to make an intensive search for creditors; if you've gone through the deceased person's papers and checkbook, you should have a good idea of who may be owed money.

In most cases, the hearing is a formality; if no one files an objection to your appointment, you probably won't even need to show up. (A court clerk or local lawyer can tell you what's customary.) If your request is approved, the court will issue documents that authorize you to act on behalf of the estate. In most places, these papers are called Letters of Authority or Letters Testamentary, or Letters of Administration if there's no will. (But they go by lots of different names in different states, including Letters of Office and Domiciliary Letters.) Probate court clerks will most likely refer to them just as your "letters." They make you the official executor, administrator, or personal representative—whatever term your state uses. The court will also issue a document called an "order," which opens the probate case.

IF YOU'RE FROM ANOTHER STATE

If you don't live in the state where you're conducting the probate, you may have some more requirements to fulfill. For example, you may need to file a document with the court in which you appoint a local resident as your "agent." This person can accept legal papers on your behalf and is subject to the authority of the court. Each state's rule about out-of-state executors is summarized in the appendix.

3. Posting a Bond

After you're appointed executor, the court may require you to post a bond—a kind of insurance policy that protects the estate from any losses you cause it, up to a certain dollar amount.

Many wills, however, specifically say that no bond is required. If the will doesn't address this issue, the judge will decide whether or not you must post a bond. If all the beneficiaries under the will agree, in writing, that it's not needed, the judge is unlikely to order it. (One potential problem: Beneficiaries under 18 can't legally waive a bond requirement.) But some courts still require a bond, even if all beneficiaries agree to waive it, if the executor lives out of state or if the person serving as executor isn't the person named in the will.

If bond is required, the amount will depend on the size of the estate. Bonding companies, most of which are divisions of insurance companies, issue a bond in exchange for a premium, usually about 10% of the face amount of the bond. You can pay for the bond from estate funds.

4. Proving the Will's Validity

If there's a will, "proving" it—that is, showing that it is valid—is always a part of probate. Usually, all you need is the statement of one or more of the witnesses who signed the will when the will-maker did.

Probate courts generally get a witness's statement in one of three ways:

- in a sworn statement called a "self-proving affidavit," signed by the witnesses in front of a notary when they witnessed the will (see Chapter 6)

- in a sworn statement signed by a witness now, or

- by having a witness come to court and testify.

If for some strange reason none of these is available (or if the will is a holographic will—that is, handwritten and unwitnessed), the court may accept other evidence of its validity, such as the testimony of someone who is familiar with the will-maker's signature. Each state has its own rules on what is sufficient.

You need a typed, English version of the will. If the will is handwritten or in a foreign language, file a typed English copy along with the original.

5. Managing Estate Property

As executor, you're in charge of keeping estate property safe during the probate process. (Chapter 9 discusses some of your responsibilities.) One part of your job is to prepare a list of the deceased person's property and, if necessary, get assets appraised. You will submit your results to the court in a document that's usually called an "inventory and appraisal." (In some states, the court may help you with this—for example, in California, a "probate referee" appointed by the court appraises the assets you list on your inventory.)

Because you have authority to conduct normal business on behalf of the estate, you probably won't have much contact with the court during this time. But if you want to do something out of the ordinary—for example, sell real estate or a business during probate—you may need to get court permission. It depends on the terms of the will and on your state's law. Many wills authorize executors to proceed under a law called the Independent Administration of Estates Act, which gives executors freedom to pay creditors' claims and sell estate property without prior court approval. In some states, executors can proceed under the Act unless the will expressly forbids it, which is extremely rare.

RUNNING A SMALL BUSINESS DURING PROBATE

If the deceased person owned a small business, and you need to take over primary responsibility for operating it during probate, your job will be made considerably more complicated. You'll probably want help from a lawyer or accountant. Chapter 9 discusses some of the issues you may encounter.

6. Paying Creditors

After you get your Letters, you'll want to promptly open a bank account in the name of the estate and transfer funds in the deceased person's bank accounts to the estate account. You can use that money to pay creditors. Some important creditors are the state, federal, and local governments—you're responsible for filing all necessary income, estate, and property tax returns. (See Chapter 11 for details on taxes and on how to open an estate account.)

Most creditors don't submit formal claims; you'll just pay obvious bills (utilities, credit cards, and so on) from the estate bank account. Creditors who do file formal claims through the probate process must submit the claims by a certain date—usually two to six months after the court issues your Letters. If they don't, they are out of luck. If you refuse to pay a formal claim, the creditor has a certain period of time to dispute your decision with the court

Some creditors will cancel bills and even refund money. If the deceased person had paid ahead for memberships or subscriptions, you may be able to get a refund. (See Chapter 4.)

7. Giving Property to Beneficiaries Early

Beneficiaries may be understandably eager to know when they will actually receive their inheritances. You can truthfully tell them that your first legal responsibility is to pay the estate's debts and taxes; only then is it clear how much property will be left for beneficiaries.

As long as you keep enough assets to pay final taxes and expenses, however, you may be able to distribute at least some assets well before the probate proceeding ends. But your state's law may put a dollar limit on the amount you can give, and you may need to get prior court approval.

Be very cautious when you consider handing over money or other property early. You must be sure the estate will have enough funds left to pay such high-priority debts as funeral expenses, expenses of the last illness, attorney fees, court fees, and state and federal taxes.

Still, there can be good reasons for distributing property sooner rather than later, especially if the estate clearly has plenty of money to pay debts. For example, if a car is left to sit in a garage, its value is likely to go down, and it's a bother for you to maintain. It's probably to everyone's advantage to turn it over to the beneficiary as soon as possible. The same may be true for household items or furniture that doesn't have much monetary value. And you may want to speed up distribution to a beneficiary who is in dire need of money (a college student, for example), keeping in mind your duty not to give away more than the estate can afford.

Always remember that you have a legal duty to be fair and impartial when dealing with beneficiaries. If you make early distributions, don't favor beneficiaries you're close to—it only invites a fight.

> **⚠ You could be personally liable for debts if you distribute property too freely and too fast.** Or you might have to bring a lawsuit to try to get the money back from the people who received it.

8. Distributing Property and Closing the Estate

When the creditor's claim period has passed, you've paid debts and filed all necessary tax returns, and any disputes have been settled, you're ready to distribute all remaining property to the beneficiaries and close the estate. Closing the estate ends the probate and releases you from your duties as executor.

Along with your request to close the estate, you'll need to submit an accounting of your activities to the probate court. The accounting shows where all the estate assets are going and shows that you've paid creditors. It also

documents any income the estate assets received during probate and any losses to the estate—for example, if an asset declined in value.

Some courts provide fill-in-the-blanks accounting forms. If yours doesn't, you can look at documents filed in other cases (probate records are public) to get an idea of what's required.

A TYPICAL PROBATE CASE, STEP BY STEP

First Month: Open Estate

1. File request (called petition or application) for probate, with original will, if there is one.
2. Publish, according to court rules, a notice of the probate in local newspaper.
3. Mail notice to beneficiaries and heirs, as required by the court.
4. File proof that you published the notice and mailed it to the required people.
5. If the will was not "self-proved," file statements from witnesses that the will is valid.
6. File other documents required by the court.

After the Court Issues Letters: Administer Estate (2 to 9 Months)

7. Get Employer Identification Number for the estate from the IRS.
8. Notify state health or welfare department of the death, if required by state law.
9. Open estate bank account.
10. Arrange for preparation of income tax returns.
11. Prepare and file inventory and appraisal of estate assets.
12. Mail notice to creditors; pay debts (state law may impose a deadline on you).
13. If court requires it, file list of creditors' claims you have approved and denied.
14. f required, file federal estate tax return within nine months after death.
15. After deadline for creditors to file claims, ask court to close estate.

Last Month: Close Estate

16. Mail notice to heirs and beneficiaries that the final hearing is coming up. (This must be done a certain period of time before the hearing; the court will have a rule.)
17. File proof that you mailed the notice as required.
18. Get court permission to distribute property.
19. Transfer assets to the new owners and get receipts.
20. After you distribute assets and all matters are concluded, file receipts and ask the court to release you from your duties.

⚠️ **Your experience will be different.** This is only a general picture of how a typical probate proceeds. Every probate court in the country has its own detailed rules about the documents it requires, what they must contain, and when they must be filed. Section F4, below discusses how to get information and instructions from your local court.

C. The Process in Uniform Probate Code States

The states listed below have adopted the Uniform Probate Code (UPC), a set of probate laws written by a group of national experts. The goal of the UPC is to make the probate process simpler, especially for small estates, and to give executors more flexibility in how they proceed. So if you're handling an estate in a UPC state, you're in luck.

STATES THAT USE THE ENTIRE UNIFORM PROBATE CODE

Alaska	Minnesota
Arizona	Montana
Colorado	Nebraska
Florida	New Mexico
Hawaii	North Dakota
Idaho	South Carolina
Maine	South Dakota
Michigan	Utah

In UPC states, there are three kinds of probate: informal, unsupervised formal, and supervised formal. Here is an overview of each.

⚠️ **Every UPC state is a little different.** States that adopt uniform laws are free to modify their provisions. So although the law is very similar in all UPC states, it isn't identical. You'll need to learn your own state's (and sometimes your own county's) particular rules.

1. Informal Probate

Most probates in UPC states are of the informal variety. This relatively simple process is designed for situations in which inheritors are getting along and you don't expect problems with creditors. Big and small estates can use informal probate. The whole process is just paperwork—there are no court hearings. In fact, it's quite similar to the "small estate" procedures discussed in Chapter 17, with the significant difference that there is no limit on the size of the estate.

a. Who Can Use Informal Probate

You can use informal probate whether or not the deceased person left a will. The important thing is that there are no disputes that need to be resolved by the court. So, for example, if you're handling your father's estate, and most or all of his property is going to you and your cooperative brother, you should be able to use informal probate. If anyone wants to contest the proceeding, however, you cannot use informal probate.

b. Getting Started

Your first step is to get permission from the probate court to begin an informal probate and serve as the personal representative (the term that UPC states use instead of executor or administrator). You can probably get a fill-in-the-blanks application from the court. You must apply more than five days, but less than three years, after the deceased person's death.

As part of the application process, you may need to speak to other people interested in the estate. For example, if there is no will, you may want other people who are entitled to serve as personal representative to sign a document giving up (waiving) their right to serve; this will clear the way for you to be appointed. And if the will does not state that no bond is required, you may also need the beneficiaries to agree, in writing, that you do not need to post a bond. The forms you file should come with instructions about these matters.

A court employee, usually called a "probate registrar" or "register," not a judge, will approve or deny your application. It should be approved unless someone objects by beginning a formal probate proceeding, you've missed the three-year deadline, or the will (if there is one) does not appear to be valid.

c. Administering the Estate

Once your application is approved, you will have official authority to act on behalf of the estate. Your authority will be granted in a document that's usually titled Letters Testamentary or Letters of Administration. People usually refer to it, though, just as "letters."

You will need to send out formal written notices of the probate to heirs, will beneficiaries, and creditors that you know about. You may also need to publish a notice in the local newspaper to alert other creditors. (Some states require that you send and publish the notice before the court actually appoints you as personal representative.) You'll also need to give the probate registrar proof that you've mailed all the right notices to the right people and that you've published the creditors' notice properly.

One of your first major tasks is to prepare an inventory and appraisal of the deceased person's assets. For some assets, you may be able to simply make a reasonable estimate of the market value; for others, you'll need an appraisal from a knowledgeable and disinterested third party. (Chapter 8 discusses how to get various kinds of property appraised.) In some states, you file this inventory with the probate registrar; in others, you can show it to the registrar and mail it to interested parties, but it doesn't have to become part of the public records.

You are responsible for keeping all estate property safe during the probate. (See Chapter 9 for more on this.)

d. Distributing Property

After it's clear that the estate has enough assets to pay debts, taxes, and expenses of administration (court and lawyer fees, for example), you can go ahead and start distributing property to the people entitled to inherit it. As a practical matter, this means that you should wait until the deadline for creditors' claims has passed—usually three or four months from the time you publish the notice to creditors.

e. Closing the Estate

After you have distributed all the property, you can end the probate (close the estate) informally.

First, you'll need to prepare a document called a final accounting, to show how you handled the estate assets. Your state may provide a fill-in-the-blanks form for this. The accounting lists any income the estate assets received during probate and any losses to the estate—for example, if an asset declined in value. It also shows the amounts you paid to creditors and how much you distributed to beneficiaries. You'll file the accounting with the court and will probably be required to send copies to interested parties, including beneficiaries and creditors.

Then, you need to file a form called a "Closing Statement" (or a similar name) stating that you have paid all debts and taxes, delivered the property to those entitled to it, and submitted the final accounting. You may also need to send a copy to each person who received property from the estate and to any creditor who hasn't been paid. Unless someone comes forward to argue about something, your job is done.

AN ALTERNATIVE: THE "FORMAL" CLOSING

If you wish, you can choose to have a formal closing to your informal probate. To get a formal closing, you'll need to submit an accounting that shows:

- all assets of the estate
- income they produced during probate, and
- how you spent estate assets or distributed them to beneficiaries.

In some states, you may have to refile the probate case in a different court. The court will review your accounting and then, if everything is satisfactory, issue an order officially approving how you handled the estate.

It's not common, but some personal representatives want a formal closing because they have an accounting question for the court to resolve, or because they want court approval to help protect themselves from possible claims that they mishandled something. For example, if you have paid yourself a good-sized but fair fee for serving as executor, you may want the court to approve it so that beneficiaries will know you handled the matter properly.

2. Unsupervised Formal Probate

Unsupervised formal probate in UPC states is a traditional court proceeding, much like the regular probate described in Section B, above. This section outlines the process; for details, see Section B.

Because it is lengthier and more expensive than informal probate, generally unsupervised formal probate is used only if there's a good reason. Here are some situations in which it may be a good idea:

- Family members or creditors with large claims want a court to resolve disagreements.

- You think beneficiaries may not trust your handling of the estate, and you want court supervision and approval to protect yourself from criticism or suspicion.

- You want the court to determine who the heirs are, because there's no valid will.

- Minors (children under 18) are inheriting significant property, and because the will does not adequately address how the property is to be managed, you want the court to decide how to best protect their interests.

- There may be more debts than assets, and you want the court to decide which debts should be paid and how you can be compensated.

Before the court appoints you as personal representative, you will have to schedule a hearing and send a formal written notice to all interested persons ahead of time. Interested persons include beneficiaries named in the will, the deceased person's heirs (surviving spouse, children, and anyone else who would inherit under state law if there were no valid will), and anyone who has formally asked the court to receive all notices connected with the case. You'll also need to publish a notice of the proceeding in a local newspaper. Anyone who learns of the proceeding and objects to your appointment can show up at the hearing to have a say.

You may need to get the court's permission before you sell the deceased person's real estate (unless the will authorizes you to do it), distribute property to beneficiaries, or pay a lawyer—or yourself—for work done on behalf of the estate. To close the estate, you'll need to file an accounting that shows how you handled all the estate's assets.

3. Supervised Formal Probate

Supervised formal probate is the rarest form of probate. It's used only if the court finds it necessary under the circumstances—for example, because a beneficiary can't adequately look after his or her own interests and needs the court's protection.

The process is generally the same as in unsupervised formal probate, described just above. But when probate is supervised, the judge can require you, as personal representative, to do whatever is necessary to safeguard the estate and get the property to its rightful inheritors. For example, the judge might order a physical inspection of estate assets or require you to submit monthly accountings. And as you would expect, you must get court approval before distributing any property.

D. Probate in Another State

If the deceased person left solely owned real estate in another state, you'll probably have to conduct a probate court proceeding there, too. That's because real estate is always governed by the law of the state in which it's situated, not the law of the state where the owner lives.

Probate in a second state is called "ancillary probate," and it's never good news, because of course it means more bother and expense. You'll probably need to find a lawyer in the other state to handle the probate for you. Usually, you start the main probate, in the state in which the deceased person lived, first. Then you open the second probate court case where the out-of-state real estate is.

Some states offer executors from other states (usually called "foreign executors") a shortcut. Instead of requesting letters of authorization from a court in the second state, someone who has already been granted authority as an executor in another state can simply file the other state's letters and a copy of the will, if any.

EXAMPLE: *Harry the executor of his father's estate. He has begun a probate proceeding in Illinois, where his father lived. But Harry's father also owned a house in Indiana, and the Illinois probate court has no authority over real estate in another state.*

Under Indiana law, Harry can acquire all the powers and responsibilities of an executor under Indiana law by filing, in the probate court of the Indiana county where the house is located, a copy of the letters issued by the Illinois probate court.

He can then go ahead and dispose of the real estate following the terms of his father's will and Indiana probate rules.

E. Disputes During Probate

Legal challenges to a will are rare—one estimate is that 99 wills out of 100 are not contested—but they are always ugly. (The 1% figure comes from Jeffrey A. Schoenblum, "Will Contests—An Empirical Study," 22 *Real Prop., Prob. & Tr. J.* 607, 611 (1987).) That's because family members are sure to be the ones doing the quarreling, causing rifts that may not heal for generations, if ever. You will do your family a great service if, in your role as executor, you can facilitate cordial—or at least civil—resolutions of simmering disputes.

This section briefly discusses the few grounds on which someone can challenge a will that was properly signed and witnessed. If you find yourself involved with an actual will contest—whether you are considering bringing one or you are fighting one off—consult an experienced lawyer, even though the dispute may not make it all the way to a trial. Some courts now automatically refer all probate disputes to mediation, in hopes that a neutral party can help people solve their own problems. This section also offers a few ideas for settling disputes outside of court.

Living trusts can be challenged, too—but it requires a lawsuit, and such challenges are even rarer than will contests. (See Chapter 19 for more on trusts.)

PAYING ATTENTION TO EMOTIONS

Many disputes are emotional, not legal. After a death, unhappy family members may threaten legal action, not realizing how hard it is to successfully contest a will. Often, their anguish has less to do with legal matters than it does with family history, and real or imagined grievances.

As executor, you will help everyone if you can defuse these kinds of conflicts. Even if you think the complaining person is nothing but a troublemaker (or worse), try to listen patiently and respectfully. If you can absorb some of the anger, you may make things much smoother for everyone over the long run.

1. Challenges to the Will

Someone who suspects that there's something fishy about a will—that it doesn't truly reflect the wishes of the person who signed it—can challenge that will in court. But the challenger has the burden of proving that the will is legally defective. It's a tough job.

a. Undue Influence Over the Will-Maker

One basis for challenging a will is that someone steered (or even coerced) the will-maker into including provisions that benefited the wrongdoer. Such actions are called exerting "undue influence," and they are a reason for voiding all or part of a will.

Just persuading someone to leave property in a certain way is not considered undue influ-ence. Undue influence is more sinister. Typically, it occurs when someone the will-maker depended on for guidance—for ex-ample, a lawyer who was supposed to give sound and impartial advice—takes advantage of the will-maker's weakness. A court is more likely to find undue influence if the will-maker was frail (because of illness or a fragile emo-tional state) and left property in a way that seems very odd under the circumstances.

EXAMPLE: *A court found undue influence by a mother over her son, who had been injured in an accident. He suffered from depression and a "narcissistic personality disorder" that made him especially susceptible to flattery. He had named his mother, instead of his own small children, as beneficiary of an annuity. (In re Estate of Bradshaw, 305 Mont. 178, 24 P.3d 211 (2001).)*

But someone who's managing day-to-day affairs reasonably well can leave property to anyone he or she chooses. It's not enough that the person changed a will late in life. For example, if an elderly woman remarries and writes a will that leaves everything to her new husband instead of her children, there is no presumption of undue influence—even if the disappointed children are sure the new husband married their mother for her money.

Anyone who wants to invalidate part or all of a will because someone unfairly influenced the person who signed it must come forward with convincing evidence of the influence. It's not an easy thing to prove.

b. Mental Competence of the Will-Maker

It's very rare that a will is challenged on the ground that the deceased person was not mentally competent when he or she signed it. Still, being "of sound mind" (or something similar) is a legal requirement for a valid will. If a will appears to have been validly signed and witnessed, a court assumes that the person who signed it had the legal capacity to make it. To prove otherwise, someone must come forward after the death with convincing evidence to the contrary.

A little forgetfulness or confusion is not enough to invalidate a will. Generally, you are considered to have the mental capacity to make a will if you:

- understand what the will is

- know generally what you own, and

- know who your close family members are—that is, the people who would be expected to inherit from you.

As one court put it, "[t]he established rule is that one who is able to understand what property he has, how he wants it to go at his death and who are the natural objects of his bounty is competent to make a will even though he may be feeble in mind and decrepit in body." (*In re Perkins' Estate,* 210 Kan. 619, 504 P.2d 564 (1972).)

One reason for having witnesses watch someone sign a will is to provide evidence, later, that the person appeared to understand what he or she was doing. What matters is how the person was functioning at that time, not before or after.

EXAMPLE: *An 82-year-old Kansas man signed his will in a care facility. Witnesses later testified that on that day, he stated or acknowledged the majority of his property, knew who his two sons were, and asked his lawyer whether this will was the same as his previous will. A few days before signing the will, however, he had been unable to recall the current season, where his room was, staff names and faces, or that he was in a nursing home. And less than two weeks after he signed the will, he did not recall that he had gone to his grandson's funeral two days earlier.*

His daughters, who were not mentioned in the will, challenged their late father's capacity. The court found that he had had sufficient capacity—at the time the will was signed—to make a valid will. (In re Estate of Farr, 49 P.3d 415 (Kan. 2002).)

c. Mistake

Sometimes a person who makes a will is mistaken about some important fact—how much property he owns, for example, or maybe even whether or not a close relative is still alive. If the will reflects this mistake, unhappy family members may later wish to argue in court that the terms of the will should be changed to reflect the will-maker's true intent.

Those relatives probably needn't bother hiring the lawyer. As long as a will is properly signed and witnessed, courts almost never agree to hear evidence about the circumstances under which it was made, except for allegations that the will-maker was unduly influenced or lacked mental capacity (discussed just above). You can't much blame the courts—if everyone were welcome to come in and argue about what Dad really wanted, the lawsuits would be endless.

Courts do, however, allow obvious mistakes in execution—that is, signing—to be corrected.

EXAMPLE: *A husband and wife signed each other's (identical) wills by mistake. After the husband died and the error was discovered, a New York probate court accepted the document the husband had actually signed, and switched the wife's and husband's names wherever they appeared in the will. (Matter of Snide, 52 N.Y.2d 193, 418 N.E.2d 656 (1981).)*

d. Fraud or Forgery

It's also possible to contest a will on the grounds of fraud. For example, someone could claim that the deceased person was tricked into signing the document, not knowing it was a purported will, or that the signature was forged.

2. Fights About Who's Entitled to Inherit

Sometimes a will does not clearly state who is to inherit—for example, there have been many lawsuits over the years about exactly what a will-maker meant by the term "children." For example, did the will-maker intend to include children born outside marriage or adopted by a stepparent? If possible beneficiaries disagree and can't work something out, then each side will present its argument to the judge, who will rule on the question based on state law. (See Chapter 6.)

3. Settling Disputes

Most disputes over wills never go before a judge. Family members settle their disagreements themselves in any way they feel is fair—saving themselves considerable money in lawyer's fees and considerable rancor among relatives.

EXAMPLE: *Charlie is 82. In his will, he leaves his house to his son and $200,000 to his daughter. But then he sells the house and, at the daughter's request, lends a chunk of the proceeds to the daughter's son to start a business. At a family gathering he says he needs to change his will to equalize things between his son and daughter—but he never gets around to it.*

After Charlie's death, his daughter doesn't feel right about how her brother has been unintentionally shut of out of the estate. She suggests that they split Charlie's estate equally.

You may want help from a mediator. A mediator is a trained, neutral third party who can help both sides reach an agreement. (Chapter 23 discusses working with a mediator.)

Arriving at your own agreement means that you won't be following the plan set out in the will. But that's okay. Even if you and other family members want to follow the will-maker's directions, you may find that doing so would involve expensive litigation, delay, and heightened family conflict, something the will-maker would not have wanted.

EXAMPLE: *When a Texas widow died, the daughter she had specifically disinherited promptly filed a lawsuit to contest the will, claiming that her mother had been unduly influenced. After two years, when the lawsuit was finally about to go to trial, the disinherited daughter settled out of court for a share of the estate.*

The executor, who did not inherit under the will, objected. The court ruled that the executor couldn't stop the settlement agreement—the beneficiaries of the will could do as they wished with their inheritance. (Matter of Estate of Hodges, 725 S.W.2d 265 (Tex. Civ. App. 1986), writ refused (1987).)

F. Working With a Lawyer—Or Going It Alone

Guiding an estate through probate takes patience, honesty, and attention to detail—but only in rare instances does it require a law degree. Whether or not you'll need help from a lawyer or other professional depends on many factors, including the kind and amount of property in the estate, how well everyone gets along, and the complexity of your state's probate procedure.

1. How Lawyers Can Help

It's important to keep in mind that there is more than one way to get help from a lawyer. Of course, a lawyer can handle the whole probate case. But you don't have to do it that way. You may want to hire an attorney just to answer some questions, help you with paper-

work, or handle one thorny aspect of a probate. Chapter 23 discusses hiring, working with, and paying lawyers while you're settling an estate.

2. When You Can Handle Things Yourself

Here's the *ideal* set of circumstances for handling a probate without turning it over to a lawyer:

- The estate isn't big enough to owe state or federal estate tax. (Only about 2% of estates pay federal estate tax.)

- Your state offers "informal probate" under the Uniform Probate Code. (This is discussed in Section C, above.)

- Some or most of the deceased person's property can be transferred outside of probate.

- You inherit most or all of the estate, so the money you save by doing the probate work yourself will be your own.

- The deceased person's property doesn't include anything potentially troublesome, such as a business you don't feel prepared to operate.

- Your local court provides fill-in-the-blanks forms, good instructions, and helpful clerks.

- You can get your hands on good self-help materials for your state (for example, they're available in Arizona and California).

That's the ideal situation. Even if your situation doesn't match it entirely, you may still want to proceed without a lawyer—or hire a lawyer only when you have questions. For example, if there are other beneficiaries in addition to you—perhaps you and your two siblings will share your mother's estate—the probate could sail through if you all get along. And even if your state doesn't offer the informal probate process, if you have a good self-help book as a guide, you could probably handle a conventional probate court case.

3. When to Hire a Lawyer

There are definitely times when an experienced lawyer's help is well worth the fee. (And remember that the estate—not you personally—pays the bill.) Here are some instances in which you should probably hire legal help:

- The estate contains unusual kinds of property that may be hard to value, sell, or distribute—for example, a valuable family business that isn't run by one of the main inheritors.

- The will contains ambiguous provisions, making it difficult for you to know who should inherit.

- The estate is large enough to that a federal estate tax return must be filed. (A CPA may also be able to help you in this situation.)

- Someone (probably someone left out of the will) is very angry and threatening to sue.

- The deceased person was in the middle of a legal proceeding—for example, a lawsuit, divorce, or real estate transaction—at the time of death.

- The estate has more debts than assets (is insolvent).

- You don't inherit very much, and handling the probate yourself means you'll spend a lot of time and effort for very little.

4. If You Go It Alone: Working With the Court

Although probate is generally a matter of state law, many counties have their own procedural rules—for example, they may dictate how documents must look or even when you must file certain notices. You need to learn as many of these local rules and customs as you can. They may seem bewildering when you first encounter them. But if you handle the probate yourself, you'll get the hang of them soon enough.

a. What You Need to Know

Here are some things you'll need to learn if you want to avoid frustrating delays in the process:

What preprinted forms are available. If you're lucky, your state will provide preprinted, fill-in-the-blanks forms for at least some steps of the probate process. Arizona, California, and Wisconsin are just a few of the states that offer this kind of help. If you're filing informal probate in a UPC state, forms will probably be available. If forms aren't available, your job will be much more difficult.

How to format court documents. If you have to type up documents from scratch, you may be required to use "pleading paper," which has numbers down the left margin. Many courts don't accept legal-size (11" x 14") paper. Some courts require you to staple court documents to a piece of stiff blue paper.

Court papers always need some blank space at the top of the first page; it gives the court clerks room to stamp the filing date and other information on them. Your court probably has exact requirements. For example, you may be required to leave a 2-inch x 2-inch blank square in the top right-hand corner of the first page, start all documents on line 10 of numbered pleading paper, and punch two centered holes at the top of each page.

When to use local forms. Your local court may have some of its own forms. For example, some probate courts provide a cover sheet, which you must fill in and submit when you file certain documents.

How to file documents. You may be able to file all your documents by mail.

b. Where to Find Forms and Information

Where can you find all these local rules? Well, if your county has a website, check it out. (For instructions on finding an official state, county, or local website, see Chapter 22.) It may contain a link to the court system website, which is likely to be a gold mine of information.

Also ask whether or not the county publishes a collection of its rules—perhaps as an instruction sheet, a booklet, or a file you can download from the court's website. These publications are usually called something like "Probate Rules" or "Probate Practice Manual."

If your state or county hasn't come up with anything for ordinary citizens, try the state or local bar association. It may have published, either on paper or online, an overview that will be at least some help.

Unfortunately, there isn't much in the way of helpful state-specific material written for nonlawyers. (Nolo's *How to Probate an Estate in California*, mentioned earlier, is an exception.) For nuts-and-bolts information, go to the local law library and look at books written for lawyers. There will almost surely be something on probate that will have forms you can use as models.

c. Finding the Right Probate Court

The court that handles probate matters in your county may simply be called probate court—or it may go by a less obvious name such as surrogate's court, circuit court, or superior court. You can probably find the correct court by looking in the phone book and calling the clerk of a likely sounding court. Or go online; see "Where to Find Forms and Information," above. If you're in a UPC state (listed in Section C, above), the kind of probate you use may determine where you file. In New Mexico, for example, informal probates may be filed in either probate court or district court, but formal probates must be filed in district court.

Large counties sometimes have one main and several branch courthouses; using a branch court may be more convenient. You'll have to check your county's rules to see whether or not you can use a branch court. ■

PART

Handling Trusts

PART 5

CHAPTER 19

Wrapping Up a Simple Living Trust

If you've been named as a successor trustee of a simple living trust, you'll take over management and control of the trust when the person who created it has died.

The job of a successor trustee is similar to that of an executor. In both roles, you distribute the deceased person's property to the people who inherit it. But when you're a trustee, the beneficiaries are named in a trust document instead of a will, and no probate is required.

There are many kinds of trusts, some of them extremely complicated tax-saving devices for the wealthy. This book discusses only these common kinds:

- revocable living trusts designed to avoid probate (simple living trusts)

- children's trusts, created in wills or living trusts to manage assets inherited by young people (see Chapter 20), and

- bypass (AB) trusts created by couples to save on estate taxes (see Chapter 21).

If you are the new trustee of any other kind of trust—for example, a QTIP or QDOT trust, or a generation-skipping trust—see an experienced attorney. You must make decisions that will have important long-term consequences, and you should have expert advice as you do so.

A. How Simple Living Trusts Work

Your first step is to make sure you have a very clear picture of how a simple living trust works. Then you can begin your job as trustee, working through the steps in this chapter one by one.

Start with the basics. A living trust is a trust that a person creates during his or her life, instead of at death. The person who creates the living trust is called the grantor. If a couple creates a trust together, each one is a grantor.

With a simple living trust designed to avoid probate, the kind of trust this chapter discusses, the grantor is also the original trustee of the trust—that is, the person who manages trust property. That way, the grantor keeps complete control over the trust assets. The grantor can even revoke the whole trust at any time for any reason.

The trust document, which sets out all the terms of the trust, also names beneficiaries. With a simple living trust, these beneficiaries don't have any rights while the grantor is alive. They inherit trust property when the grantor dies.

EXAMPLE: *Alice decides to create a simple living trust to avoid probate at her death. In the trust document, she names herself as trustee, and her grown son and daughter as beneficiaries. They will inherit trust property when Alice dies.*

When the original trustee eventually dies, someone else, named in the trust document, must step in to manage the trust. This person, usually a family member or friend, is called the successor trustee. That's now your job title. As successor trustee of a simple living trust, your job is to promptly distribute the trust property to the beneficiaries named in the trust document. In this way, the trust functions like a will, and your job parallels that of an executor.

But there is a key difference between a will and a simple living trust. The whole point of making a simple living trust is to spare survivors the delay and expense of probate. Because no probate court supervises a successor trustee, you can distribute property promptly and without red tape.

EXAMPLE: *Alice's trust document names her son Alexander as successor trustee. After Alice's death, he takes over as trustee, and, following the directions in the trust document, distributes trust property to himself and his sister.*

The law does, however, impose a strict duty on you to be scrupulously honest, keep trust property separate from your own, and faithfully distribute it according to the terms of the trust document. If you don't live up to these responsibilities, beneficiaries can sue.

Once the property has been transferred to its new owners—a process that may take only a few weeks because there is no need for probate—the trust ends, and so does the job of successor trustee. You shouldn't have any long-term management responsibilities.

TRUST TERMINOLOGY

Grantor: A person who creates a trust. Also called **settlor** or **trustor**.

Trustee: The person who's in charge of trust assets. With a simple living trust, the grantor (or grantors) is the trustee until his or her death.

Beneficiary: A person who inherits trust property when the grantor dies (or later, depending on the terms of the trust).

Living trust: A trust set up by someone during his or her life. Sometimes called an *inter vivos* trust.

Simple living trust: Our terms for a revocable living trust that is set up for the sole purpose of avoiding probate when the grantor dies. The grantor can revoke the trust at any time.

Successor trustee: The person who takes over as trustee after the original trustee (or trustees) dies. Like the executor of a will, this person is charged with distributing property to the beneficiaries. Commonly, the successor trustee is also a beneficiary.

CHECKLIST: WRAPPING UP A BASIC LIVING TRUST

1. Determine who serves as trustee.
2. Prepare an Affidavit of Assumption of Duties.
3. Determine what property is held in trust.
4. Handle assets from a pour-over will, if any.
5. Notify heirs and beneficiaries.
6. Get valuable property appraised.
7. Pay debts and expenses.
8. Transfer property.
9. End the trust.

B. If You're the Surviving Spouse

You won't have much to do if you and your spouse created a simple living trust together, and now you just want to keep the trust going as your own simple living trust.

You can follow the directions in this section and skip much of the rest of this chapter if:

- you and your spouse created a simple living trust together

- you were both original trustees

- your late spouse left his or her entire share of the trust property to you, and

- the trust document directs that trust property left to the surviving spouse stays in the trust.

In these circumstances, you are now the sole trustee of the trust. You have authority over all the trust assets. You do not need to transfer

property to any beneficiaries, because you are your deceased spouse's only trust beneficiary. Instead of transferring the assets out of the trust and ending the trust, you'll probably want to leave everything right where it is.

EXAMPLE: *To avoid probate, Millie and Max create a simple living trust together, naming themselves as trustees. They hold their house and bank accounts in the trust. Each leaves his or her half of the trust property to the other and names their daughter Debbie as the alternate beneficiary.*

When Max dies, Millie becomes sole trustee of the trust. All the trust property belongs to her, and she can do whatever she pleases with it.

Other trusts don't work this way. Again, if you and your spouse made anything but a simple living trust—for example, a QTIP or QDOT—then your situation is *not* this simple, and you should get expert advice on how to proceed. If you're dealing with a bypass (AB) trust, see Chapter 21.

1. Notifying Beneficiaries

If you are now sole trustee of the trust, and no beneficiaries are entitled to inherit anything as a result of your spouse's death, you do not need to notify any beneficiaries. The beneficiaries named in the trust document don't have any legal rights until after your death, when the trust becomes irrevocable.

If your late spouse made some specific gifts in the trust document—that is, he or she stated that certain items should go to named beneficiaries at his or her death—then it's your job to transfer those items to the beneficiaries. Section J, below, explains how.

2. Transferring Assets to Yourself

Even if you inherit everything and intend to keep the assets in your revocable trust, you may want to retitle some of the assets so that ownership is in your name as sole trustee. Doing so will make it easier for you to sell trust assets later if you wish to, and for your successor trustee to transfer them after your death.

Changing title into your name alone is much like changing title into the name of any other trust beneficiary. So just follow the process outlined in Section J, below. In general, this means taking the trust document and a certified copy of your spouse's death certificate to the holder of the records—for example, a bank, brokerage, or state motor vehicle agency.

When you get assets such as bank or brokerage accounts retitled in this way, request that your Social Security number be used as the account's taxpayer identification number, if it isn't already. This will make record keeping and tax matters less confusing.

EXAMPLE: *After her husband dies, Millie decides to reregister their jointly owned bank account, which they held in trust, in her name alone. She goes to the bank, explains that Max has died, and requests that the account be retitled as "Millie Hallbeck, trustee of the Max and Millie Hallbeck Living Trust dated June 4, 20xx."*

She then produces the trust document, which states that Millie inherits all Max's trust property, and a certified copy of Max's death certificate. She also asks the bank to use her Social Security number as the taxpayer identification number for the account.

3. Managing Your Revocable Trust

As mentioned, your trust continues to exist after your spouse's death—but now you are the sole trustee. That means you are in complete control of the trust.

If you wish, you can amend or even revoke the trust document. For example, you could change the trust beneficiaries or pick a new person to serve as successor trustee after your death. You can also add assets to the trust or sell or give away trust property.

4. Your Other Duties

Most people who create a living trust also leave a will, and if that's true in your case chances are you are the executor of your spouse's will. But even if your spouse didn't write a will, as trustee you are still in charge of wrapping up all your spouse's affairs—for example, paying debts, filing final tax returns, and distributing property that passes under state law. These tasks are discussed in Sections I and J, below, and in other chapters mentioned there.

C. Who Serves as Successor Trustee

The document that creates the trust names the successor trustee who takes over after the original grantor/trustee dies. It may appoint more than one person to serve as cotrustees. In that case, the document should also state whether each may act independently on behalf of the trust or they must all act together. If one of the cotrustees cannot serve, or declines to serve, the other(s) remain as trustee(s). If none of the people named can serve, then the alternate trustee, if the trust document named one, takes over.

If you're nominated as a successor trustee, you can decline to accept the responsibility. And if you do serve as trustee but later want to quit, you can resign from the job. In that case, though, there must be someone who will take over for you. Once you accept the job of trustee, you have legal obligations to the beneficiaries and cannot just walk away (unless the trust document allows it).

Usually, however, that's not a problem, because either a cotrustee or an alternate successor trustee (named in the trust document) can take over. A departing trustee signs a simple letter of resignation and delivers it to the person who will take over as the next successor trustee.

OBJECTIONS TO THE TRUSTEE

A beneficiary who becomes very dissatisfied with the trustee's performance may ask a court to remove that trustee. If the court agrees that the trustee should be removed, the court will appoint someone else— probably the next person in line, under the terms of the trust document—to step in.

D. The Affidavit of Assumption of Duties

As you go about your duties as successor trustee, you may be asked by banks, investment companies, or other institutions to show proof that you have authority to act on behalf of the trust. This is especially likely if you're handling real estate. Because no court is involved, you won't have the equivalent of the executor's official "letters testamentary" to show questioners.

Often, it is enough to produce the trust document (which names you as successor trustee) and the deceased person's death certificate (which shows that you're entitled to start acting as trustee). If you're taking over after the deaths of two people who created a trust together, you'll need both death certificates. And if you are an alternate trustee, you'll need proof that the first successor trustee is dead or declined to serve.

Another possibility is to create a notarized statement (affidavit) that explains why you have authority to act for the trust. You can then file (record) the affidavit in the county land records office as well as present it to institutions you deal with.

There is no legally required format for this kind of statement, but it should include:

- the name of the trust

- the date it was signed

- the fact that the trust document names you as successor trustee (or, if you are serving as the remaining cotrustee or an alternate trustee, a brief history of how this came about), and

- the date of the grantor's death.

Presenting this notarized affidavit, along with a certified copy of the death certificate and a copy of the relevant parts of the trust document itself, should reassure anyone who is reluctant to accept your authority as trustee. A sample is shown below.

SAMPLE AFFIDAVIT OF ASSUMPTION OF DUTIES BY SUCCESSOR TRUSTEE

I, Katherine Krellmer Segal, of legal age, being duly sworn, declare:

On August 14, 1999, Roberta M. and Samuel P. Krellmer created the Roberta M. and Samuel P. Krellmer Revocable Living Trust. The declaration of trust creating this trust directs that when both grantors have died, I , Katherine K. Segal, shall become trustee of the trust.

On February 22, 20xx, Samuel P. Krellmer died, as shown by the certified copy of the death certificate attached to this document.

On November 4, 20xx, Roberta M. Krellmer died, as shown by the certified copy of the death certificate attached to this document.

I hereby accept the office of trustee of the trust and am now acting as trustee.

Katherine Krellmer Segal   Date: *December 11, 20xx*

[notarization]

E. What's in the Trust

Obviously, one of your first jobs is to find out what property falls under your authority as trustee. Here's how.

1. Property Owned in the Trustee's Name

Property is subject to the terms of the trust document only if it was owned in the name of the trustee of the trust. So first, look at the trust document. It should list the items that were to be held in trust. These lists are often called "schedules" and come at the end of the trust document.

For items that don't have formal title (ownership) documents—for example, household items, electronics, or books—it's generally enough just to list them on a trust schedule. Sometimes the person who creates the trust also creates a document called an "assignment of property" (or similar name), which lists everything that's to be held in trust and states that these assets are formally being transferred to the trustee. Such a document is required in some states—New York, for example.

For items with title documents, however, it's not enough just to list the items on a trust schedule. The grantor, while alive, must have formally transferred title to the trustee's name. Common trust assets that have title documents include real estate, bank or brokerage accounts, and cars.

EXAMPLE: *Joe creates a simple living trust and names himself as trustee. He wants to put his house in the trust, so he signs and records a new deed, transferring ownership from himself as an individual to himself "as trustee of the Joseph P. Hamilton Revocable Living Trust dated June 3, 20xx."*

He also wants to hold some other valuable items, including his piano and his book collection, in the trust. These items don't have title documents, so in Joe's state, it's enough to list them on the property schedule attached to the trust document.

Unfortunately, some people who create trusts list certain items but forget to change their title documents to make the trustee the official owner of the assets. If that happened with the trust you're handling, the assets not transferred to the trustee probably don't pass under the terms of the trust—which means they may be subject to probate. (Lawyers can sometimes successfully argue, in court, that such assets should be considered part of the trust—but unless the assets are very valuable, it will likely cost you just as much to hire an attorney to make this argument as it would to take the property through probate.)

To see whether or not title was actually transferred to the trustee, carefully examine all title documents, including real estate deeds, stock certificates, and motor vehicle title slips. They should say that title is held in the person's name as trustee.

2. Assets From a Pour-Over Will

Property may also be funneled into the trust after the grantor's death, through a legal device called a pour-over will. Some people, instead of listing lots of items of property on a schedule in the trust document, make wills that leave everything (or at least everything that isn't specifically left to a named beneficiary) to their living trusts. They're called pour-over wills because property pours from the will to the trust. The property then passes under the terms of the trust.

A pour-over will, however, is treated just like any other will after the will-maker dies. So the property subject to the will may have to go through formal probate to get to the trust. Or, if the estate is small enough, you may be able to use "small estate" procedures to transfer it to the trust. (See Chapter 17.)

Once the property is formally held in trust, you, as the trustee, can distribute it to beneficiaries according to the terms of the trust document.

F. Notifying Beneficiaries

As trustee, you have a legal duty to keep trust beneficiaries informed about administration of the trust. This rule is intended to make sure that the beneficiaries have enough information to enforce their legal rights—for example, to make sure that trust assets aren't being mismanaged.

Because simple living trusts can usually be wrapped up quickly (as long as it takes for you to gather and distribute the assets), you probably won't be making many management decisions that beneficiaries can fret about—but still, as a matter of common sense and good

family relations, it's key to keep all beneficiaries up to date about what's going on. If you don't, they may worry about things that you could have easily explained to them.

If you're the surviving spouse and are now sole trustee of the trust, see Section B, above.

Questions about who is a beneficiary? If the trust document leaves property to groups of people who aren't specifically identified by name—for example, to "my children"—you may not be sure who's included in the group. See Chapter 6 for help figuring it out.

1. General Practices

If you think any beneficiaries of the trust don't know about it, you should promptly notify them when the grantor dies and you take over as trustee. A simple letter, telling the beneficiary that the trust has become irrevocable because of the grantor's death, and that you are now in charge of trust assets and will distribute them as soon as is practical, will do. A sample letter is shown below.

If a beneficiary wants to see a copy of the trust document, provide it right away. Beneficiaries who aren't familiar with living trusts may well have questions about the process of winding up the trust. You have a responsibility to keep them informed about what you're doing, so check in from time to time, especially if there's an unexpected delay. Commonly, problems arise when beneficiaries either don't know when they'll get their money, or are told when but then don't get it on time.

LETTER TO TRUST BENEFICIARY

February 13, 20xx
Judith Grandilowski
2353 Leghorn Ave.
Concord, Illinois 61399

Dear Judith:

I am writing to formally notify you that because of the death of James R. Emerson on January 24, 20xx, I am now the successor trustee of the James and Janine Emerson Revocable Living Trust. You are named as a beneficiary of that trust.
Under the terms of the trust document, dated September 23, 1998, the trust is now irrevocable. It's my job, as successor trustee, to follow the directions in the trust document and promptly distribute trust assets to the beneficiaries named in the document. I cannot distribute assets, however, until I know what debts (including taxes) must be paid. I hope to ascertain this information promptly.

I will be in touch with you soon, probably within the next 30 days, to let you know how matters are progressing. If you have any questions, or would like to see a copy of the trust document, please feel free to contact me.

Sincerely,

Jennifer Emerson
44 Bluebird Circle
Springbloom, Illinois 61357
(308) 555-1234

2. Special State Requirements

Certain states, listed below, have specific rules about how and when the successor trustee must notify beneficiaries about the existence of the trust. These states require that when a grantor dies, the successor trustee must send a notice to certain trust beneficiaries. (In California, the trustee must also notify the deceased person's heirs—the people who would inherit if there were no trust or will.) Most states that require notices give trustees 30 or 60 days to send them.

STATES THAT REQUIRE TRUSTEES TO SEND SPECIAL NOTICES

Arizona	Maine
California	Michigan
Colorado	New Mexico
Florida	South Carolina
Kansas	Wyoming

For specific rules and statutes, see your state's page in the appendix.

Several states require that notice be given to "qualified" beneficiaries. Qualified beneficiaries are those to whom the trustee could distribute assets, or who would receive assets if the trust were terminated now. For most simple living trusts, that just means all the primary beneficiaries named in the trust document. But the person who makes the trust can waive this requirement (in the trust document) for beneficiaries under age 25; read your trust document to see whether or not it contains such a waiver.

The notice must give the recipients basic facts about the trust, including:

- that the trust exists

- that they have the right to request a copy of the trust document

- the identity of the person or persons who created the trust

- the name and address of the successor trustee, and

- (in some states) that they have the right to a report from the trustee about management and distribution of trust assets.

If you must send such a notice, read your state's statute carefully to make sure you are complying with it exactly. (The citation to each state's statute and a brief summary of its provisions are listed in the appendix; Chapter 22 explains how to look up a statute online or in a law library.) If you're in doubt, consult a lawyer. There may be very strict rules about how and when the notice is to be given and exactly what it must contain. In California, for example, the notice must include certain language, and some of it must be in boldface type of a certain size.

Help for California trustees. *How to Probate an Estate in California*, by Julia Nissley (Nolo), contains a form you can use to give the required notice to heirs and beneficiaries.

G. Getting Valuable Property Appraised

If the trust contains assets such as real estate, motor vehicles, art, or jewelry worth more than a few hundred dollars, get it appraised before distributing it to the beneficiaries. Written appraisals can be important for at least three reasons.

Tax basis. Whoever inherits property gets a new tax basis (the amount on which taxable gain or loss is based) in that property: the market value at the date of death. If the property has gone up in value since the deceased person acquired it, this is called a "stepped-up" basis. The new owner needs to know his or her basis to correctly figure taxable capital gains (or losses) later, when the property is sold. (If you are the surviving spouse and already owned a half-interest in the property, you will definitely be entitled to a stepped-up basis for the half you inherit. You may even be entitled to a stepped-up basis in the entire property. (See Chapter 11.) Either way, you'll want an appraisal.

Distribution questions. It's common for a trust document to leave all the trust property to more than one beneficiary to share equally. For example, a trust may leave all trust property "to Stephen Erickson, Ramona Erickson, and Leah Erickson Rolf, in equal shares." One way for you to proceed is to transfer ownership of every asset to the new owners, so that they own everything jointly. But beneficiaries may prefer that you divvy up the property. To do that fairly, you must know the value of the trust assets.

Estate tax. If the deceased person left a large amount of property—currently, more than $1.5 million—you (or the executor) will need to file a federal estate tax return. The threshold may be lower for state estate taxes. The fact that property was left in a simple living trust has no effect on estate tax liability. So if you are dealing with a large estate, you'll need to determine the total value of the property the deceased person owned at death. If it turns out to be large enough to require a federal estate tax return, then the executor will have a choice between using the value at the date of death and the value six months later. Getting a reliable estimate now will give you something to compare to six months down the road. (Taxes are discussed in Chapter 11.)

How to get reliable appraisals for different kinds of property is discussed in Chapter 8.

H. Registering the Trust

Some states require that the trustee of a trust register the trust with the local court. But there don't appear to be any legal consequences or penalties if you don't. (Though if the court orders you to register a trust, and you refuse, you can be removed.)

STATES THAT PROVIDE FOR REGISTRATION OF LIVING TRUSTS

Alaska	Michigan
Colorado**	Missouri*
Florida*	Nebraska*
Hawaii	North Dakota
Idaho	Ohio
Maine	

* Not mandatory.

** No registration required if all trust property is distributed to the beneficiaries.

Registration of a living trust doesn't give the court any power over the administration of the trust unless there's a dispute. Registration serves to give the court jurisdiction over any disputes involving the trust—for example, if a beneficiary wants to object to the way you distribute the trust property. But even without registration, the court still has jurisdiction if a disgruntled relative or creditor files suit.

To register a trust, you file a statement with the court in the county where you live or keep trust records. The statement must include:

- the name and address of the trustee

- an acknowledgment of the trusteeship

- the name(s) of the grantor(s)

- the name(s) of the original trustee(s), and

- the date of the trust document.

A trust can be registered in only one state at a time.

Ohio has a special rule: If the trust holds any real estate, then when you take over as trustee you must file an affidavit (sworn statement) in the county where the real estate is located. The affidavit must be filed with the county auditor and county recorder. It must contain:

- the names and addresses of all the trustees

- a reference to the deed that transferred the real estate to the trustee, and

- a legal description of the property. (Ohio Code § 5302.171.)

I. Debts and Expenses

If there are no probate court proceedings, there is no formal court-supervised mechanism for paying the deceased person's debts and the expenses (for a funeral, for example) that may arise afterward. You'll need to take care of it yourself using trust funds. Commonly, this amounts to paying a few routine bills and funeral expenses and can be done in a month or two. But if the deceased person owned a business or had significant debts, it can take far longer.

The best practice is to pay valid debts before you distribute any trust property. You'll want to pay—or keep enough money reserved to pay—taxes, credit card bills, expenses of the last illness, funeral expenses, and other valid debts. Keep meticulous records of what bills you pay, when, and with what assets. Your records don't have to be anything fancy—a notebook or simple spreadsheet will do.

⚠ If you expect big bills later, protect yourself. Creditors who don't get paid have the right to press their claims with the people who inherit the trust property—or with you. If you think it's possible that big bills will surface later, you may want to actually take the estate through probate even though it isn't legally required, because probate cuts off creditors' claims after a few months. Or you may want to take advantage of a procedure offered by some states (California, for example), that lets successor trustees go to probate court and impose a deadline on creditors. Then, if creditors don't make a claim by the deadline, they lose the chance. If the prospect of big claims concerns you, see a lawyer to discuss whether or not a court procedure makes sense in your situation.

Most successor trustees who only close out a revocable living trust are not entitled, under the terms of the trust document, to payment for serving as trustee. After all, most living trusts are wound up quickly, and the successor trustee is one of the inheritors. But if the trust document states that you are entitled to a fee (as might be appropriate for a trust with lots of assets and beneficiaries), you may pay yourself a reasonable amount—whatever the trust document directs—from trust funds. Keep careful records of the hours you spend on trust matters, the rate at which you pay yourself, and the dates and amounts of all payments.

J. Transferring Trust Property

The whole point of setting up a simple living trust is to make it possible for the successor trustee to transfer trust property to the beneficiaries without probate. The trust document will tell you how, when, and to whom the trust property is to be distributed.

If you're the surviving spouse and are now sole trustee of the trust, see Section B, above.

1. Transferring in Kind or in Cash

Should you transfer trust assets directly to the beneficiaries, or sell the property and distribute the proceeds? If the trust document specifies how you are to proceed, you must follow its directions. But if the document doesn't give you any guidance, you can transfer assets to beneficiaries either in cash or in kind—that is, you can sell the asset and give beneficiaries cash, or give them the asset itself.

Generally, because you (and the beneficiaries) will want the trust wrapped up as soon as is reasonably possible, you'll find it easier to transfer the assets themselves. Such transactions may also necessitate filing a trust tax return that otherwise would not be necessary. (For more on tax rules that affect trusts, see Chapter 20.)

There are, however, several situations in which you may want to sell the asset and split the proceeds among the beneficiaries. Here are some of them:

- **Two or more beneficiaries have inherited an asset together and don't want to be co-owners.** For example, if two family members who don't get along or live on opposite sides of the country inherit a house or family business together, they'll probably want you to sell it.

- **You're not sure how to divide assets fairly.** If the trust document directs you to divide all of the trust property equally among several beneficiaries, the beneficiaries may not want to become co-owners of each and every trust asset—for example, if the trust contained works of art, jewelry, or collectibles. It follows that you'll have to give some assets to each beneficiary. Your decisions may lead to hard feelings, and even if you have the items appraised, you may not be able to ascertain whether or not you're really giving each person a fair share. By contrast, if you sell the items and divide the money equally, no one can claim you were biased or that they were treated unfairly.

- **The beneficiary can't manage the asset.** If you're pretty sure that the beneficiary doesn't have a clue about taking care of the asset he or she is about to take ownership of—whether it's a stock account or a house—it might be a good idea to sell the asset and distribute cash.

If you don't know what beneficiaries prefer, ask. Your job as executor is always to act in the best interests of beneficiaries and creditors.

2. Selling Assets and Distributing the Proceeds

If you decide to sell a trust asset and distribute the proceeds to the beneficiaries, you must keep good records of each transaction. If there's a bank account in the name of the trust, deposit the proceeds there; if not, you'll need to open one. Never, ever put trust money in your own personal account. As always, you must act in good faith and with the best interests of the beneficiaries in mind, which in this case means following a procedure designed to get the best price possible for the asset.

Keep careful records of not only what you do, but also why. You don't want to leave yourself vulnerable to criticism by beneficiaries, who might complain that you sold at the wrong time, for the wrong price, or to the wrong buyer. Just write down a brief explanation of how you made decisions: what you did to try to make a good sale and why you accepted the terms you did. (See Chapter 20 for more on this.)

You should be aware that that the sale will produce either a capital gain or a capital loss for the trust. Transferring an asset directly to a beneficiary, on the other hand, has no tax consequences for the trust. Trust tax returns are discussed in Section K, below.

3. Transferring Property to Children Younger Than 18

If any of the trust beneficiaries are minors (not yet age 18), you cannot just turn over valuable trust property to them. An adult must have legal responsibility for the property.

As always, first read the trust document carefully to see whether or not it gives you instructions. Here are a few of the possibilities for handling a child's inheritance:

The child. Generally, you can give small amounts of money or property of little mon-

etary value directly to a child old enough to handle it. More valuable property requires a more formal procedure. There are no hard and fast rules about how much is too much—you'll have to use your common sense and consult the child's parents.

Parents. A parent may accept and manage relatively small amounts of money—up to a few thousand dollars, in most states—on behalf of a child.

Custodian under the Uniform Transfers to Minors Act. The trust document may direct that property inherited by a child go to a "custodian" named in the trust document. The custodian manages the property, under a law called the Uniform Transfers to Minors Act (UTMA), which has been adopted in every state but South Carolina and Vermont. And in most states, if the grantor didn't appoint a custodian, you can.

Child's trust. The trust document may provide that property inherited by a child go into a separate child's trust or subtrust.

Property guardian. If no arrangements have been made, you may have to ask the probate court to appoint a property guardian for the child, to assume responsibility for the property.

If you don't get any guidance from the trust document, and you don't feel comfortable turning property over to the child's parents, see a lawyer.

More about property inherited by children. Chapter 10 discusses all of these options.

4. Making In-Kind Transfers

This section explains how to transfer some common kinds of trust assets.

a. Bank or Savings and Loan Accounts

If a bank or savings and loan account is held in the trust's name, transferring the funds to a trust beneficiary is usually straightforward. Financial institutions are familiar with simple living trusts and should understand that you have authority to distribute assets as successor trustee.

You'll just need to show evidence of that authority: the trust document and a certified copy of the death certificate. The bank may even have a copy of the trust document already on file. You'll also need to show proof of your identity. And if any doubt remains, produce the affidavit in which you acknowledged taking on the job of trustee. (See Section D, above.)

b. Real Estate

To transfer real estate, you need to prepare a new deed. The deed transfers title from you, in your capacity as successor trustee of the living trust that holds title to the property, to the new owner. You must record (file) the deed in the land records office in the county where the property is located.

⚠️ **Be sure the property is legally held in trust.** If the real estate isn't held in the trust—that is, the grantor never signed a deed giving ownership to himself as trustee of the living trust—then you have no authority over the real estate. The executor must transfer it as if there

were no trust, which usually means probate will be required.

Be sure to get a deed form that is valid in your state. Deed forms are available at many office supply store or title companies. States have their own requirements about what language deeds must contain and how they must be signed and notarized (and in some places, witnessed).

Before you prepare the deed, find out from the beneficiary how he, she, or they would like to take title to the property. Depending on the state, beneficiaries may have several options. Co-owners, for example, may want to own the property as joint tenants, or as tenants in common; each form has different legal consequences. Married couples typically have even more choices. (Various forms of ownership are discussed in Chapter 8; the beneficiary may want to do some research before deciding.)

If you're the successor trustee and also the trust beneficiary, you may find yourself in the odd position of signing a deed that transfers property from yourself to yourself. Strange as that process may seem, it happens every day, precisely to produce a proper public record of transfers from trustees.

EXAMPLE: *Sean creates a simple living trust and transfers his house to himself as trustee of the trust. In the trust document, he names his grown daughter Christine to inherit the house. He also makes her successor trustee.*

After Sean's death, Christine takes over as successor trustee. She prepares, signs, and records a deed that transfers the property from "Christine

Merriman, trustee of the Sean Merriman Revo-cable Living Trust dated January 17, 20xx" to *"Christine Merriman."*

The new owner will probably want to order title insurance, which protects against problems with the title. Before a title company will issue an insurance policy, it will probably require a certified copy of the death certificate and a copy of the trust document.

Special rule for Ohio trustees. If real estate is held in the trust, Ohio law requires that when a trust becomes irrevocable, the trustee must file an affidavit with the county auditor and the county recorder where the real estate is located. (Ohio Rev. Code § 5302.171.) The affidavit must contain:

- the names and addresses of all trustees

- a reference to the deed that grants ownership to the trustees, and

- a legal description of the property.

This affidavit is not required if the original trust document, or a "memorandum of trust" that complies with Ohio Rev. Code § 5301.255, was previously recorded with the county recorder.

Help for California trustees. *Deeds for California Real Estate*, by Mary Randolph (Nolo), contains tear-out deed forms you can use to transfer California real estate.

c. Brokerage and Mutual Fund Accounts

Your best bet is to contact the brokerage or mutual fund company and ask how to proceed. Start by checking its website for instructions or at least information.

The company will probably already have a copy of the trust document or a form that includes the information it needs about the trust. If not, you will probably need to send the broker a copy of the trust document (or, depending on the company's rules, just the first, last, and other relevant pages, showing the notarized signature).

You'll also need to send in:

- a certified copy of the death certificate

- a letter instructing the broker to transfer the brokerage account to the beneficiary, and

- an Affidavit of Residence (a simple, notarized form that states where the deceased person lived, shown in Chapter 13).

The company will let you know if it requires any other documents.

d. Stock Certificates and Bonds

If the deceased person kept actual stock certificates or bonds in his or her possession (most people use brokerage accounts instead), you must get the company to issue new physical certificates. The new ones will show the living trust beneficiary as the owner.

Getting this done requires some paperwork. If the stock is not publicly traded, contact the company directly. If the stock is traded on an exchange, you'll have to send several documents to the company's transfer agent (contact information should be on the back of the certificates). As a first step, get in touch with the transfer agent and ask what you need to send. Be aware that transfer agents change; you may find yourself referred to a different agent.

You'll probably need to send the agent:

- a certified copy of the death certificate

- a copy of the trust document, if the transfer agent did not receive one when the securities were transferred into the trust (the agent may require just the first, last, and other relevant pages, showing the notarized signature)

- the original certificates or bonds

- a document called a "stock or bond power," signed by you, with the signature guaranteed by an officer of a bank or brokerage firm—the stock power or bond power may be printed on the back of the certificates; if not, many office supply stores carry them

- an Affidavit of Residence, showing which state was the deceased person's residence (this form is available from banks and brokers; there's a sample in Chapter 13), and

- a letter of instructions for making the transfer from you (as trustee) to the beneficiaries; the letter should include the name, address, and Social Security number of each beneficiary.

SAMPLE LETTER OF INSTRUCTIONS FOR TRANSFER AGENT

May 19, 20xx

[name & address of transfer agent]

Re: Edward G. Ellsworth, deceased

To the Stock Transfer Department:

I am writing to instruct you to transfer shares held in the Edward G. Ellsworth Revocable Living Trust dated January 22, 20xx. Edward G. Ellsworth, who died on April 21, 20xx, was the original trustee of the trust. At his death, under the terms of the trust document, I became trustee of the trust.

Ownership of 100 shares of common stock in the Excellent Paper Company (certificate number A838929357B) was registered in Mr. Ellsworth's name as trustee of the trust. Under the terms of the trust document, those shares must now be transferred to Eric H. Ellsworth.

I have enclosed:

- the original stock certificates
- a stock power
- a certified copy of the death certificate
- an Affidavit of Domicile, and
- a copy of the trust document.

Please cancel the original certificates and issue new ones registered in the name of:

Eric H. Ellsworth
499 Regal Road
Cincinnati, Ohio 54101
Social Security Number: 999-11-9999

Sincerely,

Elana L. Crispin, Trustee
The Edward G. Ellsworth Revocable Living Trust
342 Oak Street
Fielding, OH 54000

e. Government Securities

To transfer government securities—Treasury bills or bonds, for example—you should ask the broker to contact the government agency that issued the securities, or contact the agency directly. You can download a Security Transfer Request form from www.publicdebt.treas.gov; using your authority as trustee, direct that the securities be transferred to the beneficiaries.

Finding the form. The Treasury Department's website can be difficult to navigate; try this deeper link to get to the forms section of the site: www.publicdebt.treas.gov/NC/FoRMSHome?FormType=TDF.

f. Small Business Interests

How you transfer business interests held in trust depends on how the business was organized, legally.

Transfers to outsiders. If you're transferring a business interest to someone who's not already a principal owner of the business, talk to the company's accountant or lawyer. The transfer will require coordinating many aspects of operating the business—for example, paying estimated or payroll taxes and dealing with employees and creditors.

Sole proprietorships. If the deceased person operated a business as a sole proprietor, then the assets are treated like any other assets the person owned as an individual. If the person owned a trademark or service mark, and left it in trust, you'll need to reregister it in the name of the beneficiary or surviving spouse.

More information on trademarks. *Trademark: Legal Care for Your Business & Product Name*, by Stephen Elias (Nolo), explains how to register a trademark or service mark in a new owner's name.

Corporations. If the business was incorporated, the officers of the corporation must prepare the appropriate corporate records to show that the deceased person's stock is being transferred to the beneficiary. Stock certificates must also be reissued in the beneficiary's name, or the name of the surviving spouse as sole trustee.

If the business was co-owned, check bylaws and shareholders' agreements for "buy-sell" provisions. In many small corporations, shareholders agree that when one of them dies, the others will have the right to buy that person's shares (from the trust or the inheritors) at a certain price or at an appraised value.

Limited liability companies. You'll need to transfer the deceased person's interest in the company (usually called a membership interest) to the new owner.

Before you make any transfers, however, be aware that in small companies, member-owners often agree that when one of them dies, the others will have the right to buy that person's interest at a certain price or at an appraised value. Check member agreements and the LLC's operating agreements and talk to surviving owners to see what agreements affect your actions.

 More about LLCs. *Your Limited Liability Company: An Operating Manual,* and

Form Your Own Limited Liability Company, both by Anthony Mancuso (Nolo), can help you.

Partnerships. If the deceased person owned a business that was operated as a partnership, read the partnership agreement and contact the surviving partners. They may have the right to buy out the deceased partner's ownership interest. If not, and the beneficiary wants to enter into the partnership, the partners should write and sign a new partnership agreement.

g. Copyrights

If a copyright was held in trust (registered in the original trustee's name in his or her capacity as trustee), you can transfer it to the beneficiary by signing a transfer document, and then filing it with the U.S. Copyright Office in Washington, DC.

Let the publisher know. If the deceased person was receiving royalties from a publisher, either directly or through a literary agent, be sure to notify all concerned that the copyright, and with it the right to royalty payments, has been transferred to a new owner.

More about copyrights. *The Copyright Handbook*, by Stephen Fishman (Nolo), contains sample transfer forms.

h. Patents

To transfer a patent from a living trust, you should prepare a document called an "assign-ment." You then record (file) it with the federal Patent and Trademark Office in Washington, DC. There is a small fee for recording the document.

If the patent was licensed to a company, make sure the company is notified of the death and the transfer of ownership.

More about patents. *The Inventor's Guide to Law, Business & Taxes*, by Stephen Fishman, and *Patent It Yourself*, by David Pressman (both published by Nolo), include sample assignment forms and instructions.

i. Vehicles

It's not common, but the deceased person may have owned a car or other vehicle in trust. In that case, contact the state motor vehicles department. It will have the forms you need to transfer the vehicle to the trust beneficiary.

j. Property Without Title Documents

For items that don't have title documents—furniture, for example—your job is easy. Just promptly distribute them to the beneficiaries named in the trust document. (But remember that if something is valuable, you may want to have it appraised first; see Section G, above.)

Make a list of everything you give to each beneficiary and ask him or her to sign and date it. This is not evidence of mistrust, but simply a part of your job. As a trustee, you have an obligation to keep good records of where all trust property ends up.

K. Ending the Trust

Congratulations—you're almost done. Once you've distributed the property, the trust simply ceases to exist. You don't have any papers to file with a court to mark the occasion, as you would if the property had gone through probate. You should, however, wrap up loose ends with the beneficiaries and possibly with the IRS. That process is discussed next.

1. The Final Accounting

It's a good idea to send each trust beneficiary a document that summarizes the actions you've taken as trustee and explains where all the property went. The level of detail of the document depends on the circumstances. If you're dealing with a large trust—with lots of assets and transactions—or if you're dealing with beneficiaries who are apt to be either curious or difficult, this statement should provide a meticulous accounting. With smaller trusts that have been quickly settled, it may fit on one sheet of paper.

A sample of a very basic statement is shown below.

TRUSTEE'S ACCOUNTING

I, Donald Everest, trustee of the Ella P. Everest Revocable Living Trust dated May 2, 19xx, have served as trustee since the death of Ella P. Everest on February 7, 20xx. This is a summary of the activity during that time.

Expenses. The trust had no expenses.

Income. The trust assets generated no income.

Distributions. Under the terms of the trust document, I have distributed all trust assets as follows:

Trust Asset	Distributed to	Date of transfer	Date-of-death value
House at 223 Sunrise Lane, Frankfort, KY	Donald Everest 339 Pell Street Frankfort, KY	04/21/xx	$155,000
Checking account No. 34-8889A at First Nat'l Bank, 4308 Magnolia Highway, Frankfort, KY	Julia Wright 21 Elm Street Apt. 2 Bowling Green, KY	04/29/xx	$7,430.40
Household and personal items from 223 Sunrise Lane, Frankfort, KY, including furniture, clothing, kitchenware, and hand tools	Donald Everest 339 Pell Street Frankfort, KY	04/30/xx	$5,000 (approximate)
Antique rocking chair from 223 Sunrise Lane, Frankfort, KY	Elise Smith 998 Oakley Road Frankfort, KY	04/30/xx	$350 (approximate)
			$167,780.40

Under the terms of the trust document, the trust is now terminated.

Donald Everest   Date: *April 23, 20xx*

2. The Trust Tax Return

If the trust had income or capital gains, you'll need to file a trust tax return (IRS Form 1041). Most revocable trusts that are quickly closed, however, do not require tax returns.

If you do need to file a return, you'll need to get a taxpayer ID number for the trust and file the return by April 15 following the calendar year in which the trust was terminated. Trust tax returns can be complicated. Because trust tax rates are higher than those for individuals, income is generally "passed through" to the beneficiaries, so they can report it on their individual tax returns. Capital gains may also be passed on to beneficiaries. (For more about trusts and taxes, see Chapter 11.)

Tax time is a good time to get help. If you must file a trust tax return, you'll probably want professional advice. Most trusts allow trustees to pay for such help with trust funds; read the trust document to find out whether or not yours does. ■

CHAPTER 20

Managing a Child's Trust

If you're the trustee of a child's trust, the deceased person chose you to perform a very important job: looking out for the financial well-being of someone who's not yet mature or sophisticated enough to do it alone.

You will control the trust assets for as long as the trust directs—probably until the child reaches the age specified in the trust document. While the trust exists, you will, following the terms of the trust document and state law, be responsible for investing, spending, and distributing the trust assets for the benefit of the child.

More help with trusts. Managing a child's trust—especially a large one—can be a daunting job. Fortunately there are several useful books to help you. The ones listed below discuss trust accounting, asset management, and taxes in more detail than does this chapter.

The Truth About Trusts: A Trustee's Survival Guide, by Jack W. Everett (FTCP Publishing)

The Trustee's Guide, by Pierre E. Richards and Howard I. Gross (Tower Publishing)

Executor & Trustee Survival Guide, by Douglas D. Wilson (Fiduciary Publishing).

Special needs trusts are another kettle of fish. If the young trust beneficiary has an illness or condition that will require care even after reaching adulthood, then a specialized kind of trust, generally called a special needs trust, may have been set up. These trusts have special provisions, designed to preserve eligibility for government benefits, and aren't covered here. If you have a disabled beneficiary, see a lawyer to find out whether the trust qualifies as a special needs trust or can be reformed (changed) to qualify.

A. How a Child's Trust Works

Typically, a trust for a child or children is created when a parent or grandparent dies and leaves money to one or more youngsters. The will or living trust of the deceased person (called the grantor or settlor) directs that the property a child inherits be held in trust until that child reaches a certain age. The will or trust then sets out the terms of the trust and names a trustee to manage and distribute the trust assets. If the child's trust is created as part of a living trust, it may be called a "subtrust," but it works the same way.

A child's trust comes into being only if, at the grantor's death, the young beneficiary is under the age specified by the grantor. Most grantors choose an age from 18 to about 35, but any age 18 or older is allowable. (By law, children younger than 18 must have an adult manage property for them.)

EXAMPLE: *In her will, Alma includes a provision that sets up a trust if her son Juan inherits property from her before he is 23. She names her brother, Robert, as trustee.*

When Alma dies, Juan is 19. The trust is created, and Robert manages the property for Juan until he turns 23. Then, Robert turns over the remaining trust assets to Juan outright.

Some trusts have more than one beneficiary. These are often called "pot trusts" or "family trusts." Some of these trusts end when the youngest beneficiary reaches a certain age.

EXAMPLE: *Edward sets up a simple living trust to avoid probate. In the trust document, he names his grandchildren Jacob, Jasmine, and Jenna as beneficiaries. The trust states that if they inherit while any of them is younger than 25, the money for the young beneficiaries is to go into a trust. He names their mother, Susan, as trustee.*

Edward dies when Jacob is 26, Jasmine is 23, and Jenna is 17. Under the terms of the trust, Jacob gets his money outright, but Jasmine's and Jenna's shares go into the pot trust. Susan takes over management of the property Jasmine and Jenna inherit. It's her job to decide—following the rules set out in the trust document—how to invest, manage, and spend trust assets for each child. The trust will end when Jenna turns 25.

B. The Trustee's Job

As trustee of a child's trust, your job is to manage and spend the trust assets for the benefit of the beneficiary. The trust document and state law tell you how you can invest the trust funds. The trust document also broadly spells out how you can spend trust money— commonly, for the child's education, living expenses, health care, and other necessities. Such broad language gives you a lot of discretion to use trust money for the beneficiary. When the child reaches the age specified in the trust document, or when the money runs out, the trust ends.

As trustee, your power extends only to financial matters. Unless a court has appointed you to be the child's personal guardian, you are not responsible for raising the child. You'll need to work closely with his or her parents or guardians, but you have no authority to interfere with the child's upbringing.

Serving as trustee of a child's trust is a much bigger commitment than serving as the trustee of a simple probate-avoidance living trust or even as an executor. First of all, your duties may last for years, depending on the child's age. And because you are in charge of managing and spending trust assets as long as the trust exists, you will have many more decisions to make.

1. An Overview of the Trustee's Tasks

Here are some of your duties as trustee, all of which are discussed later in this chapter:

- Protect trust property from loss or damage.

- Invest trust assets prudently.

- Establish an investment strategy and review it at least annually.

- Keep beneficiaries (or their legal guardians, if the children are minors) informed about how you're managing the trust.

- Keep meticulous records of all transactions.

- File all necessary tax returns for the trust.

- Follow terms of the trust that control how you may spend or distribute trust money.

Many trustees find it necessary to seek professional help with their duties. You might, for example, find it sensible to consult a lawyer, tax preparer, or accountant. Just a little coaching on how to make good investment decisions may ease your mind about the job you're doing. You may want to consult a lawyer at the outset to make sure you have a good understanding of your responsibilities. Under most trust documents, you can use trust funds to pay a reasonable amount for professional services.

Typically, the terms of a child's trust entitle you to compensation for serving as trustee. Payment may be a flat monthly fee, an hourly fee, a percentage of the amount of money in the trust, or simply a "reasonable" amount that you yourself determine. Many family members, however, decline payment, especially if the trust is small and the assets are not hard to manage.

2. Your Legal Duties

As trustee, you are in a very special position. You have been given control over someone else's money and property—and as a result, the law imposes a very high standard of behavior on you. (The legal term for this is a "fiduciary duty.") In other words, you have both great authority and great responsibility. You must always make decisions about trust property

with the best interests of the beneficiaries in mind. Not only must you always act honestly, you must also act in ways that will carry out the purpose of the trust.

If you take an action that violates your duties to the trust beneficiaries, they can go to court and seek to void (cancel) it. They can also seek reimbursement for any losses they suffered as a result of your action.

a. Always Put the Trust First

You must be loyal to the trust, which means you cannot engage in any conduct in which you have a conflict of interest. You cannot profit (other than collecting a reasonable fee) from your actions as trustee; you must act solely in the interests of the beneficiaries.

You may never, for example, sell yourself trust property or make loans to yourself from trust property unless the trust document authorizes it. Even if you know you'll pay back the loan quickly—even if you do in fact pay back the loan quickly, with interest—it is strictly forbidden.

Similarly, you may not make a deal that benefits someone to whom you are closely related—your spouse, children, or other very close relatives (or their spouses). The law treats these deals just the same as those that involve you directly.

If you are entitled to pay yourself for serving as trustee, document exactly what the payments are for and be prepared to explain why the amounts are reasonable. Take into consideration factors such as the size of the trust and the time you must spend to take care of trust assets and deal with beneficiaries.

b. Be Fair to All Beneficiaries

If your trust is a "pot" or "family" trust, which has two or more children as beneficiaries, you must be impartial in your dealings with them.

Being impartial does not mean treating each beneficiary exactly the same. With a typical pot trust, the trust document probably gives you discretion to act according to each beneficiary's needs. For example, a child who's injured in an accident may need more money than his or her siblings. That's why parents and grandparents set up pot trusts; they want to give the trustee flexibility to react to circumstances and the changing needs of each child. This may ease the parents' minds, but it puts a heavy burden on you.

As long as your actions further the purpose of the trust (and don't violate any other fiduciary duty), they are allowed. But there is still room for charges of favoritism if you give one beneficiary more money than another or violate one beneficiary's privacy by discussing confidential matters with another.

To prevent challenges from unhappy beneficiaries, you must do at least two things. First, have good reasons for any distribution you make, and second, write down those reasons. You should be able to explain how any action you take is authorized by the trust document and furthers the overall goals of the trust. (For more about distributing trust money to or for the beneficiaries, see Section J, below.) A third way of heading off trouble is to consult other family members before making big decisions about spending trust assets. If everyone understands your reasoning, they are more likely to support you.

C. Accepting or Declining the Trustee's Job

The job of trustee, like the job of executor, is a voluntary position. You have been nominated in a will or trust document, but you can accept or decline.

The main considerations are much the same as when deciding whether or not to serve as an executor: how large a commitment of time and energy you must make, how much conflict you can expect among family members, who will take the job if you don't, and your own feelings about what course of action is right for you and your family. (See Chapter 2 for more discussion about making this decision.)

1. Your Asset Management Duties

Obviously, the size and nature of the trust assets will have a lot to do with how much work you'll have to do. If you're going to be in charge of some CDs and mutual fund accounts, you may not have to spend a lot of time monitoring and fine-tuning.

But it's another story if the trust contains commercial or industrial property, or complicated investments that you don't completely understand. Still, if the trust has enough assets to pay for good expert help, then you may feel comfortable enough to accept the job of trustee.

⚠ Environmental hazards. One red flag that should make you think twice about accepting a post as trustee is the presence of environmental hazards in trust real estate.

Generally, this means commercial or industrial property that has been contaminated by some past activity. (Old, leaky tanks that once stored gasoline or other hazardous materials are the quintessential environmental nightmare.) The current owner—the trust—may be legally liable for the cleanup costs. That doesn't make you personally liable, but it does add a very large complication to the mix.

2. Personal Considerations

You can't really know what you're getting into until you've read the trust document and, if possible, talked to the grantor about the trust.

You must read the trust document to know how extensive your job will be, because that document gives you both authority and limits. Look to see what power you'll have. Most trusts give the trustee broad power to manage assets, so pay special attention to any language that seems tailored to the specific situation.

For example, if the trust is to have three beneficiaries, will you have authority to decide what each one receives while the trust exists? Or does the trust tie your hands and mandate equal distributions? Watch out for ambiguous conditions. For example, if the trust says you can make distributions to the beneficiaries only if they're attending college, what will you do if a beneficiary drops out of school for medical reasons, or takes just one night class at a community college?

Finally, give some thought to the emotional climate. How will it be to deal with the beneficiaries and their guardians? Are you likely to enjoy good personal relationships as you chart a sensible financial course? Or will beneficiaries, anxious to get more money, question your every decision? Ask yourself whether you are prepared to turn down a beneficiary's request for money if you decide you must. Obviously, life will be a lot more pleasant if beneficiaries accept your decisions about using trust assets for their needs and don't argue or second-guess your moves.

You're the only one who can make the decision. Difficult beneficiaries certainly make the job of trustee less attractive, but perhaps you suspect that you were chosen precisely because you're the one person in the family who can stand up to them. You may at least feel that you ought to give it a try.

3. Liability Worries

If you take the job, you may wonder whether you're opening yourself up to potential financial liability for actions you take as trustee. The answer is that you have little to fear if you act with integrity and common sense—and keep good records. If you manage assets conservatively, for example, you won't be liable even if the value of those assets goes down.

That doesn't mean you can't get yourself in trouble. You can face personal liability if you fail to accomplish any of your basic responsibilities, act in ways contrary to the trust's purpose, or carelessly mismanage trust assets. (Your management and investing duties are discussed in Section G, below.)

4. Can You Resign Later?

Even if you accept the job of trustee, you are not locked in forever; you can withdraw later. But you cannot just walk away after you've begun serving and leave the beneficiaries in the lurch. As trustee, you have a legal duty to them. So before you bow out, there must be someone waiting in the wings, ready to take over from you immediately, so that the beneficiaries do not suffer. This could be the alternate named in the trust document or someone else who is willing to step in. For more about resigning, see Section K, below.

5. Making the Job Easier

If you are reading this while the person who established the trust (the grantor) is still alive, there are some things you can do to make your future job easier. You may even want to make these steps a condition of accepting the job.

Talk to the grantor. The heart of the trustee's job is to carry out the grantor's wishes, which may not be entirely obvious from the trust language itself. Get the grantor to talk about how he or she imagines the trust will help its beneficiaries; the insights you gain will help guide your decisions later.

EXAMPLE: *In her living trust, Doris sets up a subtrust for her two grandchildren; it will come into being if Doris dies before the children have both reached age 21. She asks their mother, her daughter Amy, to be the trustee. Amy asks her mother how she envisions the trust money being spent, expecting her mother, a firm believer in higher education, to restrict it to university tuition and expenses. She is surprised when Doris explains that she hopes the trust money will help her grandchildren get through college, but that if possible, she hopes it will help them have some fun, too—maybe a trip to Europe during a summer vacation.*

Get your instructions in writing. If something surprising and important comes up when you talk with the grantor—for example, that the grantor wants you to give more money to one beneficiary than another—make sure the trust document reflects it. Otherwise you'll be in the uncomfortable position of being legally bound to follow the written terms of the trust even though you're sure they don't reflect the grantor's current wishes.

Read the trust document and ask questions if you don't understand it. You'll have to read the trust document eventually, and doing it now may save you some hassle later. Don't be surprised if you don't entirely understand your powers and duties on first reading; most trust documents are full of legal jargon. If you can't make sense of something, ask the lawyer who drafted the trust to rewrite it in plain English. You and the grantor may discover provisions you want to add, delete, or change.

Encourage the grantor to talk to the beneficiaries. A lot of anxiety can probably be prevented if the grantor sits down and talks to you and the beneficiaries (or in the case of young ones, their parents) about the trust. The grantor may want to explain why you've been chosen as trustee, and what the trust beneficiaries should—and shouldn't—expect you to do.

EXAMPLE: *Harriet sits her grandchildren down and tells them that she plans to leave them money in trust, to be used for their college educations. While they are feeling appropriately surprised and grateful, she tells them that she has picked her son Aaron to serve as trustee because she expects him to be a prudent financial manager who will do his best to make the trust money stretch until the last grandchild graduates from college. As such, she stresses, she expects him to firmly rebuff any efforts on their part to wheedle money out of him for unnecessary expenses.*

A grantor who is unwilling, for whatever reason, to have this discussion might agree to put some of this information in a letter that you could share with beneficiaries when the child's trust actually comes into being. Such a letter isn't legally binding, but it may help you when you're dealing with beneficiaries. (Of course, the letter shouldn't contradict any terms of the trust—so be sure the grantor realizes the importance of consistency.)

Get nuts-and-bolts information. Find out what assets the trust is likely to contain, and where important papers are kept. If the trust already exists, check to make sure all property that is supposed to be held in trust really has been transferred into the name of the current trustee. For example, a grantor who wants to transfer a house to a living trust must execute a new deed, showing that the real estate is held in trust. If the child's trust will be created by a will, then this isn't an issue. (Chapter 2

discusses other ways to make the trustee's job easier.)

6. Putting Your Decision in Writing

Whatever your decision about serving, it's best to put it in writing. Nothing complicated is required; a simple statement will do.

Once the trust comes into existence and you become trustee, you can use a one-page document called an Affidavit of Assumption of Duties to state that you have taken over as trustee. (Chapter 19 contains one.) If, on the other hand, you decide not to serve as trustee, you can use a letter like the one shown below.

If you decline, and the trust document names an alternate trustee to take your place, send your letter to that person, with a copy to the beneficiaries. If the trust was created by will and the will is being probated, or you don't know who is next in line to serve as trustee, you can deliver your statement to the local probate court.

DECLINATION TO SERVE AS TRUSTEE

Scott County Probate Court
98 Courthouse Square
Scottsville, Indiana 53338

Re: Michael S. Hutchinson, deceased

Michael S. Hutchinson, a resident of
Scott County, died on May 4, 20xx.
Clause 12 of his will, dated July 5, 20xx,
appointed me, Luana Kellsworth, as
trustee of the Sienna and Shawna
Hutchinson Trust.
I hereby decline to serve as trustee.

_____

Date:_____
Luana Kellsworth

D. Gathering Trust Property

The will or trust document that creates the
child's trust should tell you what property is to
be held in trust for the child or children.
Usually, everything the child inherits from the
person who set up the trust goes into the
child's trust.

Here's an example of a will clause that
creates a child's trust:

*All property left in this will to my daughter Hillary
Wilson shall be held in trust until she reaches age
22. The trustee of the Hillary Wilson Trust shall be
Alice McFeeney.*

*The trustee shall manage and distribute the trust
assets in the following manner:*

[the rest of the trust terms would appear here].

You are responsible for safeguarding all trust
property. With tangible items—a set of china
or a coin collection, for example—you must
keep them secure and protected from damage
until you sell them (as you might, if the trust
allows it and you need to raise cash) or
distribute them to one or more beneficiaries.
Get insurance if it's appropriate.

You're more likely, however, to be dealing
with intangible assets such as bank or brokerage accounts. Reregister these assets in your
name as trustee. If they're spread out over
several different accounts, consider consolidat-
ing them all into one account at a large
investment firm to greatly simplify record
keeping. You might be able to set up an
account that generates income and also lets
you write checks as needed.

Contact the bank or other institution for
instructions. You'll probably need to send a
copy of all or part of the trust document and
fill out forms provided by the account custodian.

Always, always keep trust property separate
from your own. No trust funds should ever find
their way into a bank account that belongs to
you.

Watch FDIC insurance coverage. Don't deposit assets totaling more than $100,000 with one financial institution that is FDIC insured; the excess won't be covered.

More information on taking care of property. Chapter 9 discusses safeguarding and managing property.

E. Communicating With Beneficiaries

Trustees always have a duty to keep trust beneficiaries informed about administration of the trust. This rule is intended to make sure that the beneficiaries have enough information to enforce their legal rights—for example, to make sure that trust assets aren't being mismanaged. But even if the law didn't mandate this, you would be foolish not to communicate with beneficiaries fully, honestly, and often. Good communication can head off misunderstandings, arguments, and even lawsuits.

If a beneficiary is younger than 18, send your communications to the parent or guardian who is legally responsible for that child. (It might be a good idea to send teenage beneficiaries copies of your letters, too, if only to educate them about their affairs.)

1. General Principles

Here are some general rules to follow to make sure you're staying in touch with beneficiaries as much as you should. (Section 2, below, discusses some added requirements that affect trustees in several states.)

a. The Initial Letter

Get off to a good start. When you become trustee of a children's trust, promptly notify the beneficiaries. For minors (not yet 18), notify the child's legal guardian (unless you're the child's guardian, too).

A simple letter, stating that you are now in charge of trust assets, will do. A sample is shown below. You may want the tone of your letter to be more or less formal, depending on your relationship with the beneficiaries.

INITIAL LETTER TO TRUST BENEFICIARY

February 13, 20xx
Judith Grandilowski
2353 Leghorn Ave.
Concord, Illinois 61399

Dear Judith:

I am writing to notify you that because of the death of James R. Emerson on January 24, 20xx, I have assumed the role of trustee of the James and Janine Emerson Revocable Living Trust. Your daughter Kimberly is named as a beneficiary of that trust.

Under the terms of the trust document, dated September 23, 1998, the trust can no longer be revoked. It's now my job to carefully follow the directions in the trust document and distribute trust assets on behalf of the beneficiaries for their health, welfare, and education, until the youngest beneficiary turns 21.

I will contact you again soon, probably within a month, to give you information about the assets in the trust, their value, and my plans for investing and managing them. I will also be happy to send you a copy of the trust document if you would like to see it. If you have any other questions, please feel free to contact me.

Sincerely,

Jennifer Emerson
44 Bluebird Circle
Springbloom, Illinois 61357
(308) 555-1234

---

b. Follow-Up Letter

After you've gotten a handle on how you're going to manage the trust, it's a good idea to send beneficiaries a more detailed letter outlining what they can expect from the trust and from you. In this letter, you can discuss:

- the goals of the trust

- generally, how you plan to invest trust assets

- how you will be making distributions, and

- what regular reports beneficiaries can expect.

A sample letter is shown below. You may need to include more or different information, depending on the trust document that shapes your duties. For example, if the trust document provides that you are to make distributions only from interest earned by trust assets (not the principal itself), you would want to explain that important point.

FOLLOW-UP LETTER TO TRUST BENEFICIARY

April 23, 20xx
Judith Grandilowski
2353 Leghorn Ave.
Concord, Illinois 61399

Dear Judith:

I am writing to give you some more information about the James and Janine Emerson Revocable Living Trust, dated September 23, 1998, of which your daughter Kimberly is a beneficiary.

The purpose of the trust is to provide management of assets that Kimberly and the other beneficiaries have inherited from Mr. and Mrs. Emerson. A listing of the assets and their approximate value is attached.

The trust is now irrevocable. As trustee, my job is to follow the directions in the trust document and the law of Illinois. I will manage the trust property prudently, investing conservatively so as to do my best not to lose money while making the assets produce a reasonable amount of income so that the purpose of the trust can be fulfilled.

Again, following the terms of the trust, I will distribute trust assets on behalf of the beneficiaries as needed for their "health, welfare, and education."

The trust document directs that the trust will end when the youngest beneficiary turns 21. The youngest beneficiary is now 11, so the trust will last approximately ten more years. At that time, I will divide any remaining trust assets among the beneficiaries, and the trust will cease to exist.

I will send beneficiaries quarterly statements detailing trust expenses and income, as directed by the trust document.

I hope you find this information helpful. As always, if you have any questions, please feel free to contact me.

Sincerely,

Jennifer Emerson
44 Bluebird Circle
Springbloom, Illinois 61357
(308) 555-1234

Keeping other relatives informed. It will probably make your job easier if you keep close, concerned relatives in the loop even though you have no legal obligation to do so. For example, say you're the guardian of your ten-year-old niece, whose single parent has died, and also the trustee of a trust for her. You know that several sensible members of your close extended family—grandparents and other aunts and uncles—are concerned about the girl. You might decide to keep them in the picture with fairly regular reports, even though it's not legally required.

c. Regular Statements

Your responsibility to keep beneficiaries informed about what you're doing continues as long as you are trustee. Even if beneficiaries trust your management skills completely and aren't interested in the nuances of investment choices, they (or their parents or guardians) will want to know how their trust fund is faring.

Again, check the trust document to see what it requires in the way of formal written reports—for example, you may be obligated to provide them quarterly, semiannually, or annually. State law may also require certain reports (see Section 2, below). Depending on what the beneficiaries want to see, and what the trust document requires, giving each beneficiary a copy of the annual trust tax return may be sufficient. At the other extreme, you could arrange access to online investment records, so that people could check on investments whenever they wanted. (You would still need to give them the big picture—your investment strategy.)

But even if you are not required to furnish regular written reports, you should be keeping records that would allow you to prepare such reports at any time. (See Section H, below.)

Get accounting help if you need it. If you aren't familiar with accounting principles, and especially if you need to keep careful track of the trust's income for purposes of making distributions to beneficiaries—it's probably worth it to pay an accountant to get you started on your record keeping and reporting.

Formal reports should show expenses, income, and any capital gains or losses. As part of this, you should document any purchase or sale of trust property. A simple report is shown below.

THE JAMES AND JANINE EMERSON REVOCABLE LIVING TRUST QUARTERLY STATEMENT: JANUARY THROUGH MARCH, 20XX

	Income	Expenses	Date	Balance
Beginning Principal balance				$76,998
Payment to University of Florida for fees on behalf of Kimberly Grandilowski		$750	Jan. 15, 20xx	$76,248
Dividend on 100 shares of the Midwestern Mutual Fund	$15		Feb. 28, 20xx	$76,263
Interest on money market fund #2809898 at First Nat'l Bank of Urbana	$131		Mar. 31, 20xx	$76,394
Ending balance			Mar. 31, 20xx	$76,394

---

2. Special State Laws

Certain states have very specific legal rules about how and when you must notify beneficiaries about the existence of the trust and provide subsequent reports.

a. First Notice

Several states, listed below, require that when a grantor dies and a trust becomes irrevocable (the usual way a child's trust goes into effect), you must send a notice to certain trust beneficiaries (and in California, also to the deceased person's legal heirs—the people who inherit in the absence of a valid will, trust, or other method of leaving property). Most states give trustees 60 days to send the notice.

STATES THAT REQUIRE TRUSTEES TO SEND SPECIAL NOTICES

Arizona	Maine
California	Michigan
Colorado	New Mexico
Florida	South Carolina
Kansas	Wyoming

For specific rules and statutes, see your state's page in the appendix.

Several states require that notice be given to "qualified" beneficiaries. Qualified beneficiaries are those to whom the trustee could distribute assets, or who would receive assets if the trust were terminated now. For most trusts, that means all the primary beneficiaries named in the trust document. The person who makes the trust can waive this requirement (in the trust document) for beneficiaries under age 25.

The notice must give the recipients basic facts about the trust, including:

- that the trust exists

- that they have the right to request a copy of the trust document

- the identity of the person or persons who created the trust

- the name and address of the trustee, and

- (in some states) that they have the right to a report from the trustee about management and distribution of trust assets.

If you must send such a notice, read your state's statute carefully to make sure you are complying with it exactly. (The citation to each state's statute and a brief summary of its provisions are listed in the appendix; Chapter 22 explains how to look up a statute online or in a law library.) If you're in doubt, consult a lawyer. There may be strict rules about how and when you must give the notice and exactly what it must contain. In California, for example, the notice must include certain language, and some of it must be in boldface type of a certain size.

Help for California trustees. *How to Probate an Estate in California*, by Julia Nissley (Nolo), contains a form you can use to give the required notice to heirs and beneficiaries.

b. Continuing Reports

The states listed above, which have adopted a law called the Uniform Trust Code, also require you to make certain regular reports to beneficiaries, unless the grantor waived this requirement in the trust document. Check the statute, or consult a lawyer, to find current requirements.

F. Registering the Trust

Some states require that the trustee of a trust register the trust with the local court. But there don't appear to be any legal consequences or penalties if you don't. (Though if the court orders you to register a trust, and you refuse, you can be removed.)

STATES THAT PROVIDE FOR REGISTRATION OF TRUSTS

Alaska	Michigan
Colorado**	Missouri*
Florida*	Nebraska*
Hawaii	North Dakota
Idaho	Ohio
Maine	

* Not mandatory.
** No registration required if all trust property is distributed to beneficiaries at the grantor's death.

Registration of a trust doesn't give the court any power over the administration of the trust unless there's a dispute. Registration serves to give the court jurisdiction over any disputes involving the trust—for example, if a beneficiary wants to object to the way you distribute the trust property. But even without registration, the court still has jurisdiction if a disgruntled relative or creditor files suit.

To register the trust, you file a statement with the court in the county where you live or keep trust records. Generally, the statement must include:

- the name and address of the trustee

- an acknowledgment of the trusteeship

- the name(s) of the grantor(s)

- the name(s) of the original trustee(s), and

- the date of the trust document.

A trust can be registered in only one state at a time.

For specifics on your state's law, check the summary and statute citations in the appendix.

G. Investing Trust Property

Suddenly finding yourself in charge of investing other people's money—quite a lot of it, possibly—can be understandably intimidating. But don't worry that you need to be an investment genius and bring in fantastic rates of return. The law actually requires you to be a conservative investor. If you follow some well-established rules and get good advice, you should not have to worry about either losing the beneficiaries' money or finding yourself in legal trouble because of your investment decisions.

1. Working With Experts

Many trustees turn to an investment advisor, who can help formulate a coherent investment strategy that takes into account investment goals, risk tolerance, and legal rules. Don't forget that unless the trust document forbids it (very unlikely), you can pay a reasonable amount for this kind of advice. Spending some trust money on good advice may be the most prudent action of all. Even if you consider yourself a sophisticated investor, consulting an expert can help reassure beneficiaries and protect you from second-guessing if investments don't return quite as much as you expect.

A financial advisor may recommend formalizing your investment strategy in a document called an "investment policy statement." These documents, which set out your goals and how you plan to meet them, are becoming common. They force you to do some serious thinking and planning, and let beneficiaries know what's up so that they can comment or object if they wish. They can also help take some of the emotion out of the decision-making process down the road, by giving everyone a set of agreed-upon objectives.

⚠ If you have special skills, you have a duty to use them. If you yourself have greater legal or financial skills than the average person, then you must use your expertise as you perform your duties as trustee. If beneficiaries ever question your actions, your skills will be taken into account when a court determines whether or not your actions were appropriate.

2. The Legal Rules

Most states now follow several uniform laws (laws written by panels of experts and adopted by individual states) that affect trust management. Here are two of the most important. Check the appendix to see whether or not your state has adopted one or both of them.

a. The Prudent Investor Act

This law is a change from older rules because it does not require or forbid particular kinds of investments; instead, it sets out guidelines for trustees to follow. As you can tell from its name, the law directs trustees to act prudently—in other words, to go for safety over the chance of big investment returns. (For that matter, even states that haven't adopted this law require cautious investing.) As discussed in Section 4, below, the law requires you to consider all your investments (the "portfolio") as a whole.

In states that have adopted the Act, it applies unless the trust document contradicts it. So if the trust document doesn't cover a particular issue, you should follow the provisions of the Act or other law your state follows.

b. The Uniform Principal and Income Act

Trustees often feel a tension between investing for income and investing to increase the value of the trust principal. Especially if there are two sets of beneficiaries—one that gets income and another that eventually gets the principal—this tension can be considerable. This isn't usually a problem with a child's trust, but it can arise if the trust has more than one beneficiary and their needs conflict.

Under the Uniform Principal and Income Act, now followed by most states, you can allocate traditional income to principal or principal to income. That means you can distribute principal to an income beneficiary or add income to principal if you conclude it's necessary to administer the trust impartially—in other words, to be fair to all beneficiaries. Usually, trustees exercise this power because they want to make more income available to the current income beneficiary. Trustees cannot, however, add to or change the class of beneficiaries—if one beneficiary is entitled only to income, you can't change that. And a trustee who is a beneficiary cannot exercise this power.

If you want to exercise this power, you should consider a number of factors, including how long the trust is supposed to last, what the grantor intended, the circumstances of the beneficiaries, the type of assets in the trust and fluctuations in their value, economic conditions, and tax consequences.

Lots of restrictions apply to this power. You should get the advice of an expert if you think it might be useful in your situation.

3. Coming Up With Your Investment Strategy

You must, within a reasonable time after becoming trustee, review the trust assets and decide what to keep, what to sell, and how to reinvest the proceeds of your sales. But before you can make these decisions intelligently, you need to decide on your investment goals—

what you hope to accomplish and how much risk you can tolerate.

How much risk. How much risk is acceptable? If the trust document doesn't give you any guidance, you must turn to the law, which will always tell you to be cautious. But as explained below, it's okay to make some relatively risky investments if your entire investment portfolio, considered as a whole, has an acceptable level of risk.

How much return. How much return (either income or growth in value of the principal) will satisfy the purpose of the trust? For example, if the goal is to provide money for college, estimate how much you think will be required, taking into account the expected expenses and other sources of funds. You may find that it simply isn't possible, given the low level of risk that you are in general allowed, to meet the stated goals of the trust. You'll just have to do the best you can.

4. Picking Investments

Once you have decided on your investment goals, you can devise a strategy to make them a reality. The Prudent Investor Act sets out some basic rules to keep in mind as you implement your strategy: diversify investments, keep costs low, avoid big risks, and consider the investment portfolio as a whole. This section briefly discusses these elements.

a. Consider the Portfolio as a Whole

You must exercise reasonable care and caution in managing the investment portfolio as a whole. When you evaluate particular invest-

ments, you should judge them on how they contribute to the entire investment portfolio. Not every investment has to meet your standards for return and risk, as long as the entire investment portfolio does.

If beneficiaries ever challenged your management, your investment decisions wouldn't be evaluated one at a time, in isolation. Instead, a court would look at your overall management of the trust property.

EXAMPLE: *Fred, a trustee of a trust for his nephews, invests some trust money in a mutual fund that quickly loses money. Even if that particular action turns out to have been ill-conceived, the nephews would probably not succeed in an effort to argue that Fred isn't doing a good enough job as trustee if they challenged just that decision. A court would look at Fred's overall management of the trust property.*

b. Be Cautious

You must act with prudence, which in this context means reasonable skill and caution. The emphasis is on caution: You should be careful with trust money and stay far away from risky investments. Your first job is not to lose money. Even if you would invest your own money more aggressively, you must apply a different, stricter standard to trust money.

Use your common sense to avoid excessive risk. Don't invest in small, privately owned businesses. (Just say no to Uncle Pete, who wants you to buy into his construction company.) If the trust will last more than a few years, consider investing some of its money in a conservative stock mutual fund. Again, an investment advisor can help you find safe and appropriate places to put trust money.

If you're not sure whether or not a certain action is okay—for instance, you want to put some trust funds in an uninsured account—check the trust document to see whether the action is specifically allowed or prohibited. If the trust document forbids it, that's the end of the story (even if your state's law would allow it). If the document doesn't address the issue, you are still bound by the prudent investor rule and your state's law.

c.   Diversify

Diversifying—putting money in different kinds of investments to reduce the risk to the trust if a particular kind of investment loses money—is part of being cautious when you're investing. Not putting all your eggs into one basket is a sound principle for any investor, but it's a must for a trustee. Diversification is specifically required by the Prudent Investor Act unless you have good reason to think that, under the circumstances, it isn't in the interests of the beneficiaries and won't further the purposes of the trust.

EXAMPLE: *Gary, trustee of a trust for his deceased friend's children, has done lots of research about investment and is convinced that high-tech stocks are the key to success. He invests almost all the money in the trust in stock funds that focus on high-tech companies, and he does marvelously for several years. But when a technology downturn comes, it devastates the trust assets. Because Gary didn't diversify the investments, the beneficiaries could sue him, asking a court to find that he*

violated his duty as a trustee and should compensate them for the losses.

d.   Consider All Relevant Factors

To be a prudent investor, you must consider not only the purpose and terms of the trust, but external circumstances as well. You may consider general economic conditions, possible inflation, the return you expect to get, the tax consequences of certain decisions, costs of certain investments, and of course the role each investment plays within the overall portfolio. When you're figuring out what kind of income you want to try to bring in, you may, if the trust directs, consider the beneficiaries' other income and assets.

e.   Keep Expenses Low

The Prudent Investor Act requires you to keep costs down. That means, for example, that you'll have to look very closely at investments that require you to pay a commission. If there are comparable, lower-cost investments that might bring a greater return to the trust, it's your duty as a trustee to at least investigate them.

Similarly, if you're shopping around for a checking account for the trust, look for an account with a low fee (or none), to minimize the cost to the trust. If there's enough money, and you don't plan on writing lots of checks for small amounts, you may want to use a money market account from a mutual fund company that comes with check-writing privileges. That way you can earn a bit of interest on the money. But before you sign up, there are a couple of issues to consider. First, these funds are not insured by the FDIC, so read the trust document to see whether or not that is allowed. (Several big mutual fund companies do provide extensive private insurance.) Second, find out whether the fund requires that the checks you write be for at least a certain amount—$250 is common. If you're planning to write a lot of small checks, this may be a problem.

⚠️ **Watch the fees.** If you incur bank fees because of your own carelessness—an overdraft charge, for example—you'll be personally responsible.

f. Always Keep the Trust's Purpose in Mind

Your job is to carry out the grantor's purpose in creating the trust. Obviously, that's going to influence your investment choices. For example, if the trust envisions that you will give the beneficiaries regular payments for college expenses, you won't want to lock up trust assets in long-term CDs unless the children are still years away from college. But it might make sense to keep some money in money market accounts for short-term needs while investing other funds that won't be needed for a while in a mix of investments for the long term.

g. Keep an Eye on the Money

It probably goes without saying, but you can't just implement an investment strategy—no matter how brilliant—and then walk away. Conditions change, beneficiaries' needs change, investment options change. You must

monitor your investments' performance, see how your investment strategy is panning out, and make adjustments as they're needed.

5. Conflicts With Beneficiaries

If beneficiaries object to your management decisions, and you can't work something out, they can take the matter to court—a rare development. If that happens, your conduct will be judged taking into account all the circumstances, the powers the trust document grants to you, and your duties under the law.

You cannot be found at fault just because investments haven't performed as well as you (and the beneficiaries) had hoped. If you carefully followed the prudent investor rules when making decisions, you will not be liable to beneficiaries even if your investment strategy has not been ultimately successful. The court looks at the circumstances at the time of the investment.

If you gave an investment policy statement to beneficiaries, and they didn't object to it, this will also help you fend off their objections now.

H. Keeping Good Records

Keeping clear, complete, and accurate records is an essential part of being a good trustee. Even if your own financial records are in a shoebox under the bed, you'll need to do better when it comes to trust transactions.

Just how clear, complete, and accurate must the records be? Your goal should be that a reasonably intelligent person who walked in off the street and was handed your records could understand everything you've done. The records should provide a complete picture of trust management.

All this said, the records you keep will probably be very basic ones. For example, you'll probably have a checking account in the name of the trust (remember, you cannot, ever, keep trust assets in your own personal account), and its register will provide a good record of income received and expenses paid. If you can't fit enough information in the check register, use a ledger book or a simple computer program.

Always document any discretionary distributions to beneficiaries (Section J, below), write down not just basic information such as the amount and purpose, but also who requested it (if someone did) and why you decided as you did. Refer to the trust document, if you believe that a particular clause mandates your decision. If there are multiple trust beneficiaries, explain why granting the request does, or does not, harm them.

These records can serve at least two purposes. First, you can use them to explain your actions to the beneficiary—especially if you say no. Instead of a curt dismissal, the beneficiary will receive a reasoned explanation of why you cannot, as you interpret your duties as trustee, grant the request. Second, if you are later required to defend your decision, you will have evidence that you made a conscientious choice based on the facts as you knew them.

You'll need all these records to make reports to the beneficiaries. And if you must ever

resign as trustee, the person who takes over for you will need good records. Finally, they'll be crucial in the unlikely event a beneficiary ever challenges your decisions.

SOME PAPERS TO KEEP

Bills

Correspondence about the trust (letters to and from beneficiaries, for example)

Tax returns

Check registers

Canceled checks (if the bank provides them)

Anything from the IRS

Investment policy statements

Insurance policies

Receipts from recipients of trust money

Reports to beneficiaries

Statements from all accounts

If you pay yourself, keep extra-good records. If you use trust funds to compensate yourself for serving as trustee, write down the amounts, dates, and why each payment is justified by the terms of the trust document.

I. Handling Trust Taxes

A trust must pay taxes on income it receives and doesn't distribute to beneficiaries. Under IRS rules, however, many simple trusts don't need to file a trust income tax return. This section briefly explains the rules.

1. Notifying the IRS That You're Trustee

Your first tax-related job is simply to notify the IRS that you are now acting as trustee. You do that with IRS Form 56, *Notice Concerning Fiduciary Relationship*. It's a one-page form that asks for basic information about you and about the deceased person who created the trust. File it as soon as you take over as trustee. After you do, the IRS will send you any notices that concern the trust.

2. Getting a Tax ID Number for the Trust

Before you can file a tax return for the trust, you must get the trust a taxpayer ID number. Just send Form SS-4, *Application for Employer Identification Number*, to the IRS. (For more about tax ID numbers, see Chapter 9, Section C.)

3. The Trust Tax Return

Many simple trusts don't need to file a trust income tax return (IRS Form 1041). No return is necessary if:

- the trust receives no more than $600 in annual gross income

- the trust has no taxable income (see Section 4, below), and

- all of the beneficiaries are United States citizens or permanent resident aliens.

If you do need to file a trust tax return, you'll probably want to get expert help from a CPA who is familiar with this kind of work. As you might guess, many special rules apply to trust taxes. The return will be more complicated if the trust assets include a business, if you dig into the trust assets (not just income) to make distributions, or if you sell trust property.

For filing purposes, trusts must use a calendar year. This means the return is due by April 15 for the previous calendar year. (For more about trust tax returns, see Chapter 11.)

4. Minimizing Income Taxes

A trust is taxed only on trust income that it keeps—that is, income that it doesn't pay out to beneficiaries in the year it's received.

When trust income is paid to beneficiaries, they report it on their individual tax returns. Because trusts are taxed at a higher rate, taxes on individual income are usually less than taxes on trust income, so it reduces total taxes to give all trust income to beneficiaries.

For this reason, most trust documents direct the trustee to regularly pay out income or use it on behalf of the beneficiary. Read your trust document to find out whether or not it does.

⚠ Don't miss the deadline for distributing income to beneficiaries. If you're distributing trust income to beneficiaries to reduce taxes, you'll want to pay out all the trust's income. But you won't know that exact figure until after the end of the calendar year. To solve this problem, the IRS gives you until 65 days after the year ends to make the distributions. This extra time lets you ascertain the final amount of trust income for the year.

5. Sending Beneficiaries Schedule K-1

If you distribute trust money to beneficiaries, then you must give each beneficiary an IRS form called Schedule K-1 soon after the end of each calendar year. This form shows how much the beneficiary received from the trust that year and so tells the IRS what income (and tax liability) was transferred from the trust to the beneficiary.

Because beneficiaries need their Schedule K-1 before they can prepare their own tax returns, you will earn favor by seeing to it that these forms are sent as soon as possible. If you make the beneficiaries wait until the last minute, you will make their lives harder—and they will probably do the same to you.

J. Distributing Property

Your authority to distribute trust property to beneficiaries comes from the trust document itself—so once again, it's absolutely necessary that you read the document carefully, line by line. If the trust language is vague or seems to contradict itself and you don't understand what or whom you're supposed to spend trust money for, ask an experienced lawyer for help.

As trustee of a trust for a child, you are likely to have very broad discretion to spend trust money. For example, the trust might give you the power to use trust assets for a child's "health, support, maintenance, or education."

1. Your Authority

Before you start spending trust funds, here are some issues you must understand:

Trust purposes. The most basic question: What can you spend money for? All of your decisions must further the purposes for which the trust was established. For example, if you have discretion to spend money for health, education, and living expenses, you could decide that a trip to New York City was educational and that a stint at a summer camp in the mountains was healthful.

Interest vs. principal. Are you authorized to make distributions only from interest earned by trust assets, or can you dig into principal if necessary?

Timing. Does the trust document instruct you to give beneficiaries regularly scheduled payments of certain amounts, or is it up to you to decide when to spend money on beneficiaries' behalf? Do payments depend on events—for example, when a beneficiary turns 18 or enrolls in college?

Multiple beneficiaries. If two or more beneficiaries are entitled to receive money now, does the trust document say you are obligated to spend equal amounts on all of them, or do you have the discretion to vary the amounts? (Remember that you always have a legal duty to be fair to all beneficiaries.)

Beneficiaries' other sources of income. Some trusts allow or require you to look into a beneficiary's other sources of income when you're deciding what kind of distribution to make to that beneficiary.

Taxes. As explained above (Section I), for tax purposes it's usually advantageous to distribute all trust income to beneficiaries and have them pay tax on it, instead of having the trust pay the tax. But other concerns may override taxes—for example, you may want to accumulate as much money as possible in the trust if you expect large expenses later.

2. Dealing With Beneficiaries

As discussed earlier, good communication with beneficiaries (or their guardians) will go a long way to head off difficulties. And it may seem an obvious point, but it's good to keep in mind that communication goes both ways—you must listen to beneficiaries as well as talk to them.

If a beneficiary's request for money takes you by surprise, pay attention, even if granting the request might disrupt your plan for trust management. Don't give an answer before you get all the information you need to make an informed decision, including exactly how much money the beneficiary wants, when, and what it will be used for. Then you can judge the request against the terms of the trust document and your general legal obligations of prudence, loyalty, and fairness to all beneficiaries. You may decide to deny the request, grant it in whole, or suggest something in between. Don't be pressured into making a snap decision if a beneficiary comes to you with a last-minute plea for money.

Part of your job is to hold firm against requests that you think undermine the purpose of the trust. You can soften the blow by explaining why you felt that to do so was part of your responsibility as trustee. (Section H, above, discusses why and how you should document your decisions as well.)

Sometimes there just isn't enough money to achieve all the goals set by the grantor. That's

life—whether or not there's a trust. But it may require you to make hard choices. For example, if children are young, how much should you spend on them now and how much should you save for college? No one answer is right for everybody.

A beneficiary who is dissatisfied with your decisions can challenge you in court. But a lawsuit is, of course, a last resort. If you are in regular contact with beneficiaries and explain your actions clearly to them, you should be able to placate all but the most angry and determined beneficiaries.

K. If You Want to Resign

Resignation, like virtually every other aspect of the trust, is governed by the trust document. So if you're itching to leave the role of trustee, check the document for instructions.

1. How to Resign

If you're serving with a cotrustee, that person will probably handle the job alone after you resign. The document may name an alternate trustee who will take over for you. It may direct you to name someone to serve, or allow the beneficiaries to do so. (Some trust documents allow a majority of beneficiaries to remove a trustee—in some cases, without stating any reason—and choose someone more to their liking, but that's not likely for a children's trust.)

Check the trust document for any procedures you are supposed to follow. For example, you may need to notify beneficiaries and give a certain amount of notice before your resignation becomes effective. Even if the trust doesn't require it, however, you should give beneficiaries (and the person who is next in line to serve as trustee) written notice as far in advance of the event as you can.

If the trust document doesn't have any provision anticipating a trustee's resignation, things are more complicated. You can't just abandon your responsibilities—that would be a violation of your legal duty of care (fiduciary duty) to the beneficiaries. So first, you will have to get permission from a court. The court will grant your request when a suitable replacement trustee is found. If you have an emergency, of course, a court will try to act promptly.

2. Your Responsibilities If You Resign

Try to make the transition to the new trustee's term of service as smooth as possible. Meet to discuss the challenges you've faced and what tactics have worked (or not worked) for you. And remember that until the effective date of your resignation, you are still responsible for the trust.

Here are some of the things you'll need to do to carry out your resignation and make sure that your actions cannot be questioned later:

- Formally transfer trust assets to the new trustee and get a receipt. This will probably involve changing ownership documents such as bank account registrations or, if the trust owns real estate, a deed.

- Make copies of your records (tax returns, investments, inventory of assets, and so on), and then give them to the new trustee. Get a detailed receipt. Keep the originals.

- Prepare a final accounting (covering the period from the last accounting to the day your resignation is effective) and give it to the beneficiaries.

- If beneficiaries and the new trustee don't already have a copy of your resignation, give one to each.

L. Ending the Trust

At some point it will be time to wind up the trust—probably when the trust beneficiary (or the youngest one, if there are two or more) reaches the age designated in the trust document. You'll distribute whatever trust property remains, and the trust will simply cease to exist. There shouldn't be any papers to file with a court to mark the occasion. You should, however, wrap up loose ends with the beneficiaries and with the IRS.

You should send each trust beneficiary a document that summarizes the actions you've taken as trustee and explains where all the property went. The right level of detail depends on the circumstances. If you're dealing with a large trust that involves lots of assets and transactions—or if you're dealing with beneficiaries who are apt to be either curious or difficult—this statement should provide a meticulous accounting. With smaller trusts, it can be much simpler. (An example of a regular report is shown in Section E, above.)

Keep in mind, however, that this statement is not for only the beneficiaries' benefit. It protects you, too, from later suspicions or charges that you did not carefully keep track of trust assets or use them as you should have.

You'll also need to file a final tax return with the IRS. It is due by April 15 of the year following the calendar year in which the trust ends. (See Section I, above.) ■

CHAPTER 21

Handling a Bypass (AB) Trust

Many affluent married couples who think they might someday owe federal estate tax set up bypass trusts, also called AB, marital life estate, or credit shelter trusts) to reduce the eventual tax bill. These trusts, which can currently shelter up to $3 million from federal estate tax, are a component of some living trusts. Like simple living trusts designed only to avoid probate, grantors set them up during their lifetimes. But they are considerably more complicated and potentially long-lasting than simple living trusts.

If you and your late spouse set up such a trust, and you now find yourself solely in charge of it, this chapter provides an outline of your rights and responsibilities. But these trusts often exist for many years after the first spouse dies, involve convoluted tax laws, and usually contain assets worth at least $1 million. Expert help, from an experienced lawyer or CPA, is definitely justified.

When the second spouse dies. This chapter is directed to a surviving spouse who is faced with handling a bypass trust after the first spouse dies. The situation is very different when the second spouse dies—then, the successor trustee (named in the original trust document) simply transfers the property in the A and B trusts to the final beneficiaries. This process is the same as wrapping up a simple living trust, as discussed in Chapter 19.

Some other books that may help. *The Truth About Trusts: A Trustee's Survival Guide*, by Jack W. Everett (FTPC Publishing), covers setting up, managing, and terminating simple living trusts and more complicated trusts. *Executor and Trustee Survival Guide*, by Douglas D. Wilson (Fiduciary Publishing), also discusses trusts in depth.

A. How a Bypass Trust Works

First, here is a little refresher on the basics of bypass trusts. After all, it may have been years since you and your spouse created the trust—and even then you might not have been well-versed on the details, which can be pretty confusing.

1. Setting Up the Trust

A couple hoping to avoid or reduce estate tax when the second spouse dies sets up the AB trust by signing a trust document, also called an instrument or declaration of trust. Usually, both spouses are the initial trustees, which means they both have control over the property held in trust. While both are alive, the trust is revocable—that is, the couple can revoke the trust entirely or amend its terms.

Typically, the couple transfers their major assets into the trust. This doesn't have any day-to-day consequences, but it makes a big difference when the first spouse dies.

AB TRUST TERMINOLOGY

Grantors: The couple that creates the trust. Also called settlors or trustors.

Trustee: The person who's in charge of trust assets. With an AB trust, the grantors are the trustees while they are alive.

Beneficiary: A person who inherits trust property when a grantor dies (or later, depending on the terms of the trust).

Bypass trust: The irrevocable trust created when the AB trust is split into two trusts after the death of the first spouse. The surviving spouse has limited control over the assets in this trust. Sometimes called a life estate trust.

Disclaimer trust: A special kind of AB trust that gives the surviving spouse power to decide, after the first spouse dies, whether or not to split the AB trust and create the tax-saving irrevocable bypass trust.

Final beneficiaries: The people (or charities or other entities) who inherit trust property after both spouses have died. Sometimes called remainder beneficiaries.

Survivor's trust: The revocable trust created when the AB trust is split into two trusts after the death of the first spouse. The surviving spouse has complete control over this trust. Also called the marital trust.

Successor trustee: The person who takes over as trustee after both spouses have died. Like the executor of a will, this person is charged with distributing property to the beneficiaries. Commonly, the successor trustee is also a beneficiary.

2. Splitting the Trust When One Spouse Dies

The AB trust document provides that at the death of the first spouse, ownership of the trust property is divided into two trusts: the bypass trust and the survivor's trust.

Property that goes into the bypass trust doesn't belong to the surviving spouse, but he or she has the right to use it for life. Later, when the second spouse dies, the assets in this trust will go to the "final beneficiaries" named in the original trust document—usually, the children.

The survivor's trust contains all trust property that doesn't go into the bypass trust, The survivor's trust is a revocable trust under the complete control of the surviving spouse.

DISCLAIMER TRUSTS

Some AB trusts, called disclaimer trusts, give the surviving spouse the option of not splitting the AB trust after the first spouse's death. This gives the survivor flexibility. For example, if when the first spouse dies, the survivor no longer needs a tax-saving trust because the estate tax exemption has gone up and the survivor's estate doesn't look like it will be big enough to be taxed, then the survivor isn't locked in.

If the surviving spouse does decide to go ahead and split the AB trust, creating the bypass trust and the survivor's trust, he or she "disclaims," or declines to accept, some trust property. That property goes into the bypass trust.

3. Taxation of the Bypass and Survivor's Trusts

Property of the deceased spouse that goes into the survivor's trust is not subject to federal estate tax, because all property left to a spouse is exempt from tax. (This exemption, called the unlimited marital deduction, does not apply if the surviving spouse is not a United States citizen.)

Property that goes into the bypass trust, on the other hand, does not qualify for the marital deduction and is subject to federal estate tax when the first spouse dies. But because the typical trust document provides that the bypass trust should contain no more than the amount of property that can pass free of federal estate tax ($1.5 million for deaths in 2004 or 2005), no tax is actually due when the first spouse dies.

The surviving spouse has the right to use the bypass trust property during his or her life for certain purposes. But because the survivor doesn't own these assets outright, the value of bypass trust assets never becomes part of his or her estate for estate tax purposes. So when the second spouse dies, only his or her assets—not the bypass trust assets—are taxed. As long as their value is under the estate tax threshold, no tax will be due.

With a bypass trust, a couple can pass up to $3 million (in 2004 or 2005) of property without owing any federal estate tax. By contrast, if there were no trust, and the spouses simply left everything to each other, there could eventually be a big tax bill. No tax would be due at the first spouse's death, because property one spouse leaves the other is exempt from estate tax. But when the second spouse died, all the property would be included in his or her estate—which might push its total value over the federal estate tax threshold.

THE FEDERAL ESTATE TAX THRESHOLD

Year of Death	Estate tax return must be filed if gross value of the estate exceeds:
2002 or 2003	$1 million
2004 or 2005	$1.5 million
2006, 2007, or 2008	$2 million
2009	$3.5 million
2010	*estate tax repealed*
2011	$1 million unless Congress extends repeal

HOW THE AB TRUST WORKS

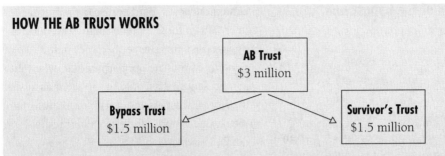

AB Trust
$3 million

Bypass Trust
$1.5 million

Survivor's Trust
$1.5 million

Surviving spouse can use this property, subject to some restrictions, for his or her lifetime, but does not legally own it. Because it was taxed when the first spouse died, it's not taxed when the surviving spouse dies.

Surviving spouse has total control over this property. At his or her death, estate tax will be due on any amount over the estate tax exemption.

EXAMPLE: *William and Kay, a married couple, add up their assets (house, life insurance, retirement accounts, and so on) and find that the total comes to about $2.5 million. They decide to set up a bypass trust to avoid estate tax liability.*

They put much of their co-owned property—their house and some valuable furniture and art—in the trust. In the trust document, Kay and William leave everything to each other, in trust, and then to their two children.

Kay dies first. William, now sole trustee, follows the trust document's directions and splits the trust into the bypass trust and the survivor's trust (Trusts A and B). The trust directs that the bypass trust should contain an amount of property equal to the estate tax exemption—for the year Kay dies, $1.5 million. To accomplish this split, William hires an experienced estate planning attorney (a certified public accountant could also help), who explains the tax consequences of dividing the

property in different ways and prepares the necessary documents.

The property that goes into the bypass trust, worth $1.5 million, is subject to federal estate tax. No tax is due, however, because the value of the trust property is under the estate tax threshold. The $1 million worth of assets that William keeps (in his revocable trust) are also not taxed, because he already owned half of the couple's property. (And if he had inherited property from Kay, it would not have been taxed, either, because of the estate tax exemption for property inherited from a spouse.)

When William dies, the property in the bypass trust and the survivor's trust passes to the couple's children. The property in the bypass trust isn't taxed, because William didn't legally own it, and it isn't part of his estate. The property in William's survivor's trust is subject to estate tax, but its value is below the federal estate tax threshold.

The net result is that Kay and William have transferred $2.5 million of property without paying any federal estate tax.

If they hadn't used a bypass trust, the whole $2.5 million would have been in William's estate when he died. Because of the estate tax exemption, $1.5 million of it could have passed tax-free. The other $1 million would have been subject to estate tax.

B. The Surviving Spouse's Rights and Duties

When one spouse dies, the survivor usually becomes sole trustee of both the bypass and survivor's trusts. This post entails a lot of responsibility. You may think of the trust property as yours—after all, you and your spouse put it in trust only to avoid estate taxes, not to keep you from using it. But now that the property is held in trust, the law gives the final beneficiaries certain rights and gives you certain rights and responsibilities.

1. Your Relationship to the Final Beneficiaries

Theoretically, there is a conflict of interest between you and the final beneficiaries: You may want to spend trust assets, while they may want you to preserve the assets so they can inherit them. Typically, however, this is not a real problem. Most beneficiaries understand that you didn't intend to give up control over the assets by setting up a tax-saving trust and that you wanted only to see that their inheritance is not reduced by large estate taxes. They should also understand that you have gone to considerable time and trouble and that they are the ones who get the primary benefit from the trust.

So although you have definite legal responsibilities to the final beneficiaries, they should not be looking over your shoulder to see that you are properly managing the bypass trust property.

Tensions are most likely to arise when there are different beneficiaries for the bypass trust and for the surviving spouse's trusts. A fairly common situation is when the deceased spouse's children from a prior marriage are the beneficiaries of the bypass trust. This usually means the trust was set up not just to avoid taxes, but to give the surviving spouse lifetime rights over property that would otherwise go directly to the deceased spouse's children.

EXAMPLE: *Ronald and Mildred set up a bypass trust soon after they marry in their 50s. Each has children from a previous marriage. The trust document provides that the property of the spouse who dies first goes into a bypass trust.*

Ronald dies first, and his property goes into a bypass trust. Mildred has certain rights over the bypass trust property while she is alive; at her death, the property goes to Ron's children. Her property (in the survivor's trust) goes to her own children.

⚠️ **If you expect scrutiny, pay attention to formalities.** If, unlike most people, you have reason to think that final beneficiaries will keep a close eye on how you manage and spend trust assets, then be sure to scrupulously follow the record-keeping and other guidelines outlined in this chapter. And consult a lawyer who can help you comply with all applicable legal rules.

2. Your Legal and Practical Duties

Here are some of the actions you must take as trustee, all of which are discussed later in this chapter:

- Get valuable trust property appraised, so you know its date-of-death value.

- Divide the trust property into two trusts: the bypass trust, which is subject to rules about how you can use it, and the survivor's trust, over which you have complete control. (Or, if your AB trust is a disclaimer trust, you must first decide whether or not to divide the AB trust.)

- Get a federal tax ID number for the irrevocable bypass trust.

- Notify beneficiaries that the bypass trust exists, if they don't already know about it or if state law requires a certain kind of notification.

- Protect bypass trust property from loss or damage.

- Invest bypass trust assets prudently.

- Keep beneficiaries (or their legal guardians, if the children are minors) informed about how you're managing the bypass trust.

- Keep meticulous records of all transactions.

- File all necessary tax returns for the bypass trust.

- Follow all terms of the bypass trust that control your rights over trust assets.

When you need professional help with any of these duties, you can use funds from the bypass trust to pay a reasonable amount for it. You will almost certainly find it sensible to consult a lawyer, tax preparer, or certified public accountant from time to time.

💡 **You may need an affidavit showing your authority.** You may be asked to show proof that you have authority to act on behalf of the bypass trust, especially if you sell or mortgage trust real estate. It will probably be enough for you to show both the trust document and your spouse's death certificate. Another way is to prepare a sworn statement (affidavit) setting out the facts that give you authority, and to file (record) it in the county land records office. A sample is shown in Chapter 19, Section D.

SPECIFIC GIFTS OF TRUST PROPERTY

If the deceased spouse left any trust property directly to other beneficiaries— that is, not to you or to the bypass trust— you must promptly (but after determining whether or not any estate tax should be paid from the property) transfer the property to the beneficiaries. See Chapter 19, Section J.

3. Your Right to Use or Spend Bypass Trust Assets

You are not only the trustee of the bypass trust—you are a beneficiary. And as a beneficiary, you have rights to the trust property. You'll need to read the trust document to find out exactly what these rights are, but most AB trusts give the surviving spouse extensive rights over bypass trust assets.

a. Income

As the surviving spouse and life beneficiary of the bypass trust, you are entitled to any income from trust property. This includes interest, dividends, rents, and other revenue generated by trust property.

b. Principal

Many surviving spouses don't find it necessary to touch any of the bypass trust principal, because their own share of the couple's property provides enough money to live on comfortably. But if you do need to spend trust principal, you'll probably have broad powers to do so.

A typical trust document gives you, the surviving spouse, the right to spend bypass trust assets (principal) if it's necessary for your "health, education, support, or maintenance," in accord with your "accustomed manner of living." This is the broadest standard the IRS allows for an AB trust. (26 CFR 20.2041-1(c)(2).) If you were given any greater powers over principal, the IRS would consider you the owner of the property—which would destroy the estate tax advantage of holding the property in trust.

As a practical matter, this gives you authority to spend bypass trust principal on anything that could be said to maintain your usual standard of living. According to the IRS, "support" does not mean only "the bare necessities of life." Unless the trust states otherwise, you do not have to use up other sources of income before spending bypass trust assets for these allowed purposes.

If this sort of language is in your trust, you can, for example, live in a house held in the bypass trust. You can sell trust property and reinvest the proceeds, take vacations, or buy new property in the name of the trust. What you can't do is build a gigantic new house, buy three new cars, or spend months lounging at luxury resorts in Europe—unless that was your standard of living before your spouse died.

You may, however, need to use the bypass trust assets to live on if your survivor's trust holds mostly nonliquid assets that don't produce the cash you need. For example, it's common (for tax reasons) to hold the family residence in the survivor's trust instead of the bypass trust.

C. What's in the Trust

Obviously, one of your first jobs is to find out exactly what property is subject to the terms of the trust. People commonly put their houses and significant nonretirement investments into an AB trust. Smaller accounts and assets such as cars, which depreciate rapidly, aren't usually transferred to into living trusts. Here's how to figure out what property is held in your trust, if you're not sure.

1. Property Owned in the Trustees' Names

First, look at the AB trust document, which should list the items that were to be held in trust. These lists are often called "schedules" and come at the end of the trust document.

For items that don't have formal title (ownership) documents—for example, household items, electronics, or books—it's generally enough just if they're listed on a trust schedule. You and your spouse may have also created a document called an "assignment of property," listing everything that's was held in trust and stating that these assets were being formally transferred to the trustee. Such a document is required in some states—New York, for example.

For items with title documents, however, title must have been transferred to the trustees' names. Common trust assets that have title documents include real estate, bank or brokerage accounts, and cars.

EXAMPLE: *Marlene and Matthew create a trust and name themselves as trustees. To put their house in the trust, they sign and record a new deed, transferring ownership from themselves as joint tenants to themselves "as trustees of the Marlene and Matthew Hamilton Revocable Living Trust dated August 3, 20xx."*

They also want to hold some other valuable items, including a piano and stamp collection, in the trust. These items don't have title documents. In their state, it's enough to list them on the property schedule attached to the trust document.

Unfortunately, some people who create trusts list certain items but forget to change their title documents to make the trustee the official owner of the assets. And assets not held in the trustees' names probably don't pass under the terms of the trust—which means they may be subject to probate.

Adding property left out by mistake. Lawyers can sometimes successfully argue, in court, that assets listed on a trust schedule but not formally transferred to the trustees should be considered part of the trust. If it's important to you to get certain omitted assets included in the trust, ask a lawyer about this possibility.

To see whether or not title was actually transferred to yourselves as trustees, carefully examine all title documents, including real estate deeds, stock certificates, and motor vehicle title slips.

2. Assets From a Pour-Over Will

Property may also be funneled into the trust after a grantor's death, through a legal device called a pour-over will. If your spouse's will directs that certain property (or perhaps everything that isn't specifically left to a named beneficiary) should go into the trust, that's a pour-over will. It's called that because property pours from the will to the trust.

A pour-over will, however, is treated no differently from any other will after the will-maker dies. So the property subject to the will may have to go through formal probate before it gets to the trust. (If the value of the property is small, however, you may be able to use simplified probate procedures; see Chapter 17.) Once the property is formally held in trust, you can handle it according to the terms of the trust document.

D. Debts and Expenses

If there are no probate court proceedings, there is no formal court-supervised mechanism for paying the deceased person's debts and the small expenses that might arise afterward. You'll need to take care of it yourself. Commonly, this amounts to paying a few routine bills and funeral expenses and can be done in a month or two. But if the deceased person owned a business or had significant debts, it can take far longer.

You'll want to pay—or keep enough money reserved to pay—taxes, expenses of the last illness, funeral expenses, and other valid debts.

Keep meticulous records of what bills you pay, when, and with what assets. Your records don't have to be anything fancy—a notebook or simple spreadsheet will do. Chapter 9 discusses paying debts and expenses.

If you expect big bills later, protect yourself. Creditors who don't get paid have the right to press their claims with the people who inherit the trust property—or with you. If you think it's possible that big bills will surface later, you may want to take advantage of a procedure offered by some states (California, for example), that lets successor trustees go to probate court and impose a deadline on creditors. Then, if creditors don't make a claim by the deadline, they lose the chance. If the prospect of big claims concerns you, see a lawyer to discuss whether or not the court procedure makes sense in your situation.

E. Getting Valuable Property Appraised

You should promptly get written appraisals of the market value of all significant trust assets, including real estate, art, or jewelry worth more than a few hundred dollars. You'll need the appraisal whether an asset will ultimately end up in the survivor's or the bypass trust.

Written appraisals are necessary for at least two reasons. First, before you can determine which assets should go into the bypass trust and which should stay in the survivor's trust, you need to know the assets' value. (This division process is discussed in Section H, below.)

Second, if the deceased person left a gross estate that exceeds the federal estate tax threshold—$1.5 million in 2004 and 2005— you'll need to file a federal estate tax return. This is true even if no tax may be due. The threshold may be lower for filing a state estate tax return. (These rules are discussed in Chapter 11.)

A related reason for getting good valuations quickly is that if you do need to file an estate tax return, you will have a choice between using the value of the estate at the date of death and the value six months later. Getting a reliable estimate now will give you something to compare to six months down the road.

How to get reliable appraisals for different kinds of property is discussed in Chapter 8.

F. Notifying Beneficiaries

As trustee, you have a legal duty to keep bypass trust beneficiaries reasonably informed about how you are administering the trust. The beneficiaries are the ultimate inheritors of the bypass trust property; if you're like many people, they're your children. They probably won't be expecting formal reports from you. Still, good communication can head off misunderstandings, arguments, and even lawsuits. Most final beneficiaries will want to know how you're managing the trust, because your actions directly affect what they will eventually inherit.

1. General Rules

Start by notifying the final beneficiaries that the trust has become irrevocable because of the death of your spouse. If a beneficiary wants a copy of the trust document, provide it promptly. A simple letter, stating that the trust has become irrevocable because of your spouse's death and that you are now in charge of trust assets, will do in most states. A sample is shown below. You may want the tone of your letter to be more or less formal, depending on your relationship with the beneficiaries.

FOLLOW-UP LETTER TO TRUST BENEFICIARY

February 13, 20xx
Judith Grandilowski
2353 Leghorn Ave.
Concord, Illinois 61399

Dear Judith:

I am writing to formally notify you that because of the death of your father, James R. Emerson, on January 24, 20xx, I am now sole trustee of the James and Janine Emerson AB Trust.

Under the terms of the trust document, dated September 23, 1998, the trust will be split into two trusts, one of which cannot be revoked. You are named as a final beneficiary of that trust, which will exist until my death. Until that time, it's my job to follow the directions in the trust document and manage trust assets. The trust document also authorizes me to receive any income generated by trust assets and authorizes me to spend trust principal for my education, health, support, or maintenance.

If you have any questions, or would like to see a copy of the trust document, please feel free to contact me.

Sincerely,

Jennifer Emerson
44 Bluebird Circle
Springbloom, Illinois 61357
(308) 555-1234

2. Special State Requirements

Some states have very specific rules about how and when you must notify beneficiaries about the existence of the trust.

STATES THAT REQUIRE TRUSTEES TO SEND SPECIAL NOTICES

Arizona	Michigan
California	New Mexico
Colorado	South Carolina
Florida	Tennessee
Kansas	Wyoming
Maine	

Generally, these notices must give basic facts about the trust and the trustee, and explain that beneficiaries have a right to a copy of the trust document. In some states, you must tell beneficiaries that they have the right to regular reports from you about management and distribution of trust assets.

Several states require that notice be given to "qualified" beneficiaries. Qualified beneficiaries are those to whom the trustee could distribute assets, or who would receive assets if the trust were terminated now. For most simple living trusts, that just means all the primary beneficiaries named in the trust document. But the trust document may waive this requirement for beneficiaries under age 25; read yours to see whether it does.

Each state's rules are summarized in the appendix, but to get the details you will need to read your state's statute. (Chapter 22 explains how to find a state statute online or in a law library.)

Help for California trustees. *How to Probate an Estate in California*, by Julia Nissley (Nolo), contains a form you can use to give the required notice.

G. Registering the Trust

Some states require that the trustee of a trust register the trust with the local court. But there don't appear to be any legal consequences or penalties if you don't. (Though if the court orders you to register a trust, and you refuse, you can be removed.) For details, see Chapter 20, Section F.

STATES THAT PROVIDE FOR REGISTRATION OF TRUSTS

Alaska	Michigan
Colorado**	Missouri*
Florida*	Nebraska*
Hawaii	North Dakota
Idaho	Ohio
Maine	

* Not mandatory.
** No registration required if all trust property is distributed to beneficiaries at the grantor's death.

H. Dividing Trust Assets

As sole trustee, it's your job to split the AB trust into two separate trusts:

- **The survivor's trust** contains your share of trust property. You have complete control over and ownership of this property, which means you can revoke or change this trust if you wish. For example, you can spend trust assets or give them away, or name different final beneficiaries.

- **The bypass trust** contains some or all of the deceased spouse's share of trust property (how much property it contains depends on what the trust document directs). You have the right to use this trust property only for the purposes stated in the trust document. You have no power to use the property for other purposes, end the trust, give away trust assets, or change its beneficiaries (unless you have been given a power of appointment that allows you to name different beneficiaries for the bypass trust). At your death, all property remaining in the trust will go to the trust's final beneficiaries.

Dividing the assets of the trust (sometimes called "funding" the bypass trust) is probably the most complicated part of using a bypass trust. To reap the greatest tax benefits, get expert help from an experienced estate planning attorney or CPA.

1. How the Trust Is Set Up

How much property goes into each trust depends in large part on what the trust document directs you to do.

a. Formula Trusts

Some AB trusts have what lawyers call a "formula clause," which instructs the surviving spouse to put into the bypass trust property with a value equal to the first spouse's entire estate tax exemption in the year of death. That amount is $1.5 million in 2004 and 2005; amounts for other years are listed in Section A, above. The goal of these trusts is to shield the maximum amount from federal estate tax when the second spouse dies.

EXAMPLE: *Isabel and Cliff, who together own assets worth about $4 million, set up an AB trust to avoid estate tax. The trust dictates that when the first spouse dies, the bypass trust should contain trust property worth the amount of the then-current federal estate tax exemption.*

Cliff dies in 2005, when the estate tax exemption is $1.5 million, and Isabel funds the bypass trust with property worth that amount. It passes free of tax because it doesn't exceed the estate tax threshold.

The rest of the property ($2.5 million) goes into Isabel's revocable survivor's trust and will be subject to tax at her death. If she also dies in 2005, the $1.5 million exemption would kick in, meaning that only $1 million of the couple's original total of $4 million would be subject to estate tax. (If she survived until 2006, only half a million would be taxed.)

b. Disclaimer Trusts

Another common situation is that the trust document leaves it up to the surviving spouse to decide how much property—if any—goes into the bypass trust. The legal mechanism is something called a "disclaimer." All the trust property is left to the surviving spouse, but whatever property he or she declines to accept (disclaims) goes into the bypass trust.

The advantage of this kind of trust is that when it comes time to fund the bypass trust, the surviving spouse knows lots of information that was impossible to predict when the couple was setting up the trust: how much the couple's assets are worth, the amount of the estate tax exemption in the year of death, and how much money the surviving spouse expects to need. This is especially valuable now, given the uncertainty in the federal estate tax laws.

To disclaim assets, the surviving spouse will have to consult a tax advisor and decide how much, if any, trust property should go into the bypass trust. Then the spouse will need to sign a formal disclaimer and file it with the IRS within nine months after the first spouse's death.

EXAMPLE: *Isabel and Cliff's trust has a disclaimer clause, so when Cliff dies in 2005, it's up to Isabel to decide how much, if anything, to put in the bypass trust.*

It turns out that because of investment downturns and wild spending, Isabel and Cliff's combined assets are worth only $2 million at Cliff's death. The estate tax exemption is $1.5 million, but Isabel *doesn't want to put that much into the bypass trust, leaving her with only $500,000 outright.*

Instead, she disclaims $1 million, which goes into the bypass trust; the other $1 million goes into the survivor's trust. No estate tax is owed.

Many legal rules apply to disclaimers. For example, the spouse cannot receive any benefit from property before disclaiming it. The surviving spouse should definitely consult a lawyer before deciding on a course of action.

c.   Other Trusts

Some other AB trusts simply state that jointly owned trust assets should be divided equally between Trust A and Trust B, so that each trust contains half of the total value of those assets. The assets can be divided in any way, as long as each trust (the survivor's trust and the bypass trust) holds assets of equal value. Every item does not have to be divided 50-50.

With this kind of trust, it's possible that the deceased person's estate may owe some estate tax.

EXAMPLE: *Let's say that Isabel and Cliff's trust document states that when the first spouse dies, the trust property should be split equally between the bypass trust and the survivor's trust.*

When Cliff dies in 2005, the trust property is worth $4 million, and the federal estate tax exemption is $1.5 million. Isabel divides the trust property equally between the two trusts. She doesn't, however, try to split every asset. For

example, after consulting an estate planning lawyer, she puts all the couple's stock, worth $300,000, into the bypass trust and their house, also worth $300,000, into the survivor's trust.

Two million dollars worth of property goes into the bypass trust. Cliff's estate will owe tax on $500,000, the amount that exceeds the $1.5 million estate tax threshold.

2.   Factors to Consider

There are several factors to consider when deciding what property goes in which trust. Here are a few of them.

Don't try this alone. This gets complicated fast. Again, it's well worth the cost to consult an expert with good real-world experience.

a.   Future Estate Tax

Usually, it's best to put assets that are likely to appreciate in the bypass trust. For example, say you put rental real estate worth $400,000 in the bypass trust, because you think it could well be worth $600,000 by the time of your death. If the value does go up, the increase won't be subject to estate tax. That's because the property, along with all the other assets assigned to the bypass trust, were already subject to tax at its value at the first spouse's death. But if you think real estate values will hold steady or even sink, you might be better off keeping the real estate in your own revocable trust—or, because nobody knows what's going to happen—to hedge your bets and split it between the bypass and survivor's trusts.

b. Stepped-Up Tax Basis

Property held in the irrevocable bypass trust does not get a stepped-up basis when the final beneficiary inherits it. Normally, someone who inherits property gets a new tax basis in the property, equal to the property's fair market value as of the date of death. In other words, if the property's value has gone up, the basis is stepped up to that value. (A higher basis is good—it results in a smaller taxable profit when the asset is eventually sold.) But for assets held in a bypass trust, the beneficiary's basis is the value as of the original owner's death, not the date that they actually inherit the property.

EXAMPLE: *Boris is the final beneficiary of his parents' AB trust. When his father dies and Boris's mother must divide the trust property between the bypass trust and the survivor's trust, she puts the couple's house into the bypass trust. Later, when she dies, Boris inherits the house. His tax basis in the house is the property's value as of the date of his father's death.*

c. Capital Gains Tax

An individual owner who sells his or her house gets a big (currently $250,000) exemption from capital gains tax; a trust does not. So if the house is held in the bypass trust, more capital gains tax may be owed if the house is sold.

3. Preparing the Paperwork

You do not need to create a new trust document to divide an AB trust into the bypass and survivor's trusts. But some paperwork is required, including:

- New lists of trust property (called property schedules), listing what's in the bypass trust and the survivor's trust.

- For property with title documents—real estate or bank accounts, for example—new title documents, showing that property is now owned by the trustee of, for example, "The John S. Donaldson and Corrine R. Donaldson AB Revocable Trust, Trust A." You sign these title documents as trustee of both trusts—for example, "Corrine R. Donaldson, Trustee of the John S. Donaldson and Corrine R. Donaldson Bypass Trust."

- For property without title documents, a new Assignment of Property, showing that these items are held in the bypass or the survivor's trust. (See Section C, above.)

I. Managing the Bypass Trust Property

As trustee of the irrevocable bypass trust, it's important to recognize your special legal position. Although it's natural to still think of the trust property as your own—and although legally, you have considerable control over it—it's important to understand that in exchange for eliminating a big chunk of estate tax, you now have legal obligations to the final beneficiaries. In a way, it's their property now, too. You owe them what the law calls a "fiduciary duty." In plain English, this means that you must always put their interests first when you make decisions about trust property.

Not only must you always act honestly, by not taking or spending trust property improperly, you must also act in ways that will carry out the purpose of the trust to ultimately benefit the final beneficiaries. Normally that means investing the money so as to preserve what you already have and, if possible, increase it. Of course, you are a beneficiary, too, and have extensive rights to the trust assets. (See Section B, above.)

If the trust document gives you specific instructions about investing trust assets, you must follow them. When matters aren't covered by the trust document, most states follow what's called the "prudent investor rule." This law does not require or forbid particular kinds of investments or actions. Instead, it judges them against the general standards of prudence (no reckless investments), loyalty, and impartiality. You may not have many liquid assets to invest—many people put only their house and some other property into their living trusts. But if you do have investments to manage, be sure to read the discussion of prudent investing rules in Chapter 20, Section G.

You must also take good care of other property. For example, you must pay, from trust assets, any real estate taxes due on trust property. (See Chapter 9.)

If you take an action that violates your duties to the trust's final beneficiaries, they can go to court and try to cancel it. But because in most cases the final beneficiaries are close family members, such lawsuits are rare. If it does happen, your conduct will be judged taking into account all the circumstances, the powers the trust document grants to you, and your duties of prudence, loyalty, and impartiality.

This section sets out some guidelines for you to follow.

Getting off on the right foot. Depending on the language of the trust document, the complexity of the trust assets, and your family situation, you may want at least some initial help from a lawyer, financial planner, or asset manager. Getting professional advice can educate you about your duties and help protect you from challenges from the beneficiaries. You may even want (or state law may require you) to prepare a written investment policy statement, setting out your investment goals and policies; if so, you'll want expert help writing it.

1. Don't Take Risks

Legally, trustees must act with prudence, which in this context means choosing investments with reasonable skill and caution. The emphasis is on caution; your main job is not to lose money. You must be careful with trust money and stay far away from risky investments. Even if you might invest your own money in volatile tech stocks, you must apply a different, stricter standard to trust money.

Many trustees stick closer to safe investments such as U.S. government securities, bank certificates of deposit, conservative stock mutual funds, or money market funds.

Your second goal is to invest trust assets so they'll grow. But it's definitely not your job to try to produce the greatest possible gain—as you know, that can't be done without taking unacceptable risks.

Use your common sense to assess risk. Generally, you don't want to invest in:

- small, privately owned businesses

- real estate that's only an investment (as compared to a home for you)

- unconventional investments such as art, antiques, or collectibles, which can be difficult to sell quickly.

If there's some specific action you want to take—for example, you want to put some trust funds in an uninsured account—check the trust document to see whether the action is specifically allowed or prohibited. If the trust document forbids it, that's the end of the story. If the document doesn't address the issue, you'll have to base your decision on your state's general principles of prudent management.

You can get help. Don't forget that unless the trust document forbids it (unlikely), you can pay a reasonable amount for investment advice. If you're not knowledgeable about investing, spending some trust money on good advice may be the most prudent action of all.

2. Be Fair to All Beneficiaries

You have a duty to be impartial, which comes into play because the bypass trust has more than one beneficiary. There is the life beneficiary (that's you) and the final beneficiaries (probably your children).

As long as your actions further the purpose of the trust—and don't violate any other fiduciary duty—they are allowed. But there may be room for charges of favoritism if you arrange things so that one beneficiary will benefit more than another.

To help prevent challenges from unhappy beneficiaries, you must do two things. First, have sound reasons for decisions you make, and second, write them down. You should be able to explain how any action you take is authorized by the trust document and furthers the overall goals of the trust.

PLAYING WITH INCOME AND PRINCIPAL: THE UNIFORM PRINCIPAL AND INCOME ACT

Trustees often feel a tension between investing for income (which benefits the life beneficiary) and investing to increase the value of the trust principal (which benefits the final beneficiaries).

The latest version of a law called the Uniform Principal and Income Act, now followed by most states, can ease this dilemma by letting a trustee allocate income to principal or principal to income. For example, a trustee who concludes that the life beneficiary isn't getting as much income as the grantor intended can distribute principal to an income beneficiary if the trustee concludes it's necessary to administer the trust impartially—in other words, to be fair to all beneficiaries.

Or a trustee may feel that to follow the requirements of the prudent investor rule (discussed above), it's necessary to change the way trust assets are reinvested—but that doing so might drastically reduce income to the life beneficiary. Distributing some principal under this power could ameliorate the effects of the shift in investments.

A trustee who is also a beneficiary, however, cannot exercise this power. That means if you are the surviving spouse and the life beneficiary, you cannot use trust principal for your own benefit except as the trust document allows. If there is a corporate trustee, however, it can exercise this power.

3. Keep Good Records

You must keep clear, complete, and accurate records to do your job as trustee. Your goal should be that a reasonably intelligent person who walked in off the street and was handed your records could understand everything you've done. The records should provide a complete picture of trust management from the time the trust begins until you die or someone else takes over as trustee.

All this said, the records you keep will probably be very basic ones. For example, a simple checking account register contains a lot of important information. You'll almost certainly have a checking account (or an investment account with check-writing privileges) in the name of the trust, and its register will provide a good record of income received and expenses paid. If you can't fit enough information in the check register, use a ledger book or a simple computer program.

Eventually, you'll use all these records to make reports to the final beneficiaries. And if you must ever resign as trustee, the person who takes over for you will need good records. Finally, they'll be crucial in the unlikely event a beneficiary ever challenges your decisions.

SOME PAPERS TO KEEP

Bills

Correspondence about the trust (letters
  to and from final beneficiaries, for
  example)

Tax returns

Check registers

Canceled checks (if the bank provides
  them)

Anything from the IRS

Investment statements

Insurance policies

Receipts from recipients of trust money

Reports to beneficiaries

Statements from all accounts

4. Keep Final Beneficiaries Informed

You have a responsibility to keep the final
beneficiaries reasonably well informed about
how you're managing the trust assets. How
much information is enough depends on what
the beneficiaries want and on the trust document itself. For example, the trust document
may require you to give the final beneficiaries a
copy of the trust's federal income tax return
each year, or to make quarterly reports. If you
manage all trust assets in a single brokerage
account (the kind offered by Schwab, Fidelity,
and other big investment companies), you
could send beneficiaries a copy of the statements you receive.

5. Compensate Yourself Fairly

Most surviving spouses don't charge anything
for managing a bypass trust, preferring that all

the bypass trust money go to the final beneficiaries. But if your trust document is typical, it
allows you to pay yourself for serving as
trustee. And if the trust document says nothing
about payment, state law may authorize it.

If you wish to take a fee, do so based on the
time you spend and the difficulty of your
duties. Make sure you document the exact
purpose of any fees you take and be prepared
to explain why the amounts are reasonable.

J. Tax Returns for the Bypass Trust

A bypass trust must pay taxes on income it
receives and keeps, so you'll need to file an
income tax return (IRS Form 1041) for the
bypass trust every year.

You won't need to file a return for the
survivor's trust as long as you're its trustee
(though of course you still have to file an
individual income tax return). If trust property
generates income, you can report it on your
personal income tax return.

1. Notifying the IRS That You're Trustee

Your first tax-related job is simply to notify the
IRS that you are now acting as trustee. You do
that with IRS Form 56, *Notice Concerning
Fiduciary Relationship*. It's a one-page form that
asks for basic information about you and about
your deceased spouse. File it as soon as you
take over as sole trustee. After you do, the IRS
will send you any notices that concern the
trust.

2. Getting a Tax ID Number for the Trust

Before you can file a tax return for the trust, you must get the trust a taxpayer ID number. Just send Form SS-4, *Application for Employer Identification Number*, to the IRS. (See Chapter 9, Section C.)

3. The Trust Tax Return

You'll need to file a trust income tax return if:

- the trust receives more than $600 in gross income

- the trust has taxable income (see Section 4, below), or

- any of the beneficiaries are nonresident aliens (people who are not United States citizens and who are not permanent residents here).

If you do need to file a trust tax return, you'll probably want to get expert help from a CPA familiar with this kind of work. As you might guess, many special rules apply to trust taxes. If the trust assets include a business, if you dig into the trust assets (not just income) to make distributions, or if you sell trust property, the return will be more complicated.

For filing purposes, trusts must use a calendar year. This means the return is due by April 15 for the previous calendar year.

(For more about tax returns that must be filed after a death, see Chapter 11.)

4. Minimizing Income Taxes

A trust is taxed only on trust income that it keeps—that is, income that it doesn't pay out to beneficiaries in the year it's received.

When trust income is paid to beneficiaries (you—or, if the trust document authorizes it, the final beneficiaries), they pay income tax on it, on their individual tax returns. Because taxes on individual income are usually less than taxes on trust income, giving all trust income to beneficiaries reduces total taxes.

For this reason, most trust documents direct the trustee to pay out income regularly. Read yours to find out whether or not it does. If you pay out all trust income within 65 days after the year ends, the trust will have no taxable income for that year.

Distributing income to reduce taxes is tricky. It's not always easy to know just how much taxable income a trust has. Talk to an accountant or lawyer who has experience with trusts.

5. Beneficiaries' Schedule K-1

If you distribute trust money to beneficiaries, then soon after the end of each calendar year, you must give each one an IRS Schedule K-1, showing how much they received from the trust that year. This shows the IRS what income (and tax liability) was transferred from the trust to the beneficiary. Beneficiaries need their Schedule K-1 before they can prepare (or have someone prepare) their own tax returns, so the sooner you can get it to them, the better.

■

Getting More Help

CHAPTER 22

Researching the Law Yourself

As you wind up the affairs of a deceased loved one, you're going to have lots of questions. This book should answer many of them—but the answers to others will depend both on your individual situation and on a thorough understanding of the law in your state (sometimes, even your county). This chapter explains some methods you can try when you want to find an answer to a legal question, without going to a lawyer.

It used to be that to do legal research, you had to find a law library open to the public—not always easy and rarely convenient. Now, lots of legal information (sometimes, it seems, too much) is available online. You may want to use both resources.

More help with research. This chapter gives just an overview of research. For a much more thorough explanation and detailed instructions for researching a legal question from start to finish, read *Legal Research: How to Find & Understand the Law*, by Steve Elias and Susan Levinkind (Nolo).

A. Libraries

Libraries, in addition to their books, offer another important source of help to the novice researcher: librarians. They are unfailingly helpful, and it's their job to help steer you to what you need.

To find out where the closest law library is, call the reference desk of the local public library. Here are the kind of materials you can expect to find in a few different kinds of libraries:

Public libraries typically have local ordinances, and most larger ones have state statutes and self-help materials as well. But except for a few excellent big-city libraries, they're not likely to contain much in the way of legal books or court information.

County law libraries, used mostly by local lawyers, are usually close by or in the main courthouse. Their quality varies considerably; in some places, you may do better at a big public library.

Public law school libraries are generally open to the public and contain all the resources you'll need.

B. Using the Internet

The Internet is a great source of legal information for executors. That's primarily because it gives you quick access to two troves of information: state statutes and government websites. That means that for most people, it's easy to go online and find out just who inherits in your state if there's no will, get the current filing fees in your local probate court, or check Social Security rules. You can also find a lawyer or get information on insurance, investing, real estate, and much more.

1. Government Websites

You're most likely to find the information you need from a government website operated by a state, local, or federal agency. You can find the websites for most states, counties, cities, and government agencies by using the formulas below. Just replace "XX" with the two-letter state postal abbreviation.

FINDING PUBLIC WEBSITES

Entity	Formula	Examples
City	www.ci.CITY_NAME.XX.us	Bakersfield, California's, website is at www.ci.bakersfield.ca.us Ann Arbor, Michigan's, website is at www.ci.ann-arbor.mi.us
County	www.co.COUNTY_NAME.XX.us	The Dutchess County, New York, website is at www.co.dutchess.ny.us The Contra Costa County, California, website is at www.co.contra-costa.ca.us
State	www.state.XX.us	The State of Georgia's website is at www.state.ga.us
Agency	www.AGENCY_ABBREVIATION.gov	The Environmental Protection Agency's website is at www.epa.gov

More and more governments are following these standards—but not all. So if you don't find the city or county you're looking for, it doesn't necessarily mean there's no website. Try one of these formulas:

County. http://directory.google.com/Top/Regional/North_America/United_States/[STATE_NAME]/Counties/[COUNTY_NAME].

EXAMPLE: *For Lane County, Oregon, the formula is: http://directory.google.com/Top/Regional/North_America/United_States/Oregon/Counties/Lane.*

City. http://directory.google.com/Top/Regional/North_America/United_States/[STATE_NAME]/Localities/[FIRST LETTER OF CITY NAME]/[CITY_NAME].

EXAMPLE: *For Lexington, Massachusetts, the formula is: http://directory.google.com/Top/Regional/North_America/United_States/Massachusetts/Localities/L/Lexington.*

2. Law Firm Websites

The Internet is sprinkled with the websites of estate planning lawyers and law firms. Some of these sites offer good information—but many of them contain only outdated, poorly written articles that are not likely to be of much help. The main reason lawyers have websites is to attract clients, so you're not likely to find more than basic information and a pitch to call the lawyer for more help. (If you're shopping for a lawyer, though, looking at a few of these websites may help you decide who you want—and don't want—to hire.)

3. State Bar Association Websites

State bar associations (lawyer groups) often publish magazines for practicing lawyers that contain good, practical information. (Most of their consumer publications—usually pamphlets—are so superficial as to be very little help.) To get to the useful stuff, start by finding the website of the state bar association in your state. A Google search may be your best bet.

4. Commercial Online Legal Databases

You'll probably be able to find the legal sources you need for free, on websites provided by states, universities, or legal organizations. If you can't, you can try Lexis (www.lexis.com) or Westlaw (www.westlaw.com), huge online databases that contain the full text of almost all published cases from state and federal courts, federal and state statutes, federal regulations, law review articles, commonly used treatises, and lawyers' practice manuals. Loislaw, Versuslaw, and Quicklaw America are smaller (and cheaper) legal databases.

5. Useful Websites

Here are many websites mentioned earlier in this book, plus some more that may be of help. Of course, this list merely scratches the surface.

SOME USEFUL WEBSITES

Organization	Website Address	What It Offers
General Legal Research, Including Statutes and Court Cases		
Nolo	www.nolo.com	Articles and products on probate and estate planning, plus access to all states' statutes, federal laws, some court cases, and court websites
Villanova University School of Law	vls.law.vill.edu/Locator/ fedcourt.html	Federal court decisions
The Legal Information Institute	www.law.cornell.edu	Directed mostly at lawyers, but a good place to find state probate statutes, federal statutes, federal court decisions, and more
National Federation of Paralegal Associations	www.paralegals.org	Links to official state home pages, state and federal courts, state and federal statutes, and more
FindLaw	www.findlaw.com	Message boards, links to statutes and cases, lawyer directory
National Center for Health Statistics	www.cdc.gov/nchswww/howto/ w2w/w2welcom.htm	How to order death certificates from state agencies
FamilyTreeMaker	http://familytreemaker.genealogy .com/countlst.html? Welcome=1065115112	Address and phone number of every county court in the country
Elder Law Attorney Dennis Toman	www.estateplanninglinks.com	Collection of links to sites on all kinds of estate planning topics
Piper Resources	www.statelocalgov.net/index.cfm	Lists of state and local government websites
University of Kansas School of Law	www.law.ku.edu/research/ prac_forms.html	Links to sources of state-specific legal forms
Looking Up Legal Terms		
Nolo	www.nolo.com	Plain-English definitions of legal terms
FindLaw	http://dictionary.lp.findlaw.com	Legal dictionary
Law.com	http://dictionary.law.com	Legal dictionary

SOME USEFUL WEBSITES (CONTINUED)

Organization	Website Address	What It Offers
Federal Government Sites		
U.S. Department of Veterans Affairs	www.va.gov	Forms and information for veterans and their families
Social Security Administration	www.ssa.gov	Forms and contact information
U.S. Government Printing Office	www.access.gpo.gov	Federal publications
Library of Congress	http://thomas.loc.gov	Pending federal legislation and other legislative information
Railroad Retirement Board	www.rrb.gov	Pension information
U.S. Postal Service	www.usps.gov	Change of address forms
U.S. Department of the Treasury	www.publicdebt.treas.gov/sav/savreiss.htm	Information and forms related to transferring savings bonds
National Archives and Administration	www.gpoaccess.gov/cfr/index.html	Code of Federal Regulations (federal agency regulations)
Internal Revenue Service	www.irs.gov	IRS forms and publications
Funerals and Grieving		
Funeral Consumers Alliance	www.funerals.org	Excellent consumer information on funerals, mortuaries, and nonprofit memorial societies
The Barr-Harris Children's Grief Center	www.barrharris.org	Information for grieving families, including lists of books, and links to related websites
General Information		
The Motley Fool	www.fool.com	Plain-English financial information and advice
Kelley Blue Book	http://kbb.com	Used car valuations
Response Insurance	www.response.com/tips_tools/great_links.asp	Links to state motor vehicle departments
Finding a Lawyer		
Martindale-Hubbell	www.martindale.com	Lawyer directory
West Publishing Co.	www.directory.findlaw.com	Lawyer directory

C. Finding Forms

There's no getting around it—probate involves a lot of forms. A lot of them will be provided by insurance companies, banks, government agencies, and the probate court. Here are some ideas on where to look for forms.

Court websites. Many courts now provide preprinted forms for probate cases. So if you're looking for a form that you intend to file with the probate court, check the court's website first. More and more courts are reaching out to provide at least some help to folks who are handling probate without a lawyer.

Many courts also put their rules online. These local rules deal with topics such as deadlines for filing certain documents, how documents must be formatted, fees, and so on. But postings are still spotty—for example, your state Supreme Court may publish its rules online, but the trial courts may not. Check your court's website. To see a list of courts, check the Nolo website's Legal Research Center. Under "Courts," click "Federal, State & Local Courts," and then choose your state.

Form books. If you can't find a preprinted form, try form books, used by lawyers. They contain sample state-specific legal documents that you may be able to copy or adapt. With a law librarian's help, you can probably find a form book for your state that has what you're looking for.

Other websites. The University of Kansas Law School website (see Section B, above), links to many sources of state-specific forms; it's a quick way to get right to the forms for your state. If the site doesn't contain a link for your state, try your court's website, as discussed just above.

Commercial websites. Thousands of legal forms are for sale on the Internet, but unless you know exactly what you're looking for, finding a form that is valid and suitable for your state can be tough. Commonly, forms sold this way are also short on instructions for filling in and using them. You won't find probate court forms, but you may find general legal forms that will be of use—for example, deed forms for your state.

D. Finding Definitions

If you're stumped by a legal term you run across, there are lots of places you can look up its meaning. First try the glossary of this book. If you don't have any luck there, go to the Nolo website, which contains plain-English definitions of many terms, or try the other online legal dictionaries listed in Section B, above.

E. Researching Specific Questions

If you want to find out exactly what your state's statutes say on a particular issue, you'll need to look up the law. Following the general research strategy outlined in this section should lead you to an answer. At the least, you should acquire enough information so that you understand the issue thoroughly and can discuss it intelligently (and efficiently) with a lawyer.

As an example, let's say you're handling the estate of a married California resident who died without a will, and you want to know who inherits his property.

1. Look for a Statute

The best place to start with this kind of question is usually by looking for a state law. If your question were more limited and local—for example, how to present papers to be filed with the local probate court—you would head instead straight to the court's rules. (Working with courts is discussed in Chapter 19.)

For this question—who inherits if there's no will—every state has a statute. You can find the citation—the abbreviation that tells you where the law is published—to your state's statute in the appendix. Armed with the citation, you should be able to put your finger on the law right away.

Here are a couple of typical statute citations and what they mean:

- Mo. Rev. Stat. § 461.025 = Missouri Revised Statutes, section 461.025

- Cal. Prob. Code § 343 = California Probate Code, section 343.

If you're looking online, start at the Nolo website and go to its Legal Research Center. You should be able to quickly find your state's statutes on the Internet. Or, if you're in a law library, a librarian can get you to the right book. Many big public libraries also have copies of the state code, or online access so you can find it online.

If you don't have a citation, make your way to a collection of your state's statutes, either online or in print at a law library. (Section B, above, lists several online sources.) Once you're there, there are two ways to find what you're after:

- Look in the table of contents under a likely heading, such as probate, wills, nonprobate transfers, or taxation.

- Search online by keyword—for example, "joint tenancy" or "transfer on death."

For our example, the key term is "intestate succession." That's the legal term for inheritance in the absence of a valid will. If you search for that term in the statutes, you'll find California Probate Code section 6401, which lists who inherits when a California resident dies without a valid will.

When you're searching legal materials, try as many terms as you can think of. Lawyers often classify information in ways that are not obvious to anyone who hasn't sat through three years of law school.

Once you find a statute, make sure you're reading the most recent version. Statutes change, so always check the date of the statute. If you're online, there should be a date that tells you what session of the legislature is covered. If you're reading a book, check the "pocket part" inserted into the back cover for updates.

2. See How Courts Interpret the Statute

Once you've found a statute, the next step is to see whether any courts have ruled on what it means—or at least, on the part of it you're interested in. Statutes typically have many sections and subsections, and you may care only about one of them.

The easiest way to find cases interpreting a statute is to look up the statute in what's called an "annotated code." The annotations following the text of the statute list, and briefly summarize, any court decisions that discuss the statute.

Unfortunately, most of the collections of state statutes you're apt to find online aren't annotated unless you use a commercial database. But the sets of statutes you'll find in libraries are likely to be annotated.

Continuing with our example of the California law on intestate succession, when you read the statute you see that it says a surviving spouse is entitled to a certain share of the deceased spouse's property. Sounds straightforward enough. But to make matters a little more complex, let's say the deceased person's widow had gone to court while both were alive, and gotten a decree of legal separation. But the couple hadn't actually divorced. Is the widow considered a "surviving spouse," entitled to inherit under the statute?

Looking at the annotations following the text of the statute, you find a 1999 decision by a California court, ruling that in these circumstances, a surviving spouse is not entitled to inherit under the California intestate succession law.

If you want to read the case to see whether or not it really applies to your situation, you can get its citation from the annotation. The citation tells you where the case is published. You should have no trouble finding your case in a law library. Looking online is less of a sure thing.

If the case you're looking for was decided within the last few years, you may be able to find it for free on the Internet. A good place to start is FindLaw.com. If the case is older, you can still find it online, but you will probably have to pay a private company for access to its database. (See Section B, above.)

If you're looking in a library, you'll find that state appellate court opinions are published in their own sets of books—for example, California cases are in the California Reporter. Many states' decisions are found only in regional collections—for example, the Northeastern or Southern Reporter. A librarian can help you find a case in one of these reporters.

> ⚠️ **Make sure a case hasn't been overruled.**
> Before you rely on a court decision, check to see whether or not the case is still valid—a higher court could have overruled it. You can use a service called Shepard's. If you're in a law library, ask a librarian for instructions—it can be very confusing when you're not used to it. You can also use it online for about $4.

3. If There's No Statute

If you can't find a statute that answers (or at least addresses) your question, you'll probably want to look for court opinions that do. But it's not always easy. When cases are published, they are not arranged by topic. So to find citations to cases that may help you, look in:

- treatises on your topic (especially in footnotes)

- articles in periodicals, such as those published by bar associations

- commercial databases, where you can search by keyword (see Section B, above)

- digests—books arranged by topic that contain summaries of cases and are available in law libraries, or

- *American Law Reports* (A.L.R.), a collection of case summaries arranged by narrow legal topic. ■

CHAPTER 23

Lawyers and Other Experts

Most executors and trustees need expert help at one time or another. So if you have legal or practical questions and you can't find the answers yourself, get help right away—don't wait until you feel totally over your head. The cost can be well worth it. Almost all will and trust documents anticipate that expert help will be needed, and authorize the executor or trustee to pay for it from estate or trust funds.

This short chapter focuses on working with lawyers, but also discusses other experts who may give you the help you need and charge less than a lawyer, too.

A. When to Get Help

If you've got reliable and complete information about the law and custom in your state, you may be able to go it alone. This is especially likely if the estate is small or the deceased person arranged matters so that assets can pass without probate.

Lots of situations, many of them flagged throughout this book, justify getting help. Here are some situations in which it's definitely a good idea to call in an expert:

- Someone threatens to contest the will or trust in court.

- The estate is large enough to require a state or federal estate tax return.

- The deceased person owned a business, alone or with someone else.

- The death was accidental or intentional.

- The deceased left any kind of trust more complicated than a simple probate-avoidance living trust—for example, a bypass (AB), QTIP, QDOT, generation-skipping, or charitable trust.

B. What Kind of Expert Do You Need?

Lawyers aren't the only people who can provide aid as you wrap up the affairs of a deceased loved one. For many questions and tasks, in fact, there is no need to hire an expensive lawyer. For example, if you have an estate tax question, an experienced accountant may be your best bet.

C. Deciding What You Want From a Lawyer

Although many consumers (and some lawyers) haven't realized it yet, the way lawyers and their customers structure their relationships is changing very fast. Lawyers used to insist on taking responsibility (and fees) for handling a whole probate proceeding from start to finish. But in what has become a very competitive market for legal services, many lawyers now offer piecemeal services, tailored to just what a customer wants.

This means you no longer have to walk into a lawyer's office, turn over your legal problems, and wait for an answer (and a bill). Instead, you can buy what you need. You may want a

CHOOSING AMONG THE EXPERTS

Kind of Expert	What They Can Help You With
Accountants	Preparing tax returns, valuing businesses, preparing trust or estate accountings, making tax planning decisions that may save beneficiaries a bundle
Appraisers	Putting a value on assets
Financial advisors	Putting together an investment plan if you're going to be managing assets over the long term
Insurance agents	Determining what coverage estate or trust assets need, helping with claiming life insurance proceeds, providing insurance for executor; not a good source of disinterested investment advice
Lawyers	Explaining how the law applies to your particular situation, advising you on legal decisions, representing you in court, handling probate court paperwork
Mediators	Solving disputes among survivors before they escalate into a lawsuit
Paralegals	Preparing and filing paperwork, under your direction
Probate court clerks	Answering questions about court paperwork and procedure. They are forbidden from giving anything resembling legal advice
Real estate brokers	Estimating the value of real estate or selling it; but because they make money only from transactions, not a good source of unbiased advice about whether or not to sell
Stockbrokers	Buying and selling securities, and getting title transferred into survivors' names; but because they make money on transactions, not a good source of disinterested investment advice
Therapists	Working out family problems that are getting in the way of wrapping up an estate peacefully and quickly

lawyer just to coach you through the probate process, answering your legal questions as they come up. The lawyer might also do some research, prepare a particularly difficult document, or look over court papers before you file them.

If you adopt this approach, you and the lawyer should sign an agreement that clearly sets out your roles and states that the lawyer is not acting in a traditional role, but instead giving you only limited representation.

Without this kind of agreement, lawyers fear that dissatisfied clients might later hold them responsible for more than they actually agreed to take on. The agreement should make things clear to you, too, so you know what to expect.

You're still free, of course, to turn the probate or trust administration over to the lawyer. This is the traditional choice for executors who just don't want to deal with the probate process. And if you aren't going to inherit much from the estate, it's perfectly reasonable for you to hire a lawyer who can be paid with estate funds.

Even if you do hire a lawyer to do all the paperwork, you will still have ultimate responsibility for making decisions—for example, whether or not to sell a certain asset. You cannot delegate these matters to anyone, and, as discussed throughout this book, you have a legal duty to make careful decisions that are in the best interests of the beneficiaries and creditors.

Before you talk to a lawyer, decide what kind of help you really need. (If you've read much of this book, you should have a good idea of what the executor's job entails—and how much time and energy you can devote to it.) If you don't clearly tell the lawyer what you want, you may find yourself turning over all your work.

Advice by phone. For about $40, you can call a lawyer licensed in your state and talk as long as you want about a single matter. This "Ask an Attorney" service is offered by ARAG, a large provider of prepaid legal insurance, at www.aragdirect.com. The lawyers who staff the phones must be licensed and in good standing with their state bar association. There's a money-back guarantee if you're not satisfied.

D. Finding a Lawyer

There are certainly lots of lawyers in the world—just look at the "Attorneys" section of the Yellow Pages—but how do you know which ones can give you reliable help at a reasonable fee? Here are some ideas on finding the right lawyer.

But first, an important point: You do not need to hire the lawyer who drafted the will, even if the will instructs you to hire that person. It's up to you to decide whom you want to work with.

LAWYERS MAY FIND YOU

Lawyers spent $311.3 million on television commercials in 2002, a 75% increase from 1999, according to the Television Bureau of Advertising, an industry trade group.

1. Personal Recommendations

The best way to find a lawyer (or plumber or doctor, for that matter) is to get a recommendation from someone you trust. So ask your relatives and friends—especially those who have been through a probate court proceeding or handled a trust.

If they can't help, try some other sources:

- probate court clerks—they know who's good and who isn't, and although they aren't really supposed to make recommendations, a discreet plea for help may get you a name

- people who work in the trust department of a bank

- long-term volunteers at a local senior center, and

- local lawyers you know and respect (or who are recommended to you) who don't handle estates and trusts—they probably know someone who does.

2. Group Legal Plans

Some unions, employers, and organizations offer group legal plans to their members or employees. If you are a member of such a plan, check with it first to see whether you can get legal assistance free or for low rates. If you are satisfied with the lawyer you are referred to (make sure he or she is knowledgeable about probate or trusts), this route is probably a good choice.

Some plans, however, give you only a slight reduction in a lawyer's fee. In that case, you may be referred to a lawyer whose main virtue is the willingness to reduce fees in exchange for a high volume of referrals. Chances are you can find a better lawyer outside the plan and negotiate a similar fee.

3. Referral Services and Directories

Many state and local bar associations (lawyer groups) offer referral services, which will give you the name of a lawyer whose practice includes probate. The quality of these lists is an unknown—usually, there is little or no screening. You may end up with a good

lawyer, or one who just needs to drum up more clients.

Lawyer directories—lists of lawyers that you can browse through—may give you a little more information about each lawyer than do referral services or advertisements. Looking at online directories is an efficient way to get the names of lawyers in your area who you may want to talk to. But be aware that as in the Yellow Pages, not every lawyer is listed.

Online lists of lawyers. Attorney directories are available online at www .martindale.com and www.directory.findlaw .com. You may be able to find out some useful background information about lawyers on these sites.

E. Choosing a Lawyer

Once you have the names of two or three likely lawyers, find out all you can about them from the people who recommended them, from online lawyer directories (see Section D3, just above), or from the lawyer's own website, if any. (To find a website, just enter the firm or the lawyer's name in Google or another search engine.)

Then schedule an appointment, with the goal of talking to the lawyer but not making any commitment about hiring him or her. When you make the appointment, be sure to ask what the fee will be for your first meeting. Some lawyers offer a short free initial consultation, but experienced ones generally don't.

Before you go, write down your legal questions as specifically as you can, and take paper and pen to jot down answers. It's almost impossible to remember everything later. Even lawyers who are good communicators are likely to use jargon that you're not familiar with, and especially if you are grieving, it's simply hard to take in a lot of new information.

To make your first meeting with the lawyer more productive, it's a good idea to gather some basic information (listed below) and take it with you. Bring the will and any trust documents along, too—but don't hand them over to the lawyer until you've made your final choice about hiring.

WHAT THE LAWYER WILL WANT TO KNOW

- Names of the deceased person's surviving family members: spouse, children, grandchildren
- Names of deceased children, if any
- Previous marriages, if any, and how they ended (death or divorce)
- What the deceased person owned— the kinds of assets and an estimate of how much they are worth (from the inventory from Chapter 8)
- Debts the deceased person owed (also on the inventory form)
- Whether or not the deceased person owned a business
- Whether or not there is a will, and who it names as executor
- Whether or not there is a trust, and who the trust document names as successor trustee
- Life insurance policies and who is named as beneficiary
- Any potential complications you see— disputes among family members or business associates, for example.

Pay attention to the lawyer's attitude when you meet. You want someone who's respectful of your knowledge and opinions—someone you will feel comfortable working with over many months. Does the lawyer really appear to be listening to your questions and concerns? You won't get good advice if the lawyer doesn't know what you want.

If the lawyer doesn't give you clear, concise answers to your questions, ask for clarification. If that doesn't help, then you'll want to try someone else. If the lawyer says little but promises to handle everything—for a substantial fee, of course—watch out. You're either dealing with someone who doesn't know the answer and won't admit it (common) or someone who finds it impossible to let go of the "me expert, you plebeian" philosophy (even more common).

QUESTIONS YOU MAY WANT TO ASK AT THE FIRST MEETING

- What is your experience in handling probate cases?
- Are you willing to work with me if I want to handle much of the probate work myself?
- About how long do you think it will take to go through probate and distribute all the property?
- About how much do you think it will cost?
- How do you determine your fees? (See Section G, below.)

F. Working With a Lawyer

Good lawyers explain to their clients just what to expect; they lay out when it will happen and how much it will cost. If your lawyer answers every question you've got like this before you even ask, consider yourself very lucky. Most

people may need to do a little prodding. Here are some tips:

Make sure you know how the work is divided up. Are you responsible for calling an expert to appraise the value of the deceased person's coin collection, or is the lawyer? Will you or the lawyer file the deceased person's final tax return? So many details swirl around a probate proceeding that it's essential to settle these questions in writing.

Ask for a written list of deadlines. This will be a great help not only to you, but also to the beneficiaries and creditors who will call you and demand to know what's up with the probate or trust administration.

Decide who will talk to beneficiaries. Should beneficiaries call the lawyer with questions or go through you? (If everything seems straightforward and everyone gets along, it will be cheaper and potentially less confusing if the lawyer communicates only or primarily with you.) If you write regular letters to keep beneficiaries up to date, consider having the lawyer review them to make sure they're accurate.

On tasks you're going to handle alone, consider checking in with the lawyer. For example, you'll be paying bills and keeping financial records for the estate or trust. It's a good idea to send the lawyer a copy of the records you're keeping a month or two into the process, to see if what you're doing is enough.

Save up your questions—but ask before you act. It's more efficient for everyone if you save up a few questions for each phone call or visit with the lawyer instead of picking up the phone every time a question occurs to you. But don't wait too long—there's no use in asking about an act after you've done it.

G. Paying a Lawyer

You, personally, won't pay the lawyer, because you can use estate funds to do that. But you do have a legal duty to try to keep costs reasonable—not always easy, given what many lawyers charge for routine paperwork.

Don't be penny-wise. The way to save money as an executor or trustee is to do as much of the routine work as possible yourself. Once you've decided you need a lawyer's advice, don't skimp. An expensive expert who will work well with you may be a bargain compared to a beginner who charges a lower hourly rate.

1. How Lawyers Charge for Probate Work

Probate lawyers charge an hourly rate, a lump sum, or a percentage of the value of the estate.

a. Hourly Fees

An hourly rate of $150 to $250 is common. But fees vary, of course, depending on where you live. Expect rates of $175 and up in an urban area; you might pay a little less in a rural area or small town.

The fee of an experienced specialist is higher than that of a general practitioner, but the specialist will probably produce results more efficiently and save you money in the long run. After all, you want the work done right.

Much of the work required for a probate court proceeding is commonly done by paralegals who work for the lawyer. Their time should be billed at a significantly lower rate. (See Section 2, below.)

b. Flat Fee

Some lawyers have figured out how much work it takes to do a typical probate and simply charge a flat fee, usually a few thousand dollars. This does offer you the advantages of simplicity and certainty, but you'll have to make your best estimate of whether or not you would be better off with an hourly rate.

The basic fee is for basic work. It usually doesn't include extra costs such as filing and appraisal fees. And if your probate turns out to involve complications—a will contest or a federal estate tax return, for example—the bill will go up accordingly.

c. Percentage of the Estate

In a few states, listed below, state law authorizes the lawyer to take a certain percentage of the gross value of the deceased person's estate. (Other states have dropped this compensation method and now allow "reasonable" compensation for the lawyer.)

These fee schedules are optional—they are in no way required by law. You can negotiate a lower payment structure. Unless you expect a complicated probate, hourly fees are usually a better deal, because the price is related to actual work done.

Here's how a percentage fee works. The lawyer may collect a percentage of the gross value of the probate estate. Gross value means the total value of the asset, without subtracting any amounts owed on it. So if the deceased person left a house that's worth $400,000 on the open market, its gross value is the entire $400,000 even if the deceased person owed $200,000 on a mortgage. The probate estate includes all the property that must go through probate. It doesn't include nonprobate property such as joint tenancy property or life insurance proceeds that are payable directly to a beneficiary.

In California, the allowed fee is:

- 4% of the first $100,000 of the gross value of the probate estate

- 3% of the next $100,000

- 2% of the next $800,000

- 1% of the next $9 million

- ½% of the next $15 million, and

- a "reasonable amount," determined by the court, for anything above $25 million.

So, if the probate estate has a gross value of $500,000, the allowable lawyer's fee is $13,000. At $150 an hour, that's more than 80 solid hours of work. Especially if you are willing to do some of the work yourself, you might get by with far fewer lawyers' hours.

2. Getting a Written Fee Agreement

Be sure you settle your fee arrangement in writing at the start of your relationship with the lawyer. A written fee agreement is required by law in some states; it's always a good idea.

Make sure the agreement clearly spells out:

- hourly fees of the lawyer and of any paralegals

- how much work will be done by paralegals

- an estimate of the total cost or number of hours

- other costs you should expect, such as copying, postage, filing fees, costs of publication, appraisals, or messenger service

- how often you will be billed (or, if it's a flat fee, when you'll pay it), and

- how detailed the bill will be (so you'll know exactly what was done on the estate's behalf, instead of getting a bill for $2,000 worth of "legal services").

H. Problems With Your Lawyer

Working with a lawyer isn't always a smooth process. And although administering an estate or trust is a legal process, it's also an emotional one. As executor or trustee, you may field a lot of anxious inquiries from relatives who want to know what's going on and why things aren't happening sooner. If your lawyer isn't responsive or doesn't do quality work, it makes your life that much harder.

The problems you're likeliest to encounter fall into three categories: communication, poor work, or fees.

1. Communication Problems

Probably the most common complaint voiced by clients is that their lawyers don't keep them well enough informed on what's going on with their legal matter.

Sometimes this kind of problem can be solved fairly easily. If your lawyer isn't returning your phone calls or has been out of touch for too long, write a polite letter setting out your concerns. Say you'll be calling for an appointment so you can get answers to your questions, and then follow up.

If the problem lies in the actual communications—you don't understand what the lawyer tells you or the lawyer doesn't seem to get what you are talking about—start by letting your lawyer know there's a problem. Your lawyer, used to speaking in legal jargon, may not know there's a problem. Ask your lawyer to rephrase the information, or explain that you aren't sure your questions or concerns are being heard.

Once you bring it up, your lawyer will probably work harder to communicate clearly.

If these efforts don't work, consider switching lawyers unless you're convinced that the lawyer—despite poor communication skills—is doing a high-quality and efficient job of handling your legal work.

2. Concerns About Quality

If you're not a lawyer, it's often hard to know whether or not you're getting really good legal help. But if something's confusing or just doesn't seem right, don't hesitate to bring it up to the lawyer.

Even generally competent lawyers make mistakes. According to one law professor who has studied malpractice by estate planning lawyers, a "startling" number of cases involve "very basic errors, such as having an insufficient number of witnesses sign a will or having a beneficiary witness the will." ("Estate Planning Malpractice," Bradley E.S. Fogel, *Probate & Property*, July/August 2003.) So don't assume everything is being done right.

If you are confused by the advice you're getting or if you disagree with it, ask for an explanation of why the lawyer has offered this particular advice, and also ask what other options are available. You're free to disregard a lawyer's advice if it just isn't right for you and your family. If you still feel confused, get a second opinion.

If you find what you think is a mistake in any document your lawyer prepares, point it out right away. Give the lawyer a copy of the document with the mistakes noted and keep a copy for yourself so you can double check that the errors have been fixed.

3. Fee Disputes

A written fee agreement should stave off most fee disputes—but no agreement anticipates every issue that can come up.

As always, try talking first. There may be a misunderstanding that the lawyer can explain.

If that doesn't help, you may be able to get help from a local or state bar association. In some places, a panel of volunteer lawyers will review your dispute and offer an opinion.

Visit Nolo's website for more information. You can find articles about working with a lawyer in the Lawsuits & Mediation section of www.nolo.com. ∎

Appendix:
State Information

This appendix summarizes some state rules that you may be interested in as you settle a loved one's estate or trust. When you look up information for your state, please keep in mind two important considerations:

- **This table includes only summaries of state laws.** Citations to the laws are included so that you can look up and read the law itself. It may contain details that are critical in your situation.

- **Laws change.** Before you rely on any statute listed here, make sure it hasn't changed since this book was printed. To take just one example, as the average size of an estate goes up, states respond by increasing the limit on what they consider a "small estate" eligible for probate shortcuts.

Chapter 22 explains how to look up a statute and how to dig deeper if necessary to answer your question.

Alabama

TOPIC	STATE RULE	CHAPTER
Out-of-state executors or administrators	Nonresident can't be appointed as administrator unless he or she is the executor or administrator of the same estate in some other state. Ala. Code § 43-2-22	2, 18
Surviving spouse's allowance rights	Ala. Code § 43-8-110 and following	5
System of protecting surviving spouse from disinheritance	Traditional spousal share. Ala. Code § 43-8-70	6
Holographic will	Not valid unless valid in the state where it was executed. Ala. Code §§ 43-8-131, 135	6
Can will refer to separate memorandum leaving tangible items?	No	6
Priority for appointment as administrator (after named executor, if any)	Spouse; next of kin entitled to inherit; creditor with the largest claim. Ala. Code § 43-2-42	7
Intestate succession	Ala. Code §§ 43-8-41, 42, 44	7
Uniform Transfers to Minors Act	1. If custodian appointed in will or trust, custodianship ends at age 21. 2. If custodian appointed by executor, transfers to custodian cannot exceed $10,000 in value; custodianship ends at age 19. Ala. Code §§ 35-5A-1 and following	10
State inheritance tax	No	11
State estate tax	No	11
State taxing authority website	www.ador.state.al.us	11
Community property	No	14
Uniform Transfer-on-Death Securities Act	Yes	16
Affidavit procedure for small estates	No	17
Summary probate for small estates	Yes. No real estate and a value of no more than $3,000. Ala. Code §§ 43-2-690 and following	17
Uniform Probate Code	No	18
Trustee must send special notice after grantor dies	No	19-21
Trust registration	No	19-21
Uniform Prudent Investor Act	No	20-21
Uniform Principal and Income Act	Ala. Code §§ 19-3A-101 and following	20-21
State law sets rates lawyers can charge for probate, based on estate value	No	23

Alaska

TOPIC	STATE RULE	CHAPTER
Out-of-state executors or administrators	No restrictions	2, 18
Surviving spouse's allowance rights	Alaska Stat. § 13.12.402 and following	5
System of protecting surviving spouse from disinheritance	Surviving spouse can claim share of augmented estate. Alaska Stat. § 13-13-201 and following	6
Holographic will	Valid. Alaska Stat. §§ 13.12.502, 504	6
Can will refer to separate memorandum leaving tangible items?	Yes. Alaska Stat. § 13.12.513	6
Priority for appointment as administrator (after named executor, if any)	Alaska Stat. §§ 13.12.102, 103	7
Intestate succession	Spouse if he or she inherits under the will; other will beneficiaries; spouse if he or she doesn't inherit under the will; other heirs; and 45 days after the death of the decedent, any creditor. Alaska Stat. § 13.16.065	7
Uniform Transfers to Minors Act	1. If custodian appointed in will or trust, custodianship ends at age 18 to 25. 2. If custodian appointed by personal representative, transfers exceeding $25,000 must be authorized by court, and custodianship ends at age 18. Alaska Stat §§ 13.46.010 and following	10
State inheritance tax	No	11
State estate tax	No	11
State taxing authority website	www.revenue.state.ak.us	11
Community property	Yes, if married couples sign an agreement making their property community property. Alaska Stat §§ 34.77.030, 34.77.090	14
Uniform Transfer-on-Death Securities Act	Estates of up to $15,000, less liens and encumbrances; 30-day waiting period. Alaska Stat. § 13.16.680	16
Affidavit procedure for small estates	Value of entire estate, less liens and encumbrances, does not exceed homestead allowance, exempt property, family allowance, costs and expenses of administration, funeral expenses, and medical and hospital expenses of the last illness. Alaska Stat. §§ 13.16.690, 695	17
Summary probate for small estates	Yes	17
Uniform Probate Code	Yes	18
Trustee must send special notice after grantor dies	No	19-21
Trust registration	Yes. Alaska Stat. §§ 13.36.05 and following	19-21
Uniform Prudent Investor Act	Alaska Stat. §§ 13.36.200 and following	20-21
Uniform Principal and Income Act	No	20-21
State law sets rates lawyers can charge for probate, based on estate value	No	23

Arizona

TOPIC	STATE RULE	CHAPTER
Out-of-state executors or administrators	No restrictions	2, 18
Surviving spouse's allowance rights	Ariz. Rev. Stat. § 14-2402 and following	5
System of protecting surviving spouse from disinheritance	Community property. Ariz. Rev. Stat. § 14-3101	6
Holographic will	Valid. Ariz. Rev. Stat. § 14-2503	6
Can will refer to separate memorandum leaving tangible items?	Yes. Ariz. Rev. Stat. § 14-2513	6
Priority for appointment as administrator (after named executor, if any)	Spouse who inherits under the will; other will beneficiaries; spouse; other heirs; if the deceased was a veteran or the spouse or child of a veteran, the department of veterans' services; 45 days after the death, any creditor; the public fiduciary. Ariz. Rev. Stat. §§ 14-3203	7
Intestate succession	Ariz. Rev. Stat. §§ 14-2102, 2103	7
Uniform Transfers to Minors Act	1. If custodian appointed in will or trust, custodianship ends at age 21. 2. If custodian appointed by personal representative, transfers exceeding $10,000 must be authorized by court, and custodianship ends at age 18. Ariz. Rev. Stat. §§ 14-7651 to 13.46.195	10
State inheritance tax	No	11
State estate tax	No	11
State taxing authority website	www.revenue.state.az.us	11
Community property	Yes	14
Uniform Transfer-on-Death Securities Act	Yes	16
Affidavit procedure for small estates	1. Value of all personal property in estate, less liens and encumbrances, is $50,000 or less. 30-day waiting period. Ariz. Rev. Stat. Ann. § 14-3971.B 2. Value of all Arizona real property in the estate, less liens and encumbrances, is $50,000 or less at the date of death, and all debts and taxes have been paid. Ariz. Rev. Stat. Ann. § 14-3971.E	17
Summary probate for small estates	Value of entire estate, less liens and encumbrances, does not exceed allowance in lieu of homestead, exempt property, family allowance, costs of administration, funeral expenses, and expenses of the last illness. Six-month waiting period. Ariz. Rev. Stat. Ann. §§ 14-3973, 3974	17
Uniform Probate Code	Yes	18
Trustee must send special notice after grantor dies	Yes. Ariz. Rev. Stat. Ann. § 14-7303	19-21
Trust registration	No	19-21
Uniform Prudent Investor Act	Ariz. Rev. Stat. Ann. §§ 14-7601 and following	20-21
Uniform Principal and Income Act	Ariz. Rev. Stat. Ann. §§ 14-741 and following	20-21
State law sets rates lawyers can charge for probate, based on estate value	No	23

Arkansas

TOPIC	STATE RULE	CHAPTER
Out-of-state executors or administrators	Allowed, but must appoint agent who lives in county where probate is conducted. Ark. Code Ann. § 28-48-101	2, 18
Surviving spouse's allowance rights	Ark. Code Ann. § 28-39-201 and following	5
System of protecting surviving spouse from disinheritance	Traditional spousal share. Ark. Stat. Ann. § 28-39-401 and following	6
Holographic will	Valid. Ark. Code Ann. § 28-25-104	6
Can will refer to separate memorandum leaving tangible items?	Yes. Ark. Stat. Ann. § 28-25-107	6
Priority for appointment as administrator (after named executor, if any)	Spouse or person chosen by spouse; people who inherit. Ark. Stat. Ann. § 28-48-101	7
Intestate succession	Ark. Code Ann. §§ 28-9-201 and following	7
Uniform Transfers to Minors Act	1. If custodian appointed in will or trust, custodianship ends at age 18-21. 2. If custodian appointed by executor, transfers exceeding $10,000 must be authorized by court, and custodianship ends at age 18. Ark. Code Ann. §§ 9-26-201 and following	10
State inheritance tax	No	11
State estate tax	Yes	11
State taxing authority website	www.arkansas.gov/dfa	11
Community property	No	14
Uniform Transfer-on-Death Securities Act	Yes. Ark. Code Ann. §§ 28-14-101 and following	16
Affidavit procedure for small estates	None	17
Summary probate for small estates	1. Personal property does not exceed that to which the widow, if any, or minor children, if any, are by law entitled free of debt, as dower or curtesy and statutory allowances. Probate court can order entire estate to widow and/or minor children. Ark. Code Ann. § 28-41-103 2. Value, less encumbrances, of all property owned by the decedent, excluding the homestead of and the statutory allowances for the benefit of a spouse or minor children, if any, does not exceed $50,000. 45-day waiting period. Ark. Code Ann. § 28-41-101	17
Uniform Probate Code	No	18
Trustee must send special notice after grantor dies	No	19-21
Trust registration	No	19-21
Uniform Prudent Investor Act	Ark. Code Ann. §§ 24-3-417 and following	20-21
Uniform Principal and Income Act	Ark. Code Ann. §§ 28-70-101 and following	20-21
State law sets rates lawyers can charge for probate, based on estate value	Yes. Ark. Code Ann. § 28-48-108	23

California

TOPIC	STATE RULE	CHAPTER
Out-of-state executors or administrators	No restrictions	2, 18
Surviving spouse's allowance rights	Cal. Prob. Code §§ 654, 6520 to 6526	5
System of protecting surviving spouse from disinheritance	Community property. Cal Prob. Code §§ 100, 101	6
Holographic will	Valid. Cal. Prob. Code § 6111	6
Can will refer to separate memorandum leaving tangible items?	No	6
Priority for appointment as administrator (after named executor, if any)	Spouse or registered domestic partner; children; grandchildren; other descendants; parents; brothers and sisters; descendants of brothers and sisters; grandparents; grandparents' issue; children of predeceased spouse or domestic partner; other issue of predeceased spouse or domestic partner; other next of kin; parents of a predeceased spouse or domestic partner; issue of parents of a predeceased spouse or domestic partner; conservator or guardian of the estate; public administrator; creditors. Cal. Prob. Code § 8461	7
Intestate succession	Cal. Prob. Code §§ 6401 and following	7
Uniform Transfers to Minors Act	1. If custodian appointed in will or trust, custodianship ends at age 18-25. 2. If custodian appointed by executor, transfers exceeding $10,000 must be authorized by court unless the custodian is a trust company or is an individual designated as a trustee by a trust instrument that does not require a bond; custodianship ends at age 18-25. Cal. Prob. Code §§ 3900 and following	10
State inheritance tax	No	11
State estate tax	No	11
State taxing authority website	www.sco.ca.gov, www.ftb.ca.gov	11
Community property	Yes	14
Uniform Transfer-on-Death Securities Act	Yes	16
Affidavit procedure for small estates	1. For personal property in estates up to $100,000 in value, as calculated using exclusions listed in "summary probate" section, below; 40-day waiting period. Cal. Prob. Code §§ 13050, 13100 and following 2. For real estate up to $20,000 in value. Six-month waiting period. Cal. Prob. Code §§ 13200 to 13208	17
Summary probate for small estates	Value up to $100,000. Excluded from calculating value: real estate outside California; joint tenancy property; property that goes outright to a surviving spouse; life insurance, death benefits, and other assets not subject to probate that pass to named beneficiaries; multiple-party accounts and payable-on-death accounts; any registered manufactured or mobile home; any numbered vessel; registered motor vehicles; salary up to $5,000; amounts due decedent for services in the armed forces; property held in trust, including a living trust. Cal. Prob. Code §§ 13150 and following	17
Uniform Probate Code	No	18

Trustee must send special notice after grantor dies	Yes. Must notify trust beneficiaries and deceased person's heirs (people who would inherit under state law in the absence of a will or trust). Cal. Prob. Code §§ 16060.5-16061.8	19-21
Trust registration	No	19-21
Uniform Prudent Investor Act	Cal. Prob. Code, §§ 16045 and following	20-21
Uniform Principal and Income Act	Cal. Prob. Code, §§ 16320 and following	20-21
State law sets rates lawyers can charge for probate, based on estate value	Yes. Cal. Prob. Code §§ 10810	23

Colorado

TOPIC	STATE RULE	CHAPTER
Out-of-state executors or administrators	No restrictions	2, 18
Surviving spouse's allowance rights	Colo. Rev. Stat. §§ 38-41-204, 15-11-402 and following	5
System of protecting surviving spouse from disinheritance	Augmented estate. Col. Rev. Stat. Ann. §§ 15-11-201 and following	6
Holographic will	Valid. Col. Rev. Stat. Ann. § 15-11-502	6
Can will refer to separate memorandum leaving tangible items?	Yes. Col. Rev. Stat. Ann. § 15-11-513	6
Priority for appointment as administrator (after named executor, if any)	Spouse who inherits under the will; other will beneficiaries; spouse; other heirs; 45 days after the death, any creditor. Col. Rev. Stat. Ann. § 15-12-203	7
Intestate succession	Col. Rev. Stat. Ann. §§ 15-11-100 and following	7
Uniform Transfers to Minors Act	1. If custodian appointed in will or trust, custodianship ends at age 21. 2. If custodian appointed by personal representative, transfers exceeding $10,000 must be authorized by court, and custodianship ends at age 21. Col. Rev. Stat. Ann. §§ 11-50-101 and following	10
State inheritance tax	No	11
State estate tax	No	11
State taxing authority website	www.revenue.state.co.us/main/home.asp	11
Community property	No	14
Uniform Transfer-on-Death Securities Act	Yes	16
Affidavit procedure for small estates	Estates where fair market value of property that is subject to disposition by will or state intestate succession law, less liens and encumbrances, is $50,000 or less. (This excludes joint tenancy property, property in a living trust, payable-on-death bank accounts, and other kinds of property that don't pass under a will.) Ten-day waiting period. Col. Rev. Stat. Ann. § 15-12-1201	17
Summary probate for small estates	Value of entire estate, less liens and encumbrances, does not exceed the value of personal property held by the decedent as fiduciary or trustee, exempt property allowance, family allowance, costs of administration, funeral expenses, and medical expenses of last illness. Colo. Rev. Stat. § 15-12-1203	17
Uniform Probate Code	Yes	18
Trustee must send special notice after grantor dies	Yes. Colo. Rev. Stat. 15-16-303	19-21
Trust registration	Yes. Colo. Rev. Stat. §§ 15-16-01 and following	19-21
Uniform Prudent Investor Act	Colo. Rev. Stat. §§ 15-1.1-101 and following	20-21
Uniform Principal and Income Act	Colo. Rev. Stat. §§ 15-1-401 and following	20-21
State law sets rates lawyers can charge for probate, based on estate value	No	23

Connecticut

TOPIC	STATE RULE	CHAPTER
Out-of-state executors or administrators	Allowed, but nonresident must agree that probate court judge is his or her agent. Conn. Gen. Stat. Ann. § 52-60	2, 18
Surviving spouse's allowance rights	Conn. Gen. Stat. Ann. § 45a-320	5
System of protecting surviving spouse from disinheritance	Traditional spousal share. Conn. Gen. Stat. Ann. § 45a-436	6
Holographic will	Not valid unless valid in the state where it was executed. Conn. Gen. Stat. Ann. § 45a-251	6
Can will refer to separate memorandum leaving tangible items?	No	6
Priority for appointment as administrator (after named executor, if any)	Spouse or next of kin. Conn. Gen. Stat. Ann. § 45a-290	7
Intestate succession	Conn. Gen. Stat. Ann. §§ 45a-437, 438	7
Uniform Transfers to Minors Act	1. If custodian appointed in will or trust, custodianship ends at age 21. 2. If custodian appointed by executor, transfers exceeding $5,000 must be authorized by court, and custodianship ends at age 21. Conn. Gen. Stat. §§ 45a-557 and following	10
State inheritance tax	Will be phased out by 2008. Conn. Gen. Stat. Ann. § 12-344	11
State estate tax	No	11
State taxing authority website	www.drs.state.ct.us	11
Community property	No	14
Uniform Transfer-on-Death Securities Act	Yes	16
Affidavit procedure for small estates	No	17
Summary probate for small estates	No real estate (except real estate held in survivorship form), estate not exceeding $20,000 in value. Conn. Gen. Stat. § 45a-273	17
Uniform Probate Code	No	18
Trustee must send special notice after grantor dies	No	19-21
Trust registration	No	19-21
Uniform Prudent Investor Act	Conn. Gen. Stat. Ann. § 45a-541	20-21
Uniform Principal and Income Act	Conn. Gen. Stat. Ann. § 45a-542	20-21
State law sets rates lawyers can charge for probate, based on estate value	No	23

Delaware

TOPIC	STATE RULE	CHAPTER
Out-of-state executors or administrators	Nonresident must designate county Register of Wills as agent. Del. Code Ann. tit. 12, § 1506	2, 18
Surviving spouse's allowance rights	Del. Code Ann. tit. 12, § 2308	5
System of protecting surviving spouse from disinheritance	Traditional spousal share. Del. Code Ann. tit. 12, §§ 901 and following	6
Holographic will	Not valid unless valid in the state where it was executed. Del. Code Ann. tit. 12, §§ 202, 1306	6
Can will refer to separate memorandum leaving tangible items?	Yes. Del. Code Ann. tit. 12, § 212	6
Priority for appointment as administrator (after named executor, if any)	Spouse; children; parents; siblings. Del. Code Ann. tit. 12, § 1505	7
Intestate succession	Del. Code Ann. tit. 12, § 503	7
Uniform Transfers to Minors Act	1. If custodian appointed in will or trust, custodianship ends at age 21. 2. If custodian appointed by executor, transfers exceeding $50,000 must be authorized by court, and custodianship ends at age 18. Del. Code Ann. tit. 12, §§ 4501 and following	10
State inheritance tax	No	11
State estate tax	No	11
State taxing authority website	www.state.de.us/revenue/index.htm	11
Community property	No	14
Uniform Transfer-on-Death Securities Act	Yes	16
Affidavit procedure for small estates	Estates without solely owned Delaware real estate and a value of no more than $20,000. (Jointly owned property, and death benefits that pass outside of probate, such as insurance or pension proceeds, are not counted toward the $20,000 limit.) 30-day waiting period. Available only to spouse, certain relatives, or funeral director. Del. Code Ann. tit. 12, § 2306	17
Summary probate for small estates	No	17
Uniform Probate Code	No	18
Trustee must send special notice after grantor dies	No	19-21
Trust registration	No	19-21
Uniform Prudent Investor Act	No	20-21
Uniform Principal and Income Act	No	20-21
State law sets rates lawyers can charge for probate, based on estate value	No	23

District of Columbia

TOPIC	STATE RULE	CHAPTER
Out-of-state executors or administrators	Nonresident must designate probate register as agent. D.C. Code Ann. § 20-303	2, 18
Surviving spouse's allowance rights	D.C. Code Ann. §§ 19-101.02 to 19-101.04	5
System of protecting surviving spouse from disinheritance	Traditional spousal share. D.C. Code Ann. § 19-112 and following	6
Holographic will	Not valid. D.C. Code Ann. § 18-103	6
Can will refer to separate memorandum leaving tangible items?	No	6
Priority for appointment as administrator (after named executor, if any)	Spouse if there is a will, or spouse or children if there's no will; residuary beneficiary; children if there's a will; grandchildren; parents; brothers and sisters; next of kin; other relations; largest creditor who applies. D.C. Code Ann. § 20-303(a)	7
Intestate succession	D.C. Code Ann. §§ 19-302 and following	7
Uniform Transfers to Minors Act	1. If custodian appointed in will or trust, custodianship ends at age 18 to 21. 2. If custodian appointed by executor, transfers exceeding $10,000 must be authorized by court, and custodianship ends at age 18. D.C. Code Ann. §§ 21-301 and following	10
State inheritance tax	No	11
State estate tax	Yes. D.C. Code Ann. §§ 47-3701 and following	11
State taxing authority website	http://cfo.dc.gov/etsc/main.shtm	11
Community property	No	14
Uniform Transfer-on-Death Securities Act	Yes	16
Affidavit procedure for small estates	Deceased person owned nothing but one or two motor vehicles. D.C. Code Ann. § 20-357	17
Summary probate for small estates	Property subject to administration in D.C. has value of $40,000 or less. D.C. Code Ann. §§ 20-351 and following	17
Uniform Probate Code	No	18
Trustee must send special notice after grantor dies	No	19-21
Trust registration	No	19-21
Uniform Prudent Investor Act	D.C. Code Ann. §§ 28-4701 and following	20-21
Uniform Principal and Income Act	D.C. Code Ann. §§ 28-4801.1 and following	20-21
State law sets rates lawyers can charge for probate, based on estate value	No	23

Florida

TOPIC	STATE RULE	CHAPTER
Out-of-state executors or administrators	Allowed only if the nonresident is: (1) a legally adopted child or adoptive parent of the decedent; (2) related by lineal consanguinity to the decedent; (3) a spouse or a brother, sister, uncle, aunt, nephew, or niece of the decedent, or someone related by lineal consanguinity to any such person; or (4) the spouse of a person otherwise qualified. Fla. Stat. Ann. § 733.304	2, 18
Surviving spouse's allowance rights	Fla. Stat. Ann. § 732.401 and following	5
System of protecting surviving spouse from disinheritance	Traditional spousal share. Fla. Stat. Ann. §§ 732.2065 and following	6
Holographic will	Not valid. Fla. Stat. Ann. § 732.502(2)	6
Can will refer to separate memorandum leaving tangible items?	Yes. Fla. Stat. Ann. § 732.515	6
Priority for appointment as administrator (after named executor, if any)	If there is a will: Person chosen by majority in interest of people who inherit; someone who inherits under will. If there is no will: spouse; person chosen by majority in interest of heirs; most closely related heir. Fla. Stat. Ann. § 733.301	7
Intestate succession	Fla. Stat. Ann. §§ 732.100 and following	7
Uniform Transfers to Minors Act	1. If custodian appointed in will or trust, custodianship ends at age 21. 2. If custodian appointed by executor, transfers exceeding $10,000 must be authorized by court, and custodianship ends at age 18. Fla. Stat. Ann. §§ 710.101 and following	10
State inheritance tax	No	11
State estate tax	No	11
State taxing authority website	http://sun6.dms.state.fl.us/dor	11
Community property	No	14
Uniform Transfer-on-Death Securities Act	Yes	16
Affidavit procedure for small estates	No	17
Summary probate for small estates	1. No real estate, and all property is exempt from creditors' claims except amounts needed to pay funeral and two months' last illness expenses. Upon letter to court, court will authorize transfer of property to people entitled to it. Fla. Stat. Ann. § 735.301 2. Value of entire estate subject to administration in Florida, less the value of property that is exempt from creditors' claims, doesn't exceed $75,000, OR decedent has been dead more than two years. Petition must be filed with court. Fla. Stat. Ann. §§ 735.201 and following	17
Uniform Probate Code	Yes	18
Trustee must send special notice after grantor dies	Yes. Fla. Stat. Ann. § 737-303	19-21
Trust registration	Yes. Fla. Stat. Ann. §§ 737.101 and following	19-21
Uniform Prudent Investor Act	Fla. Stat. Ann. §§ 518.11 and following	20-21
Uniform Principal and Income Act	Fla. Stat. Ann. §§ 738.101 and following	20-21
State law sets rates lawyers can charge for probate, based on estate value	Yes. Fla. Stat. Ann. § 733.6171	23

Georgia

TOPIC	STATE RULE	CHAPTER
Out-of-state executors or administrators	No restrictions	2, 18
Surviving spouse's allowance rights	Ga. Code Ann. § 53-3-1	5
System of protecting surviving spouse from disinheritance	Traditional spousal share. Ga. Code Ann. § 55-2-1	6
Holographic will	Not valid. Ga. Code Ann. § 53-4-20	6
Can will refer to separate memorandum leaving tangible items?	No	6
Priority for appointment as administrator (after named executor, if any)	Spouse (unless couple was getting divorced at time of death); next of kin; creditor. Ga. Code Ann. § 53-6-24	7
Intestate succession	Ga. Code Ann. § 53-2-1	7
Uniform Transfers to Minors Act	1. If custodian appointed in will or trust, custodianship ends at age 21. 2. If custodian appointed by executor, transfers exceeding $10,000 must be authorized by court, and custodianship ends at age 18. Ga. Code Ann. §§ 44-5-110 and following	10
State inheritance tax	No	11
State estate tax	No	11
State taxing authority website	http://www2.state.ga.us/Departments/DOR	11
Community property	No	14
Uniform Transfer-on-Death Securities Act	Yes	16
Affidavit procedure for small estates	No	17
Summary probate for small estates	There is no will, estate owes no debts, and all heirs have amicably agreed on how to divide the property. Ga. Code Ann. §§ 53-2-40 and following	17
Uniform Probate Code	No	18
Trustee must send special notice after grantor dies	No	19-21
Trust registration	No	19-21
Uniform Prudent Investor Act	No	20-21
Uniform Principal and Income Act	Ga. Code Ann. §§ 53-12-210 and following	20-21
State law sets rates lawyers can charge for probate, based on estate value	No	23

Hawaii

TOPIC	STATE RULE	CHAPTER
Out-of-state executors or administrators	No restrictions	2, 18
Surviving spouse's allowance rights	Haw. Rev. Stat. § 560:2-402	5
System of protecting surviving spouse from disinheritance	Augmented estate. Haw. Rev. Stat. § 560:2-202	6
Holographic will	Valid. Haw. Rev. Stat. § 560:2-502	6
Can will refer to separate memorandum leaving tangible items?	Yes. Haw. Rev. Stat. § 560:2-513	6
Priority for appointment as administrator (after named executor, if any)	Spouse or reciprocal beneficiary who inherits under the will; others who inherit under the will; spouse or reciprocal beneficiary; other heirs; 45 days after the death, any creditor. Haw. Rev. Stat. § 560:3-203	7
Intestate succession	Haw. Rev. Stat. § 560:2-402	7
Uniform Transfers to Minors Act	1. If custodian appointed in will or trust, custodianship ends at age 21. 2. If custodian appointed by personal representative, transfers exceeding $10,000 must be authorized by court, and custodianship ends at age 18. Haw. Rev. Stat. §§ 553A-1 and following	10
State inheritance tax	No	11
State estate tax	No	11
State taxing authority website	www.state.hi.us/tax	11
Community property	No	14
Uniform Transfer-on-Death Securities Act	Yes	16
Affidavit procedure for small estates	Value of property deceased person owned in Hawaii is $100,000 or less. Can transfer motor vehicles this way regardless of value of estate. Haw. Rev. Stat. §§ 560:3-1201 and following	17
Summary probate for small estates	Value of all property deceased person owned in Hawaii doesn't exceed $100,000. Haw. Rev. Stat. §§ 560:3-1205 and following	17
Uniform Probate Code	Yes	18
Trustee must send special notice after grantor dies	No	19-21
Trust registration	Yes. Haw. Rev. Stat. §§ 560:7-101 and following	19-21
Uniform Prudent Investor Act	Haw. Rev. Stat. §§ 554C-1 and following	20-21
Uniform Principal and Income Act	Haw. Rev. Stat. §§ 557A-101 and following	20-21
State law sets rates lawyers can charge for probate, based on estate value	No	23

Idaho

TOPIC	STATE RULE	CHAPTER
Out-of-state executors or administrators	No restrictions	2, 18
Surviving spouse's allowance rights	Idaho Code §§ 15-2-403, 404	5
System of protecting surviving spouse from disinheritance	Community property. Idaho Code §§ 15-3-101 and following	6
Holographic will	Valid. Idaho Code § 15-2-503	6
Can will refer to separate memorandum leaving tangible items?	Yes. Idaho Code § 15-2-513	6
Priority for appointment as administrator (after named executor, if any)	Spouse who inherits under the will; other person who inherits under the will; spouse; other heirs; 45 days after the death of the decedent, any creditor; the public administrator. Idaho Code § 15-3-203	7
Intestate succession	Idaho Code §§ 15-2-102 and following	7
Uniform Transfers to Minors Act	1. If custodian appointed in will or trust, custodianship ends at age 21. 2. If custodian appointed by personal representative, transfers exceeding $10,000 must be authorized by court, and custodianship ends at age 18. Idaho Code §§ 68-801 and following	10
State inheritance tax	No	11
State estate tax	No	11
State taxing authority website	http://www2.state.id.us/tax	11
Community property	Yes	14
Uniform Transfer-on-Death Securities Act	Yes	16
Affidavit procedure for small estates	Fair market value of property subject to probate, wherever located, less liens and encumbrances, is $75,000 or less. 30-day waiting period. Idaho Code §§ 15-3-1201 and following	17
Summary probate for small estates	1. Value of all property deceased person owned, less liens and encumbrances, doesn't exceed the homestead allowance, exempt property, family allowance, costs of administration, funeral expenses, and medical expenses of the last illness. Idaho Code §§ 15-3-1203 and following 2. A surviving spouse who inherits everything can file petition with court, which will issue a decree to that effect. Idaho Code § 15-3-1205	17
Uniform Probate Code	Yes	18
Trustee must send special notice after grantor dies	No	19-21
Trust registration	Yes. Idaho Code § 15-7-101	19-21
Uniform Prudent Investor Act	Idaho Code §§ 68-501 and following	20-21
Uniform Principal and Income Act	Idaho Code §§ 68-10-101 and following	20-21
State law sets rates lawyers can charge for probate, based on estate value	No	23

Illinois

TOPIC	STATE RULE	CHAPTER
Out-of-state executors or administrators	Court may require executor to post bond even if will says it's not required. 755 Ill. Comp. Stat. § 5/6-13	2, 18
Surviving spouse's allowance rights	755 Ill. Comp. Stat. §§ 5/15-1 to 15-4	5
System of protecting surviving spouse from disinheritance	Traditional spousal share. 755 Ill. Comp. Stat. § 5/2-8	6
Holographic will	Not valid. 755 Ill. Comp Stat. § 5/4-3	6
Can will refer to separate memorandum leaving tangible items?	No	6
Priority for appointment as administrator (after named executor, if any)	Spouse; people who inherit under the will, with preference for children; grandchildren; parents; brothers and sisters; next of kin; representative of estate of deceased ward; public administrator; creditor. 755 Ill. Comp. Stat. § 5/9-3	7
Intestate succession	755 Ill. Comp. Stat. § 5/2-1	7
Uniform Transfers to Minors Act	1. If custodian appointed in will or trust, custodianship ends at age 21. 2. If custodian appointed by executor, transfers exceeding $10,000 must be authorized by court, and custodianship ends at age 18. 760 Ill. Comp. Stat. §§ 20/1 and following	10
State inheritance tax	No	11
State estate tax	Beginning in 2006, state estate tax separate from federal estate tax. 35 Ill. Comp. Stat. § 405/3	11
State taxing authority website	www.revenue.state.il.us	11
Community property	No	14
Uniform Transfer-on-Death Securities Act	Yes	16
Affidavit procedure for small estates	Gross value of all deceased person's property that passes under a will or by state law, excluding real estate, is $100,000 or less. 755 Ill. Comp. Stat. § 5/25-1	17
Summary probate for small estates	Gross value of property subject to probate in Illinois does not exceed $100,000. All heirs and beneficiaries must consent in writing. 755 Ill. Comp. Stat. § 5/9-8	17
Uniform Probate Code	No	18
Trustee must send special notice after grantor dies	No	19-21
Trust registration	No	19-21
Uniform Prudent Investor Act	760 Ill. Comp. Stat. §§ 5/5, 5/5.1	20-21
Uniform Principal and Income Act	760 Ill. Comp. Stat. § 15/1	20-21
State law sets rates lawyers can charge for probate, based on estate value	No	23

Indiana

TOPIC	STATE RULE	CHAPTER
Out-of-state executors or administrators	Nonresident must appoint resident agent and post bond. Ind. Code Ann. § 29-1-10-1	2, 18
Surviving spouse's allowance rights	Ind. Code Ann. § 29-1-4-1	5
System of protecting surviving spouse from disinheritance	Traditional spousal share. Ind. Code Ann. § 29-1-3-1	6
Holographic will	Not valid. Ind. Stat. § 29-1-5-2	6
Can will refer to separate memorandum leaving tangible items?	No	6
Priority for appointment as administrator (after named executor, if any)	Spouse who inherits under the will; other person who inherits under the will; spouse or person spouse nominates; heir or person heir nominates. Ind. Code Ann. § 29-1-10-1	7
Intestate succession	Ind. Code Ann. § 29-1-2-1	7
Uniform Transfers to Minors Act	1. If custodian appointed in will or trust, custodianship ends at age 21. 2. If custodian appointed by executor, transfers exceeding $10,000 must be authorized by court, and custodianship ends at age 21. Ind. Code Ann. §§ 30-2-8.5-1 and following	10
State inheritance tax	Yes. Ind. Code Ann. § 6-4.1-11-5	11
State estate tax	No	11
State taxing authority website	www.state.in.us/dor	11
Community property	No	14
Uniform Transfer-on-Death Securities Act	Yes	16
Affidavit procedure for small estates	Value of gross probate estate, less liens and encumbrances, does not exceed $25,000. 45-day waiting period. Ind. Code § 29-1-8-1	17
Summary probate for small estates	Value of property subject to probate does not exceed $25,000. Ind. Code Ann. §§ 29-1-8-3 and following	17
Uniform Probate Code	No	18
Trustee must send special notice after grantor dies	No	19-21
Trust registration	No	19-21
Uniform Prudent Investor Act	Ind. Code Ann. § 30-4-3.5-1	20-21
Uniform Principal and Income Act	Ind. Code Ann. §§ 30-2-14	20-21
State law sets rates lawyers can charge for probate, based on estate value	No	23

Iowa

TOPIC	STATE RULE	CHAPTER
Out-of-state executors or administrators	Resident must serve as coexecutor unless court allows otherwise. Iowa Code § 633.64	2, 18
Surviving spouse's allowance rights	Iowa Code §§ 633.240, 633.374	5
System of protecting surviving spouse from disinheritance	Traditional spousal share. Iowa Code § 633.238	6
Holographic will	Not valid unless valid in the state where it was executed. Iowa Code §§ 633.279, 633.283	6
Can will refer to separate memorandum leaving tangible items?	Yes. Iowa Code § 633.276	6
Priority for appointment as administrator (after named executor, if any)	Spouse; heirs; creditors. Iowa Code §§ 633.227-228	7
Intestate succession	Iowa Code §§ 633.212, 633.219	7
Uniform Transfers to Minors Act	1. If custodian appointed in will or trust, custodianship ends at age 21. 2. If custodian appointed by executor, transfers exceeding $10,000 must be authorized by court, and custodianship ends at age 21. Iowa Code §§ 565B.1 and following	10
State inheritance tax	Yes. Iowa Code § 450.10	11
State estate tax	No	11
State taxing authority website	www.state.ia.us/tax/index.html	11
Community property	No	14
Uniform Transfer-on-Death Securities Act	Yes	16
Affidavit procedure for small estates	No real estate (or real estate passes to spouse as joint tenant) and gross value of the deceased person's personal property is $25,000 or less. 40-day waiting period. Iowa Code § 633.356	17
Summary probate for small estates	1. If deceased person is survived by a spouse or child: Available if gross value of property subject to Iowa jurisdiction (basically, everything but real estate outside Iowa) doesn't exceed $50,000. 2. If deceased person is survived by parents or grandchildren: Available if gross value of property subject to Iowa jurisdiction (basically, everything but real estate outside Iowa) doesn't exceed $15,000. 3. If deceased person is survived by more distant relatives: Available if gross value of property subject to Iowa jurisdiction (basically, everything but real estate outside Iowa) doesn't exceed $10,000. Iowa Code § 635.1	17
Uniform Probate Code	No	18
Trustee must send special notice after grantor dies	No	19-21
Trust registration	No	19-21
Uniform Prudent Investor Act	Iowa Code §§ 633.4301 and following	20-21
Uniform Principal and Income Act	Iowa Code §§ 637.101 and following	20-21
State law sets rates lawyers can charge for probate, based on estate value	Yes. Iowa Code §§ 633.197, 633.198	23

Kansas

TOPIC	STATE RULE	CHAPTER
Out-of-state executors or administrators	Nonresident must appoint someone who lives in the county where the probate takes place as an agent. Kan. Stat. Ann. § 59-1706	2, 18
Surviving spouse's allowance rights	Kan. Stat. Ann. § 59-6a215	5
System of protecting surviving spouse from disinheritance	Augmented estate. Kan. Stat. Ann. § 59-6a202	6
Holographic will	Not valid. Kan. Stat. Ann. § 59-606	6
Can will refer to separate memorandum leaving tangible items?	Yes. Kan. Stat. Ann. § 59-623	6
Priority for appointment as administrator (after named executor, if any)	Spouse or next of kin or both, or person they select; creditors or someone they nominate. Kan. Stat. Ann. § 59-705	7
Intestate succession	Kan. Stat. Ann. §§ 59-502 and following	7
Uniform Transfers to Minors Act	1. If custodian appointed in will or trust, custodianship ends at age 21. 2. If custodian appointed by executor, transfers exceeding $10,000 must be authorized by court, and custodianship ends at age 18. Kan. Stat. Ann. §§ 38-1701 and following	10
State inheritance tax	No	11
State estate tax	Yes. Kan. Stat. Ann. §§ 79-15,000 and following	11
State taxing authority website	www.ksrevenue.org	11
Community property	No	14
Uniform Transfer-on-Death Securities Act	Yes	16
Affidavit procedure for small estates	Value of total assets of the deceased person's estate is $20,000 or less. Kan. Stat. Ann. § 59-1507b	17
Summary probate for small estates	Simplified estate procedure available if court approves it, based on size of estate, wishes of heirs, and other factors. Kan. Stat. Ann. §§ 59-3202 and following	17
Uniform Probate Code	No	18
Trustee must send special notice after grantor dies	Yes. Must notify qualified trust beneficiaries. Kan. Stat. Ann. ch. 58a	19-21
Trust registration	No	19-21
Uniform Prudent Investor Act	Kan. Stat. Ann. §§ 58-24a01 and following	20-21
Uniform Principal and Income Act	Kan. Stat. Ann. §§ 58-9-101 and following	20-21
State law sets rates lawyers can charge for probate, based on estate value	No	23

Kentucky

TOPIC	STATE RULE	CHAPTER
Out-of-state executors or administrators	Nonresident must be related to the deceased person by blood, marriage, or adoption or be the spouse of a person so related. Ky. Rev. Stat. Ann. § 395.005	2, 18
Surviving spouse's allowance rights	Ky. Rev. Stat. Ann. § 391.030	5
System of protecting surviving spouse from disinheritance	Traditional spousal share. Ky. Rev. Stat. Ann. §§ 392.020, 392.080	6
Holographic will	Valid. Ky. Rev. Stat. Ann. § 394.040	6
Can will refer to separate memorandum leaving tangible items?	No	6
Priority for appointment as administrator (after named executor, if any)	Spouse or someone the spouse nominates; someone else who inherits; after 60 days, creditor or other person. Ky. Rev. Stat. Ann. § 395.040	7
Intestate succession	Ky. Rev. Stat. Ann. §§ 391.010 and following	7
Uniform Transfers to Minors Act	1. If custodian appointed in will or trust, custodianship ends at age 18. 2. If custodian appointed by executor, transfers exceeding $10,000 must be authorized by court, and custodianship ends at age 18. Ky. Rev. Stat. Ann. §§ 385.012 and following	10
State inheritance tax	Yes. Ky. Rev. Stat. Ann. § 140.010	11
State estate tax	No	11
State taxing authority website	http://revenue.ky.gov	11
Community property	No	14
Uniform Transfer-on-Death Securities Act	Yes	16
Affidavit procedure for small estates	No	17
Summary probate for small estates	No will leaves personal property, and there is a surviving spouse and value of property subject to probate is $15,000 or less, or if there is no surviving spouse and someone else has paid at least $15,000 in preferred claims. Ky. Rev. Stat. Ann. §§ 391.030, 395.455	17
Uniform Probate Code	No	18
Trustee must send special notice after grantor dies	No	19-21
Trust registration	No	19-21
Uniform Prudent Investor Act	No	20-21
Uniform Principal and Income Act	Ky. Rev. Stat. Ann. § 396.010	20-21
State law sets rates lawyers can charge for probate, based on estate value	No	23

Maine

TOPIC	STATE RULE	CHAPTER
Out-of-state executors or administrators	No restrictions	2, 18
Surviving spouse's allowance rights	Me. Rev. Stat. Ann. tit. 18-A, §§ 2-401 and following	5
System of protecting surviving spouse from disinheritance	Augmented estate. Me. Rev. Stat. Ann. tit. 18-A, § 2-201	6
Holographic will	Valid. Me. Rev. Stat. Ann. tit. 18-A, § 2-503	6
Can will refer to separate memorandum leaving tangible items?	Yes. Me. Rev. Stat. Ann. tit. 18-A, § 2-513	6
Priority for appointment as administrator (after named executor, if any)	Spouse who inherits under the will; other people who inherit under the will; spouse; other heirs; 45 days after the death, creditors; six months after the death, State Tax Assessor. Me. Rev. Stat. Ann. tit. 18-A, § 3-203	7
Intestate succession	Me. Rev. Stat. Ann. tit. 18-A, §§ 2-101 and following	7
Uniform Transfers to Minors Act	1. If custodian appointed in will or trust, custodianship ends at age 18-21. 2. If custodian appointed by personal representative, transfers exceeding $10,000 must be authorized by court, and custodianship ends at age 18. Me. Rev. Stat. Ann. tit. 33, §§ 1651 and following	10
State inheritance tax	No	11
State estate tax	Yes. Me. Rev. Stat. Ann. tit. 36, §§ 4062 and following	11
State taxing authority website	www.state.me.us/revenue	11
Community property	No	14
Uniform Transfer-on-Death Securities Act	Yes	16
Affidavit procedure for small estates	Value of entire estate, wherever located, less liens and encumbrances, does not exceed $10,000. 30-day waiting period. Me. Rev. Stat. Ann. tit.18-A, §§ 3-1201, 1202	17
Summary probate for small estates	Value of entire estate, less liens and encumbrances, does not exceed homestead allowance, exempt property, family allowance, costs of administration, reasonable funeral expenses, and reasonable medical expenses of the last illness. Me. Rev. Stat. Ann. tit.18-A, § 3-1203	17
Uniform Probate Code	Yes	18
Trustee must send special notice after grantor dies	Yes. Me. Rev. Stat. Ann. tit. 18-A, § 7-303	19-21
Trust registration	Yes. Me. Rev. Stat. Ann. tit. 18-A, § 7-101	19-21
Uniform Prudent Investor Act	Me. Rev. Stat. Ann. tit. 18-A, §§ 7-302 and following	20-21
Uniform Principal and Income Act	Me. Rev. Stat. Ann. tit. 18-A, §§ 7-701 and following	20-21
State law sets rates lawyers can charge for probate, based on estate value	No	23

Maryland

TOPIC	STATE RULE	CHAPTER
Out-of-state executors or administrators	Nonresident must appoint resident agent. Md. Code Ann. [Est. & Trusts] § 5-105	2, 18
Surviving spouse's allowance rights	Md. Code Ann. [Est. & Trusts] § 3-201	5
System of protecting surviving spouse from disinheritance	Traditional spousal share. Md. Code Ann. [Est. & Trusts] § 3-203	6
Holographic will	Only if made outside U.S. by person serving in U.S. armed forces; void a year after discharge. Md. Code Ann. [Est. & Trusts] § 4-103	6
Can will refer to separate memorandum leaving tangible items?	No	6
Priority for appointment as administrator (after named executor, if any)	Spouse and children, or spouse if there's a will; residuary beneficiaries; children if there's a will and they inherit; grandchildren who inherit; parents who inherit; brothers and sisters who inherit; other relatives; largest creditor who applies; any other person interested in the estate. Md. Code Ann. [Est. & Trusts] § 5-104	7
Intestate succession	Md. Code Ann. [Est. & Trusts] §§ 3-101 and following	7
Uniform Transfers to Minors Act	1. If custodian appointed in will or trust, custodianship ends at age 21. 2. If custodian appointed by executor, transfers exceeding $10,000 must be authorized by court, and custodianship ends at age 21. Md. Code Ann. [Est. & Trusts] §§ 13-301 and following	10
State inheritance tax	Yes. Md. Code Ann. [Tax-Gen.] §§ 7-201 and following	11
State estate tax	Yes. Md. Code Ann. [Tax-Gen.] §§ 7-301 and following	11
State taxing authority website	www.comp.state.md.us/default.asp	11
Community property	No	14
Uniform Transfer-on-Death Securities Act	Yes	16
Affidavit procedure for small estates	No	17
Summary probate for small estates	Property subject to probate in Maryland has a value of $30,000 or less, or if surviving spouse is the only beneficiary, $50,000 or less. Md. Code Ann. [Est. and Trusts] §§ 5-601 and following	17
Uniform Probate Code	No	18
Trustee must send special notice after grantor dies	No	19-21
Trust registration	No	19-21
Uniform Prudent Investor Act	No	20-21
Uniform Principal and Income Act	Md. Code Ann. [Est. & Trusts] §§ 15-501 and following	20-21
State law sets rates lawyers can charge for probate, based on estate value	No	23

Massachusetts

TOPIC	STATE RULE	CHAPTER
Out-of-state executors or administrators	Nonresident must appoint resident agent. Mass. Gen. Laws ch. 195, § 8	2, 18
Surviving spouse's allowance rights	Mass. Gen. Laws ch. 196, §§ 1 and following	5
System of protecting surviving spouse from disinheritance	Traditional spousal share. Mass. Gen. Laws ch. 191, § 15	6
Holographic will	Not valid. Mass. Gen. Laws ch. 191 § 1	6
Can will refer to separate memorandum leaving tangible items?	No	6
Priority for appointment as administrator (after named executor, if any)	Spouse; next of kin; creditors; public administrator. Mass. Gen. Laws ch. 193, § 1	7
Intestate succession	Mass. Gen. Laws ch. 190, §§ 1 and following	7
Uniform Transfers to Minors Act	1. If custodian appointed in will or trust, custodianship ends at age 21. 2. If custodian appointed by executor, transfers exceeding $10,000 must be authorized by court, and custodianship ends at age 21. Mass. Gen. Laws ch. 201A, §§ 1 and following	10
State inheritance tax	No	11
State estate tax	Yes. Mass. Gen. Laws ch. 65C, §§ 1 and following	11
State taxing authority website	www.dor.state.ma.us	11
Community property	No	14
Uniform Transfer-on-Death Securities Act	Yes	16
Affidavit procedure for small estates	No	17
Summary probate for small estates	Value of estate doesn't exceed $15,000 and doesn't include real estate. Mass. Gen. Laws ch. 195, §§ 16, 16A	17
Uniform Probate Code	No	18
Trustee must send special notice after grantor dies	No	19-21
Trust registration	No	19-21
Uniform Prudent Investor Act	Mass. Gen. Laws ch. 203C, §§ 1 and following	20-21
Uniform Principal and Income Act	No	20-21
State law sets rates lawyers can charge for probate, based on estate value	No	23

Michigan

TOPIC	STATE RULE	CHAPTER
Out-of-state executors or administrators	No restrictions	2, 18
Surviving spouse's allowance rights	Mich. Comp. Laws §§ 700.2402 and following	5
System of protecting surviving spouse from disinheritance	Mich. Comp. Laws §§ 700.2202, 700.2102, 700.1210	6
Holographic will	Valid. Mich. Comp. Laws § 700.2502	6
Can will refer to separate memorandum leaving tangible items?	Yes. Mich. Comp. Laws § 27.12513	6
Priority for appointment as administrator (after named executor, if any)	Spouse who inherits under will; other person who inherits under will; spouse; other heir; someone creditor nominates at least 42 days after death; public administrator. Mich. Comp. Laws §§ 700.3203	7
Intestate succession	Mich. Comp. Laws §§ 700.2101 and following	7
Uniform Transfers to Minors Act	1. If custodian appointed in will or trust, custodianship ends at age 18-21. 2. If custodian appointed by executor, transfers exceeding $10,000 must be authorized by court, and custodianship ends at age 18. Mich. Comp. Laws §§ 554.521 and following	10
State inheritance tax	No	11
State estate tax	No	11
State taxing authority website	www.michigan.gov/treasury	11
Community property	No	14
Uniform Transfer-on-Death Securities Act	Yes	16
Affidavit procedure for small estates	Estate does not include real estate, and value of the entire estate, less liens and encumbrances, doesn't exceed $15,000. 28-day waiting period. Mich. Comp. Laws § 700.3983	17
Summary probate for small estates	1. Value of gross estate, after payment of funeral and burial costs, is $15,000 or less. Court can order property turned over to surviving spouse or heirs. Mich. Comp. Laws § 700.3982 2. Value of entire estate, less liens and encumbrances, does not exceed homestead allowance, family allowance, exempt property, costs of administration, and reasonable expenses of last illness and funeral. Mich. Comp. Laws § 700.3987	17
Uniform Probate Code	No (but the state has adopted large parts)	18
Trustee must send special notice after grantor dies	Yes. Mich. Comp. Laws § 700.7303	19-21
Trust registration	Yes. Mich. Comp. Laws § 700.7101	19-21
Uniform Prudent Investor Act	Mich. Comp. Laws § 700.1501	20-21
Uniform Principal and Income Act	No	20-21
State law sets rates lawyers can charge for probate, based on estate value	No	23

Minnesota

TOPIC	STATE RULE	CHAPTER
Out-of-state executors or administrators	No restrictions	2, 18
Surviving spouse's allowance rights	Minn. Stat. Ann. §§ 524.2-402 and following	5
System of protecting surviving spouse from disinheritance	Augmented estate. Minn. Stat. Ann. § 524.2-202	6
Holographic will	Not valid unless valid in the state where it was executed. Minn. Stat. Ann. § 524.2-506	6
Can will refer to separate memorandum leaving tangible items?	Yes. Minn. Stat. Ann. § 524.2-513	6
Priority for appointment as administrator (after named executor, if any)	Spouse who inherits under the will; other people who inherit under the will; spouse; other heirs; 45 days after the death, any creditor; 90 days after the death, conservator of the deceased person. Minn. Stat. Ann. § 524.3-203	7
Intestate succession	Minn. Stat. Ann. §§ 524-2-101 and following	7
Uniform Transfers to Minors Act	1. If custodian appointed in will or trust, custodianship ends at age 21. 2. If custodian appointed by personal representative, transfers exceeding $10,000 must be authorized by court and custodianship ends at age 21. Minn. Stat. Ann. §§ 527.21 and following	10
State inheritance tax	No	11
State estate tax	Yes. Minn. Stat. Ann. §§ 291.005 and following	11
State taxing authority website	www.taxes.state.mn.us	11
Community property	No	14
Uniform Transfer-on-Death Securities Act	Yes	16
Affidavit procedure for small estates	$20,000 limit for entire probate estate, wherever located, including any contents of a safe deposit box, less liens and encumbrances. 30-day waiting period. Minn. Stat. § 524.3-1201	17
Summary probate for small estates	If court determines that no property is subject to creditors' claims (because it is exempt from claims or must be set aside for the spouse and children), can order estate closed without further proceedings. Minn. Stat. Ann. § 524.3-1203	17
Uniform Probate Code	Yes	18
Trustee must send special notice after grantor dies	No	19-21
Trust registration	No	19-21
Uniform Prudent Investor Act	Minn. Stat. §§ 501B.151 and following	20-21
Uniform Principal and Income Act	Minn. Stat. §§ 501B.59 and following	20-21
State law sets rates lawyers can charge for probate, based on estate value	No	23

Mississippi

TOPIC	STATE RULE	CHAPTER
Out-of-state executors or administrators	No restrictions	2, 18
Surviving spouse's allowance rights	Miss. Code Ann. §§ 91-1-19 and following	5
System of protecting surviving spouse from disinheritance	Traditional spousal share. Miss. Code Ann. § 91-5-25	6
Holographic will	Valid. Miss. Code Ann. § 91-5-1	6
Can will refer to separate memorandum leaving tangible items?	No	6
Priority for appointment as administrator (after named executor, if any)	Spouse; relatives who inherit; after 30 days, creditors. Miss. Code Ann. § 91-7-63	7
Intestate succession	Miss. Code Ann. §§ 91-1-3 and following	7
Uniform Transfers to Minors Act	1. If custodian appointed in will or trust, custodianship ends at age 21. 2. If custodian appointed by executor, transfers exceeding $10,000 must be authorized by court, and custodianship ends at age 18. Miss. Code Ann. §§ 91-20-1 and following	10
State inheritance tax	No	11
State estate tax	No	11
State taxing authority website	www.mstc.state.ms.us	11
Community property	No	14
Uniform Transfer-on-Death Securities Act	Yes	16
Affidavit procedure for small estates	No	17
Summary probate for small estates	Value of estate is $500 or less. Miss. Code Ann. § 91-7-147	17
Uniform Probate Code	No	18
Trustee must send special notice after grantor dies	No	19-21
Trust registration	No	19-21
Uniform Prudent Investor Act	No	20-21
Uniform Principal and Income Act	No	20-21
State law sets rates lawyers can charge for probate, based on estate value	No	23

Missouri

TOPIC	STATE RULE	CHAPTER
Out-of-state executors or administrators	Nonresident must appoint resident agent. Mo. Rev. Stat. § 473.117	2, 18
Surviving spouse's allowance rights	Mo. Rev. Stat. §§ 474.250 and following	5
System of protecting surviving spouse from disinheritance	Traditional spousal share. Mo. Rev. Stat. § 474.160	6
Holographic will	Not valid. Mo. Rev. Stat. § 474.320	6
Can will refer to separate memorandum leaving tangible items?	Yes. Mo. Rev. Stat. § 474.333	6
Priority for appointment as administrator (after named executor, if any)	Spouse; person who inherits; someone the spouse or inheritor nominates. Mo. Rev. Stat. § 473.110	7
Intestate succession	Mo. Rev. Stat. §§ 474.010 and following	7
Uniform Transfers to Minors Act	If custodian appointed in will or trust, custodianship ends at age 21. Mo. Rev. Stat. §§ 404.005 and following	10
State inheritance tax	No	11
State estate tax	No	11
State taxing authority website	http://dor.state.mo.us	11
Community property	No	14
Uniform Transfer-on-Death Securities Act	Yes	16
Affidavit procedure for small estates	No	17
Summary probate for small estates	Value of entire estate, less liens and encumbrances, is $40,000 or less. Mo. Rev. Stat. § 473.097	17
Uniform Probate Code	No	18
Trustee must send special notice after grantor dies	No	19-21
Trust registration	Yes. Mo. Rev. Stat. §§ 456.400 and following	19-21
Uniform Prudent Investor Act	Mo. Rev. Stat. §§ 456.900 and following	20-21
Uniform Principal and Income Act	Mo. Rev. Stat. §§ 469.401 and following	20-21
State law sets rates lawyers can charge for probate, based on estate value	Yes. Mo. Rev. Stat. § 473.153	23

Montana

TOPIC	STATE RULE	CHAPTER
Out-of-state executors or administrators	No restrictions	2, 18
Surviving spouse's allowance rights	Mont. Code Ann. §§ 72-2-412 and following	5
System of protecting surviving spouse from disinheritance	Augmented estate. Mont. Code Ann. § 72-2-221	6
Holographic will	Valid. Mont. Code Ann. § 72-2-522	6
Can will refer to separate memorandum leaving tangible items?	Yes. Mont. Code Ann. § 72-2-533	6
Priority for appointment as administrator (after named executor, if any)	Spouse who inherits under the will; custodial parent if deceased person was under 18; others who inherit under the will; spouse; other heirs; public administrator; 45 days after death, creditors. Mont. Code Ann. § 72-2-503	7
Intestate succession	Mont. Code Ann. §§ 72-2-112 and following	7
Uniform Transfers to Minors Act	1. If custodian appointed in will or trust, custodianship ends at age 21. 2. If custodian appointed by personal representative, transfers exceeding $10,000 must be authorized by court, and custodianship ends at age 18. Mont. Code Ann. §§ 72-26-501 and following	10
State inheritance tax	No	11
State estate tax	No	11
State taxing authority website	www.state.mt.us/revenue/css/default.asp	11
Community property	No	14
Uniform Transfer-on-Death Securities Act	Yes	16
Affidavit procedure for small estates	Value of entire estate, wherever located, less liens and encumbrances, is $20,000 or less. 30-day waiting period. Mont. Code Ann. § 72-3-1101	17
Summary probate for small estates	Value of entire estate, less liens and encumbrances, doesn't exceed homestead allowance, exempt property, family allowance, costs of administration, funeral expenses, and medical expenses of the last illness. Mont. Code Ann. § 72-3-1103	17
Uniform Probate Code	Yes	18
Trustee must send special notice after grantor dies	No	19-21
Trust registration	No	19-21
Uniform Prudent Investor Act	Mont. Code Ann. §§ 72-34-601 and following	20-21
Uniform Principal and Income Act	Mont. Code Ann. §§ 72-34-421 and following	20-21
State law sets rates lawyers can charge for probate, based on estate value	Yes. Mont. Code Ann. §§ 72-3-631, 72-3-633	23

Nebraska

TOPIC	STATE RULE	CHAPTER
Out-of-state executors or administrators	No restrictions	2, 18
Surviving spouse's allowance rights	Neb. Rev. Stat. §§ 30-2322 and following	5
System of protecting surviving spouse from disinheritance	Augmented estate. Neb. Rev. Stat. § 30-2313	6
Holographic will	Valid. Neb. Rev. Stat. § 30-2328	6
Can will refer to separate memorandum leaving tangible items?	Yes. Neb. Rev. Stat. § 30-2338	6
Priority for appointment as administrator (after named executor, if any)	Spouse who inherits under the will; others who inherit under the will; spouse; other heirs; 45 days after death, creditors. Neb. Rev. Stat. § 30-2412	7
Intestate succession	Neb. Rev. Stat. §§ 30-2302 and following	7
Uniform Transfers to Minors Act	1. If custodian appointed in will or trust, custodianship ends at age 21. 2. If custodian appointed by personal representative, transfers exceeding $10,000 must be authorized by court, and custodianship ends at age 18. Neb. Rev. Stat. §§ 43-2701 and following	10
State inheritance tax	Yes. Neb. Rev. Stat. §§ 77-2001 and following	11
State estate tax	Yes. Neb. Rev. Stat. §§ 77-2101 and following	11
State taxing authority website	www.revenue.state.ne.us	11
Community property	No	14
Uniform Transfer-on-Death Securities Act	Yes	16
Affidavit procedure for small estates	Value of entire estate, wherever located, less liens and encumbrances, is $25,000 or less. 30-day waiting period. Neb. Rev. Stat. § 30-24,125	17
Summary probate for small estates	Value of entire estate, less liens and encumbrances, doesn't exceed homestead allowance, exempt property, family allowance, costs of administration, funeral expenses, and medical expenses of the last illness. Neb. Rev. Stat § 30-24,127	17
Uniform Probate Code	Yes	18
Trustee must send special notice after grantor dies	No	19-21
Trust registration	Yes. Neb. Rev. Stat. §§ 30-2801 and following	19-21
Uniform Prudent Investor Act	Neb. Rev. Stat. §§ 8-2201 and following	20-21
Uniform Principal and Income Act	Neb. Rev. Stat. §§ 30-3116 and following	20-21
State law sets rates lawyers can charge for probate, based on estate value	No	23

Nevada

TOPIC	STATE RULE	CHAPTER
Out-of-state executors or administrators	Nonresident administrator must appoint resident coadministrator. Nev. Rev. Stat. Ann. § 132.040	2, 18
Surviving spouse's allowance rights	Nev. Rev. Stat. Ann. §§ 146.010 and following	5
System of protecting surviving spouse from disinheritance	Community property. Nev. Rev. Stat. Ann. § 123.250	6
Holographic will	Valid. Nev. Rev. Stat. Ann. § 133.090	6
Can will refer to separate memorandum leaving tangible items?	Yes. Nev. Rev. Stat. § 133.045	6
Priority for appointment as administrator (after named executor, if any)	Spouse; children; parents; brothers or sisters; grandchildren; relatives who inherit; public administrator; creditors; other relatives. Nev. Rev. Stat. Ann. § 139.040	7
Intestate succession	Nev. Rev. Stat. Ann. §§ 134.010 and following	7
Uniform Transfers to Minors Act	1. If custodian appointed in will or trust, custodianship ends at age 18-25. 2. If custodian appointed by executor, transfers exceeding $10,000 must be authorized by court, and custodianship ends at age 18. Nev. Rev. Stat. Ann. §§ 167.010 and following	10
State inheritance tax	No	11
State estate tax	No	11
State taxing authority website	http://tax.state.nv.us	11
Community property	Yes	14
Uniform Transfer-on-Death Securities Act	Yes	16
Affidavit procedure for small estates	No Nevada real estate, and gross value of property in Nevada doesn't exceed $20,000. Only surviving spouse, children, grandchildren, parents, or siblings can use affidavits. 40-day waiting period. Nev. Rev. Stat. Ann. § 146.080	17
Summary probate for small estates	1. Gross value of estate doesn't exceed $200,000, if court approves. Nev. Rev. Stat. Ann. §§ 145.020 and following 2. Gross value of estate, less encumbrances, doesn't exceed $75,000. Court can set aside all property for surviving spouse or minor children, or if there are neither, to pay debts. Nev. Rev. Stat. Ann. § 146.070	17
Uniform Probate Code	No	18
Trustee must send special notice after grantor dies	No	19-21
Trust registration	No	19-21
Uniform Prudent Investor Act	No	20-21
Uniform Principal and Income Act	No	20-21
State law sets rates lawyers can charge for probate, based on estate value	No	23

New Hampshire

TOPIC	STATE RULE	CHAPTER
Out-of-state executors or administrators	Nonresident must appoint resident agent. N.H. Rev. Stat. Ann. §§ 553:5 and following	2, 18
Surviving spouse's allowance rights	N.H. Rev. Stat. Ann. §§ 560:1 and following	5
System of protecting surviving spouse from disinheritance	Traditional spousal share. N.H. Rev. Stat. Ann. § 560:10	6
Holographic will	Not valid. N.H. Rev. Stat. Ann. § 551:2	6
Can will refer to separate memorandum leaving tangible items?	No	6
Priority for appointment as administrator (after named executor, if any)	Spouse or next of kin or one one of them nominates; someone who inherits under the will or a creditor. N.H. Rev. Stat. Ann. § 553:2	7
Intestate succession	N.H. Rev. Stat. Ann. § 561:1	7
Uniform Transfers to Minors Act	1. If custodian appointed in will or trust, custodianship ends at age 21. 2. If custodian appointed by executor, transfers exceeding $10,000 must be authorized by court, and custodianship ends at age 18. N.H. Rev. Stat. Ann. §§ 463-A:1	10
State inheritance tax	No	11
State estate tax	No	11
State taxing authority website	www.state.nh.us/revenue	11
Community property	No	14
Uniform Transfer-on-Death Securities Act	Yes	16
Affidavit procedure for small estates	No	17
Summary probate for small estates	No real estate, and gross value of all property doesn't exceed $10,000. N.H. Rev. Stat. Ann. § 553:31	17
Uniform Probate Code	No	18
Trustee must send special notice after grantor dies	No	19-21
Trust registration	No	19-21
Uniform Prudent Investor Act	No	20-21
Uniform Principal and Income Act	No	20-21
State law sets rates lawyers can charge for probate, based on estate value	No	23

New Jersey

TOPIC	STATE RULE	CHAPTER
Out-of-state executors or administrators	Nonresident must post bond unless will waives the requirement. N.J. Stat. Ann. § 3B:15-1	2, 18
Surviving spouse's allowance rights	N.J. Stat. Ann. § 3B:3-30	5
System of protecting surviving spouse from disinheritance	Augmented estate. N.J. Stat. Ann. § 3B:8-1	6
Holographic will	Valid. N.J. Stat. Ann. § 38:3-3	6
Can will refer to separate memorandum leaving tangible items?	No	6
Priority for appointment as administrator (after named executor, if any)	Spouse; other heir. N.J. Stat. Ann. § 3B:10-2	7
Intestate succession	N.J. Stat. Ann. §§ 3B:5-1 and following	7
Uniform Transfers to Minors Act	1. If custodian appointed in will or trust, custodianship ends at age 18 to 21. 2. If custodian appointed by executor, transfers exceeding $10,000 must be authorized by court, and custodianship ends at age 18. N.J. Stat. Ann. §§ 46:38A-1 and following	10
State inheritance tax	Yes. N.J. Stat. Ann. §§ 54:33-1 and following	11
State estate tax	Yes. N.J. Stat. Ann. §§ 54:38-1 and following	11
State taxing authority website	www.state.nj.us/treasury/taxation	11
Community property	No	14
Uniform Transfer-on-Death Securities Act	Yes	16
Affidavit procedure for small estates	No	17
Summary probate for small estates	Two procedures, available only if there is no valid will: 1. If value of all property doesn't exceed $10,000, surviving spouse is entitled to all of it without probate. N.J. Stat. Ann. § 3B:10-3 2. If value of all property doesn't exceed $5,000 and there is no surviving spouse, one heir, with the written consent of the others, can file affidavit with the court and receive all the assets. N.J. Stat. Ann. § 3B:10-4	17
Uniform Probate Code	No	18
Trustee must send special notice after grantor dies	No	19-21
Trust registration	No	19-21
Uniform Prudent Investor Act	N.J. Stat. Ann. § 3B:20-11.1	20-21
Uniform Principal and Income Act	N.J. Stat. Ann. § 3B:19B-1	20-21
State law sets rates lawyers can charge for probate, based on estate value	No	23

New Mexico

TOPIC	STATE RULE	CHAPTER
Out-of-state executors or administrators	No restrictions	2, 18
Surviving spouse's allowance rights	N.M. Stat. Ann. §§ 45-2-402, 403	5
System of protecting surviving spouse from disinheritance	Community property. N.M. Stat. Ann. § 45-2-805	6
Holographic will	Not valid unless valid in the state where it was executed. N.M. Stat. Ann. §§ 45-2-502, 506	6
Can will refer to separate memorandum leaving tangible items?	Yes. N.M. Stat. Ann. § 45-2-513	6
Priority for appointment as administrator (after named executor, if any)	Spouse who inherits under the will; other will beneficiaries; spouse; other heirs; interested person. N.M. Stat. Ann. § 45-3-203	7
Intestate succession	N.M. Stat. Ann. §§ 45-2-101 and following	7
Uniform Transfers to Minors Act	1. If custodian appointed in will or trust, custodianship ends at age 21. 2. If custodian appointed by personal representative, transfers exceeding $10,000 must be authorized by court, and custodianship ends at age 18. N.M. Stat. Ann. §§ 46-7-11 and following	10
State inheritance tax	No	11
State estate tax	No	11
State taxing authority website	www.state.nm.us/tax	11
Community property	Yes	14
Uniform Transfer-on-Death Securities Act	Yes	16
Affidavit procedure for small estates	1. For real estate: If married couple owns principal residence, valued for property tax purposes at $100,000 or less, as community property, surviving spouse may file affidavit with county clerk if no other assets require probate. Six-month waiting period. N.M. Stat. Ann. § 45-3-1205 2. For other property: Value of entire estate, wherever located, less liens and encumbrances, is $30,000 or less. 30-day waiting period. N.M. Stat. Ann. § 45-3-1201	17
Summary probate for small estates	Value of entire estate, less liens and encumbrances, doesn't exceed personal property allowance, family allowance, costs of administration, funeral expenses, and medical expenses of the last illness. N.M. Stat. Ann. § 45-3-1203	17
Uniform Probate Code	Yes	18
Trustee must send special notice after grantor dies	Must notify qualified trust beneficiaries after taking over as trustee. N.M. Stat. Ann. § 46A-8-813	19-21
Trust registration	No	19-21
Uniform Prudent Investor Act	N.M. Stat. Ann. §§ 45-7-601 and following	20-21
Uniform Principal and Income Act	N.M. Stat. Ann. §§ 46-3A-1901 and following	20-21
State law sets rates lawyers can charge for probate, based on estate value	No	23

New York

TOPIC	STATE RULE	CHAPTER
Out-of-state executors or administrators	No restrictions	2, 18
Surviving spouse's allowance rights	N.Y. Est. Powers & Trusts Law § 5-3.1	5
System of protecting surviving spouse from disinheritance	Traditional spousal share. N.Y. Est. Powers & Trusts Law § 5-1.1-A	6
Holographic will	Not valid unless made by (1) member of armed services (or someone who accompanies armed services) during period of armed conflict, in which case it becomes invalid a year after discharge or (2) by mariner at sea, in which case it becomes invalid three years after it is made. N.Y. Est. Powers & Trusts Law § 3-2-2	6
Can will refer to separate memorandum leaving tangible items?	No	6
Priority for appointment as administrator (after named executor, if any)	Spouse; children; grandchildren; parent; brothers or sisters; others who inherit, with preference given to the largest inheritor. N.Y. Surr. Ct. Proc. Act § 1001	7
Intestate succession	N.Y. Est. Powers & Trusts Law § 4-1.1	7
Uniform Transfers to Minors Act	1. If custodian appointed in will or trust, custodianship ends at age 21. 2. If custodian appointed by executor, transfers exceeding $50,000 must be authorized by court, and custodianship ends at age 18. N.Y. Est. Powers & Trusts Law §§ 7-6.1 and following	10
State inheritance tax	No	11
State estate tax	Yes, for estates greater than $1 million. N.Y. Tax Law §§ 152 and following	11
State taxing authority website	www.tax.state.ny.us	11
Community property	No	14
Uniform Transfer-on-Death Securities Act	No	16
Affidavit procedure for small estates	No	17
Summary probate for small estates	Property, excluding real estate and amounts that must be set aside for surviving family members, has a gross value of $20,000 or less. N.Y. Surr. Ct. Proc. Act § 1301	17
Uniform Probate Code	No	18
Trustee must send special notice after grantor dies	No	19-21
Trust registration	No	19-21
Uniform Prudent Investor Act	N.Y. Est. Powers & Trusts Law § 11-2.3	20-21
Uniform Principal and Income Act	N.Y. Est. Powers & Trusts Law §§ 11-A-1.1 and following	20-21
State law sets rates lawyers can charge for probate, based on estate value	No	23

North Carolina

TOPIC	STATE RULE	CHAPTER
Out-of-state executors or administrators	Nonresident must appoint resident agent. N.C. Gen. Stat. § 28A-4-2	2, 18
Surviving spouse's allowance rights	N.C. Const. Art. X, § 2	5
System of protecting surviving spouse from disinheritance	Traditional spousal share. N.C. Gen. Stat. § 30-3	6
Holographic will	Valid only if found after the death in place intended for safekeeping. N.C. Gen. Stat. § 31-3.4	6
Can will refer to separate memorandum leaving tangible items?	No	6
Priority for appointment as administrator (after named executor, if any)	Spouse; anyone who inherits under the will; any heir; any next of kin; any creditor. N.C. Gen. Stat. § 28A-4-1	7
Intestate succession	N.C. Gen. Stat. §§ 29-1 and following	7
Uniform Transfers to Minors Act	1. If custodian appointed in will or trust, custodianship ends at age 18-21. 2. If custodian appointed by executor, Transfers exceeding $10,000 or to the executor as custodian must be authorized by court, and custodianship ends at age 18. N.C. Gen. Stat. §§ 33A-1 and following	10
State inheritance tax	No	11
State estate tax	Yes. N.C. Gen. Stat. § 105-32.2	11
State taxing authority website	www.dor.state.nc.us	11
Community property	No	14
Uniform Transfer-on-Death Securities Act	No	16
Affidavit procedure for small estates	No	17
Summary probate for small estates	Value of personal property, less liens and encumbrances, is $10,000 or less ($20,000 if the surviving spouse is the sole heir). N.C. Gen. Stat. §§ 28A-25-1 and following	17
Uniform Probate Code	No	18
Trustee must send special notice after grantor dies	No	19-21
Trust registration	No	19-21
Uniform Prudent Investor Act	N.C. Gen. Stat. § 36A-161	20-21
Uniform Principal and Income Act	No	20-21
State law sets rates lawyers can charge for probate, based on estate value	No	23

North Dakota

TOPIC	STATE RULE	CHAPTER
Out-of-state executors or administrators	No restrictions	2, 18
Surviving spouse's allowance rights	N.D. Cent. Code §§ 47-18-01, 30.1-07-02	5
System of protecting surviving spouse from disinheritance	Augmented estate. N.D. Cent. Code § 30.1-05-01	6
Holographic will	Valid. N.D. Cent. Code § 30.1-08-02	6
Can will refer to separate memorandum leaving tangible items?	Yes. N.D. Cent. Code 30.1-08-13	6
Priority for appointment as administrator (after named executor, if any)	Spouse who inherits under will; other person who inherits under will; spouse; other heirs; a trust company; after 45 days, creditors. N.D. Cent. Code § 30.1-13-03	7
Intestate succession	N.D. Cent. Code §§ 30.1-04-02, 03	7
Uniform Transfers to Minors Act	1. If custodian appointed in will or trust, custodianship ends at age 21. 2. If custodian appointed by personal representative, transfers exceeding $10,000 must be authorized by court, and custodianship ends at age 18. N.D. Cent. Code §§ 47-24.1-01 and following	10
State inheritance tax	No	11
State estate tax	No	11
State taxing authority website	www.state.nd.us/taxdpt	11
Community property	No	14
Uniform Transfer-on-Death Securities Act	Yes	16
Affidavit procedure for small estates	Value of entire estate subject to probate, less liens and encumbrances, is $15,000 or less. 30-day waiting period. N.D. Cent. Code § 30.1-23-01	17
Summary probate for small estates	Value of the entire estate, less liens and encumbrances, does not exceed the homestead, plus exempt property, family allowance, costs of administration, funeral expenses, and medical expenses of the last illness. N.D. Cent. Code § 30.1-23-03	17
Uniform Probate Code	Yes	18
Trustee must send special notice after grantor dies	No	19-21
Trust registration	Yes. N.D. Cent. Code § 30.1-32-01	19-21
Uniform Prudent Investor Act	N.D. Cent. Code §§ 59-02-08.1 and following	20-21
Uniform Principal and Income Act	N.D. Cent. Code §§ 59-04.2.1 and following	20-21
State law sets rates lawyers can charge for probate, based on estate value	No	23

Ohio

TOPIC	STATE RULE	CHAPTER
Out-of-state executors or administrators	Nonresidents may not be administrators. Nonresidents may be executors if they are nominated in the will and they are either related to the deceased person or live in a state that allows nonresident executors. Ohio Rev. Code Ann. § 2109.21	2, 18
Surviving spouse's allowance rights	Ohio Rev. Code Ann. §§ 2106.01, 2106.10 and following	5
System of protecting surviving spouse from disinheritance	Traditional spousal share. Ohio Rev. Code Ann. § 2106.01	6
Holographic will	Not valid. Ohio Rev. Code Ann. § 2107.03	6
Can will refer to separate memorandum leaving tangible items?	No	6
Priority for appointment as administrator (after named executor, if any)	Spouse if state resident; one of next of kin if state resident. Ohio Rev. Code Ann. § 2113.06	7
Intestate succession	Ohio Rev. Code Ann. § 2105.06	7
Uniform Transfers to Minors Act	If custodian appointed in will or trust, custodianship ends at age 18-21. Ohio Rev. Code Ann. §§ 1339.39 and following	10
State inheritance tax	No	11
State estate tax	Yes. Ohio Rev. Code Ann. §§ 5731.21 and following	11
State taxing authority website	http://tax.ohio.gov	11
Community property	No	14
Uniform Transfer-on-Death Securities Act	Yes	16
Affidavit procedure for small estates	No	17
Summary probate for small estates	Available if either: • value of the estate is $35,000 or less, or • surviving spouse inherits everything, either under a will or by law, and value of the estate is $100,000 or less. Ohio Rev. Code Ann. § 2113.03	17
Uniform Probate Code	No	18
Trustee must send special notice after grantor dies	No	19-21
Trust registration	Yes. If trust holds real estate, trustee must file an affidavit in the county where real estate is located. Affidavit must contain names and addresses of all trustees, a reference to the deed that transferred the real estate to the trustee, and a legal description of the property. Ohio Rev. Code Ann. § 5302.171	19-21
Uniform Prudent Investor Act	Ohio Rev. Code Ann. §§ 1339.52 and following	20-21
Uniform Principal and Income Act	Ohio Rev. Code Ann. §§ 1340.40 and following	20-21
State law sets rates lawyers can charge for probate, based on estate value	No	23

Oklahoma

TOPIC	STATE RULE	CHAPTER
Out-of-state executors or administrators	Nonresident executor must appoint an agent living in the county where the probate is conducted. Okla. Stat. Ann. tit. 58, § 162	2, 18
Surviving spouse's allowance rights	Okla. Stat. Ann. tit. 58, §§ 311 and following	5
System of protecting surviving spouse from disinheritance	Traditional spousal share. Okla. Stat. Ann. tit. 84, § 44	6
Holographic will	Valid. Okla. Stat. Ann. tit. 84, § 54	6
Can will refer to separate memorandum leaving tangible items?	No	6
Priority for appointment as administrator (after named executor, if any)	Spouse or person spouse nominates; children; mother or father; brother or sister; grandchildren; next of kin entitled to inherit; creditors. If deceased was member of a partnership, surviving partner may not be appointed. Okla. Stat. Ann. tit. 58, § 122	7
Intestate succession	Okla. Stat. Ann. tit. 84, §§ 212 and following	7
Uniform Transfers to Minors Act	1. If custodian appointed in will or trust, custodianship ends at age 18-21. 2. If custodian appointed by executor, transfers exceeding $10,000 must be authorized by court, and custodianship ends at age 18. Okla. Stat. Ann. tit. 58, §§ 1201 and following	10
State inheritance tax	No	11
State estate tax	Yes. Okla. Stat. Ann. tit. 68, §§ 802 and following	11
State taxing authority website	www.oktax.state.ok.us	11
Community property	No	14
Uniform Transfer-on-Death Securities Act	Yes	16
Affidavit procedure for small estates	No	17
Summary probate for small estates	Available if value of estate is $60,000 or less. Okla. Stat. Ann tit. 58, § 241	17
Uniform Probate Code	No	18
Trustee must send special notice after grantor dies	No	19-21
Trust registration	No	19-21
Uniform Prudent Investor Act	Okla. Stat. Ann. tit. 60, §§ 175.60 and following	20-21
Uniform Principal and Income Act	Okla. Stat. Ann. tit. 60, §§ 175.101 and following	20-21
State law sets rates lawyers can charge for probate, based on estate value	No	23

Oregon

TOPIC	STATE RULE	CHAPTER
Out-of-state executors or administrators	No restrictions	2, 18
Surviving spouse's allowance rights	Or. Rev. Stat. § 114.005 and following	5
System of protecting surviving spouse from disinheritance	Traditional spousal share. Or. Rev. Stat. §§ 114.105, 114.125	6
Holographic will	Not valid. Or. Rev. Stat. § 112.235	6
Can will refer to separate memorandum leaving tangible items?	No	6
Priority for appointment as administrator (after named executor, if any)	Spouse or person spouse nominates; nearest next of kin or person he or she nominates; if deceased person received public assistance and there is a claim for it against the estate, the Director of Human Services; if deceased person was a veteran and a protected person under state law, the Director of Veterans' Affairs. Or. Rev. Stat. § 113.085	7
Intestate succession	Or. Rev. Stat. §§ 112.025 and following	7
Uniform Transfers to Minors Act	1. If custodian appointed in will or trust, custodianship ends at age 21-25. 2. If custodian appointed by executor, transfers exceeding $30,000 must be authorized by court, and custodianship ends at age 21. Or. Rev. Stat. §§ 126.805 and following	10
State inheritance tax	No	11
State estate tax	Yes (but called inheritance tax) Or. Rev. Stat. § 118.160	11
State taxing authority website	www.dor.state.or.us	11
Community property	No	14
Uniform Transfer-on-Death Securities Act	Yes	16
Affidavit procedure for small estates	No	17
Summary probate for small estates	Fair market value of the estate is $140,000 or less, and not more than $50,000 of the estate is personal property and not more than $90,000 is real estate. Or. Rev. Stat. §§ 114.505 and following	17
Uniform Probate Code	No	18
Trustee must send special notice after grantor dies	No	19-21
Trust registration	No	19-21
Uniform Prudent Investor Act	Or. Rev. Stat. §§ 128.192 and following	20-21
Uniform Principal and Income Act	Yes. 2003 Oregon Laws ch. 279	20-21
State law sets rates lawyers can charge for probate, based on estate value	No	23

Pennsylvania

TOPIC	STATE RULE	CHAPTER
Out-of-state executors or administrators	Probate register may refuse to allow a nonresident to serve as administrator. 20 Pa. Cons. Stat. Ann. § 3157	2, 18
Surviving spouse's allowance rights	20 Pa. Cons. Stat. Ann. § 3121	5
System of protecting surviving spouse from disinheritance	Traditional spousal share. 20 Pa. Cons. Stat. Ann. § 2203	6
Holographic will	Valid. 20 Pa. Cons. Stat. Ann. §§ 2502, 2504.1	6
Can will refer to separate memorandum leaving tangible items?	No	6
Priority for appointment as administrator (after named executor, if any)	Those who inherit residuary estate; spouse; people who inherit under intestate law, with preference for those who inherit the largest share; creditors. Any of these people who declines may nominate someone else. If none of the above are available and the deceased was incapacitated and under a guardianship, a guardianship support agency. 20 Pa. Cons. Stat. Ann. § 3155	7
Intestate succession	20 Pa. Cons. Stat. Ann. §§ 2102 and following	7
Uniform Transfers to Minors Act	1. If custodian appointed in will or trust, custodianship ends at age 21-25. 2. If custodian appointed by executor, transfers exceeding $25,000 must be approved by court, and custodianship ends at age 18. 20 Pa. Cons. Stat. Ann. §§ 5301 and following	10
State inheritance tax	72 Pa. Cons. Stat. Ann. §§ 9101 and following	11
State estate tax	No	11
State taxing authority website	www.revenue.state.pa.us/revenue/site/default.asp	11
Community property	No	14
Uniform Transfer-on-Death Securities Act	Yes	16
Affidavit procedure for small estates	No	17
Summary probate for small estates	Property (not counting real estate, certain payments the family is entitled to, and funeral costs) is worth $25,000 or less. 20 Pa. Cons. Stat. Ann. § 3102	17
Uniform Probate Code	No	18
Trustee must send special notice after grantor dies	No	19-21
Trust registration	No	19-21
Uniform Prudent Investor Act	20 Pa. Cons. Stat. Ann. §§ 7201 and following	20-21
Uniform Principal and Income Act	20 Pa. Cons. Stat. Ann. §§ 8101 and following	20-21
State law sets rates lawyers can charge for probate, based on estate value	No	23

Rhode Island

TOPIC	STATE RULE	CHAPTER
Out-of-state executors or administrators	Nonresident must appoint resident agent. R.I. Gen. Laws § 33-18-9	2, 18
Surviving spouse's allowance rights	R.I. Gen. Laws §§ 33-10-1 and following	5
System of protecting surviving spouse from disinheritance	Traditional spousal share. R.I. Gen. Laws §§ 33-35-2 to 33-35-5	6
Holographic will	Not valid unless valid in the state where it was executed or if made by soldier in actual military service or mariner at sea. R.I. Gen. Laws §§ 33-5-5, 33-5-6, 33-5-7	6
Can will refer to separate memorandum leaving tangible items?	No	6
Priority for appointment as administrator (after named executor, if any)	If no will: spouse or next of kin or both; R.I. Gen. Laws § 33-8-8. If there is a will but executor cannot serve: some suitable person. R.I. Gen. Laws § 33-8-4	7
Intestate succession	R.I. Gen. Laws §§ 33-1-5 and following	7
Uniform Transfers to Minors Act	1. If custodian appointed in will or trust, custodianship ends at age 21. 2. If custodian appointed by executor, transfers exceeding $10,000 must be authorized by court, and custodianship ends at age 18. R.I. Gen. Laws §§ 18-7-1 and followiing	10
State inheritance tax	No	11
State estate tax	R.I. Gen. Laws §§ 44-22-1 and following	11
State taxing authority website	www.tax.state.ri.us	11
Community property	No	14
Uniform Transfer-on-Death Securities Act	Yes	16
Affidavit procedure for small estates	No	17
Summary probate for small estates	No real estate, and value of property that would be subject to probate (not counting tangible personal property) doesn't exceed $15,000. R.I. Gen. Laws § 33-24-1	17
Uniform Probate Code	No	18
Trustee must send special notice after grantor dies	No	19-21
Trust registration	No	19-21
Uniform Prudent Investor Act	R.I. Gen. Laws §§ 18-15-1 and following	20-21
Uniform Principal and Income Act	No	20-21
State law sets rates lawyers can charge for probate, based on estate value	No	23

South Carolina

TOPIC	STATE RULE	CHAPTER
Out-of-state executors or administrators	No restrictions	2, 18
Surviving spouse's allowance rights	S.C. Code Ann. §§ 15-41-30, 62-2-401	5
System of protecting surviving spouse from disinheritance	Traditional spousal share. S.C. Code Ann. § 62-2-201	6
Holographic will	Not valid unless valid in the state where it was executed. S.C. Code Ann. §§ 62-2-502, 62-2-505	6
Can will refer to separate memorandum leaving tangible items?	Yes. S.C. Code Ann. § 62-2-512	6
Priority for appointment as administrator (after named executor, if any)	Spouse who inherits under the will; other person who inherits under the will; spouse; other heirs; 45 days after the death, creditors. S.C. Code Ann. § 62-3-203	7
Intestate succession	S.C. Code Ann. §§ 62-2-101 and following	7
Uniform Transfers to Minors Act	No	10
State inheritance tax	No	11
State estate tax	No	11
State taxing authority website	www.sctax.org/default.htm	11
Community property	No	14
Uniform Transfer-on-Death Securities Act	Yes	16
Affidavit procedure for small estates	Value of property passing by will or under law, less liens and encumbrances, is $10,000 or less. Probate judge must approve affidavit. 30-day waiting period. S.C. Code Ann. § 62-3-1201	17
Summary probate for small estates	Value of property passing by will or under law, less liens and encumbrances, is $10,000 or less (not counting exempt property, funeral expenses, and medical expenses of last illness). S.C. Code Ann. § 62-3-1203	17
Uniform Probate Code	Yes	18
Trustee must send special notice after grantor dies	Yes. S.C. Code Ann. § 62-7-303	19-21
Trust registration	No	19-21
Uniform Prudent Investor Act	S.C. Code Ann. §§ 62-7-302 and following	20-21
Uniform Principal and Income Act	S.C. Code Ann. §§ 62-7-401 and following	20-21
State law sets rates lawyers can charge for probate, based on estate value	No	23

South Dakota

TOPIC	STATE RULE	CHAPTER
Out-of-state executors or administrators	No restrictions	2, 18
Surviving spouse's allowance rights	S.D. Codified Laws Ann. §§ 29A-2-402, 43-31-13, 43-45-3 and following	5
System of protecting surviving spouse from disinheritance	Augmented estate. S.D. Codified Laws Ann. § 29A-2-202	6
Holographic will	Valid. S.D. Codified Laws Ann. § 29A-2-502	6
Can will refer to separate memorandum leaving tangible items?	Yes. S.D. Codified Laws § 29A-2-513	6
Priority for appointment as administrator (after named executor, if any)	Spouse who inherits under the will; other person who inherits under the will; spouse; other heirs; 45 days after the death, any qualified person. S.D. Codified Laws Ann. § 29A-3-203	7
Intestate succession	S.D. Codified Laws Ann. § 29A-2-102 and following	7
Uniform Transfers to Minors Act	1. If custodian appointed in will or trust, custodianship ends at age 18. 2. If custodian appointed by personal representative, transfers exceeding $10,000 must be authorized by court, and custodianship ends at age 18. S.D. Codified Laws Ann. §§ 55-10A-1 and following	10
State inheritance tax	No	11
State estate tax	No	11
State taxing authority website	www.state.sd.us/drr2/revenue.html	11
Community property	No	14
Uniform Transfer-on-Death Securities Act	Yes	16
Affidavit procedure for small estates	Value of entire estate, less liens and encumbrances, is $50,000 or less. S.D. Codified Laws §§ 29A-3-1201 and following	17
Summary probate for small estates	"Informal probate" available regardless of value of estate. 30-day waiting period. S.D. Codified Laws Ann. §§ 29A-3-301 and following	17
Uniform Probate Code	Yes	18
Trustee must send special notice after grantor dies	No	19-21
Trust registration	No	19-21
Uniform Prudent Investor Act	No, but follows prudent investor rule. S.D. Codified Laws Ann. §§ 55-5-7 and following	20-21
Uniform Principal and Income Act	No	20-21
State law sets rates lawyers can charge for probate, based on estate value	No	23

Tennessee

TOPIC	STATE RULE	CHAPTER
Out-of-state executors or administrators	Nonresident spouse, issue, parent, grandparent or issue of a grandparent of the deceased person or of the deceased person's spouse, or the spouse of any such relative, may serve; and any other nonresident may serve if the court approves. Nonresident must appoint resident personal representative to serve with him or her. Tenn. Code Ann. § 35-50-107	2, 18
Surviving spouse's allowance rights	Tenn. Code Ann. §§ 30-2-102, 31-1-104	5
System of protecting surviving spouse from disinheritance	Traditional spousal share. Tenn. Code Ann. § 31-4-101	6
Holographic will	Valid. Tenn. Code Ann. § 32-1-105	6
Can will refer to separate memorandum leaving tangible items?	No	6
Priority for appointment as administrator (after named executor, if any)	Spouse; next of kin; creditor. Tenn. Code Ann. § 30-1-106	7
Intestate succession	Tenn. Code Ann. §§ 31-2-101 and following	7
Uniform Transfers to Minors Act	1. If custodian appointed in will or trust, custodianship ends at age 21-25. 2. If custodian appointed by executor, transfers exceeding $25,000 must be authorized by court, and custodianship ends at age 21-25. Tenn. Code Ann. §§ 35-7-201 and following	10
State inheritance tax	Tenn. Code Ann. §§ 67-8-201 and following	11
State estate tax	No	11
State taxing authority website	www.state.tn.us/revenue	11
Community property	No	14
Uniform Transfer-on-Death Securities Act	Yes	16
Affidavit procedure for small estates	No	17
Summary probate for small estates	Value of property, not counting property held jointly with right of survivorship or real estate, is $25,000 or less. Tenn. Code Ann. §§ 30-4-102 and following	17
Uniform Probate Code	No	18
Trustee must send special notice after grantor dies	Must notify the life beneficiary and all final beneficiaries of the details of AB trust. Tenn. Code Ann. § 35-50-119	19-21
Trust registration	No	19-21
Uniform Prudent Investor Act	Tenn. Code Ann. §§ 35-14-101 and following	20-21
Uniform Principal and Income Act	Tenn. Code Ann. §§ 35-6-101 and following	20-21
State law sets rates lawyers can charge for probate, based on estate value	No	23

Texas

TOPIC	STATE RULE	CHAPTER
Out-of-state executors or administrators	Nonresident must appoint resident agent. Tex. Prob. Code Ann. § 78	2, 18
Surviving spouse's allowance rights	Tex. Prob. Code Ann. §§ 270, 273, 286 to 292	5
System of protecting surviving spouse from disinheritance	Community property. Tex. Fam. Code Ann. §§ 3.101, 3.102	6
Holographic will	Valid. Tex. Prob. Code Ann. § 60	6
Can will refer to separate memorandum leaving tangible items?	No	6
Priority for appointment as administrator (after named executor, if any)	Spouse; principal inheritor; other inheritor; next of kin; creditor. Tex. Prob. Code Ann. § 77	7
Intestate succession	Tex. Prob. Code Ann. § 38	7
Uniform Transfers to Minors Act	1. If custodian appointed in will or trust, custodianship ends at age 21. 2. If custodian appointed by executor, transfers exceeding $10,000 must be authorized by court, and custodianship ends at age 18. Tex. Prop. Code Ann. §§ 141.001 and following	10
State inheritance tax	No	11
State estate tax	No	11
State taxing authority website	www.cpa.state.tx.us	11
Community property	Yes	14
Uniform Transfer-on-Death Securities Act	No	16
Affidavit procedure for small estates	There is no will, and value of entire estate, not including homestead and exempt property, is $50,000 or less. Probate judge must approve affidavit. Can be used to transfer homestead, but no other real estate. 30-day waiting period. Tex. Prob. Code Ann. § 137	17
Summary probate for small estates	1. Value of property doesn't exceed that needed to pay family allowance and certain creditors. Tex. Prob. Code Ann. § 143 2. "Independent administration" available, regardless of value of estate, if requested in the will or all inheritors agree to it. Tex. Prob. Code Ann. § 145	17
Uniform Probate Code	No	18
Trustee must send special notice after grantor dies	No	19-21
Trust registration	No	19-21
Uniform Prudent Investor Act	Tex. Prop. Code Ann. §§ 117.001 and following	20-21
Uniform Principal and Income Act	Tex. Prop. Code Ann. §§ 116.001 and following	20-21
State law sets rates lawyers can charge for probate, based on estate value	No	23

Utah

TOPIC	STATE RULE	CHAPTER
Out-of-state executors or administrators	No restrictions	2, 18
Surviving spouse's allowance rights	Utah Code Ann. §§ 75-2-402 and following	5
System of protecting surviving spouse from disinheritance	Augmented estate. Utah Code Ann. § 75-2-202	6
Holographic will	Valid. Utah Code Ann. § 75-2-502	6
Can will refer to separate memorandum leaving tangible items?	Yes. Utah Code Ann. § 75-2-513	6
Priority for appointment as administrator (after named executor, if any)	Spouse who inherits under the will; other person who inherits under the will; spouse; other heirs; 45 days after the death, creditor. Utah Code Ann. § 75-3-203	7
Intestate succession	Utah Code Ann. §§ 75-2-102 and following	7
Uniform Transfers to Minors Act	1. If custodian appointed in will or trust, custodianship ends at age 21. 2. If custodian appointed by personal representative, transfers exceeding $10,000 must be authorized by court, and custodianship ends at age 18. Utah Code Ann. § 75-5a-101	10
State inheritance tax	No	11
State estate tax	No	11
State taxing authority website	http://tax.utah.gov	11
Community property	No	14
Uniform Transfer-on-Death Securities Act	Yes	16
Affidavit procedure for small estates	Value of entire estate subject to probate, less liens and encumbrances, is $25,000 or less. May also transfer up to four boats, motor vehicles, trailers or semi-trailers if value of estate subject to probate, excluding the value of the vehicles, is $25,000 or less. 30-day waiting period. Utah Code Ann. § 75-3-1201	17
Summary probate for small estates	Value of entire estate, less liens and encumbrances, does not exceed the homestead allowance, exempt property, family allowance, costs of administration, funeral expenses, and medical expenses of the last illness. Utah Code Ann. § 75-3-1203	17
Uniform Probate Code	Yes	18
Trustee must send special notice after grantor dies	No	19-21
Trust registration	No	19-21
Uniform Prudent Investor Act	Utah Code Ann. §§ 75-7-302 and following	20-21
Uniform Principal and Income Act	Utah Code Ann. §§ 22-3-1 and following	20-21
State law sets rates lawyers can charge for probate, based on estate value	No	23

Vermont

TOPIC	STATE RULE	CHAPTER
Out-of-state executors or administrators	Court may in its discretion appoint nonresident executor. Court may not appoint nonresident administrator unless requested to do so by the deceased person's spouse, adult children, parents, or guardian, in that order. Nonresident must appoint resident person as agent. Vt. Stat. Ann. tit. 14, § 904	2, 18
Surviving spouse's allowance rights	Vt. Stat. Ann. tit. 14, §§ 461, 462	5
System of protecting surviving spouse from disinheritance	Traditional spousal share. Vt. Stat. Ann. tit. 14, § 402	6
Holographic will	Not valid. Vt. Stat. Ann., tit. 14, § 5	6
Can will refer to separate memorandum leaving tangible items?	No	6
Priority for appointment as administrator (after named executor, if any)	Spouse, next of kin, or both; person spouse or next of kin nominates; after 30 days, a principal creditor. Vt. Stat. Ann. tit. 14, § 903	7
Intestate succession	Vt. Stat. Ann. tit. 14, §§ 401 and following	7
Uniform Transfers to Minors Act	No	10
State inheritance tax	No	11
State estate tax	Vt. Stat. Ann. tit. 32, §§ 7442a and following	11
State taxing authority website	www.state.vt.us./tax	11
Community property	No	14
Uniform Transfer-on-Death Securities Act	Yes	16
Affidavit procedure for small estates	No	17
Summary probate for small estates	Deceased is survived by a spouse or children and owned no real estate, and value of personal property is $10,000 or less. Vt. Stat. Ann., tit. 14, § 1902	17
Uniform Probate Code	No	18
Trustee must send special notice after grantor dies	No	19-21
Trust registration	No	19-21
Uniform Prudent Investor Act	Vt. Stat. Ann., tit. 9. §§ 4651 and following	20-21
Uniform Principal and Income Act	Vt. Stat. Ann., tit. 14, §§ 3301 and following	20-21
State law sets rates lawyers can charge for probate, based on estate value	No	23

Virginia

TOPIC	STATE RULE	CHAPTER
Out-of-state executors or administrators	Nonresident must appoint probate court clerk or other resident as agent. Va. Code Ann. § 26-59	2, 18
Surviving spouse's allowance rights	Va. Code Ann §§ 64.1-151.1, 64.1-16.4	5
System of protecting surviving spouse from disinheritance	Traditional spousal share. Va. Code Ann. § 64.1-16	6
Holographic will	Valid. Va. Code Ann. § 64.1-49	6
Can will refer to separate memorandum leaving tangible items?	Yes. Va. Code Ann. § 64.1-45.1	6
Priority for appointment as administrator (after named executor, if any)	During first 30 days after death, sole inheritor or person he or she nominates; any inheritor (or person he or she nominates) who gets agreement of other inheritors. After 30 days, the first inheritor who requests it. After 60 days, creditor or other person. Va. Code Ann. § 64.1-118	7
Intestate succession	Va. Code Ann. §§ 64.1-1, 64.1-11	7
Uniform Transfers to Minors Act	1. If custodian appointed in will or trust, custodianship ends at age 18-21. 2. If custodian appointed by executor, transfers exceeding $10,000 must be authorized by court, and custodianship ends at age 18. Va. Code Ann. §§ 31-37 and following	10
State inheritance tax	No	11
State estate tax	Yes. Va. Code Ann. §§ 58.1-902 and following	11
State taxing authority website	www.tax.state.va.us	11
Community property	No	14
Uniform Transfer-on-Death Securities Act	Yes	16
Affidavit procedure for small estates	1. Entire personal probate estate $15,000 or less. Will, if any, must be filed with probate court. 60-day waiting period. Va. Code Ann. § 64.1-132.2 2. Amounts of less than $15,000 that are owed the decedent for wages, union death benefits, state or federal benefits, or from a trust or estate; vessels registered with the U.S. Bureau of Customs; and securities worth less than $15,000 can be transferred to surviving spouse or inheritors without probate. 60-day waiting period. Va. Code Ann. §§ 64.1-123 and following	17
Summary probate for small estates	No	17
Uniform Probate Code	No	18
Trustee must send special notice after grantor dies	No	19-21
Trust registration	No	19-21
Uniform Prudent Investor Act	Va. Code Ann. §§ 26-45.3 and following	20-21
Uniform Principal and Income Act	Va. Code Ann. §§ 55-277.5 and following	20-21
State law sets rates lawyers can charge for probate, based on estate value	No	23

Washington

TOPIC	STATE RULE	CHAPTER
Out-of-state executors or administrators	Nonresident must appoint as agent someone who lives in the county where the probate court proceeding is conducted. Wash. Rev. Code Ann. 11.36.010	2, 18
Surviving spouse's allowance rights	Wash. Rev. Code Ann. §§ 11.54.020 and following	5
System of protecting surviving spouse from disinheritance	Community property. Wash. Rev. Code Ann. §§ 11.02.070, 26.16.220, 26.16.230	6
Holographic will	Not valid unless valid in the state where it was executed. Wash. Rev. Code Ann. § 11.12.020	6
Can will refer to separate memorandum leaving tangible items?	Yes. Wash. Rev. Code § 11.12.260	6
Priority for appointment as administrator (after named executor, if any)	Spouse or person he or she chooses; next of kin in this order: children, parents, brothers or sisters, grandchildren, nephews or nieces; trustee named in living trust instrument or will, guardian of the deceased person's estate or person, or attorney in fact appointed by deceased person, if any of them controlled substantially all of the deceased person's assets; someone who inherits; director of revenue if deceased person's property is going to the state; one or more principal creditors. Wash. Rev. Code § 11.28.120. For community property: for 40 days after death, spouse. Wash. Rev. Code § 11.28.030.	7
Intestate succession	Wash. Rev. Code Ann. § 11.04.015	7
Uniform Transfers to Minors Act	1. If custodian appointed in will or trust, custodianship ends at age 21. 2. If custodian appointed by executor, transfers exceeding $30,000 must be authorized by court, and custodianship ends at age 18. Wash. Rev. Code Ann. §§ 11.114.010 and following	10
State inheritance tax	No	11
State estate tax	Yes. Wash. Rev. Code Ann. §§ 83.100.010 and following	11
State taxing authority website	http://dor.wa.gov	11
Community property	Yes	14
Uniform Transfer-on-Death Securities Act	Yes	16
Affidavit procedure for small estates	Value of assets subject to probate, not counting surviving spouse's community property interest, less liens and encumbrances, is $60,000 or less. 40-day waiting period. Wash. Rev. Code §§ 11.62.010 and following	17
Summary probate for small estates	Solvent estates of any size. Wash. Rev. Code Ann. §§ 11.68.011 and following	17
Uniform Probate Code	No	18
Trustee must send special notice after grantor dies	No	19-21
Trust registration	No	19-21
Uniform Prudent Investor Act	Wash. Rev. Code Ann. §§ 11.100.010 and following	20-21
Uniform Principal and Income Act	Wash. Rev. Code Ann. §§ 11.104A.101 and following	20-21
State law sets rates lawyers can charge for probate, based on estate value	No	23

West Virginia

TOPIC	STATE RULE	CHAPTER
Out-of-state executors or administrators	Clerk of the county commission of the county where the probate is conducted serves as a nonresident's agent. W. Va. Code Ann. § 44-5-3(c)	2, 18
Surviving spouse's allowance rights	W. Va. Const. Art. 6, § 48, W. Va. Code Ann. § 44-1-17	5
System of protecting surviving spouse from disinheritance	Augmented estate. W. Va. Code Ann. § 42-3-1	6
Holographic will	Valid. W. Va. Code § 41-1-3	6
Can will refer to separate memorandum leaving tangible items?	No	6
Priority for appointment as administrator (after named executor, if any)	Spouse; someone who inherits; after 30 days, creditors or other persons. W. Va. Code § 44-1-4	7
Intestate succession	W. Va. Code §§ 42-1-3, 42-1-3a	7
Uniform Transfers to Minors Act	1. If custodian appointed in will or trust, custodianship ends at age 21. 2. If custodian appointed by executor, transfers exceeding $10,000 must be authorized by court, and custodianship ends at age 18. W. Va. Code §§ 36-7-1 and following	10
State inheritance tax	No	11
State estate tax	No	11
State taxing authority website	www.state.wv.us/taxdiv	11
Community property	No	14
Uniform Transfer-on-Death Securities Act	Yes	16
Affidavit procedure for small estates	No	17
Summary probate for small estates	Value of estate, not counting real estate, is $100,000 or less; or if the personal representative is the sole beneficiary of the estate; or if surviving spouse is the sole beneficiary of the estate; or if all the beneficiaries state that no disputes are likely, there are enough assets to pay debts and taxes, and the executor agrees. W. Va. Code § 44-3A-5	17
Uniform Probate Code	No	18
Trustee must send special notice after grantor dies	No	19-21
Trust registration	No	19-21
Uniform Prudent Investor Act	W. Va. Code §§ 44-6C-1 and following	20-21
Uniform Principal and Income Act	W. Va. Code §§ 48B-1-101 and following	20-21
State law sets rates lawyers can charge for probate, based on estate value	No	23

Wisconsin

TOPIC	STATE RULE	CHAPTER
Out-of-state executors or administrators	Nonresident must appoint resident agent. Wis. Stat. Ann. § 856.23.	2, 18
Surviving spouse's allowance rights	Wis. Stat. Ann. §§ 861.31 and following	5
System of protecting surviving spouse from disinheritance	Marital (community) property. Wis. Stat. Ann. §§ 861.01, 861.02	6
Holographic will	Not valid unless valid in the state where it was executed. Wis. Stat. Ann. §§ 853.03, 853.05	6
Can will refer to separate memorandum leaving tangible items?	Yes. Wis. Stat. Ann. § 853.32	6
Priority for appointment as administrator (after named executor, if any)	Any person interested in the estate or a person he or she nominates; after 30 days, the guardian of the deceased person, any creditor, anyone with a cause of action against the estate, or anyone who has in interest in property that may be in the estate. Wis. Stat. Ann. §§, 856.07, 856.21	7
Intestate succession	Wis. Stat. Ann. § 852.01	7
Uniform Transfers to Minors Act	1. If custodian appointed in will or trust, custodianship ends at age 21. 2. If custodian appointed by executor, transfers exceeding $10,000 must be authorized by court, and custodianship ends at age 18. Wis. Stat. Ann. §§ 880.61 and following	10
State inheritance tax	No	11
State estate tax	Yes. Wis. Stat. Ann. §§ 72.02 and following	11
State taxing authority website	www.dor.state.wi.us	11
Community property	Yes (marital property)	14
Uniform Transfer-on-Death Securities Act	Yes	16
Affidavit procedure for small estates	Decedent's solely owned property in Wisconsin is worth $20,000 or less. Wis. Stat. Ann. § 867.03	17
Summary probate for small estates	Value of estate, less mortgages and encumbrances, is $50,000 or less and decedent is survived by a spouse or minor children. Also available if value of estate, less mortgages and encumbrances, does not exceed costs, expenses, allowances, and claims. Wis. Stat. Ann. § 867.01	17
Uniform Probate Code	No	18
Trustee must send special notice after grantor dies	No	19-21
Trust registration	No	19-21
Uniform Prudent Investor Act	No	20-21
Uniform Principal and Income Act	No	20-21
State law sets rates lawyers can charge for probate, based on estate value	No	23

Wyoming

TOPIC	STATE RULE	CHAPTER
Out-of-state executors or administrators	Nonresident must appoint resident agent. Wyo. Stat. § 2-11-301	2, 18
Surviving spouse's allowance rights	Wyo. Stat. §§ 2-5-501 and following	5
System of protecting surviving spouse from disinheritance	Traditional spousal share. Wyo. Stat. § 2-5-101	6
Holographic will	Valid. Wyo. Stat. § 2-6-113	6
Can will refer to separate memorandum leaving tangible items?	Yes. Wyo. Stat. § 2-6-124	6
Priority for appointment as administrator (after named executor, if any)	Spouse or person spouse nominates; children; parents; brothers or sisters; grandchildren; next of kin; creditors. Relatives are entitled to appointment only if they inherit. Wyo. Stat. § 2-4-201	7
Intestate succession	Wyo. Stat. §§ 2-4-101 and following	7
Uniform Transfers to Minors Act	1. If custodian appointed in will or trust, custodianship ends at age 21. 2. If custodian appointed by executor, transfers exceeding $10,000 must be authorized by court, and custodianship ends at age 18. Wyo. Stat. § 34-13-114	10
State inheritance tax	No	11
State estate tax	No	11
State taxing authority website	http://revenue.state.wy.us	11
Community property	No	14
Uniform Transfer-on-Death Securities Act	Yes	16
Affidavit procedure for small estates	Value of entire estate, less liens and encumbrances, is $150,000 or less. Must file affidavit with county clerk. 30-day waiting period. Wyo. Stat. § 2-1-201	17
Summary probate for small estates	Value of entire estate, including real estate and mineral interests, is $150,000 or less. Wyo. Stat. § 2-1-205	17
Uniform Probate Code	No	18
Trustee must send special notice after grantor dies	Must notify qualified trust beneficiaries. Wyo. Stat. § 4-10-813	19-21
Trust registration	No	19-21
Uniform Prudent Investor Act	Wyo. Stat. Ann. §§ 4-9-101 and following	20-21
Uniform Principal and Income Act	Wyo. Stat. Ann. §§2-3-801 and following	20-21
State law sets rates lawyers can charge for probate, based on estate value	Yes. Wyo. Stat. § 2-7-804	23

Glossary

If you don't find a term here, consult www.nolo.com, another online legal dictionary (see Chapter 22), or a printed legal dictionary.

AB trust. See "Bypass trust."

Abatement. A reduction in one or more gifts left in a will. Abatement is necessary if the deceased person didn't leave enough property to fulfill all the bequests made in the will and also pay taxes and debts, which are higher-priority obligations.

Ademption. The failure of a gift made in a will because the will-maker no longer owns the property at death. Usually, ademption occurs when someone leaves a specific item to a beneficiary in his or her will, and then sells or gives away the item before death.

Administration of an estate. The process of collecting and distributing the probate estate of a deceased person, supervised by the probate court.

Administrator. Someone a probate court appoints to act on behalf of an estate, just like an executor, when no will names an executor or the named executor cannot serve.

Administrator *de bonis non*. The Latin term for an administrator who takes over for a previous administrator or executor.

Administrator with will annexed. An administrator appointed by a court because the executor named in the will cannot serve. Also called by the Latin term, administrator *cum testamento annexo* or administrator CTA.

Adult. Legally, someone 18 or older.

Advancement. What happens when someone leaves property to a beneficiary in a will and then gives the beneficiary that property while still alive.

Affidavit. A written statement, signed under oath in front of a notary public.

Age of majority. The age at which someone gains the rights of adulthood— the right to manage his or her own property, make a will, vote, and enter into binding contracts, for example. In most states, the age of majority is 18.

Alien. Someone who is not a citizen of the United States.

Alternate beneficiary. A beneficiary who inherits only if the primary beneficiary has died or does not accept the inheritance.

Ancillary probate. A probate proceeding conducted in a different state from the one the deceased person resided in at the time of death. Usually, ancillary probate is necessary if the deceased person owned real estate in another state.

Annuity. A contract between an individual and an insurance company under which the person pays premiums in return for later receiving regular payments (monthly, quarterly, semiannual, or annual) for a certain period of time, usually during retirement.

Anti-lapse statute. A state law that provides that under certain circumstances, if a will beneficiary does not survive the will-maker, the property the beneficiary would have inherited goes instead to the beneficiary's children.

Appraisal. An opinion of an asset's market value.

Attestation. The act of watching someone sign a legal document, such as a will, and then signing as a witness. Witnesses don't need to know anything about the contents of the document; they are there to provide evidence that it was willingly signed by the person whose name is on the signature line, and that the person appeared to know what he or she was signing.

Augmented estate. Generally, property belonging to both a deceased and surviving spouse, plus property the deceased spouse gave away shortly before death. The augmented estate is calculated only if the surviving spouse wants to claim the "elective share" allowed by state law.

Basis. See "Tax basis."

Beneficiary. A person or organization who is legally entitled to receive property under a will, trust, life insurance policy, or other arrangement.

Bequest. A gift, made in a will, of personal property—that is, anything but real estate.

Bond. A kind of insurance policy that protects beneficiaries and heirs from any losses caused by the executor's dishonesty or recklessness.

Bypass trust. A trust for couples, designed to save on federal estate taxes at the death of the second spouse. Also called AB trust, marital life estate trust, or credit shelter trust. When an AB trust is split into Trusts A and B at the first spouse's death, one of the trusts is called the bypass trust because its property bypasses taxation when the second spouse dies.

Certified copy. A copy of a document issued by a court or government agency, guaranteed to be an exact copy of the original. Banks, life insurance companies, and government agencies require certified copies of a death certificate as proof of a person's death.

Class. A group of people who inherit property through a will or trust—for example, "my children."

Codicil. A document that supplements an existing will. A codicil may explain, change, or revoke provisions in a will. It must be signed in front of witnesses, just like a will.

Common-law marriage. In some states, couples may be considered married if they live together and intend to be husband and wife.

Community property. Certain property owned by married couples in Alaska, Arizona, California, Idaho, Louisiana, New Mexico, Nevada, Texas, Washington, and Wisconsin. Very generally, all property acquired during the marriage is considered community property, belonging equally to both spouses, except for gifts to and inheritances by one spouse. Spouses can, however, enter into an agreement to the contrary. (In Alaska, community property exists only if the couple signed an agreement making it so. Wisconsin calls its system marital property, but it's essentially the same as community property.)

Community property with right of survivorship. A way for married couples to hold title to property, available in Alaska, Arizona, California, Nevada, and Wisconsin. It allows one spouse's half-interest in community property to pass to the surviving spouse without probate.

Consanguinity. The relationship between blood relatives—that is, people who have a common ancestor.

Conservator. Someone appointed by a court to manage the affairs of a person who can no longer make decisions about day-to-day care and other matters. In some states, this person is called a guardian.

Contingent beneficiary. See "Alternate beneficiary."

Corpus. Property held in trust. This is the Latin word, sometimes used by lawyers; most people call trust property the "principal."

Creditor. A person or institution to whom money is owed.

Curtesy. See "Dower and curtesy."

Custodian. A person named to manage property left to a minor under the Uniform Transfers to Minors Act. The custodian uses the property for the minor's health, education, and support until the minor reaches the age at which state law says he or she must receive it.

Decedent. A deceased person.

Deed. The document that transfers real estate. See also "Transfer-on-death deed."

Devise. A gift made in a will. Traditionally, the term referred only to gifts of real estate, but it is now often used for any gift made by will.

Devisee. Someone who inherits a devise.

Discharge. In a probate court proceeding, the court order that releases the executor from his or her duties.

Disclaim. To refuse all or part of an inheritance, so that it passes to the alternate beneficiary (or sometimes, to a trust). Inheritors sometimes disclaim property to reduce the overall tax paid by family members.

Disclaimer trust. A kind of AB trust that gives the surviving spouse the option of *not* splitting the AB trust after the first spouse's death, if it's not necessary to save on estate taxes. A surviving spouse who decides to split the AB trust "disclaims," or declines to accept, some trust property. That property goes into the bypass trust.

Domicile. A person's place of residence, where the person intends to live permanently.

Dower and curtesy. The right of a surviving spouse to receive or have the use of a portion of the deceased spouse's property (usually one-third to one-half) if the surviving spouse is not left at least that share. (Dower is the widow's right, curtesy the widower's.) In most states, the elective share has replaced dower and curtesy, though in some places both exist.

Durable power of attorney. A power of attorney that remains effective even if the person who created it (called the "principal") becomes incapacitated. The person authorized to act (called the "agent" or "attorney-in-fact") can make decisions on behalf of the principal. There are two kinds of durable powers of attorney: financial and health care.

Elective share. This is the share of a deceased spouse's property that a surviving spouse is entitled to claim. Every state has different rules about what a surviving spouse can claim.

Encumbrance. A debt that is attached to a particular asset—for example, a mortgage or lien on a particular piece of real estate.

Equity. The difference between the market value of an asset and how much the owner owes on it.

Escheat. The forfeit of all property to the state when a person dies without heirs.

Estate. Generally, all the property someone owns at death. There are, however, different kinds of estates, including the probate estate (the property that goes through probate) and the taxable estate (property subject to estate tax).

Estate tax. See "Federal estate tax."

Executor. The person (or more than one) named in a will and appointed by a court to wind up the affairs of a deceased person. Called the "personal representative" in some states.

Executrix. A female executor. The term isn't much used anymore; most courts simply use "executor" or the gender-neutral "personal representative."

Expenses of administration. The costs of wrapping up an estate and distributing property. They may include attorney fees, appraisal costs, and probate court fees.

Fair market value. The value of an item of property on the open market.

Federal estate tax. A federal tax levied on estates of a certain size—in 2004, more than $1.5 million.

Fiduciary. Someone who owes a special duty of honesty and fairness to someone else. For example, an executor owes a fiduciary duty to the people who are entitled to the deceased person's property.

Final beneficiary. The beneficiary who receives trust property when a trust's life

beneficiary dies. For example, when a couple sets up a bypass trust, usually the life beneficiary is the surviving spouse, and the final beneficiaries are the couple's children.

Forced share. See "Elective share."

Funding a trust. Transferring ownership of property to the trustee's name.

General bequest. A bequest of money in a will.

Grantor. A person who establishes a trust. Also called settler or trustor.

Gross estate. For federal estate tax purposes, the value of all property a deceased person owned, without subtracting any debts or encumbrances on the property.

Guaranteed signature. A signature that has been witnessed by a person—commonly, a bank employee—who is qualified to guarantee signatures. Companies often require guaranteed signatures on documents requesting the reregistration of stocks in a new owner's name.

Guardian. An adult who has legal authority, granted by a court, to raise a minor or be responsible for the minor's property. Someone who is appointed by a court to look after an incapacitated adult may also be known as a guardian, but in most states is called a conservator.

Guardian of the estate. See "Property guardian."

Guardian of the person. See "Personal guardian."

Heir. Someone who inherits in the absence of a valid will.

Holographic will. A handwritten will, signed but usually not witnessed. Holographic wills are valid in about half the states.

In terrorem **clause.** See "No-contest clause."

Income in respect of decedent. Any income a deceased person would have received, had he or she lived.

Inheritance tax. A state tax imposed on people who inherit property. Most states don't impose inheritance tax.

Insolvent estate. An estate that has more debts than assets.

Intangible property. Property that cannot be physically touched—for example, an ownership share in a corporation. Documents—for example, a stock certificate—are evidence of intangible property.

Inter vivos trust. See "Living trust."

Intestate. The condition of dying without a will.

Intestate succession. Inheritance under state law, in the absence of a valid will. In most states, the surviving spouse, children, parents, siblings, nieces and nephews, and next of kin inherit, in that order.

Inventory. A list of all property in an estate, usually required by the probate court.

Issue. Direct descendants—children, grandchildren, and so on. See also "Lawful issue."

Joint tenancy. A way for two or more people to hold title to property. When one owner dies, the survivor(s) automatically own the property. No probate is necessary to change title into the name of the surviving owners.

Keogh plan. A qualified retirement plan for self-employed people.

Lapse. The failure of a gift left through a will because the beneficiary has died and the will doesn't contain any provisions (a clause naming an alternate beneficiary, for example) to deal with this situation. Under state anti-lapse statutes, the property may go to the beneficiary's offspring. See also "Anti-lapse statute."

Lawful issue. As used in a will, direct descendants who were born to a married couple.

Legacy. A gift made in a will.

Legatee. Someone who inherits a legacy.

Letters of administration. The document a probate court issues to the administrator of an estate, authorizing him or her to act on behalf of the estate.

Letters testamentary. The usual term for the document that a probate court uses to authorize someone to serve as the executor of an estate when there is a will.

Lien. A secured creditor's right to take a specific item of property if its owner doesn't pay a debt. Common liens include mortgages, car loans, judgment liens (liens filed by a creditor who has won a lawsuit), and tax liens.

Life beneficiary. A person entitled to use certain property only for his or her lifetime. A life beneficiary does not have the right to pass the property to someone at his or her death.

Life estate. The right to the use and enjoyment of certain property for life only. For example, someone who inherits a life estate in a house may live in the house for his or her life, but has no right to sell it or to leave it at his or her death.

Lineal descendant. A direct descendant. Same as "Issue."

Living trust. A trust created during the grantor's lifetime, usually to avoid probate and sometimes to avoid estate tax as well.

Marital deduction. A tax law provision that allows a married person to leave any amount of property to his or her surviving spouse free of federal estate tax. (If, however, the surviving spouse is not a U.S. citizen, the marital deduction does not apply.)

Marital property. The name for Wisconsin's property system, which is essentially the same as community property.

Minor. A child younger than 18.

Next of kin. The person most closely related to a deceased person.

No-contest clause. A will provision that states that any beneficiary who contests the will automatically loses whatever he or she would have inherited through the will. Also called *"in terrorem"* clause.

Nonprobate transfer. A transfer, without involvement of the probate court, of a deceased person's property to the person who inherits it.

Nuncupative will. An oral will, which is legal only in some states and in very unusual circumstances, such as imminent death.

Payable-on-death (POD) bank account. An account for which the owner named a beneficiary on a form provided by the bank. The beneficiary has no rights while the account owner is alive, but inherits any money in the account, without probate, when the account owner dies.

Per capita. A way of dividing property among heirs if a beneficiary has died. Each heir in a group inherits an equal share, regardless of how closely related he or she was to the deceased person. For example, if children and grandchildren all inherited, each would receive an equal share. Compare "Right of representation."

Per stirpes. See "Right of representation."

Personal effects. Items that the deceased person wore or carried, or that have some very close connection to him or her.

Personal guardian. An adult who has court-granted legal authority to raise a child, including making decisions about the child's physical, medical, and educational needs. Also called guardian of the person.

Personal property. Anything that isn't real estate.

Personal representative. Another term for executor or administrator, used in states that have adopted the Uniform Probate Code and some other states.

Petition. A document requesting something from a court.

POD. Abbreviation for "payable-on-death." A POD beneficiary is named to inherit certain kinds of property—for example, bank accounts—and inherits it without probate.

Posthumous child. A child born after the death of his or her father.

Pot trust. A trust that has more than one beneficiary. Parents often create a pot trust for all their children and give the trustee authority to spend trust assets as needed for each child. Also called a family pot trust or sprinkling trust.

Pour-over will. A will that "pours over" property into a trust. Property left through the will must generally go through probate before it goes into the trust.

Prenuptial agreement. An agreement made by a couple before marriage that controls the management and ownership of their property. Also known as a premarital or antenuptial agreement.

Pretermitted heir. A child (or the child of a deceased child) who is either not named or (in some states) not provided for in a will. In certain circumstances, such children may be entitled to a share of the estate.

Pro per. Someone who goes to court without a lawyer. Also called pro se.

Probate. The court-supervised process following a person's death that includes proving the authenticity of the deceased person's will, appointing an executor to handle the deceased person's affairs, inventorying the deceased person's property, paying debts and taxes, identifying heirs, and distributing the deceased person's property according to the will or, if there is no will, according to state law.

Probate estate. The property of a deceased person that goes through probate.

Property guardian. Someone who has been given authority to look after a child's property. Also called guardian of the estate.

Public administrator. Someone hired by a probate court to administer an estate if no relatives or creditors are available to do it.

Quasi-community property. In a few community property states, property acquired in another state that would have been a couple's community property had it been acquired in the community property state. Quasi-community property is treated just like community property when one spouse dies. Wisconsin has a similar concept but calls the property deferred marital property.

Real property. Land and things permanently attached to land, such as houses. Also called real estate.

Recording. The process of filing a copy of a deed or other document with the county land records office. Recording creates a public record of all ownership of real estate in the state.

Residence. See "Domicile."

Residuary beneficiary. The will beneficiary who receives any property not specifically left to beneficiaries by the will or other method.

Residuary estate. Property that goes to the residuary beneficiary. Also called residue.

Right of representation. The right of children to inherit in the place of their deceased parent, who would inherit if he or she were still alive. For example, if a deceased person's children and grandchildren inherited, the children would inherit a larger share; the grandchildren would split their deceased parent's share. Compare "Per capita."

Right of survivorship. The right of a surviving co-owner to automatically inherit the property when one owner dies. When property is held in joint tenancy, tenancy by the entirety, or community property with right of survivorship, co-owners have the right of survivorship.

Schedule. A list of property attached to a trust document, showing what property is held in trust.

Schedule K-1. An IRS form that a trustee uses to notify trust beneficiaries of how much they received from the trust in the previous calendar year.

Secured creditor. Someone who has a security interest in certain property.

Security interest. An interest in property that exists because of an agreement between a creditor and a borrower that gives the creditor the right to seize the property if the borrower doesn't repay the loan.

Self-proving affidavit. A notarized statement signed by the witnesses to a will. It makes it easier to prove the will's authenticity in probate court after the will-maker has died.

SEP or **SEP-IRA.** Simplified employee pension; an IRA (individual retirement account) for the self-employed.

Separate property. In community property states, property only one spouse owns. It includes all property that one spouse owned before marriage, inherited, or received as a gift.

Settlor. See "Grantor."

Signature guarantee. Verification from a bank or broker that a signature is genuine. It's similar to notarization, but notarization is *not* a substitute for a guarantee.

Small estate. An estate that contains property with a value small enough to be eligible, under state law, for simplified probate procedures or out-of-court transfers of the deceased person's property.

Specific bequest. An item of property specifically left to a named beneficiary in a will or trust.

Spousal share. See "Elective share."

Sprinkling trust. See "Pot trust."

Statutory share. See "Elective share."

Stepped-up basis. An increased basis (value used to determine taxable gain or loss when property is sold) given to inherited property that went up in value before the new owner inherited it. The new owner's tax basis is "stepped up" to the market value of the property at the time of the previous owner's death. As a result, if the new owner eventually sells the property, there will be less taxable gain.

Succession. Inheritance in the absence of a will.

Successor trustee. The person who takes over as trustee of a trust after the original trustee dies or becomes incapacitated.

Summary probate. A streamlined probate procedure available to "small estates," as defined by each state.

Taking against the will. The choice, by a surviving spouse, to demand a certain share (in most states, one-third to one-half) of the deceased spouse's property instead of accepting whatever was left to the surviving spouse by will. See "Elective share."

Tangible property. Property that can be touched. Compare "Intangible property."

Tax basis. The amount on which you base your profit or loss from the sale of an asset. If you inherit property, generally your tax basis is that property's fair market value at the date of death. So if you inherit property that's worth $20,000 at the death of its former owner, then your tax basis is probably $20,000. If you later sell the property for $35,000, your taxable profit is $15,000. See also "Stepped-up basis."

Taxable estate. The property left by a deceased person that is subject to estate tax. The taxable estate is calculated by taking the gross estate (everything the deceased person owned at death) and subtracting deductions allowed by law, such as debts owed by the deceased person, expenses of the last illness and funeral, and costs of administering the estate.

Tenancy by the entirety. A way that married couples (and in Hawaii and Vermont, same-sex couples who have registered with the state) can hold title to property. It's available in about half the states. When one spouse dies, the surviving spouse automatically owns 100% of the property.

Tenancy in common. A way two or more people can own property together. Unlike joint tenants, each owner can leave his or her interest to beneficiaries of his choosing; the surviving owners don't automatically inherit. Ownership shares need not be equal.

Testamentary. Having to do with a will. For example, a testamentary trust is a trust that's created in a will and takes effect at the will-maker's death.

Testate. The condition of dying with a will.

Testator. Someone who leaves a will.

Testatrix. A woman testator. The term isn't used much anymore.

TOD. Abbreviation for "transfer-on-death." Ownership to certain kinds of property—for example, securities accounts and cars—can in many states be owned in TOD form. The TOD beneficiary inherits the asset without probate.

Totten trust. A bank account that is held in trust for a beneficiary, who inherits

any money in the account when the account owner dies, without probate. Works just like a payable-on-death bank account.

Transfer agent. The person or company that handles the paperwork when a corporation's stock is transferred to a new owner.

Transfer-on-death deed. A deed that takes effect at death, allowed in only a few states.

Trust. An arrangement under which one person, a trustee, manages property for a beneficiary. See "Living trust."

Trustee. The person who manages assets held in trust. A trustee's job is to safeguard the trust property and distribute trust income or principal as directed in the trust document.

Trustor. See "Grantor."

Undue influence. Improper influence over a will-maker. Typically, it occurs when the will-maker is susceptible to pressure because of illness or emotional state, and is taken advantage of by someone he or she depends on for guidance—for example, a lawyer or close family member.

Uniform Principal and Income Act. A statute, adopted by most states, that in its most recent version allows some trustees to make adjustments that were not formerly allowed—for example, distributing principal to income beneficiaries if it's necessary to carry out the purpose of the trust.

Uniform Probate Code. A set of laws governing wills, trusts, and probate. Almost all states have adopted some parts of the UPC, but only 15 have adopted it in its entirety.

Uniform Prudent Investor Act. A statute that sets out guidelines for trustees to follow when investing trust assets.

Uniform Transfer-on-Death Securities Registration Act. A statute, adopted by almost all states, that allows securities owners to register their stocks and bonds in transfer-on-death (TOD) or beneficiary form. When the owner dies, the named beneficiary inherits the securities, without probate.

Uniform Transfers to Minors Act. A statute, adopted by almost all states, that provides a method for leaving property to minors and arranging for an adult (called a "custodian") to manage it until the child is old enough to receive it.

Will. A document in which a person directs who is to inherit his or her property at death. A will usually names an executor and, if the will-maker has young children, names a guardian to raise them if neither parent can.

Witness. Someone who watches another person sign a document (a will, for example) and then signs it as well, to confirm ("attest") that the signature is genuine. ■

Index

Benefits of HALT Membership

✓ A free copy of *Using a Lawyer: And What To Do If Things Go Wrong*

✓ Action Alerts reporting on legal reform developments in your state

✓ HALT's quarterly newsletter, *The Legal Reformer*

✓ The HALT *eJournal*, containing breaking legal reforms news and interesting information, delivered via e-mail twice a month

✓ A voice for your concerns about the lack of accessibility and affordability of America's civil justice system

- -

JOIN OUR FIGHT FOR REFORM

Since 1978, HALT has provided a powerful voice—working on your behalf in Washington and across the nation—to help Americans navigate the legal system with or without a lawyer. And we need your help. Join HALT to help us allow more people to settle their legal affairs simply and affordably.

☐ YES!

I want to help reform America's civil justice system. Enclosed is a check or money order for my membership dues of:

- ☐ $25 *(minimum)*
- ☐ $35
- ☐ $50
- ☐ $100
- ☐ $250
- ☐ $500

Or, I prefer to charge my contribution to:

- ☐ Visa   ☐ MasterCard
- ☐ American Express

Credit Card #_____

Expiration Date_____

Signature_____

Name_____

Address_____

City, State, Zip_____

Phone_____

E-mail_____

1612 K Street, NW, Suite 510
Washington, DC 20006
(202) 887-8255
Fax: (202) 887-9699
E-mail: halt@halt.org
Web: www.halt.org

NOTES